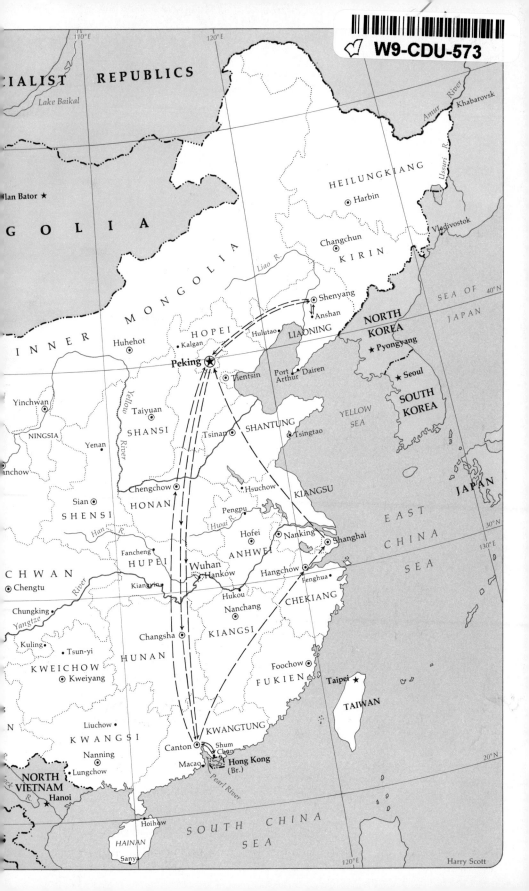

JOURNEY BETWEEN TWO CHINAS

A *Cass Canfield* BOOK

JOURNEY
BETWEEN
TWO CHINAS

Seymour Topping

HARPER & ROW, PUBLISHERS

NEW YORK

EVANSTON

SAN FRANCISCO

LONDON

1817

Maps by Harry Scott

FIRST EDITION

STANDARD BOOK NUMBER: 06–014329–0

LIBRARY OF CONGRESS CATALOG CARD NUMBER: 70–181649

Designed by Sidney Feinberg

l- 17 -73

For Audrey and our daughters,
Susan, Karen, Lesley, Rebecca and Joanna

CONTENTS

Sections of photographs follow page 114 and page 274.

ACKNOWLEDGMENTS

This book is intended to contribute to the literature illuminating aspects of the history of China from the period of the civil war (1946–49) to the visit of President Nixon in February 1972. Most of the material relates to personal experience, but I am indebted to many sources for facts which provided continuity and perspective. I am most grateful to Chester A. Ronning and my wife, Audrey, for their help and for having shared with me their experience. My thanks to Philip Fugh for enabling me to include fresh material of historical importance describing the work and career of John Leighton Stuart, the last American Ambassador to Nationalist China on the mainland. All the opinions expressed, however, are entirely my own, and I accept full responsibility for them and for the reliability and presentation of factual information.

Like so many of his colleagues in the field, I am bereaved by the death this year of Edgar Snow, and I salute his pioneer research and his reporting, which have been of so much value to all of us.

My thanks also to Arthur Ochs Sulzberger, the Publisher of the *New York Times*, for making my 1971 assignment to China possible, and for use of the research facilities of the paper. The dispatches of the correspondents of the *Times* were a mainstay, particularly those of Henry R. Lieberman and Tillman Durdin. I am indebted to the Associated Press for opening its archives to me, particularly to Ben Bassett, who made the arrangements, and Arnold Fox, who assisted me in the research. The East Asian Institute Library of Columbia University was of great help. For assistance in research I am especially indebted to Armida Gaeta, and also to Marian Underhill, Marvine Howe and Gray Peart. My thanks to Harold K. Milks for his recollections of Nanking.

I am also most grateful to O. Edmund Clubb for his reading of the manuscript and his many useful suggestions, and also to Henry R. Lieberman, Donald Klein and Gerald Gold, who read sections of it. My appreciation also to the editors of Harper & Row: Cass Canfield, Sr., for nudging me into writing this book; M. S. Wyeth, Jr. and Henry Reath, for their thoughts and encouragement; and Richard E. Passmore, who edited the manuscript with such skill and sympathy.

My thanks to Kay Lieberman for deciphering my longhand and typing the manuscript.

Apart from the sources cited in the text, I found the following books to be among the most useful references: Patrick O'Donovan, *For Fear of Weeping,* London, 1950; F. F. Liu, *A Military History of Modern China,* Princeton, 1956; Bernard B. Fall, *The Two Viet-Nams,* New York, 1963; O. Edmund Clubb, *Twentieth Century China,* New York, 1964, and *China and Russia,* New York, 1971; Lionel Max Chassin, *The Communist Conquest of China,* Cambridge, 1965; John F. Melby, *The Mandate of Heaven,* Toronto, 1968; Ezra Vogel, *Canton Under Communism,* Cambridge, 1969; John King Fairbank, *The United States and China,* Cambridge, 1971; Theodore Shabad, *China's Changing Map,* New York, 1971; Gordon A. Bennett and Ronald N. Montaperto, *Red Guard,* New York, 1971; and Donald W. Klein and Anne B. Clark, *Biographic Dictionary of Chinese Communism, 1921–1965,* Cambridge, 1971.

JOURNEY BETWEEN TWO CHINAS

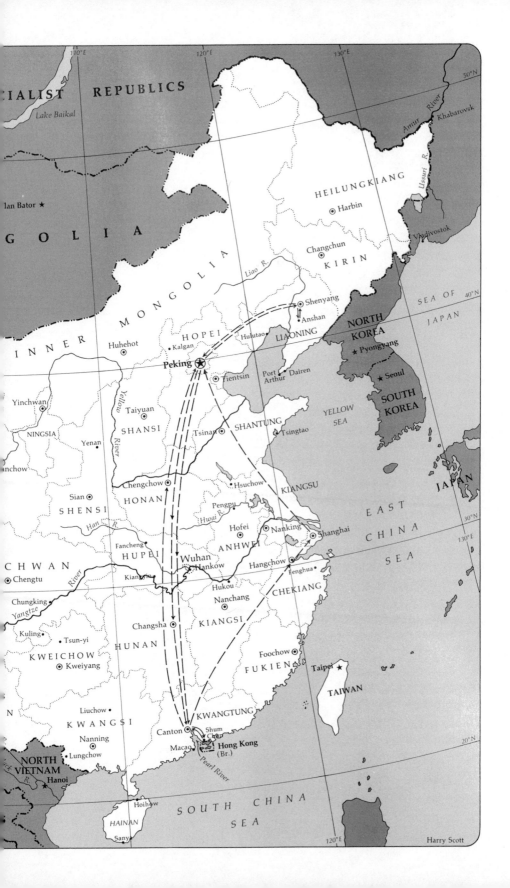

PROLOGUE

I strode through the lobby of the Commodore Hotel toward the Windsor Ballroom where I was to lecture to the New York Rotary Club on China, muttering unkind words about the retired *New York Times* advertising executive who had prodded me into this speaking chore. Should I delight them with tales of my wife's adventures in China or should I read to them from my yellowed clippings of two decades ago? I thought, almost relishing my savage frustration. It was May 13, 1971, and one week since Audrey, my wife, visiting China with her diplomat father, had cabled from Peking: "Chou En-lai says you can come to China." The Chinese Premier had asked that I contact Hsu Chung-fu, the Chargé d'Affaires of the Chinese Embassy in Ottawa. Since the arrival of Audrey's message at the *New York Times,* where I was the Assistant Managing Editor, I had impatiently telephoned the embassy each day, only to be told that no authorization for a visa had yet arrived from Peking. Now, I agonized that something had gone wrong and that I would not return to China.

How I had longed these many years to see again the panorama of the villages, the tile-roof dwellings, enclaved by the checkered green and brown fields unfolding endlessly beyond the horizon, and the cities surging with the torrential energies of a people unlike any other. I had witnessed their revolution, 500 million people being lifted violently from feudalism, walked among the dead on the civil war battlefields hidden in the vastness of the great plains, spoken to the peasant soldier survivors, recorded their hurt, anger and hopes. To behold revo-

1

lution, then immersed in its turbulence . . . the catharsis, the cruelty, the exaltation . . . the insights gained from a society in transition at the very moments of defeat and triumph and the beginnings of transformation . . . the rush of understanding and the maturing of self before the vision and the reality. Nothing eclipsed that experience as I went to the French Indochina War, to London, Berlin, Moscow and finally to partake of the agony of my own people in Vietnam.

In September of 1946 I had arranged my discharge from the U.S. Army in Manila and flown to Peking to become a language student and part-time correspondent. I was twenty-four. Two months later, in November, I flew in the plane of the American mediators in the civil war to Yenan, in the brown hills of Shensi in the northwest where Mao Tse-tung and other Chinese Communist leaders lived, blockaded by the Nationalist troops of Generalissimo Chiang Kai-shek. For a week, in the cave dwellings overlooking the river valley, I spoke to Mao's followers, questioning them in my naïveté. At the University of Missouri I had studied about China in hopes of going there. When I was an infantry officer in the war, there were always books about China in my duffel. But these readings had not prepared me for China in revolution.

In Yenan, discussing the Communist land reform program with several members of the Party's Central Committee, I said: "You know people in the United States are suspicious of Communists. Why don't you change the name of your party to the Agrarian Reform Party or something like that?" The Central Committee members, men in blue caps and tunics, most of them lean, deeply bronzed by years in the field fighting against Chiang Kai-shek's forces and the Japanese, looked at each other, concealing their astonishment and amusement, and one said gently: "We call ourselves Communists because we are Communists."

In Yenan, one had only to read the volumes made of yellow grass paper, containing the writings of Mao Tse-tung and other political literature available in English, to know that these men were Marxist-Leninists bent on a peasant revolution to transform China by stages into a Communist state. Mine was an innocent question, but also there was implicit in it the typical foreign arrogance toward the Chinese. Like the Czarist generals, the British gunboat captains, the Yankee traders, the Comintern agents, and most recently American diplomats mediating in their civil war, I was telling the Chinese to accommodate their society to foreign attitudes. Change your name to make Americans *happy. But this, too, was ending in the caves of Yenan.*

"Stand up, and be the masters of your own fate," Mao Tse-tung was telling his people. Before I left Yenan, I began to perceive the commitment and fervor of Maoist ideology. In the night, the sides of the hills were streaked with light as the people, bearing lanterns, weaved down the narrow paths to the meeting hall in the valley where the leaders spoke of the struggle for a Communist China. But it was not yet clear to me and other Americans what this meant for the relationship of China to the United States. There would be a time in 1949 in a village hut on a great battlefield in Central China, after a confrontation with a Communist commissar who had held me prisoner, when I would rest my head against a sack of grain and weep, when I knew that China and its people would go down a path that would veer sharply away from the United States and its people, and that it would be a generation or more before they could come together again.

And now it was more than two decades and the time of parley and reunion was approaching. The signal had come a month ago from the Chinese in an invitation of comic spirit but serious intent to an American table tennis team to visit Peking. China had entered upon a new historical era in its foreign policy. After years of isolation and virtually no contact with the United States, Peking was reacting to a shift in the balance of forces in the world. The ideological and national antagonisms between China and the Soviet Union had sharpened, and the Chinese were viewing apprehensively the re-emergence of Japan as a great world power. The United States was withdrawing from Indochina, and a new relationship between Peking and Washington had become feasible. Within China, the convulsive phase of the Great Proletarian Cultural Revolution was ended, and Mao, satisfied that his people were once more traveling the ideological path to the classless society he had defined in Yenan, had turned over the day-to-day management of the country's affairs to the astute, practical Chou En-lai. I was consumed with the compulsion to go back to China to see what had transpired in the vastest of experiments in human engineering.

Audrey had been in China seventeen days when she forwarded to me the message from Chou En-lai.

She was traveling with her father, Chester A. Ronning, a retired Canadian diplomat considered by many to be his country's leading expert on China. Ronning, born in China, an old friend of Chou En-lai and a long-time advocate of recognition of Peking, had been invited to visit China as a guest of the government soon after Canada and China entered into diplomatic relations in October 1970.

Ronning had been sent on two confidential government missions to Hanoi in 1966 to get peace negotiations started between North Vietnam and the United States. Secretly, he had brought back the first Hanoi offer to open peace talks with the United States if the Johnson Administration would halt the bombing of North Vietnam, a move which President Johnson did not make for another two and a half years. Earlier Ronning had served for six years as Counselor and then Chargé d'Affaires of the Canadian Embassy in China. He closed the embassy in 1951 and left Nanking, the Nationalist capital, two years after the Communists occupied the city. It was in Nanking in 1947 that I had met Audrey, a slender blonde girl of eighteen.

Ronning, now at seventy-six a tall, vibrant man of unflagging energy, was traveling about China with Audrey, her sister Mrs. Sylvia Cassady, and an entourage of Chinese officials and a Canadian television team that was doing a documentary on his return to his birthplace, Fancheng in Hupei Province. In Fancheng, a town three hundred miles up the Han River from Hankow, as the river winds, Ronning's Lutheran missionary parents had established a church and school. Audrey's grandmother, whom she resembles, died there when she was thirty-six. Hannah Ronning, a tall slim woman with piercing blue eyes and long chestnut hair drawn into a bun, was the mother of seven children and a spirited, dedicated missionary. Christian and non-Christian Chinese, remembering her as a teacher and the woman who had tended the infant girls she often found abandoned on the village streets, thronged to her funeral when she was buried in Fancheng.

On May Day, Ronning had his first meeting with Premier Chou, who welcomed him as "my old friend" in the Great Hall of the People on T'ien-an-men Square where a half-million people were gathered in a gay, festive celebration. It was a jovial meeting. The Premier, wearing a gray tunic suit and offering tea and Central Flowery Kingdom cigarettes to his guests, laughingly chided Ronning for retiring. When Ronning protested that he left the diplomatic service at seventy-one, although the compulsory retirement age was sixty-five, the seventy-three-year-old Premier quipped: "Well, you and I are exceptions to the rule. Take me, now. Why should I retire?"

During that first meeting Audrey, a free-lance photographer and writer for the *New York Times* and *National Geographic Magazine,* took a series of portraits of Chou that were to be widely published.

It was after a dinner for twelve given four days later by Chou for Ronning in the Kiangsu Room of the Great Hall of the People, where the Premier did most of his official entertaining and diplomatic business, that the question of my visa had arisen. The sumptuous twelve-course Chinese dinner was attended by two of Chou's most important aides on Canadian and American affairs. I knew them personally: Huang Hua, the newly appointed Ambassador to Canada who would become Permanent Representative to the United Nations in the fall, and Ch'iao Kuan-hua, the Vice Minister of Foreign Affairs, whom I had once known as Ch'iao Mu, his journalistic pen name. Ch'iao would head the first Peking delegation to the General Assembly of the United Nations. At the end of the two-and-a-half-hour dinner, as Chou bade farewell to Audrey and her sister, Audrey asked permission to write about the private dinner, and the Premier graciously replied: "That is your freedom." Audrey, in her dispatch to the *Times,* wrote with equal finesse about Chou's discussion of Sino-Soviet tensions and the food, dishes from her father's native Hupei Province, topped off by the exquisite Eight Heavens dessert.

Ronning, who speaks fluent Chinese, his first language, stayed that night for an hour's tête-à-tête with Chou. The Chinese leader, eager for firsthand impressions of Canada and the United States, and their leading political personalities, had many questions, but Ronning found time to raise the matter of the visa application submitted by A. M. Rosenthal, the Managing Editor of the *Times,* on behalf of James Reston, the columnist and a vice president of the paper, and myself. The *Times* strategy in offering the two names was to give the Chinese the option of granting admission to the most prestigious columnist in the United States or myself, a news executive who could negotiate on the question of opening a bureau in Peking and who was also a reporter well known to the Chinese Communists from civil war days. All the first wave of reporters admitted with the American Ping-Pong players, led by John Roderick of the Associated Press and John Rich of the National Broadcasting Company, had been in China during the civil war, 1946–49. It was during this private talk that Ronning was told by Chou En-lai that Reston and I would be granted visas.

This I did not know as I gloomily entered the Windsor Ballroom of the Hotel Commodore and paused to pick up my ticket for the Rotary

Club luncheon. My metabolism rate spurted when the receptionist said there had been an urgent call from my assistant at the *Times*, Armida Gaeta. Yao Jen-liu, the Cultural Attaché at the Chinese Embassy in Ottawa, had telephoned my office and asked me to call back as soon as possible. "We have received a message from Peking that you may go to China as you have requested," Yao told me, "and please inform Mr. Reston that he may also have a visa as requested by Mr. Rosenthal." Elated, I returned to the luncheon, rose to speak to the Rotarians, all of them magically transformed into beautiful people, told them of my good fortune, and with their applause following me and feeling like a soap opera hero sallying forth, I dashed across town to the West Forty-third Street office of the *Times*.

When Rosenthal telephoned Reston at his Washington office, Scotty generously agreed immediately that I should go first to China and he would follow at the end of my stay, so that the *Times* would have the most extended period of news coverage. Both visas were good for three weeks at any time within three months. That night, I flew to Ottawa, checked into the Skyline Hotel at 2 A.M. and at 9 A.M. walked out of the elevator in the Juliana Apartments onto the closed twelfth floor housing the Chinese Embassy chancery, past painters and carpenters who were still decorating the new offices, into a bare reception room where Yao, a young, slim Chinese who spoke excellent English, smilingly greeted me. Yao soon handed me back my American passport with a card inserted on which a visa was stamped, rather than in the passport itself, the customary practice when admitting a citizen of a country with whom Peking had no diplomatic relations.

We were joined by Lao Hsu, a slightly built Chinese of serious mien who spoke French but little English. He was the deputy to Hsu, the Chargé d'Affaires, who was ill. I had met Lao on a previous visit as well as Hsu, a good-humored man who welcomed me in English as "an old friend of China." There appeared to be only about a half-dozen Chinese diplomatic staffers in the embassy, which was hopelessly trying to sort out hundreds of visa applications from Americans and Canadians.

Lao asked about public opinion in the United States and attitudes toward Peking. I told him that opinion was divided. As I rose to go, the conversation turned to my immediate plans. Lao said, with a shy laugh, that it would be nice if Audrey and I could go together to Nanking, where we had met. I told him it was my plan to leave for Hong Kong three days hence, cross over into Canton on May 20 and join Audrey on the following day, her birthday. Unbeknownst to me, Lao began to hatch a Communist plot on behalf of sentiment.

As Lao and Yao, who had acted as interpreter, saw me to the elevator door, Lao remarked, thinking back on our conversation about American public opinion, that it must be the "monopoly-capitalists" in the United States who were opposing Peking's claim to being the sole government representing China. I glanced at him startled. It was an observation I had read many times in translations of the Peking press, but it rang strange in Ottawa, so close to the United States. What were Chinese diplomats abroad telling Peking about America? They looked at us through an ideological prism, but there was also the twenty-year lapse in communication and direct contact. Peking would need sophisticated reporting of America if China's leaders were to understand and engage with Washington.

Jay Walz, the *Times* correspondent in Ottawa, drove me to the airport. Formerly our correspondent in Cairo, Walz was delighted to find Ottawa, his rather quiet post, bustling with activities associated with the Chinese. Prime Minister Pierre E. Trudeau was determined, one of Trudeau's senior aides told me, that Canada was not going to become simply an intermediary between Washington and Peking, but would develop relations independently and fully with China on a bilateral basis. Nevertheless, it was obvious that Huang Hua had been assigned to Ottawa as Chou's overseer for North America and that he might be paying more attention to events in the United States and American contacts than to Canada despite Trudeau's sensitivities. Walz remarked that he was surprised that the American Embassy in Ottawa had not been beefed up with China experts. Walz and I agreed to keep in close touch on Chinese developments, and I flew back to New York.

The same Friday afternoon, I went into Rosenthal's office at the *Times* to say goodbye. Abe, in his warm, effusive manner, was enthusiastic about my return to China and understanding my impatience insisted that I go immediately. But we were both, in fact, troubled by the timing of the trip. A crisis was impending that would stir the country and pose a fundamental challenge to the *Times*. I was disturbed about leaving Rosenthal.

When I returned to New York in 1966 to become Foreign Editor, I hardly knew Rosenthal, a brilliant, intuitive newspaperman who had been summoned three years earlier from Tokyo to become Metropolitan Editor. In the following years, we collaborated closely on *Times* projects and found we worked well together. When Rosenthal became Managing Editor in September 1969, he selected me as his deputy. We headed the News Department, whose seven hundred members produce the news matter that goes into the daily paper except for the editorial pages and certain sections of the Sunday edition. Rosenthal and I worked in close tandem. When one of us was away or involved in corporate business or on a special project, the other supervised the news operation.

My China visa had arrived as we were involved in a momentous undertaking. The *Times* had obtained the top-secret documents concerning the United States role in Indochina, documents which later became known as the Pentagon Papers. Under maximum security arrangements, we were preparing the Papers for publication. June 14 was the target date for printing the first article. My China visa would expire June 10 and I intended to be back in New York before we went to press. Nevertheless, as Rosenthal and I talked in his office, I worried about the pressures which would mount on him. Formidable obstacles remained to be surmounted before we could publish the Pentagon Papers. We agreed, if he needed my help urgently, to communicate using Lloyd, the middle name of our Foreign Editor, James L. Greenfield, as our code reference. We said goodbye warmly, but I remained troubled as I went home to pack. In the end, the Pentagon Papers affair would affect my trip to China.

On Sunday, I said goodbye to our five daughters. Audrey had already been in China for four weeks, and now was out of contact as she traveled up the Han River in Central China to Fancheng. But the girls were troupers and cheered my going. Susan, our twenty-year-old, came home to Scarsdale from Sarah Lawrence College. The oldest, she had been born in Saigon, had learned ballet in Moscow, and was already performing with the La MaMa Company off-Broadway. Karen, the eighteen-year-old, born in London, who, like her sister, had attended a Soviet public school in Moscow, telephoned from Franklin and Marshall College, where she was taking Russian studies. Lesley, fifteen, was born in London, and Rebecca, thirteen, in a Berlin military hospital. Joanna, the four-year-old, the only one born in the United States, held a photo of her mother sitting on the Great Wall of China, and pretended she could pop into the scene at will. This would be the first time that Audrey and I would be traveling abroad on assignment without the girls. So the girls and I walked in the garden of our old, white-shingled house under the willow trees and remembered. I recalled Moscow during the Cuban missile crisis when I would come into the tiny bedroom where they slept in double-deckers and look at them wondering if a nuclear missile from our own country would end it all for us. We laughed about the time in Germany when I was summoned home on three days' notice to become Foreign Editor, how we piled into three taxis to go to the airport, baggage, four cats, one Australian cockatoo, four daughters, one pregnant wife and the German driver who asked in all seriousness: "Are you a traveling circus?"

The girls stood on the stone steps, Joanna in the arms of Blanca, our Uruguayan housekeeper, waving goodbye as my taxi went down the driveway. I looked back once. Soon I would see Audrey in China. I was traveling in space and time. Memories of China possessed me.

PART I

THE NATIONALIST

COLLAPSE

CHAPTER 1

NANKING

It was the morning of November 23, 1948, and I stood on the bleak airfield in the southeast district of Nanking, chilled by the damp wind off the Yangtze, watching the Australian Air Force plane lift over the old brick city wall, circle and then head east toward Tokyo. On board was my fiancée, Audrey Ronning, her mother, a sister, Kjeryn, her ten-year-old brother, Harmon, and other women and children of the Canadian and Australian embassies. Advance elements of the Chinese Communist armies had approached the north bank of the Yangtze River and the families were being evacuated before the battle for the Nationalist capital began. As the plane disappeared into the clouds, I climbed into my jeep and waved goodbye to T. C. Davis, the Canadian Ambassador, who had come to the airfield to see his wife off. Davis, a gregarious, bluff man in his sixties, looked more like a Toronto bank manager than a diplomat holding the fort amid a civil war. Audrey's father, Chester Ronning, the Counselor of the Canadian Embassy, was at home ill. Moodily I drove across the airfield, glancing at the Chinese Air Force transports being unloaded. For weeks, the transports had been flying in from the north, evacuating the families, concubines, gold bars, furniture and other personal possessions of senior Nationalist officers. The civil war, in the third year of uninterrupted conflict, had become a Nationalist rout.

Isolated Nationalist-held cities were toppling one after the other before the onrushing Communist armies, which had been left free to maneuver, concentrate and pick off at will the seemingly paralyzed Nationalist garrisons. The walled city of Tsinan, capital of Shantung, had

13

fallen on September 24, with the loss of eighty thousand troops. In the far north, Lin Piao's crack red columns had swept through Manchuria in October taking Changchun, the capital of the former Japanese state of Manchukuo, and Mukden, the great industrial center of the region.

In the Manchurian disaster, Chiang Kai-shek had lost seven armies, more than 400,000 men, including some of his best American-equipped and -trained divisions. In early March, when the Communists had withdrawn to regroup after their winter offensive, Major General David Barr, the head of the Joint United States Military Advisory Group (JUSMAG), had advised the Generalissimo to withdraw the 60,000-man garrison at Changchun and the 200,000 troops holding Mukden, to pull them back into North China. The Generalissimo declined, politely turning aside Barr's advice as he had done so often. In September, when Lin Piao opened his offensive with a force of 600,000 men, it was too late. Lin Piao's columns, facilitated by the treachery of some of the Nationalist commanders, overran Changchun and Mukden, destroying the units trying to break out and the reinforcements sent north to relieve them.

Chiang had flown to Peking to personally direct Nationalist operations, bypassing the Ministry of Defense and the normal field command structure, as he often did to the confusion of the general staff. When it was over at the end of October and the Communists were still counting their vast booty in captured American weapons and supplies, the Generalissimo returned to Nanking and asserted: "The loss of Manchuria is discouraging, but it relieves the government of a formidable burden, so far as military defenses are concerned, and allows it to concentrate its war effort to the south of the Great Wall." Soon, Lin Piao would move south in overwhelming force from Manchuria into North China against the Peking-Tientsin line, held by General Fu Tso-yi.

Like scavengers the Nationalist Air Force transports swooping in from the north with the personal loot of generals were always the harbingers of the fall of some city to the Communists. I had been with the Mukden garrison toward the end of the siege of the Manchurian metropolis, and now I swore as I thought of what the transports might have done for the thousands of Nationalist troops who died trapped in the Communist encirclement on the frozen Manchurian plain when they made their final futile breakout toward North China.

Not a shot had yet been fired across the turbulent brown waters of the broad Yangtze, but already as I drove into the center of Nanking, I could feel the pervasive sense of dissolution and abandonment that clutched at the city. Twenty years after Chiang Kai-shek had marched north from Canton and established his capital in Nanking, the Kuomintang dream of a new, modern unified China was dying in the drafty, littered offices of the government buildings along Chungshan Lu which the cabinet ministers no longer regularly attended. The Kuomintang revolution had been left unfinished, and so was its capital.

There had not been much time to transform this city of 1.2 million people, the "Southern Capital" of the Ming emperors, 150 miles from the sea in a bend of the Yangtze River, into a proud city. In 1931, only four years after Generalissimo Chiang Kai-shek had marched to Peking and compelled the northern warlords to join in a unified government, the Japanese attacked in Manchuria and then, in 1932, at Shanghai. The Japanese renewed their advance in 1937, seizing Nanking and slaughtering more than 60,000 of its civilians and raping thousands of women. The Chiang Government fled to the interior, where it was to remain until 1946. (One hot afternoon in 1947, I went outside of the city to a large dusty field and watched without being able to feel pity as several of the Japanese generals who had entered Nanking in 1937 were hauled roughly from the back of a truck, their hands tied behind their backs. They were forced to their knees and executed, each with a single pistol shot to the back of his shaven head, while a Chinese mob jostled and jeered behind a cordon of Nationalist soldiers.)

The Nationalist capital was still encased by a twenty-two-mile-long brick wall built by the Ming emperors. The Chiang Government had slashed broad pretentious boulevards across the city and put up government office buildings whose blue- and green-tiled roofs were a poor acknowledgment of the classical heritage. The city lacked the grace and splendor of Peking, and the dynamism of industrial Shanghai or commercial Canton. Many of the narrow, twisting cobbled side streets remained as they had been for hundreds of years, the only additions being two-story slapdash buildings and the refugee shacks. Within the walls there were great dreary patches of fields, plowed by water buffalo. The stagnant ponds dotting Nanking came mercifully alive with color when the giant lotus bloomed. The city was accursed with a foul climate, four months of unbearably humid heat in the summer and a dank winter of penetrating cold. Only when the spring came, and the fruit trees blossomed and the little hills adorned with temples and shrines turned vivid green, did the successors of the emperors who resided here seem to enjoy the Mandate of Heaven bestowed on the former imperial rulers.

I drove into Hsinchiehkow, the central district of the city, where many of the government offices and shops were situated. Hundreds of Nationalist soldiers, stragglers and deserters from the defeated armies in the north, in their padded, disheveled, lice-ridden yellow uniforms wandered aimlessly in the streets, some still holding their rifles, dodging the Chinese Army trucks that raced through. Thousands of refugees were camped on the sidewalks, huddled up against buildings for shelter from the cold and wet. Each morning the city sanitation trucks came through the central districts picking up the bodies of those who had died of hunger or cold in the night.

Suddenly, ample rice stocks and other food, hoarded by the speculators, appeared in the shops. Only two weeks ago, there had been food riots, with the milling crowds battering down the fronts of the rice shops. Now so many thousands of the middle-class and the wealthy had left that the hoarders had brought out hidden stocks to dispose of them before the Communists came. But for the refugees without money there was nothing unless they could clutch a ration when it was handed out from American aid stocks at the relief stations.

Six days before, in the middle of the night and in a frenzied rush, the eight hundred officers and men of JUSMAG, which had supervised American military aid to the Nationalist Army, had been evacuated with their families and what possessions they could carry. The order had come unexpectedly from the Chief of Staff in Washington, who feared that a Communist entry into the city was imminent. The JUSMAG families left behind tons of supplies and personal possessions, from record players to draperies, all abandoned in the elaborate apartment buildings and compounds which had been erected to house them. Within hours their former Chinese servants and other looters had carried off most of the leavings. Now the swank Officers Club stood empty. The Post Exchange and club, trappings of American affluence, which had so irritated the Chinese, vanished overnight without ceremony or tears.

The Nationalist economy had come unstuck, paralyzing business in Nanking. In August, when the inflated national currency was valued at more than twelve million yuan to the American dollar, a new gold yuan had been introduced at four to the dollar. But the currency inflation was again out of control, and once more we were carrying sacks of currency to pay restaurant bills.

The city was under martial law, and an atmosphere of insecurity permeated everywhere as power blackouts grew more frequent and shots were heard in the darkness. Policemen patrolled the intersections with fixed bayonets. The great iron gates of the city which pierced the walls at a dozen points were slammed shut to traffic at 9:30 P.M. By 11 P.M. the streets were deserted, and the apprehensive population, struggling against its nightmares, slept.

The political currents in Nanking swirled around two lonely men, President Chiang Kai-shek and the American Ambassador, John Leighton Stuart.

Imperturbable, the Generalissimo sat amid panicky ministers at his massive desk in a modern office building erected in an inner courtyard of a T'ai P'ing Palace on Kuo Fu Road in the center of the city. His Vice President, Li Tsung-jen, and most of the government were ready for peace talks and coalition government with the Communists, but the towering, uncompromising figure of the Generalissimo thwarted their efforts. A lean, erect, indomitable man, the sixty-one-year-old Chiang still considered himself, despite the visible disintegration of his republic, the destined national leader of China who would lead its people to salvation over the bodies of the Communist foes. He was the heir of Dr. Sun Yat-sen, the founder of the Kuomintang revolution who had enunciated the San Min Chu I, the Three Principles of the People, a promise made in the 1920s but still unfulfilled:

1. Nationalism: drive the foreigners out of the concessions and restore unity and sovereignty.

2. People's Democracy: the village masses would become literate and vote for their government.

3. People's Livelihood: socialization of industry and land to the tillers.

Chiang had ruled in fact more with a philosophy blended of the warlord politics of the professional Chinese Army officer, the anti-imperialist principles of Leninism learned in Moscow in 1923 where one of Dr. Sun's Russian advisers had sent him for six months of indoctrination, Confucian authoritarianism, and a leavening of Christianity. He joined the Methodist Church in 1931, one of the conditions for marriage stipulated by Madame Chiang, the beautiful former Soong Mei-ling, the Wellesley-educated sister of T. V. Soong, the banker and, intermittently, Minister of Finance. In a morass of official corruption, Chiang had stood as the incorruptible ascetic, but incapable or unwilling to stem the thievery and nepotism that engulfed the Nationalist Government and Army, even tainting his own family.

In the dying Nationalist capital, he was manipulating the levers of control over government and army in the warlord style which earlier had kept him in power. The unity that Chiang had forged in China had been only a coalition of warlord generals. From 1926, when his revolutionary army marched north, until 1937, when the war against Japan began, Chiang had been engaged in civil war. He had survived only by employing the tactics and intrigue of the warlord, always relying on the "Whampoa clique," a group of generals who had graduated from the Whampoa Military Academy in Canton, and had remained personally loyal to Chiang, their former commandant. Even as his armies crumbled, and his American advisers pleaded with him to put more efficient generals in command, he favored the Whampoa clique, tolerating their ineptitude and corruption. The bungling generals had wasted an overwhelming superiority in troops and arms over the armies of Mao Tsetung. Faced with defeat, in desperation Chiang was once more seeking American military aid, looking up the road to the two-story white villa where John Leighton Stuart lived. Madame Chiang Kai-shek had just left for Washington to make a personal appeal to President Truman and Secretary of State George C. Marshall for massive assistance. There had been many such requests, but this was to be a cry for help at the brink of the precipice.

In the cream-colored sitting room of the villa on the edge of the large American Embassy compound, Dr. Stuart was receiving a procession of Chinese visitors. They were former students of the Ambassador, intellectuals and liberals who were being hounded by the Kuomintang police, politicians seeking American support for an accommodation with the Communists, and old friends who wanted a haven for their families in the United States. They sipped pale Chinese tea set out on the beautiful old rosewood side tables, admired the lovely scrolls on the walls, received the sympathy of the Ambassador, and left without the encouragement which in conscience he could not provide. The visitors could not know that John Leighton Stuart was no longer in fact functioning as a dutiful State Department diplomat. He was conducting himself more as the Christian missionary he had once been. Desperate to halt the civil war and the killing in any way he could, Stuart was taking independent actions that had estranged him from the State Department.

Stuart had been born in Hangchow in 1876, the son of an American missionary. In 1904, two years after he graduated from the Union Theological Seminary in Richmond, Virginia, he returned to Hangchow with his bride, a New Orleans girl, as a missionary for the Southern Presbyterian Church. Stuart became a missionary educator in a growing system of colleges supported in part by twenty-one Protestant organizations and a dozen American universities. In 1919 he helped to found and became the first president of Yenching University, "Harvard in China," outside of Peking, the greatest of some thirteen Protestant educational institutions. It became a center for the espousal of liberal Western thought. Except for the interruption of World War II, Stuart remained at Yenching until 1946, happy and revered by his students. On June 24, 1946, Stuart, now a widower, celebrated his seventieth birthday, a thin spare man with angular features, dark cavernous eyes under heavy eyebrows, gray hair that receded from a high forehead, and long slender, nervous hands. His Chinese friends spoke of him as a "Christ-like man." Only ten days after his festive seventieth birthday party at Yenching, at the urging of General George C. Marshall, Special Representative of President Truman in China, Stuart agreed to become ambassador. Marshall had arrived in China in December 1945, delegated by Truman to bring to bear the influence of the United States to the end that the "unification of China by peaceful and democratic methods" might be achieved as soon as possible and the civil war terminated. Marshall's only leverage, apart from his great personal prestige, was the power to grant or withhold American economic and military aid, and he thought he needed the personal influence of the Yenching president with the Chinese and the benefit of Stuart's familiarity with the country.

As for Stuart's role, in his words: "General Marshall had originally brought me into his efforts to form a coalition government because of my reputation as a liberal American, friendly to the Chinese people as a whole, and with no pronounced sympathy for any one faction or school of thought. This included the Communists, several of whose leaders I had known fairly well." The Marshall mission, begun in December 1945, ended in January 1947 in bitterness and frustration shared by Nationalists, Communists and Americans alike. General Marshall became mired in the complexities of Chinese politics and in the deep-seated hates and ambitions of both camps. The Generalissimo and Mao Tse-tung sought to exploit his mediation mission for political advantages and tactical gains on the battlefields.

During World War II, Americans had sought in Chungking and in Yenan to bring the Nationalists and Communists together in the common struggle against Japan. An enforced and sporadic cooperation existed in the last years, but it dissolved in late 1945 as the two armies raced each other to occupy territory relinquished by the defeated Japanese forces. The United States, caught in the middle, decided to aid the Nationalist Government by airlifting Chiang Kai-shek's troops into the principal cities of North China and Manchuria. The Russians, withdrawing slowly from their occupation of Manchuria, where they had disarmed the Japanese armies, gave much less help to the Communists. When Marshall arrived, the two armies were already clashing and the Communists were furiously complaining about American assistance to Chiang Kai-shek.

If Mao entertained seriously Marshall's proposal of peace and coalition government, it was discarded by the summer of 1946 as his troops, strengthened by Japanese weapons turned over by the Russians in Manchuria, gained in force. Mao remembered too well the last attempt at coalition, which had ended in 1927 with the slaughter of the Communist workers in Shanghai, and the "bandit extermination campaigns," which finally in 1934 drove the remnants of his army out of Kiangsi on the 6,000-mile "Long March," from South China to the new Yenan base area in the northwest province of Shensi. Nor did Chiang, at this moment in history the world symbol of Chinese resistance against Japan, have serious intention of sharing power with his mortal enemies. The truce arranged by Marshall expired on June 30, 1946, and the civil war raged uninterrupted thereafter.

After the Marshall mission, the Truman Administration turned away from the policy of mediation in the civil war in China. The Truman Doctrine, proclaimed by the President on March 12, 1947, committed the United States to a policy of containment of Communism in Greece and Turkey, and by implication in Eastern Europe and elsewhere. With the Communist takeover from within in Czechoslovakia in February 1948, Washington's pursuit of a coalition government in China of the Kuomintang and Communist parties became a painful political embarrassment. The policy was abandoned.

But Stuart, agonizing over the human devastation about him and the dissipation of his vision of a new liberal China, stubbornly pursued mediation and peace through a coalition government. On August 12,

1948, Marshall, who had become Secretary of State, specifically instructed the embassy in Nanking to dissuade the Nationalist Government from seeking a coalition with the Communists. "You should, of course, overlook no suitable opportunity to emphasize the pattern of engulfment which has resulted from coalition governments in Eastern Europe." Nevertheless, Stuart persisted in what he later called "my dream of China peaceful, united and progressive, helped in this by American technical advice and financial grants or loans." Ignoring the opposition of Marshall, and the embassy staff, headed by Lewis Clark, the Minister-Counselor, Stuart continued to explore the possibilities of mediation, turning at times to the Soviet Embassy, which encouraged him to believe that Russian help in peacemaking might be forthcoming. Angered, Marshall virtually reprimanded Stuart. The Ambassador was instructed on October 28, 1948, to tell the Generalissimo that the mediation proposals were his own and did not have the approval of the State Department. The only person who remained close to the Ambassador politically was Philip Fugh, his long-time Chinese secretary and confidant, whom he regarded as an adopted son. Fugh kept in touch with Vice President Li Tsung-jen, who was a member of the Kwangsi clique and distrusted by Chiang. In November, Stuart was searching for ways to persuade the Generalissimo to retire so that Li Tsung-jen could take power and make peace with the Communists. Stuart had received no encouragement from Mao Tse-tung, who saw total victory in reach. Yet the lonely missionary struggled on, convinced that he knew what was best for China.

Thoughts of what was transpiring at the embassy were turning in my mind as I drove my jeep to the Associated Press compound at 101 Kaoloumen in the northern district of the city. Harold Milks, the chief AP correspondent, lived there in a two-story brick house, which belonged to Judge Hsu Mo, China's representative on the International Court of Justice at The Hague. I had just joined the AP after two years with the International News Service in Peking and Nanking. INS had paid me barely enough to live, and when an offer came from the AP, just as the INS reduced my living allowance in another of its economy waves, I had gladly joined the agency, with which I was to remain ten good years until I joined the *Times* in 1959. I was about to move from the dreary press hostel into the AP house. Milks was preparing to go on home leave, and his wife, Evelyne, had already left for the United States.

Standing in the courtyard of the compound, I looked to the east where Purple Mountain loomed up beyond the city wall. Audrey and I had driven there often. In my jeep, we would drive through the Great Peace Gate, pausing at Lotus Lake. The placid, lotus-filled waters lapped at the foot of the wall. On the other shore was a garden park where pleasure-seekers strolled shopping in the tiny kiosks, gliding on the lake in gaily decorated sampans beneath vividly colored canopies or dining at the small floating restaurants. Musicians went from boat to boat singing and playing their Chinese instruments for tips. We would also go to the Ming Tombs, walk down the avenue of mythical animal statuary, pose on the stone elephant or the camel who guarded the graves of the emperors. Then we would drive back to picnic on the slope of Purple Mountain or drive up to the curious old observatory on the peak. One evening in the spring of 1948, atop Purple Mountain, I asked Audrey to marry me. Later in the summer she and her family sailed on a river boat up the Yangtze to Kiukiang in Kiangsi Province and then went into the Lu Mountains to Kuling, the cool, green hill station where the Generalissimo, Marshall and Stuart would often go on weekends to escape the Nanking heat. They would fly to the airfield on the river bank opposite Kiukiang, motor across to the foot of the mountain, and then in swaying sedan chairs be carried up the narrow paths cut as steps in the mountainside to Kuling. That same summer of 1948, I came up the railroad from Canton to Hankow on the Yangtze, seeing the havoc of that year's terrible floods, and then traveled by river boat down to Kiukiang. I felt guilty about riding the sedan chair on the backs of four men up the mountain until I saw the coolies, fighting for their rice, struggle among themselves for a turn to carry the foreigner. In Kuling, Audrey and I walked among the lovely pines. One day, her father and I climbed a mountainside, and I told him Audrey and I wished to marry. After that she wore my ring.

Now I wondered if I would see her again. That morning her little brother, Harmon, as he cheerfully said goodbye, chirped, as I winced: "I suppose we will never see you again." It had been a strange coming together, Audrey and I. She, of a Lutheran missionary family, always knowing within herself surely that one day she would leave Alberta in western Canada to go to China where her grandmother was buried. And I, the son of East European immigrant Jews, who for no discernible reason had been determined from the time that I was a boy to go to China. At sixteen, the editor of my New York high school paper, I decided to become a correspondent in China, and later went to the School of Journalism at the University of Missouri because of its many associations with the Far East. Three and a half years in the army, and my decision to take my terminal leave in Manila and go to China had followed. When I met Audrey, she was a student at the University of Nanking.

Now the university was dying like the capital. In the spring and the summer, the students had demonstrated violently against the government and American policy until a ban had been imposed on further meetings and marches. Police agents swarmed over the campus beating up and arresting militant students. Many of the boys and girls had abandoned their studies.

As Audrey boarded a Norwegian freighter at Yokohama bound for Vancouver, I plunged into coverage of the war. With a group of other correspondents, I flew north to the Communist-encircled city of Hsuchow.

CHAPTER *2*

THE BATTLE OF
THE HWAI-HAI

On October 11, 1948, when the Nationalist military debacle in Manchuria was nearing its end, Mao Tse-tung sent instructions to his Eastern China and Central Plains Field Armies to make ready for the Hwai-Hai campaign, which would become the climactic battle of the civil war. A half-million Nationalist troops stood north of the Hwai River blocking the way to Nanking.

The Battle of the Hwai-Hai, upon which the fate of Nanking and Shanghai would turn, would be fought over a great plain extending into the provinces of Kiangsu, Shantung, Anhwei and Honan. It would pivot on Hsuchow, a city of 300,000 population, 175 miles north of Nanking, situated at the juncture of the Tientsin-Nanking Railroad and the Lunghai Railroad which ran westward to Kaifeng and eastward to the East China Sea. The battle would take its name from the Hwai River which flowed west to east about a hundred miles north of Nanking and from the first syllable of Haichow, a town on the eastern spur of the Lunghai.

The Generalissimo met with his generals November 4 to 6 to plan their strategy. His leading military commanders argued for a defense line along the Hwai River. It was Chiang who finally made the fateful decision that the Communist armies would be confronted on the plain around Hsuchow.

Mao, in his field orders issued on October 11, stated: "You are to complete the Hwai-Hai campaign in two months, November and December. Rest and consolidate your forces next January. . . . By autumn your main force will probably be fighting to cross the Yangtze."

24

When we flew to Hsuchow on November 25, the Communists had already successfully completed—three days earlier—the first phase of their campaign, which had begun on November 6. Mao Tse-tung had committed about 600,000 men to the battle divided into columns under Ch'en Yi, Liu Po-ch'eng and Ch'en Keng. The Nationalist forces, some 55 divisions, totaling about 600,000 men, commanded by General Liu Chih, were strung out in static positions centered on Hsuchow east and west along the Lunghai Railroad and along the rail line to the south. Moving in from the east, Ch'en Yi's columns had snapped a pincer around Nienchuangchi, overwhelming and destroying the ten divisions of the Seventh Group Army commanded by General Huang Po-t'ao. A relief column pushing out from Hsuchow, thirty miles to the west, had been blocked by Ch'en Yi. Our Chinese Army transport circled over the smoking ruin of Nienchuangchi before landing at the airfield within the Hsuchow perimeter. The ancient town had been shielded by two brick and mud concentric walls and moats. A network of trenches radiated out from the edge of the outer moat, now dotted with corpses and shattered equipment. The town had been General Huang's headquarters, and he had been fatally wounded, presumably in the final tank-led assault which overran the town. Only about three thousand of Huang's ninety-thousand-man force had escaped to join with the armored relief column which had been battered to a halt ten miles to the west. On the outskirts of Nienchuangchi and near the shattered villages, clusters of mud houses amid fields sown with winter wheat, we glimpsed shreds of parachutes used in the supply airdrops to the doomed troops.

The Nationalists enjoyed unchallenged command of the air. The Chinese Air Force transports, C-47s and C-46s, the P-51 Mustang fighters, and the B-25 and B-24 bombers paraded up from Nanking in hundreds of sorties over the Hsuchow region. To the despair of their American instructors and advisers, the Chinese pilots persisted in operating only at safe altitudes, and as a result had no decisive effect on the Nienchuangchi action, nor would they influence the outcome of the Hwai-Hai campaign.

We found Hsuchow, an ugly old market town of rutted roads and dilapidated two-story buildings, overrun with refugees, the hospitals jammed with untended wounded, the airfield crowded with panicky civilians battling each other and attempting to bribe their way into the outgoing transports which had brought in supplies. In an army truck, we were driven to the headquarters of General Li Mi, the commander of the Thirteenth Group Army, which held Hsuchow. We were briefed on the rapidly deteriorating Nationalist position. The deputy chief of staff, Major General Chang Yu-chin, told us that General Chu Te, the Communist Commander-in-Chief, had committed 27 columns, and 6 independent brigades, more than 600,000 men, into the struggle for Hsuchow.

We piled into a truck and rode out to the front which bulged to the east and northeast. The dusty, rutted road twisted from village to village. Some of the peasants had remained with their mud huts, their fields, and a pig or two, although shells from Li Mi's 75- and 105-mm guns were screaming overhead toward the Communist-held villages. Abruptly, we were at the front in a village, with Nationalist soldiers, in their winter caps, with earflaps up, padded yellow tunics and leg wrappings, looking at us curiously. Beyond the village there were some trenches and foxholes, but there was no sense of close engagement with the enemy until we walked to a nearby field. The Communists had attacked the village during the night and had been repulsed. The bodies of some twenty Communist soldiers lay there. They had been dragged in behind jeeps and ponies from the fields beyond the outer defenses. In dress and appearance, the dead men, their features gray and frozen, looked no different from the Nationalist soldiers about us. Henry R. Lieberman, the *New York Times* correspondent, noticed that some of the dead had secondary wounds, pistol shots in the backs of their heads. Angrily, he asked if the men had been executed. A Nationalist officer shrugged. There were no adequate medical facilities for the Nationalist wounded, certainly not for the Communists found on the battlefield. As we drove back from the village to Hsuchow, we passed the body of a soldier lying beside the road, his head split open like a ripe cantaloupe. No one knew whether he was a Communist or a Nationalist.

We flew back the next day to Nanking. It was the same day that Ch'en Yi's columns racing southwest from Nienchuangchi had joined with Liu Po-ch'eng, the "One-Eyed Dragon," in an encirclement of the Nationalist Twelfth Group Army, commanded by General Huang Wei. The Group Army, made up of 11 divisions and a mechanized column, about 125,000 men, had been ordered to the relief of Hsuchow. The Communists had thrown 13 columns, about 250,000 men, across the southern line of retreat of the Hsuchow garrison, holding Suhsien, where Huang was to have joined with Li Mi's forces. Ringed by artillery, Huang's Twelfth Group Army was being pounded to bits. The Hsuchow garrison, which had not yet begun its withdrawal, was ordered by

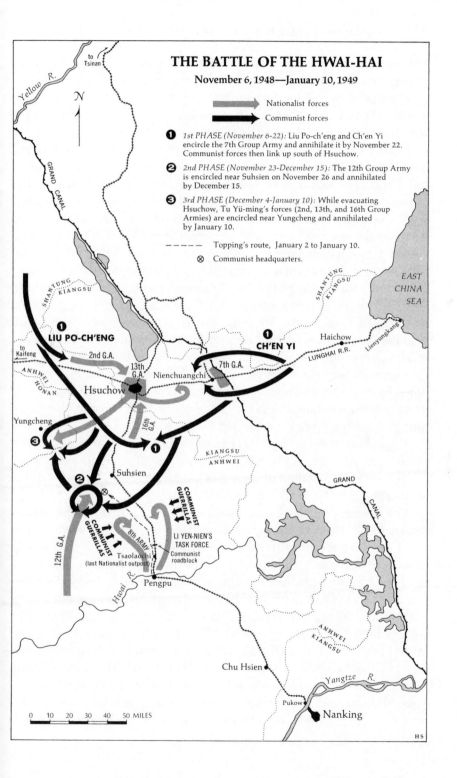

THE BATTLE OF THE HWAI-HAI

November 6, 1948—January 10, 1949

➡ Nationalist forces

➡ Communist forces

❶ *1st PHASE (November 6-22):* Liu Po-ch'eng and Ch'en Yi encircle the 7th Group Army and annihilate it by November 22. Communist forces then link up south of Hsuchow.

❷ *2nd PHASE (November 23-December 15):* The 12th Group Army is encircled near Suhsien on November 26 and annihilated by December 15.

❸ *3rd PHASE (December 4-January 10):* While evacuating Hsuchow, Tu Yü-ming's forces (2nd, 13th, and 16th Group Armies) are encircled near Yungcheng and annihilated by January 10.

– – – – – Topping's route, January 2 to January 10.

⊗ Communist headquarters.

to Tsinan

Yellow R.

GRAND CANAL

SHANTUNG
KIANGSU

SHANTUNG
KIANGSU

EAST
CHINA
SEA

❶ LIU PO-CH'ENG

to Kaifeng

2nd G.A.

❶ CH'EN YI

Haichow

Lienyungkang

LUNGHAI R.R.

ANHWEI
HONAN

13th
G.A.

Nienchuangchi

7th G.A.

Hsuchow

Yungcheng

16th
G.A.

❸

①

KIANGSU
ANHWEI

GRAND

Suhsien

⊗

❷

CANAL

COMMUNIST
GUERRILLAS

LI YEN-NIEN'S
TASK FORCE

12th G.A.

COMMUNIST
GUERRILLAS

8th ARMY

Tsaolaochi
(last Nationalist outpost)

Communist
roadblock

Hwai R.

Pengpu

ANHWEI
KIANGSU

Chu Hsien

Yangtze R.

Pukow

Nanking

0 10 20 30 40 50 MILES

H 5

Chiang to move out at once and break through to the encircled Twelfth Group Army at Shwangchiaochi, sixty-five miles to the southwest.

On November 27 the Sixteenth Group Army, commanded by General Sun Yuan-liang, which had been holding the southern sector of the Hsuchow perimeter, began the march south. The following day General Liu Chih, the Commander-in-Chief of the Hwai-Hai operations, flew out to the safety of Pengpu, a rail town on the southern bank of the Hwai. He was accompanied by General Chiang Wei-kuo, the Generalissimo's son, who was in command of the Armored Corps. During the next two days, the Armored Corps and Li Mi's Thirteenth Group Army in the main column, and General Ch'iu Ching-ch'uan's Second Group Army, which had been holding the western sector, also moved out. The long columns of marching men, heads bowed against the sharp cold wind, moved alongside of big American-made trucks, slowly southwest across the desolate plain, with Communist guerrillas harassing their flanks. General Tu Yü-ming, the Deputy Commander-in-Chief, who had been given his post despite his responsibility for the disaster in Manchuria, led the rear guard out. On December 1, the next day, Communists occupied Hsuchow, as the Nationalist garrison, weighed down by heavy armor, artillery, the families of some of the officers and men, and Kuomintang officials, clanked toward a collision with a Communist blocking force commanded by Ch'en Yi.

When I returned to Nanking, I went to Harold Milks with a plan that would get me back to the front. Milks, a friendly, chipper Midwesterner, who was a talented newsman of long experience, listened sympathetically.

In Pengpu, a hundred miles north on the Hwai River, there was an Italian Jesuit Mission. The retreating Hsuchow garrison seemed destined for destruction in the next weeks, and the Communists would then seize Pengpu. My plan was to enter the Jesuit Mission, wait there until the Communists took Pengpu, and then emerge. I would ask the Communists to allow me to cover their advance on Nanking and Shanghai and to send out my dispatches over their radio system. There was a precedent. John Roderick of the AP had two years earlier been permitted to stay in Yenan. His dispatches had been broadcast and monitored by the AP listening station on the West Coast. At this stage of the war, there were no independent Western newsmen with the Communists. Milks agreed to the plan, which I confided also to Chester Ronning. Chester provided me with a supply of Chinese silver dollars which would be acceptable currency in the Communist areas.

On December 12, the day following my twenty-seventh birthday, I got into a jeep beside Milks, threw my heavy duffel in the rear and we drove through the Northwest Gate to Siakwan, the Nanking quay on the Yangtze. We took the rail ferry across to Pukow, the terminus on the Yangtze of the railroad coming down from Tientsin through Hsuchow and Pengpu. The ferry slipped past motorized junks and the two Nationalist gunboats anchored in the dark, sullen water of the river. In the waiting room of the railway station, packed with ragged refugees from the north, smelling of sweat and urine, I showed my internal travel visa to a guard and then bought a ticket for a passenger train—a rather futile gesture. Troop trains, with thirty or forty cars attached to the wheezing locomotives, were coming down from the north packed with soldiers, sick and wounded, and hundreds of refugees who had clambered aboard at Pengpu or along the way. Despite the bitter wind, women dressed in ragged tunics over trousers, with babies on their backs, sat on top of the train beside their menfolk clutching bundles of their remaining possessions, often strapped to their bodies. Some were jammed into the vestibules between cars. I saw one old bearded man hanging out of a vestibule holding a straw cage of quacking white ducks. There was always a half-dozen refugees hanging onto the iron cowcatchers at the front of each of the locomotives.

Ordinarily, the trip to Pengpu took five hours on the single-track line, but now it was taking twenty hours. Most of the troop traffic was still going north, and I found a place in a boxcar with some friendly soldiers who helped me aboard with my duffel. There were bags of rice stacked against the sides of the car. If the Communist guerrillas hit the train during the night, as they often did, the rice sacks would absorb some of the fire. Despite the cold, the doors were left ajar as the train jerked out of Pukow. We slipped into the countryside, moving slowly through the brown fields covered with the stubble of the rice, broken where the winter wheat had been sown. On hills along the tracks there were blockhouses shielded by barbed wire or moats, to protect the trains from guerrilla attack. We rolled past bodies of men, women and children, looking like broken rag dolls, lying beside the tracks. They were refugees who, their hands numb from the cold, had lost their grip and slipped in the night from the tops or sides of trains.

At dusk, the endless expanse of the plains engulfed me. A strangeness pervaded, leaving me apprehensive and in doubt that I would ever see friends and familiar places again. The soldiers were eating their evening meal, squatting, holding bowls and with their chopsticks shoveling down cold rice sprinkled with a piquant sauce. A young officer offered me a bowl, and I gladly took it, for the company more than for the rice. At night, the doors of the boxcar were slammed shut. I wrapped myself in a blanket I had brought, and spent the night, half awake, staring into the darkness, the rancid odors of the press of bodies enveloping me as the train jostled from stop to stop. At dawn, we were in Pengpu. The train no longer went beyond the Hwai River just north of the city. From Pengpu, General Li Yen-nien had marched north with his Sixth Army, reinforced by General Liu Ju-ming's Eighth Army, a total force of eleven divisions, to attempt to break the encirclement of Huang's Twelfth Group Army at Shwangchiaochi, forty-five miles northwest of Pengpu.

I had to fight my way out of the boxcar through a frantic mob of several hundred refugees trying to clamber on board for the return journey away from the fighting zone. The soldiers used the butts of their rifles to clear a path so they could unload the supplies and equipment in the car. As I walked across the tracks to the small dingy station, hoisting my duffel, I looked back and saw the tide of ragged, desperate humanity flow over the train, covering it. Women were pushing their weeping children, many of them covered with open sores and scabs on their pinched faces, into the boxcars. Some were already atop the cars tying themselves and their bundles to every iron protrusion.

Pengpu was a market town, with a population of about 250,000 people, which gathered in the crops of Anhwei Province. In times of peace, the produce had gone up the railway to Peking and Tientsin, and south to Nanking and Shanghai. The peasants brought their rice, wheat, corn and squealing pigs into the market in carts pulled by bullocks, donkeys or small horses whose bones showed beneath shrunken flanks. In the open market squares the peasants bought cheap manufactured goods, padded cotton tunics and trousers, canvas shoes, simple farm implements from hawkers or in the shops in the jerry-built one- and two-story buildings on the cobbled side streets. There were small coal mines nearby and flour mills and tobacco factories in Pengpu but no other significant industry.

I got into a ricksha, pulled by an eager young Chinese, who wore a dirty gray towel as a turban and sandals despite the cold, and asked him to take me to the Jesuit Mission. At a trot, he pulled me through the muddied streets to the mission compound, which suddenly loomed up behind tall gray walls. There were about twenty buildings in the compound, mostly brick, a few clay, which clustered about a red-brick Gothic church. As I dismounted from the ricksha, paying the ricksha man extra for bearing my heavy duffel, I asked him if the Communists would come soon. "Yes, the people say they will come soon."

"Are you afraid?"

"No, it will be better. When the fighting stops, the rice will be cheaper."

I went into the mission, where an Italian priest in a long black gown greeted me and took me to the Bishop. In his office, a cold, bare room with simple furniture, and pictures of the Saints on the walls, the Bishop of Pengpu served me strong, black coffee and listened sympathetically. "You are welcome to share our bread and shelter," he said. The Bishop was a kindly, cultured man, about fifty-four years old, portly, with a trim graying beard. He wore a black skullcap and a heavy crucifix over his long black gown that swept the stone floor. He spoke Italian, French, Chinese and a few words of English, and we managed to carry on our conversation in several languages. His name was Cipriano Cassini, and he was from San Remo. He had come to China sixteen years earlier and been appointed Bishop by the Vatican in 1936.

I had seen others of these Catholic missionaries living lonely, spartan lives, much less comfortable than their Protestant counterparts. Once in the early spring of 1947, I had traveled to Kalgan in the northwest where General Fu Tso-yi then ruled as warlord, and gone onto the barren plain where Inner Mongolia began. I stayed with a Belgian Catholic priest whose job it was to send supplies farther into the interior to solitary priests who worked as farmers while they taught school and preached. The Belgian priest was up each dawn laboring on the supply shipments. One midnight I saw a lantern shining in the courtyard and found him in the freezing cold hauling water from the well. I went out, offered to help and asked how he endured the days and nights of unending labor. "Oh, I have had good news," he said. "The Vatican is sending me another priest to help." "Good," I said. "When do you expect him?" "He will come, perhaps, in two years," the priest replied.

The Bishop of Pengpu readily agreed to allow me to stay in the mission without worrying that the presence of an American might bring political retaliation by the Communists. He was hopeful that the Communists would not come south of the Hwai River, but if they did

—he shrugged. "We will trust to God. We have seen many things here," he said. He led me to the refectory for the noon meal and seated me at the head table at his side under a large cross. The priests sat on wooden benches at their dining table, a large chunk of bread beside each plate of thick soup. They ate in silence as a priest read in Latin from the Scriptures. There were fifty-two priests, Italians mainly and a few Chinese, in the mission.

In the mission compound there was a primary school for 800 Chinese youngsters and a middle, or secondary, school for 1,000 boys. The mission ran six other middle schools outside the compound, making a total of 10,000 boys in attendance at the Catholic schools. There was also a mission hospital, staffed by 12 doctors who cared for 150 patients and treated about 800 out-patients daily. One of the school buildings had been taken over by the Nationalists as a prison for captured Communists. In the compound across the road, there was a nunnery, which operated an orphanage and middle school for girls. The nuns took in hundreds of infant girls abandoned by impoverished families which could not afford the luxury of daughters. Thousands more died untended where they were left, in fields, on refuse piles and in the streets. The nuns also ran a nursery school and hospital, with 12 European nurses on duty. The mission did its work in a region which had a population of 9.5 million. "This is the center of civilization in this area," one of the fathers said.

In the afternoon, I went to call on General Liu Chih, the Commander-in-Chief for "Bandit Suppression" in the Hwai-Hai campaign, who had flown here from encircled Hsuchow on November 28. I found him in a gray-brick villa, abandoned by a wealthy rice merchant. The General, fleshy in plain padded uniform that emphasized his rotundity, flashed a gold-toothed smile as he welcomed me in an upstairs room adorned with suitable maps and an open coal brazier that heated the damp room unevenly. "We are closing a trap on Ch'en Yi and Liu Po-ch'eng," the General said, waving at a situation map on the wall. The plan was that the Sixth and Eighth Armies now marching north from Pengpu would batter the Communist columns against the anvil of the Twelfth Group Army, which the Communists had encircled.

Two days later, on December 15, his troops and tanks having been torn apart by the encircling Communist artillery, and after one of his twelve infantry divisions had defected, General Huang surrendered the remnants of his Twelfth Group Army. On the following day, General

Li Yen-nien's Sixth and Eighth Armies, which had advanced only seventeen miles against heavy harassment on their flanks by Communist guerrillas, turned and fell back toward Pengpu. On the bank of the Hwai River I watched the tanks and the truck convoys rattle over the railway bridge, followed by long lines of infantry, to the safety south of the river line.

The Hsuchow garrison was also bogging down in its flight to the southwest. The Sixteenth Group Army, commanded by General Sun Yuan-liang, which had led the retreat from Hsuchow, surrendered as it was enveloped by the Communist blocking force. General Sun escaped dressed as a beggar.

The survivors of the Hsuchow garrison, the Second, Thirteenth and Sixteenth Group Armies and the Armored Corps, some 200,000 men, commanded by General Tu Yü-ming, were harried by the Communists as they withdrew to the west. Finally, in desperation, they drew up in a defensive ring northeast of Yungcheng, a town about a hundred miles northwest of Pengpu. They had succeeded in marching only sixty miles from Hsuchow. On the edge of the perimeter, Tu's divisions dug their large American six-by-six trucks into the crusted brown soil, and scooped trenches and foxholes behind them. The tanks and artillery were drawn into the center to lay down protective fire around the perimeter. Within, the families of soldiers, government officials, students and other civilians who had accompanied the garrison crouched, pelted by the freezing December rain and snow.

On December 17, Mao Tse-tung broadcast a message urging Tu Yü-ming to surrender, guaranteeing life and safety to officers and men:

"For more than ten days, you have been surrounded ring upon ring and received blow upon blow, and your position has shrunk greatly. You have such a tiny place, only a little more than ten li square [about one square mile], and so many people are crowded together that a single shell from us can kill a lot of you. Your wounded soldiers and the families who have followed the army are complaining to high heaven. Your soldiers and many of your officers have no stomach for any more fighting. You, as deputy commander-in-chief, as commanders of armies, corps, divisions and regiments, should understand and sympathize with the feelings of your subordinates and families, hold their lives dear, find a way out for them as early as possible and stop sending them to a senseless death."

Tu Yü-ming did not reply.

I waited in the mission for the Communists to come. During the day, I would wander in the town speaking to the people. There was not much concern about the Communists. There was more worry about Pengpu's bridge across the Hwai River. It was known that the Nationalist garrison had put demolition charges under the 1,823-foot, nine-span bridge. It was to be blown up to delay the Communists when they approached Pengpu. The townspeople had gone to the garrison to plead for the bridge. Built in 1910, it had bestowed relative prosperity on Pengpu. It had brought in the railroad, making Pengpu the central market for the region, and elevated it from a mud village into a town of a quarter of a million people. "If it is blown up," a bearded shopkeeper in a fur hat told me, "we shall be back in the mud. It would take more than a year to rebuild the bridge. It doesn't belong to the Kuomintang or the Communists. It belongs to us." Many of the townspeople were hoping that the Communists would snap up Pengpu one night before the demolition charges went off.

The days dragged and suddenly it was Christmas Eve. I spoke to Harold Milks in Nanking on the single telephone line out of Pengpu and told him if the Communists did not come soon, I would try to cross the Hwai River line. That night, Milks sent a dispatch in which he described me as "the loneliest Associated Press staff member in the whole world this Christmas Eve." But it was not that lonely because in the afternoon, near the railway station, I ran into another newspaperman, Bill Sydney Smith of the London *Daily Express*, a short, quiet, but highly competitive correspondent, whom I had met before in Shanghai. He had traveled to Pengpu with Lachie MacDonald, a bespectacled New Zealander who worked for the London *Daily Mail*, and Patrick O'Donovan, a brooding thirty-one-year-old Irishman who wrote beautiful prose for the *Observer*. To celebrate the gathering, I went out to a Chinese provision shop, joyfully found a fifth of Johnny Walker Black Label, for which I paid the equivalent of twenty dollars, and brought it back to the mission, where we all stayed that night. In one of the four cold bedrooms assigned us, with the portraits of the Saints staring down on us, I doled out the precious Scotch into tea mugs, and with cries of "Cheers!" we downed it. All promptly spat on the stone floor groaning. I had been taken. The Johnny Walker bottle had been filled with evil-tasting tea and resealed. Then someone scrounged a bottle of Italian red wine from one of the priests, so we had our Christmas drink. Donovan was a Catholic, and I accompanied him to midnight Mass when the Bishop asked him if he would join in taking the Sacrament. The twenty-year-old church, draped in festive red cloth, was filled with about two hundred worshipers, mostly Chinese, who had come with their bedding and would spend the night. There was a curfew in the town after nightfall, and nervous sentries patrolling the snow-covered streets opened fire on slight provocation. The Italian priests in the unheated church were wearing long black overcoats. One of them, standing before the altar, set up a huge book of music emblazoned with Chinese characters and led the congregation in "Adeste Fideles" sung in Chinese. Donovan, a burly figure in a red plaid woolen jacket, knelt with the Chinese as the Bishop said Mass. Altar boys in red cassocks swung incense lamps. A choir sang carols in Chinese, and as shots were heard distantly in the town, Christmas dawned.

On Christmas Day an officer brought us a message from General Liu Chih urging us to leave Pengpu on his train. My companions of the night decided to leave for Nanking. It was obvious that the Nationalists did not intend to defend the Hwai River line, and Liu Chih was moving his headquarters south to Chu Hsien. I told the others I would stay and went to the railway station to say goodbye. They left on an armored train with tank turrets fixed atop the cars, the locomotive pushing an open car lined with steel plates and with soldiers manning mounted machine guns. I walked back to the mission, shouldering through the crowds of refugees and soldier stragglers, many of them wounded and on crutches, thronging the streets. I felt very alone.

On New Year's Day, after another week of impatient waiting, I decided to cross the Hwai River line into the Communist areas. I wangled a travel permit from an officer at the garrison headquarters who was beyond caring about the activities of a crazy American. One of the priests found two railroad workers who were eager to return to their homes north of the Hwai and agreed to carry my baggage for a small payment. I hoped to remain for months with the Communists and therefore carried considerable supplies in addition to clothing, a typewriter and camera. A third railway worker, also eager to return home, joined the party.

We set forth from the mission early on the morning of January 2. The railway workers were dressed in their customary black work uniforms, and two of them carried my duffel on a pole between them. I wore a U.S. Army pile jacket and a khaki wool hat. We were met at the Hwai

River Bridge by a Nationalist Army lieutenant who examined my papers, looked at me curiously, and then led us across the span to the last outpost at Tsaolaochi, ten miles north of Pengpu. Ahead of us lay no-man's land, and the most dangerous leg of the journey. Bandits, many of them Nationalist deserters, preyed on the villages and travelers, killing for a trinket or a silver coin, in this stretch between the Nationalist lines and the first Communist outpost. North of that outpost, the Communists were in control of the entire plain except for the flaming perimeter held by Tu Yü-ming's Nationalist troops, ninety miles to the northwest of Tsaolaochi.

As we began walking north, a steady stream of Nationalist planes droned overhead, on the way to drop supplies to Tu Yü-ming's troops or to strike at the encircling Communists. They were my sign, day by day, that the surrounded divisions of Tu Yü-ming were still resisting.

The Hwaipei plain, brown stubble fields flecked with snow drifts, stretched to the horizon. The villages, spaced a half-mile or less apart, clusters of mud houses with straw and tile roofs, each of about fifty to one hundred households, spotted the dull, windswept landscape. Yapping packs of mongrel dogs signaled our progress, each halting at the limits of its village's fields, another picking us up as we approached its universe.

About five miles north of Tsaolaochi we could see a barrier across the road, and men with guns who had stopped some peasants ahead of us. Two peasants returning from the barrier passed us, one of them mumbling something about "bad men," and I was afraid. Bandits. It was too late to turn back, the armed men had seen us, and so we walked slowly forward. There were four of them in peasant dress, and the leader seemed to be a sharp-faced man, oddly wearing a crumpled gray fedora. He held an American Thompson submachine gun, which he pointed at me. When I asked him in Chinese "Who are you?" he shouted back "Who are you?" and thrust the tommy gun at me. "I am an American correspondent," I said. He did not seem to understand, and angrily shouted again, "Who are you?" He slipped the safety catch on the tommy gun and, as if in a trance, I watched wide-eyed as his fingers wrapped around the trigger. One of my baggage carriers shouted: "He is an American correspondent." The sharp-faced one searched us for weapons, and motioned us to sit down. Suddenly, two soldiers in uniform stood up about 150 yards off to the west of the tracks. They had been covering the barrier with a machine gun. We were in the hands of Communist militia. I was taken to one of the uniformed militiamen, whom I showed a letter in Chinese which had been prepared in Nanking, identifying me and asking permission for me to remain with the Chinese Communist armies and to proceed to the headquarters of Mao Tse-tung for an interview with the Party Chairman. I also showed him a photograph which had been taken in Yenan in October 1946 when I had visited there and posed with General Yeh Chien-ying and other leaders at a dinner. The militiaman, a broad-faced peasant with a pistol strapped around the waist of his padded uniform, looked at the photograph uncomprehendingly and shook his head at the letter. He could not read.

With an escort of a half-dozen riflemen, accompanied by my baggage carriers and three other railway workers who had been nabbed at the barrier, we were marched the balance of the afternoon to a village militia headquarters. This was the area in which Communist militia fighters had attacked the flanks of the Sixth and Eighth Nationalist Armies before they were turned back to Pengpu. Scores of decomposed bodies of soldiers still lay in the fields, picked at by black flocks of cawing crows and village dogs. There were slit trenches and foxholes everywhere that had been dug by the Nationalists. Some of the willow trees, carefully husbanded near each hamlet, had been cut down to make clear fields of fire. Peasants were fashioning mud bricks to rebuild walls and thatch new roofs on houses smashed by artillery fire. We saw dozens of wounded Nationalist soldiers, whom the Communists farther north had released allowing them to limp back to their homes in the south.

All the villages in the region had been under Communist control for many months before the start of the Hwai-Hai campaign. I was told proudly by the militia leader, who pounded his chest with the flat of his hand, that the peasants now owned the land, and the landlords had been dealt with.

The villages of this region had slumbered without a dream of change until one day the Communists had suddenly appeared, coming down from North China and Shantung. At first there had been no soldiers, only many Communist cadres, political workers, some of them only students. Teams of about a half-dozen cadres had gone to each village, speaking not of Marxism-Leninism but of the peasants' grievances against the corrupt Kuomintang officials and local gentry who were the landlords. About one-fourth of the land was owned by the gentry, many of them Kuomintang officials or army officers who had bought up or seized the land from peasants impoverished in the turmoil of the war with the Japanese.

For the rich, the land had been the best hedge against the inflation. The landlords of the Hwaipei plain had not respected the Kuomintang law of 1930—hardly observed anywhere in the country—which restricted rents to 37.5 percent of the crop. Rents were mainly at a traditional 50 percent, but many landlords on this good land charged as much as 60 or 70 percent. Some of the gentry had ruled as petty despots, their men beating up peasants who could not pay the rents or the usurious interest on loans. It was common for a landlord to press a peasant into forced labor, or take his daughter as a slave maid or concubine, in lieu of unpaid rents. In Nanking, the Generalissimo spoke of the principles of San Min Chu I, but feudalism flourished on the land.

At first the Hwaipei peasants were afraid of the Communist cadres, apprehensive that association with them would bring retribution from the gentry or punishment by the Nationalist soldiers who might be summoned from the garrison towns. Then the peasants, their burdens and hatreds outweighing their fears, began to organize, and violent demonstrations against the landlords erupted. There were mass trials and the landlords were accused of "crimes against the people." In the village where the militia headquarters was situated, the local landlord, who owned more than fifty acres, had been denounced and humiliated at a trial. In the neighboring village, a landlord accused of killing one of his tenants had been stoned to death. The Communist cadre supervised the redistribution of the landlord's land. The rich peasants who owned several acres and tilled their own fields were left undisturbed. The distribution of the land was according to its quality. But on the average, each adult member of a household received about two mow of land, or one-third of an acre. The landlord's house, a three-room dwelling, larger but not much different from some of the other houses in the village, was used as a militia headquarters and meeting place. The landlord and his family had left for a city in the south.

Several weeks after the land reform, the first Communist Army units came into the villages. They were not like the Nationalist soldiers, who requisitioned whatever they wanted. They paid for the food supplied them by the peasants in Communist currency, issued by the Farmers Bank of Chung-chou, which could be exchanged for Nationalist yuan or silver dollars. The soldiers organized and trained "self-defense" militia units and distributed weapons and some uniforms. In the fall of 1948, when Ch'en Yi and Liu Po-ch'eng's columns came into the region to prepare for the Hwai-Hai campaign, the villages were already well organized. Thousands of willing peasants were recruited to carry supplies and to dig trenches that were used to block the retreat of the Nationalist armies. When the Sixth and Eighth Nationalist Armies marched north to the relief of Huang's Twelfth Group Army, the peasant guerrillas struck ferociously at them, slowing the advance until the encircled Nationalists were overrun. When I asked the militia leader how his men had fought against the tanks and artillery of General Li Yen-nien, he said: "These are our fields."

The land reforms on the Hwaipei plain were similar to programs elsewhere in the Communist-held areas of the country. The Kuomintang, preoccupied with the cities and the civil war, had done little to ease the plight of the peasants. Mao Tse-tung found the raw power of his revolution in the villages. As early as 1927, Mao had looked to the peasants as the mainspring of revolution, staging the peasant "autumn harvest uprisings." These rural insurrections, organized at a time when the Chinese Communist Party was still under the direction of the Stalin-dominated Comintern, were unsuccessful. Later, breaking with the Leninist concept, dogmatically required by the Comintern, that revolution must be led by the urban proletariat with the peasants only in a secondary role, Mao Tse-tung established his foundation for revolution in the countryside. He proclaimed the heresy, which the Chinese Communist Party finally adopted as its successful strategy, that the "revolutionary vanguard" shall be drawn from the poor peasants. In May 1946, as prospects of coalition with the Nationalists waned, the Communist Party put into effect a radical land reform program. During the war and in the immediate postwar period, the Communists had contented themselves with organizing cooperatives on the land, reducing rents while encouraging a united front among the people. The May 1946 directive resumed the redistribution of land and class warfare against the rural gentry. The land reform smashed the classes which were the natural political foes of the Communists and gave the poor peasants, who made up the bulk of the rural population, a vested interest in Communist victory. The land reform program was not always carried out in a uniform, orderly manner. Mao Tse-tung and other leaders conceded later that there had been "leftist excesses" at times. In Nanking and in my travels in the north, I had spoken to Chinese who witnessed the terror rampant in some areas, especially in Hopei and

Shantung. Thousands of landlords and some rich peasants had been slaughtered by mobs who seized their possessions. The mobs ignored the Communist land decrees which granted those landlords not convicted of "crimes against the people" the right to retain land on the scale of the average holdings and which also extended protection to those rich peasants who tilled their own fields.

In 1950, after the conquest of the mainland, the Party stated that 100 million peasants had been involved in the land reform program, including 4 million landlord families whose rented land had been seized and redistributed. The peasants who received this land made up the base on which Mao built his revolution. Land, not ideology, attracted the loyalty of the peasant masses. The second banner of nationalism raised by the Communists against foreign concessions in China and in the war against the Japanese rallied intellectuals as well as peasants.

My first night in the "Liberated Area" was spent in the militia headquarters village sleeping in a small mud-walled shed used to store grain. I stretched out on the kaoliang grain sacks with a blanket over me. In the night, I heard the scurryings of mice and rats, and felt them tread my blanket. I pulled my U.S. Army wool knit hat over my face, and was awakened by the rodents running over my covered features. I was glad to see the morning, and the militiaman who brought in a feast of fresh hen's eggs, steaming hot brown kaoliang bread and tea.

We marched north all the next day, and at sundown came into a village where I was greeted by the commander of a unit of Liu Po-ch'eng's columns. It was my first contact on the Hwaipei with a regular army unit. The commander, who wore no badge or identification, was a lean, strong man with a friendly, compassionate manner about him. "We will escort you to Suhsien," he said. "You will go by horse tomorrow." He released the six railway workers with me, and told them they could go where they liked. The next morning, on horses led by one rifleman and with another leading a horse laden with baggage, we rode out of the village. A cluster of youngsters from the village, the boys with shaven heads, gathered to watch the exit. Their large dark eyes stared in amazement at the first "foreign devil" they had seen. The commander waved goodbye. I would see him again and come to like him more than anyone else I met in the Communist area. We rode well away from the railroad. Nationalist fighters and bombers passed overhead on the way to or returning from the Yungcheng encirclement of Tu Yü-ming's forces seventy-five miles to the northwest. Each village seemed like the other as our horses picked their way across the monotonous plain, following paths through the fields and along the banks of irrigation ditches. We stopped for the night at a village, thirty miles south of Suhsien. I shared a hut with my escort and other soldiers, who played cards and sang over a small fire. One of the songs referred to Chiang Kai-shek as "a running dog of the Americans," and with a grin, one of the soldiers in friendly fashion asked me: "Why is Truman helping Chiang?" I shook my head. It was too much for my Chinese. I was awakened in the morning by the soldiers drilling outside my hut and singing, "On to Nanking and strike down Chiang Kai-shek."

Our journey continued and took us through the eastern edge of the area where Huang's Twelfth Group Army had been destroyed three weeks earlier. Desolate and silent, except for the cawing crows who perched on the unburied bodies of the soldier dead, the battlefield stretched into the pale gold of the setting sun. The fields were cratered by artillery shells and bombs dropped by Nationalist B-25s and B-24s on the encircling Communist positions. Demolished American vehicles, tires and salvageable parts already stripped, lay rusting at a distance in the deserted fields. Thousands of Huang's troops who survived the final artillery bombardment had been marched off to prisoner encampments in long lines. The bulk of Liu Po-ch'eng's and Ch'en Yi's columns had already marched north to join the encirclement of Tu Yü-ming's forces, which had been whittled down to about 130,000 troops.

The final episode in one of the largest and most decisive battles in modern history was unfolding, and yet there was no way for me to send a dispatch which would record the details, and perhaps arouse some indignation about the destruction, or some sentiment for the clumps of dead now frozen into the brown unyielding earth. I never saw anyone weep for the dead on this battlefield, and I could not find the tears myself, although I bore away with me the anguish of that forgotten tract.

It was dusk, the evening of January 5, when we reached our destination, a headquarters about ten miles southwest of Suhsien. I was escorted to a hut. Soon, a round-faced man, named Wu, whom some addressed as Deputy Commissar, dressed like the others in a plain uniform, arrived to question me. Wu looked me over rather suspiciously as he questioned me in Chinese. He would tell me nothing of himself, his rank or unit, except that he was from Hopei Province. He was obviously an intelligent, well-educated man. A young Chinese wearing black horn-rimmed glasses, who looked like a student, joined us and examined my baggage and papers. He left with my typewriter and camera. "I cannot take responsibility," Wu said, "for allowing you to pass into the Liberated Area. Your case must be referred to my superiors." He took my letter requesting permission to proceed to Mao Tsetung's headquarters, and I was escorted to another house, one of the larger ones in the village, with two rooms, one of them used for grain storage, where I slept on the sacks.

In the morning, I found myself under the guard of three friendly soldiers, armed with American carbines. I walked out the door to look at a cold but beautiful morning. The frost glistened on the stubble in the fields. Without any warning a Nationalist Mustang fighter flashed overhead on a strafing run. In fascination I watched its machine-gun fire stitch across the field several hundred yards away. It did not occur to me to duck for cover, nor did the incident excite my guards, who presented me with a breakfast of duck eggs, rice and tea. Wu returned, very polite but still suspicious, to tell me that my letter had been forwarded, and that when a reply came, I would be notified.

My afternoon was enlivened by a wedding ceremony at the next house. With firecrackers popping, a grinning bridegroom brought home his bride, who sat cross-legged on a sled decorated with red silk and drawn by a small donkey and an ox. The bride, wearing an embroidered hat, a padded gown with huge mandarin sleeves over an embroidered satin wedding skirt, sat with head bowed modestly. The groom wore a long, fleece-lined gown and mandarin hat. There was a feast that evening, with the peasants singing and eating steamed bread, man-t'ou, and drinking bai-ghar, a strong clear vodka-like drink distilled from kaoliang grain.

The same day Communist troops launched their final assault on Tu Yü-ming's encircled armies. In the distance I heard the steady thudding of the artillery through the night.

At 11 o'clock the next morning, Wu returned and said to me firmly: "In regard to your mission, we ask you to return. This area is a war zone and it is not convenient for you to proceed." I interjected: "But if it is a question of danger, I don't care."

"You don't care, but we do care about you passing through here," Wu snapped back.

I turned abruptly and walked into the other room, where the grain was stored. The accumulated tensions and the disappointment were too much. I leaned against one of the grain sacks and wept. When I was composed, I returned to face Wu, who stood waiting impatiently. I asked if he would allow me to proceed via Tsinan in Shantung to Tsingtao, where the U.S. Navy was still based. He declined. When I asked for an explanation in writing, he shook his head and said: "It is enough that you have asked and we have refused." He said he did not know whether my request for an interview with Mao Tse-tung had been referred directly to the Party leader.

Stung by Wu's hardness, I said bitterly: "You know I came here to tell your side of the story." Wu's features relaxed for the first time. "You cannot help us," he said softly. "The horses are waiting."

Outside the hut there was an escort officer already mounted, waiting for me. Wu returned my typewriter and camera. Two soldiers put my belongings on two horses and mounted two others. As I climbed on my horse, Wu came up to me, put his hand on my saddle, and said gently, speaking for the first time in English: "I hope to see you again. Peaceful journey. Goodbye."

As we rode out of the village, I became aware that the artillery in the northwest had stopped. There was an almost eerie stillness. I turned to my escort officer and said: "The artillery has stopped. Are the Hsuchow troops finished?"

"Yes," he replied. "Just about finished." It was January 7 and Communist troops had charged and pierced one section of Tu Yüming's perimeter. The 130,000 survivors of the Hsuchow garrison had been ringed by 300,000 Communist troops. The airdrops made from above two thousand feet could not supply the garrison adequately. Many of the parachutes caught in the stiff plains winds drifted into the Communist camp. Horses were slaughtered for food. The soldiers scrounged for bark and roots in the fields. Women and children froze to death in the crowded village huts, which had no fuel for fires. On the edge of the perimeter, Communist loudspeakers offered the Nationalist soldiers food and safety if they would surrender. "There is no escape," the loudspeakers boomed before the final artillery barrage opened on January 6. Panic spread among the Nationalist troops at the news that there had been discussion in Nanking of bombing their equipment, especially the tanks of the Armored Corps, to prevent them from falling into Communist hands. The Second Group Army surrendered first, then the Thirteenth Group Army and the Armored Corps followed. By January 10 the

Communists had mopped up and the Battle of the Hwai-Hai was ended.

Tu Yü-ming, disguised as an ordinary soldier, pretended to be a prisoner of his bodyguard, who were dressed as Communists, but he was captured as they tried to slip away. General Li Mi, commander of the Thirteenth Group Army, escaped disguised as a merchant and was taken through the Communist lines in a wheelbarrow. I was to encounter him again.

For the Communists, the Hwai-Hai campaign had lasted sixty-five days, from November 6, 1948, to January 10, 1949. They were confronted by a Nationalist force of about the size of their army, but better equipped with tanks, artillery and vehicles and with complete command of the air. Yet the Communists won total victory. They wiped out 56 divisions of the Nationalists' best troops, including the Armored Corps, comprising 555,000 men. They took 327,000 prisoners. Four and a half divisions defected to the Communists. The military equipment captured was beyond counting. The way was now open to Nanking and Shanghai as soon as the Communists could regroup for the Yangtze River crossing.

The disaster on the Hwaipei plain would be attributed by military historians to the failure of the Generalissimo's leadership. First, he had elected to stand on the Hsuchow salient instead of holding behind the barrier of the Hwai River line. Second, instead of assigning command of the Hsuchow forces to General Pai Ch'ung-hsi, the Central China Commander, who was his best strategist, he had turned it over to Generals Liu Chih and Tu Yü-ming, two notorious incompetents. Once again it had been a matter of passing over Pai, a Kwangsi general, in favor of Chiang's Whampoa clique.

On the journey back, I followed the same line of villages to the south. With my soldier escort, I reached my first station at 5:45 P.M. after dark, and we joined a group of soldiers sitting about cooking fires, who shared their rice and bits of pork with us.

In every village it seemed that the night was alive with high-spirited soldiers singing. Every Communist soldier seemed to have been briefed by commanders and political officers about the general strategy of the Hwai-Hai campaign and the next move against the Yangtze in the summer.

The soldiers were intensely curious about American gadgets. They crowded around as I demonstrated my typewriter and camera. A young infantryman surprised me by asking about automat restaurants, of which he had read. "Twenty years after all China is Communist, we shall have automat restaurants," he said.

The fires were low when I went to a hut, wrapped myself in a blanket and lay in a corner, listening to the snores of the others, utterly dejected about the rebuff at the Communist headquarters. Pompously, I had written that morning in my diary: "I felt, in a sense, that I had been the first envoy of the United States to Communist China, and I had been spurned." Staring into the darkness, I became wiser. The realization came that we were beyond the crossroads, that Mao was traveling his revolutionary road and that my own people were on another, going in a different direction. I knew now that the time of Americans mixing freely with the Communists was over. There would be no more friendly dinners in Yenan and jovial ideological debates. Mao Tse-tung was bent on his revolutionary course, and foreigners, Americans or Russians for that matter, would not deflect him. "When would Americans and Chinese come together again?" I asked the question of myself without being able to answer.

We made seventeen miles the next day and I was back at the village headquarters of the first regular army commander I had met, whom I liked so much. He listened to me sympathetically, and at the evening meal, sitting around the fire, we shared a delicious fish fried in a pungent sauce. He asked me about the two-party political system and about the status of Negroes in the United States. He told me that he had been with the People's Liberation Army since 1936 and had seen his wife and family only once since then. In the morning, before I left, he wrote on the flyleaf of my diary in fine Chinese characters: "We would like to fight to the end with our American friends for democracy, freedom and happiness." He signed his name T'ien Wu-chang without indicating his rank.

Another day's journey, and on the morning of January 10 I was taken to within about five miles of the Hwai River Bridge. The Nationalist Tsaolaochi outpost had been pulled back behind the river line. My escort found me two peasants to help with my baggage, waved goodbye and rode back to the north. I approached the Nationalist bridge outpost waving a white handkerchief, and they took me in.

I stayed the night in the Jesuit Mission, saying goodbye in sadness to the Bishop and the other priests. They were stoical, but I knew the mission would not survive long. The Communists would never tolerate leaving the education of their young in the care of foreigners. At the railway station, I fought my way into a boxcar jammed with refugees and soldiers who had abandoned their weapons, and went back to Nanking.

Pengpu was evacuated by its skeleton garrison on January 15. Nationalist troops looted the town's shops, and blew up the Pengpu bridge, killing thirty civilians who were on the span when the demolition charges went off without warning.

Many years later I learned from Padre Mario Francesconi, the last of the Pengpu Mission's superiors, what happened to the town and the Jesuits.

"When the Communists first came, they preached freedom," Padre Mario said. "For the first year, the people kept quiet because they believed. Then the Communists made everyone sign statements if they had cooperated with the old government. Worse, everyone was asked to write his own autobiography many times and answer three terrible questions: One: What do you think of Communism? Two: Give the names of your friends and enemies. Three: What evil deeds have you done to the people? Then began the wave of denunciations and executions of 'the enemies of the people.'

"The mission did not escape this process. The Communists didn't want to expel the missionaries outright but were determined to find 'evidence' of their wrongdoings so that the people would denounce them or they would leave of their own accord.

"It was a process to try to break down the missionaries, and it was this continual harassment that in the end killed the Bishop. The Communists would come in day and night and ask for the mission's accounts. They had already frozen the mission's money in the banks. They first came to the mission on January 19, 1950, asking for one room, to put their agent in to report everything that went on in the mission. Later they took over the whole second floor of the mission headquarters to house foreign guests, such as a group of Russian engineers who came in to rebuild the bridge which had been blown up by the Nationalists. When there were foreign guests in the building, the priests were confined to their quarters and only allowed out for a short time when it was certain that they would not meet with other foreigners. Once there was a delegation from the Italian Communist Party—but there were no contacts allowed.

"One evening a Chinese priest arrived at the mission by river boat without official permission. The police agent reported his visit and the

Bishop had to spend three nights in jail as punishment. Worse, the Bishop was forced to buy an advertisement in the local paper to say he had been wrong to receive a visitor without authorization and that the Communists were good because they had kept him in prison only three days. There was no limit to the charity of the Bishop. When the Communists came, they took everything he had, and when he had nothing more to give, he died. He died in the mission, sitting upright in his room with his breviary in his hands, on June 13, 1951.

"Things got worse when the Bishop died. The Communists tried to say that the Bishop had committed suicide, taken too much opium. But the missionaries were able to get a statement from the doctors that he had died of a heart attack.

"When the Bishop died, the Communists closed the church, defaced its façade to make it look like a bank, removed Gothic decorations and turned it into a theater. The priests were forced to move out of their residence and went to the nunnery. The bishop was buried in an area south of the compound near the seminary. Some two thousand Chinese Catholics came to his funeral. The Communists asked for their names. It was at this point that the mission decided to burn all its own records. At this time, too, the Communists banned baptism, but the priests did not heed this ruling. They opened two new chapels in the nunnery and received more Chinese Catholics than before.

"When the Communists took over the mission schools, I went to teach at the seminary.

"The Communist line to the missionaries was: 'We protect the mission, but the people want you to leave.' At least a thousand meetings were held with the people to try to get them to denounce the 'foreign dogs.' But the people, who had been cared for by the mission hospital and whose sons had gone to their school, steadfastly refused to denounce the missionaries.

"Then the Communists tried intimidation. They called in one of the forty Chinese nurses and told her that her father was to be shot but that she could save his life. She was asked to testify that I had done some fault, to give the names of the best Catholics of the mission and admit that there was a section of the Legion of Mary (which to Chinese minds sounded paramilitary) in the mission—which wasn't true. She finally agreed so as to save her father, and was told to bring in her photo and not to tell anyone about the police pressure. But she came to me crying and told me everything. I counseled her to tell the police that everything she had said was false—which she did. She was then forced to report to the police daily, but nothing happened to her father.

"Finally, the police picked on a former seminarist who had been a soldier in the Nationalist Army and was working at the mission and took pictures of him with me, holding a Latin grammar and next to a crucifix. To me the police pointed out Article 12 of the Constitution that says those who keep traitors must suffer the same punishment as traitors. This was intended to frighten me and make me leave of my own free will. But I only laughed and the next morning gave the police my written answer: 'If I have gone against Chinese laws, I must do penance in China.' The police were very angry. Then they said that if I did not sign a statement saying, 'I leave China freely,' five Chinese would be put in jail. Only then did I agree to sign—but the five Chinese were put in jail anyway. This happened in January 1953. I was the last of the superiors in the Pengpu Mission."

NANKING AWAITS
THE COMMUNISTS

The Nanking to which I returned in January 1949 lay cowering in hopelessness and despair as it waited for the Communists. Chiang Kai-shek had decided to retire, saying he would yield the government to Vice President Li Tsung-jen. On Christmas Eve, the Generalissimo had driven in his black Cadillac to the "Song of Victory" church, an official residence converted by Madame Chiang into a place of worship for Christians in the government, and there, near the Sun Yat-sen Mausoleum, he sang carols in his native Chekiang accent. The next morning, he told his subordinates that he would announce his resignation on New Year's Day. There was reason enough for him to go.

In 1948 alone, Nationalist military power had been reduced by heavy losses from an estimated strength of 2,723,000 troops to 1,500,-000, of which approximately 500,000 were service troops. Communist strength, swelled by Nationalist defections, went in the same period from an estimated 1,150,000 to 1,622,000, virtually all combat-effectives.

General Barr, the last JUSMAG commander, would leave Nanking at the end of January, and in his final summary to Washington would say:

I believe that the Government committed its first politico-military blunder when it concentrated its efforts after V-J Day on the purely military reoccupation of the former Japanese areas, giving little consideration to long established regional sentiments or to creation of efficient local administrations which could attract wide popular support in the liberated areas. Moreover, the Nationalist

49

Army was burdened with an unsound strategy which was conceived by a politically influenced and militarily inept high command. Instead of being content with consolidating North China, the Army was given the concurrent mission of seizing control of Manchuria, a task beyond its logistic capabilities. The Government, attempting to do too much with too little, found its armies scattered along thousands of miles of railroads, the possession of which was vital in view of the fact that these armies were supplied from bases in central China. In order to hold the railroads, it was also necessary to hold the large cities through which they passed. As time went on, the troops degenerated from field armies, capable of offensive combat, to garrison and lines of communication troops with an inevitable loss of offensive spirit. Communist military strength, popular support, and tactical skill were seriously under-estimated from the start. It became increasingly difficult to maintain effective control over the large sections of predominantly Communist countryside through which the lines of communication passed. Lack of Nationalist forces qualified to take the field against the Communists enabled the latter to become increasingly strong. The Nationalists, with their limited resources, steadily lost ground against an opponent who not only shaped his strategy around available human and material resources, but also capitalized skillfully on the Government's strategic and tactical blunders and economic vulnerability. . . .

It must be understood that all through the structure and machinery of the Nationalist Government there are interlocking ties of interest peculiar to the Chinese—family, financial, political. No man, no matter how efficient, can hope for a position of authority on account of being the man best qualified for the job; he simply must have other backing. In too many cases, this backing was the support and loyalty of the Generalissimo for his old army comrades which kept them in positions of high responsibility regardless of their qualifications. A direct result of this practice is the unsound strategy and faulty tactics so obviously displayed in the fight against the Communists.

Madame Chiang had found the doors shut in Washington when she arrived to plead for more aid. Marshall was already seriously ill and Dean Acheson, who was to become Secretary of State, shared Washington's general skepticism and disillusionment with the Generalissimo. There was no interest in Chiang's offer that American officers, perhaps General Douglas MacArthur or General Mark Clark, join in staff direction of the Nationalist war effort. The United States had already allocated about $3 billion in military and economic aid, much of the military equipment having wound up in the hands of the Communists.

General Barr had reported on November 18 that "no battle has been lost since my arrival due to lack of ammunition or equipment. Their military debacles in my opinion can all be attributed to the world's worst leadership and many other morale destroying factors that lead to a complete loss of will to fight." The Generalissimo had refused or had proved incapable of acceding to the demands for military, political and economic reforms which Marshall and his advisers in China deemed essential to an efficient Nationalist war effort against the Communists.

On March 29, 1948, the first constitutional session of the National Assembly was convened, but its outcome was a travesty. There had been a freshet of hope for democracy when a revolt among the delegates had elected Li Tsung-jen as Vice President over the furious opposition of the Generalissimo. But when the Assembly was dismissed in April, the Kwangsi General found himself powerless, with no one to complain to except Ambassador Stuart, and the Generalissimo still in complete dictatorial control of the army, Kuomintang and government.

On August 19 Draconian economic reform decrees to curb currency speculation and hoarding and black marketing were issued. General Chiang Ching-kuo, the Generalissimo's son, was put in charge in Shanghai, and he sternly enforced the regulations, executing some offenders on the streets of the city. Chiang Ching-kuo soon ran into opposition as business became depressed. He had the support of K. C. Wu, the ebullient, courageous Mayor of Shanghai, but Ching-kuo locked horns with Tu Yueh-sheng, the notorious leader of the underworld, a member of the Green Gang secret society, whose influence extended to Chiang Kai-shek. The irrepressible Ching-kuo also crossed his stepmother, Madame Chiang. His agents uncovered a huge cache of prohibited goods in the warehouses of the Yangtze Development Corporation, controlled by H. H. Kung, the banker husband of Madame Chiang's elder sister. Ching-kuo raided the warehouses and threatened to arrest David Kung, the banker's son, who was in charge. Madame Chiang flew to Shanghai, and soon after, David Kung left for the United States amid a great scandal. Restraints on prices and wages were removed on October 31. Ching-kuo resigned his post on November 1, and Shanghai was again in the toils of, in the General's words, the "unscrupulous merchants, bureaucrats, politicans and racketeers." T. V. Soong, the brother of Madame Chiang, was another member of the family whose participation in government and private business manipulations became indistinguishable in the peculiar bureaucratic capitalism that scandalized Nationalist China.

In contrast to other members of the family, Madame Sun Yat-sen, the second sister of Madame Chiang and the widow of the father of the Chinese Revolution, was respected and popular among the people. She lived in Shanghai, heading the China Welfare Institute. With the help of a young American, Gerald Tannebaum, who was executive director, she distributed medical and other relief supplies to thirty-eight organizations in the Nationalist and Communist areas. Estranged from Chiang Kai-shek, it was only her personal prestige and the funding of American and other Western charities which gave her the license to operate in Communist as well as Nationalist areas. When the Communist Government was founded, she became one of six vice chairmen of the Government Council, the highest organ of state authority.

On New Year's Day, the Generalissimo issued his statement of resignation, but stipulated obviously unacceptable conditions for his retirement and peace negotiations. He had been sharply stung by the Communist broadcast of a list of forty-five war criminals, naming himself and Madame Chiang as the prime culprits. But the pressures were becoming unbearable for Chiang. The Generalissimo drove again out the Great Peace Gate of the city to the Sun Yat-sen Mausoleum on the slope of Purple Mountain. From the foot of the white stone stairway, I watched as the slim uniformed figure in the military cloak and cap walked up the steps of the tomb leaning on a walking stick. Before entering the tomb, he took off his cloak and handed it to an aide. Upon entering he bowed three times before the white marble statue of the seated Sun Yat-sen. When the Generalissimo emerged, he paused at the entrance and looked down for the last time at his walled capital to the west. Then he walked down the steps, saluting and nodding to the thousands of soldiers massed about the tomb, re-entered his Cadillac and sped back to the T'ai P'ing Palace. A few days later, on January 22, he flew to Fenghua, his birthplace, a lovely town in Chekiang Province near the coast. Ostensibly, the Generalissimo had retired in Confucian humility to the life of a country squire. In reality, he was feverishly preparing for his retreat to the Taiwan redoubt. It was not the first time that Chiang had withdrawn to the country, supposedly to dabble in rural delights, but actually to confound his enemies. Li Tsung-jen, the Generalissimo's political opponent, was left behind in Nanking as the Acting President, to deal with the Communists, but without control over the bulk of the armed forces, the government or its finances. Chiang continued to manipulate the levers of power from Fenghua. When Li sent representatives to Fenghua to plead for authority over the remaining resources of the government needed to organize the defenses south of the Yangtze, he was rebuffed. The Generalissimo, meanwhile, making ready his ultimate refuge on Taiwan, transferred air force and naval units to the island, a hundred miles off the Fukien coast. Some of the best remaining Nationalist divisions, commanded by generals personally loyal to Chiang, were also sent there and United States military aid shipments were diverted to Taiwan. These shipments were from the last aid allocation passed reluctantly by Congress on April 2, 1948, providing $338 million for economic rehabilitation and $125 million which could be used to buy military equipment and supplies. After December 1948 virtually the entire Nationalist reserve of gold and silver bullion and other foreign exchange, as well as national art treasures, were moved to the island.

The Generalissimo also clamped tighter military and police control over the restive eight million Taiwanese. Taiwan had been ruled as a colony of Japan for fifty years, having been ceded by China in 1895 following defeat in the Sino-Japanese War. At the end of World War II, the Allied Command transferred authority over the island to the Chiang Government pending conclusion of a peace treaty with Japan.

The Nationalist troops sent in by Chiang Kai-shek to occupy Taiwan looted and stripped the island, which had been developed with Japanese capital. Many Kuomintang officials expropriated land from Taiwanese for themselves. In February and March 1947, the Taiwanese demonstrated against the sacking of their island, demanding that the Nationalist Governor, Ch'en Yi, reform his corrupt, dictatorial administration. Ch'en Yi's response was to bring in additional troops from the mainland and put down the demonstrations in an orgy of killing in which between ten and twenty thousand Taiwanese were massacred, including several thousand of the island's political and economic leaders and intellectual elite. On the Generalissimo's orders, Ch'en Yi eventually was shot for his excesses, but the population of the island, to which Chiang would eventually flee, remained hostile to the mainlanders.

In January 1949, Ambassador Stuart was still tirelessly striving to mediate in the civil war. His confidant, Philip Fugh, had once again discussed the prospect of a peace settlement, this time with Chang Chih-chung. A thin, hatchet-faced man and skillful political intriguer, Chang Chih-chung had been a close associate of Chiang Kai-shek since their days at the Whampoa Academy. Now a minister without portfolio in the Nationalist cabinet, he was acting on behalf of Li Tsung-jen as the key intermediary in negotiations with the Chinese Communists and the Soviet Embassy on moves to end the civil war. Secretly, he had been in touch with Chou En-lai, with whom he had an old personal tie. Directly, and through Chang Chih-chung, Stuart had contacted the Soviet Ambassador, General N. V. Roshchin, a number of times, seeking Russian assistance in persuading the Communists to negotiate a peace settlement. Some of these contacts had not been reported to the State Department. Roshchin, a gregarious, bluff soldier, who previously had been Military Attaché in Nanking, repeatedly had expressed interest in a mediation effort.

On January 4 Ambassador Stuart wrote in his personal diary, extracts* of which have not been published previously:

> Philip saw Chang Chih-chung who said CCP [Chinese Communist Party] determination to fight on is not due to Soviet who advise them to stop at the Yangtze.

The diary entry indicated that the Russians had tried to persuade Mao Tse-tung to check his armies at the Yangtze and to consolidate his gains while leaving the south to the Nationalists, at least for the time being. Stalin had a stake in preserving some vestige of the Nationalist Government.

Apart from allowing the Chinese Communists to take over the weapons of the surrendered Japanese forces in Manchuria, Moscow had not given Mao Tse-tung any significant assistance in the civil war. Mao, in an unpublished speech before the Tenth Plenary Session of the Eighth Central Committee of his Party on September 24, 1962, discussed the attitude of the Russians at that time. Referring to the Sino-Soviet ideological dispute, Mao said:

> The roots for [the conflict] were laid earlier. The episode occurred a long time ago. They did not allow China to make revolution. This was in 1945, when Stalin tried to prevent the Chinese Revolution by saying there should not be any civil war and that we must collaborate with Chiang Kai-shek. At that time we did not carry this into effect, and the revolution was victorious. After the victory, they again suspected that China would be like Yugoslavia and I would become a Tito.

Stalin had already gained important concessions in Manchuria, at the expense of the Nationalist Government, as a consequence of the understanding reached by Stalin, Roosevelt and Churchill at Yalta in February 1945. On August 14 Nationalist China and the Soviet Union

---

*Entries quoted here have been edited slightly for clarity.

signed a treaty implementing the Yalta understanding, which gave Moscow joint ownership and operation of the Chinese Eastern and Manchurian Railways, use of Port Arthur as a naval base and lease of half of the port facilities of Dairen. In the exchange of notes, the Soviet Union promised to give moral support and military aid entirely to the "National Government as the central government of China." Confronted by the prospect of civil war with the Chinese Communists, Chiang Kai-shek was quite satisfied to yield the Manchurian concessions to the Russians in return for Soviet recognition of the legitimacy of his government. In any case, Soviet armies were already in occupation of Manchuria without the presence of a single Nationalist soldier, and the Sino-Soviet treaty like the Yalta agreement was tacit recognition of what Stalin intended to take by force if he could not obtain the rights by a stroke of the pen. The Chinese also were being prodded by the United States and Britain to give effect to the agreement concluded at Yalta.

In January 1949, as the Chinese Communists stood on the banks of the Yangtze, Stalin was tempted to salvage his war gains through mediation between the Nationalists and Communists. To entice the Russians further, Chang Chih-chung flew to Sinkiang and attempted to negotiate an agreement that would have given Moscow special trading rights in that Central Asia border province and brought it in effect under Soviet influence.

On January 23, Vice President Li, trying every device to reach a peace accord with the Communists, informed Stuart that he had reached a tentative understanding with Roshchin for Russian intercession. The price was a pledge to maintain China's strict neutrality in any future international conflict, eliminate American influence from China to the greatest extent possible, and establish a new basis for effective cooperation between China and the Soviet Union. When Li asked for American approval of this negotiating approach, Stuart was told by the State Department to inform the Vice President that it considered it "incredible that Li Tsung-jen should seek a United States statement indicating support for the purpose of strengthening his position while at the same time arranging a tentative agreement with the Russians calling for elimination of American influence from China."

In early February, the Soviet Ambassador left for Canton following Premier Sun Fo, who had installed his cabinet, including the Foreign Ministry, in the southern metropolis while the Acting President remained in Nanking to deal with the Communists. The Soviet Union was thus the first of the great powers to transfer its embassy from Nanking to Canton as requested by the Nationalist Government. It was a clever ploy. From the standpoint of strict protocol, Roshchin was behaving correctly. The jump to Canton also put him in position to salvage any possible gain from the wreckage of Nationalist China. Stalin was given additional leverage to bargain with the Chinese Communists.

However, Mao Tse-tung impassively withstood the Soviet maneuvers, aware that he was on the verge of total victory. When the inevitable flight of the Nationalist Government from the mainland took place, and the Chinese Communist Government was founded in Peking (called Peiping by the Nationalists), it was promptly accorded Soviet recognition. The agile Roshchin became the first ambassador to the People's Republic. But in 1955, as Stalin had anticipated, embarrassed by the anomaly of retaining a colonial position on the territory of a fellow Socialist state, Moscow was compelled to give up its rights in Manchuria.

In Nanking, as the Communist onslaught across the Yangtze grew more imminent, the entries in Stuart's diary reflected the rivalries and divisions which persisted within the Nationalist Government despite its desperate predicament.

JAN. 7—Meanwhile Formosa is being prepared as an "arsenal for democracy." All the people and most of those in the Government want peace but the will of CKS [Chiang Kai-shek] and his failure to understand the non-military aspects of Communism—or even the military—and the truculence of CP [Communist Party] are combining to lengthen a futile and disastrous conflict.

All Stuart's hopes for peace now rested on the two Kwangsi generals, Li Tsung-jen and Pai Ch'ung-hsi, the Central China Commander, with headquarters at Hankow, who had some 350,000 troops, the only force that the Vice President could count on.

JAN. 22—CKS has left but problem of status of Li not clear. CKS on Formosa raises many problems.
Peiping fighting over.

While Nationalist armies were being chewed up in the Hwai-Hai region of East-Central China, a great but less bloody military disaster befell the Nationalists in the Peking-Tientsin area of North China. Since early December, General Fu Tso-yi, the Nationalist commander, had secretly been negotiating with Lin Piao advancing from Manchuria. The delaying actions culminated with a face-saving siege of Peking during which the Communists pumped a few 75-mm shells into the city, mainly duds, so as not to damage its historical treasures, and on January 23 a Communist regiment marched into the city after a moderate surrender document had been signed. The Generalissimo had opposed the surrender, but Li Tsung-jen had agreed. The Vice President dispatched Ho Ssu-yuan, a former Mayor of Peking, to the northern capital to meet with the Communists, but he was assassinated by the Kuomintang secret police before making the contact.

The twenty-five divisions of Fu Tso-yi were absorbed into Communist armies. Officers were allowed to retain their current rank, and those who chose to leave the army were allowed to go with three months' pay and their personal belongings. Fu Tso-yi, a popular general with millions of people who had never felt close to Chiang Kai-shek, became a member of the Communist administration. The treatment accorded Fu Tso-yi and his troops became an inducement to other Nationalist commanders and soldiers to defect.

Stuart noted in his diary on January 23:

Li sent for Philip—he will do his utmost for just peace—if C.P. are intractable he will withdraw to Pearl River [Kwangtung] to carry on.

JAN. 24—C.P. 6 or 7 columns 10 miles from Pukow [the railway station on the northern bank of the Yangtze].

JAN. 27—C.P. broadcast Li if sincerely for peace must hand over CKS and long list war criminals—again claims U.S. instigating Li—distinction between real and false peace—Li and whole Government caught therefore in dilemma —they must go all way either with CKS or coalition that is anti-Chiang—they all timid, irresolute—prefer easy solution of compromise nature—avoid extreme measures.

North Atlantic Group [Western ambassadors] met at 11 A.M., met again 5:30 P.M. my home—I announced message from Washington my instructions—[Minister Lewis] Clark to go to Canton. I stay here expecting all North Atl to do the same.

On January 29 Clark, Livingston Merchant, the embassy economic counselor and a group of other officers left for Canton to open an embassy office, leaving Stuart behind with a skeleton staff. Fred Schultheis, the station chief of the CIA, drove to Shanghai.

JAN. 31—Call from French Ambassador—Paris worried over Soviet Ambassador going to Canton. Fear for Indochina.

FEB. 1—Li is making a brave effort for peace—thwarted by Kuomintang diehards and C.P. suspicions.

FEB. 2—CKS wrote Li his intention not to take office with present term (5 more years)—giving Li free hand.

Stuart flew to Tsingtao, the site of the U.S. naval base on the Shantung coast, on February 7 for a conference on economic aid attended by Roger Lapham, head of the Economic Cooperation Administration in China (ECA), and one his deputies, Allen Griffin. The Ambassador was told that there had been a cabinet meeting in Washington during which it was decided unanimously that economic aid would not be continued under the Communists.

The Truman Administration was also becoming worried about getting entangled with Chiang Kai-shek on Formosa. On February 10 Stuart noted in his diary:

Problems of Formosa become acute over plans of CKS there and ECA program—In Tsingtao and with [embassy officer J. Wesley] Jones—Merchant I advocated either take our trusteeship in some form for islanders and go whole way or stay out completely—might make exception of J.C.R.R. [Joint China Rural Reconstruction aid program]. J.C.R.R. should also be pushed in Southern provinces.

FEB. 13—Growing cleavage between Li and Sun Fo in Canton—CKS insists he supporting Li yet orders Hu Tsung-nan [one of the Generalissimo's generals] and 200,000 troops fly Canton to block Li's influence—CKS pays CAT [General Claire Chennault's airline] hard cash.

FEB. 20—Message from Ho Ying-ch'in [leading Nationalist General] wanting U.S. to help get CKS out of China.

FEB. 21—Pai Ch'ung-hsi came 1½ hours same problem of getting CKS out of China.

On March 2 the Nationalist cruiser *Chunking*, donated by Britain a year earlier, and now the pride of the navy, slipped away from its mooring at Shanghai and defected to the Communists. Nationalist bombers found it off Hulutao on March 19 and sank it.

Premier Sun Fo, attacked by members of the Legislative Yuan, the Nationalist Parliament, for moving the cabinet to Canton and selling his house in Shanghai at an excessive price, resigned on March 8. The Nationalist generals holding regions south of the Yangtze were now operating as virtually independent warlords. On March 11 the Generalissimo was confronted at a secret conference at Hsi K'ou by a group of rebellious Nationalist leaders who asked him to leave the country.

On March 11 Stuart noted in his diary:

Chang Chih-chung back from Hsi K'ou. CKS refused to be pressed to go abroad—got angry—blamed Li—scoffed at democracy—said the essential thing was to have power. Li baffled—double fight against CP and Fascism—Ho Ying-ch'in hesitating to be premier because CKS still active—Li's best hope is winning public support against both.

MARCH 12—Li told Philip of conference last evening 8:30–1:30 after return of Chang Chih-chung from Hsi K'ou. All present. They telephoned CKS about going abroad—he agreed but blamed Li for U.S. publicity—wants his intention kept secret.

MARCH 18—Li left tonight for Shanghai—K. C. Wu resigning because tension with Mao Sen Garrison Commander whose policies harshly Fascist—also Li to persuade liberals to join [Ho Ying-ch'in] cabinet.

MARCH 20—Premier came to ask for U.S. currency stabilization loan—fiscal situation desperate—if this cabinet falls—CP has free field—I promised consult Counsellors and see what could be done. Ho looked harassed.

MARCH 21—Various callers—main concern problem of U.S. loan or aid to help currency—serious dilemma. (1) To give new aid would anger CP might injure peace talks. Question of strength and worth of this government. But (2) not to give aid mean early collapse and leave whole of China open to CP.
Terrific problem—I have asked for Merchant and Parker come from Taiwan for consultation.

MARCH 22—A busy day—
Li asked me to call—explained difficulty getting first class men or even second for cabinet—I replied better any cabinet quickly get on with Peace—Then he asked me to sound out my government on his going to Moscow. Reported to Washington.

Meanwhile, the Communists had agreed to receive in Peking a Nationalist peace delegation of six members headed by Chang Chih-chung.

MARCH 28—Call on Li Tsung-jen—suggested Li go with peace delegation. Discussed munitions shipments to Canton—escape Gimo [Chiang] control Taiwan.

MARCH 29—Peace is the one thought in all our minds—opinions vary from stark pessimism to qualified hopefulness.
Currency desperate—will ECA help?

APRIL 2—Message from Department strengthening fear ECA aid for Taiwan may arouse anti-American feeling. ECA should be concentrated on bolstering up this government.
Premier told Philip Peace Delegation would be recalled if CP crossed Yangtze—asked again about U.S. loan.

APRIL 4—Call on Li—concerned over crossing of Yangtze—I urged government to defend it without interference of CKS.
What should I do if Nanking falls? All others would follow U.S.A.

Stuart's unsteady handwriting in this notation revealed his strain and extreme agitation.

APRIL 6—CP broadcast mentions me twice as representing American Imperialism—Li and Ho must break with CKS and me and come to them.
CP sent Li ultimatum Peace must be settled by 12th. Kan Chieh-hou [li's representative] came at once to report and I went to meeting (11:00 A.M.) North Atlantic Group to report the news. Meeting was to discuss our action if CP cross Yangtze—Very serious question what I should do—all others follow us—

APRIL 7—Wrote draft of message against my removal to Canton.

APRIL 10—Conference on ECA aid—We were all disappointed at inability to help fiscal crisis. Should not carry on any projects especially in Taiwan. Hold funds at discretion of President.
This evening Philip went to see Li—gave him bad news. No U.S. aid—urged him to insist draw on Taiwan reserves.

APRIL 12—British Ambassador [Sir Ralph Stevenson] brought news from his Foreign Office. I stay in Nanking. This came later in direct.
CP have extended deadline three days after today.

APRIL 13—Final Missionary Conference on Communism—I led discussion.
News of Department decision reply to our Embassy message, confirmed previous one. I stay Nanking. I am very much pleased.
Peace move slightly more hopeful.
Li asked Department make some pronouncement on CP crossing Yangtze —or unofficial comment through news agency.

APRIL 14—Li sent Kan to tell me that CP had demanded to cross Yangtze at Kiangyin and to occupy nine hsien [counties] across from An-ch'ing—He asked me: What could USA do? He was ready for me to think it over. Kan would return the next morning for reply.
Later I told Kan I would make no official reply nor give advice. But encouraged him take a firm stand—refuse permission—take consequences—his place in history would not suffer. But his real problem was CKS. Ho Ying-ch'in should face CKS on (1) Unified control in Ministry National Defense (2) Release all funds for Li and Ho to use at their discretion.

APRIL 15—CP threat discussed at staff meeting. They may not try to force crossing.
Yen Hsi-shan [warlord governor of Shansi Province] failed to persuade CKS to release bullion.
Give up military interference.

APRIL 17—CP demand to occupy all Yangtze provinces Hunan East.

5:00 P.M. Preached at Sage Chapel—large attendance (Easter service).

8:30 Li, Kan—British, Australian, French Ambassadors—my home presented CP ultimatum deadline April 20—Very very serious crisis.

APRIL 18—Pai Ch'ung-hsi called—Li had decided to force CKS either (1) to take over completely and fight or (2) to leave the country—we discussed his going on mission Southeast Asia anti-Communist crusade. If CKS left China Kan might be Ambassador in Washington where Madame CKS, [Ambassador Wellington] Koo and others had been working to get CKS back.

Li sent for Philip to advise I go to Canton—he intended to fight but will leave at last moment—gave all the reasons why I should—lead diplomatic body to Canton.

APRIL 20—Li determined to refuse CP terms—CKS apparently ready to cooperate.

British called—told of sinking of *Amethyst* near Chinkiang.

Kan came to report Government rejected CP terms—deadline tonight unchanged by CP.

CHAPTER *4*

THE FALL OF NANKING

Beleaguered on all sides, Li Tsung-jen sent a delegation to Peking on April 1 to negotiate for peace. Once it got there, the Communists handed it an "Agreement on Internal Peace," which stipulated eight conditions tantamount to complete surrender. When the Acting President in Nanking rejected the Agreement charging that it would give the Communists "military control of the entire nation," Chang Chih-chung, the head of the Nationalist delegation, defected to the Communists. At midnight April 20 the Communist ultimatum expired, and an "Order to the Army for the Country-wide Advance," signed by Mao Tse-tung and Chu Te sent Communist armies across the Yangtze. The order stated: "After the People's Liberation Army has encircled Nanking, we are willing to give the Li Tsung-jen Government at Nanking another opportunity to sign the Agreement on Internal Peace, if that government has not yet fled and dispersed and desires to sign it."

The Communist armies, jammed aboard thousands of junks, sampans and motor launches, breached the Yangtze without significant resistance on a front of about 325 miles extending from Hukou, northeast of Kiukiang, 250 miles southwest of Nanking, to the river fortress of Kiangyin, about 90 miles downriver midway between the capital and Shanghai. The Second Field Army commanded by Liu Po-ch'eng crossed west of Nanking while the Third Field Army under Ch'en Yi crossed on the east. About 350,000 Nationalist troops were concentrated in the Nanking-Shanghai area, but only token resistance was offered and the Communist crossing was facilitated by large-scale defections, especially at Kiangyin. At the Kiangyin fortress, guarding the Yangtze narrows, the Communists succeeded in bribing the commander, General Tai Yung-kwan, who turned his heavy guns on the Nationalist river gunboats, preventing them from blocking the Communist crossings. At Nanking, Commodore Lin Tsun defected to the Communists with his naval squadron.

The crossings were complicated by an unexpected international clash. On the morning of April 20, the British frigate *Amethyst*, proceeding up the Yangtze to Nanking, came under the fire of Communist assault troops who were poised on the mist-covered north bank waiting for the order to cross the river. The frigate was struck fifty-three times. Of its 183-man crew, 23 were killed and 31 wounded. The *Amethyst* had been en route to Nanking to relieve the destroyer *Consort* on station there and to furnish protection and provisions to the British Embassy. The *Consort*, coming from Nanking, and the cruiser *London* and frigate *Black Swan*, racing up from Shanghai to the aid of the *Amethyst*, also came under Communist fire, suffered damage, and withdrew to Shanghai without being able to succor the crippled frigate. Medical teams traveling overland from Nanking and sea planes managed to reach the *Amethyst* with help for the wounded, but the vessel remained trapped for 101 days because the captain, Lieutenant J. S. Kerans, refused to sign a Communist document acknowledging responsibility for "criminally invading Chinese territorial waters." The frigate, which had sailed for Nanking with the usual letter of authority from a Nationalist admiral, finally escaped under fire on July 30, using a passing Chinese vessel as a screen, and reached the mouth of the Yangtze. There was never any explanation for the Communist attack on the *Amethyst*, although it was questionable judgment on the part of the British admirals to send a naval vessel up the river line which the Communists had just announced they were about to assault. There was some speculation that the Communists had mistaken the *Amethyst* for a Nationalist gunboat coming from Kiangyin.

One Communist radio broadcast which the AP office in Nanking monitored on the afternoon of April 23 said that the Communist troops were not aware until the afternoon of April 21 that the ships they had engaged on the morning of April 20 were British. The radio accused the British of "direct participation in China's civil war."

Mao Tse-tung, replying to statements by Prime Minister Clement Atlee and Winston Churchill in the House of Commons, said on April 30 that the Communists had suffered 252 casualties in the exchange of fire and Peking was right in demanding an apology and compensation for an illegal intrusion. Mao demanded withdrawal of the naval and air units and Marines of Britain, France and the United States from China's ports and inland waterways.

On April 22, with Communist troops swarming across the Yangtze, Acting President Li, accompanied by Premier Ho Ying-ch'in and General Pai Ch'ung-hsi, flew to Hangchow from Nanking for a conference with the Generalissimo. A joint communiqué issued in Nanking on their return the same day pledged unity and a "fight to the end," with Premier Ho Ying-ch'in empowered to exercise a unified command over the armed forces. But in reality there remained basic differences between the Generalissimo and Li. Chiang looked to Taiwan as a final redoubt where he had already transferred 300,000 troops as well as air and naval units. Li still hoped to defend the South, falling back on his native Kwangsi, and Kwangtung. The Generalissimo also pulled back the Central Army troops of General T'ang En-po from the lower Yangtze line for defense of Shanghai and to hold them ready for transfer to Taiwan rather than allow T'ang's forces to join in coordinated defense with the troops of Pai Ch'ung-hsi in Central China.

At dawn, on the morning of April 23, I was awakened by gunfire and explosions in the northern district of Nanking. I had been sleeping in the Associated Press house. Harold Milks, the chief correspondent, had left China in March on three months' home leave, believing the Communists would not seize the capital before his return. I dressed hastily, clambered into my jeep, drove to Chungshan Lu, the principal thoroughfare, and headed north toward the sounds of explosions coming from the Siakwan quays on the Yangtze.

The Nationalist garrison had abandoned the city, and the municipal police had fled with them. The Twenty-sixth Army, which had been ordered into the city to defend it, never arrived.

Mobs of Chinese were already looting the palatial residences of Nationalist officials, including those of Li Tsung-jen, Ho Ying-ch'in and Mayor Teng Chieh. The Mayor, trying to escape in his car loaded with 300 million gold yuan from the city treasury, had been beaten up by his chauffeur and bodyguards, his legs broken, then captured by the Communists on the highway south of the city. By the next day, the gold yuan was valued on the Nanking market at 1.5 million to one U.S. dollar, making the Mayor's intended haul worth only $200.

The looters, mostly shabbily dressed men, women and children who had swarmed up from the slums of Fu Tze Miao, the old Chinese quarter in the southern district, were going about their thievery good-humoredly, laughing and shouting to each other. From the upper floors of the two-story villas, they were hurling sofas, carpets and bedding to the lawns below. The household goods were being hauled away on peasant carts and on the backs of excited men, women and children. A grinning soldier, who had thrown away his rifle, gingerly carried off a lamp in each hand. An old woman, her gray hair pulled back in a bun, wearing a ragged black tunic and hobbling away on tiny feet, bound in the old custom, happily carried off four elaborately embroidered cushions. Hundreds of looters had ransacked the huge Executive Yuan building and the Ministry of Communications, bearing away everything, including window sashes.

Thousands of refugees and exhausted, disheveled Nationalist soldiers, some still grouped in units, poured south along Chungshan Lu, coming from the Yangtze, which they had crossed during the night. They were fleeing south away from the flashes of Communist artillery fire creeping up to the north bank of the river. They were grabbing every Chinese vehicle in sight. Some of the soldiers had commandeered rickshas and bicycle-pulled pedicabs, and the ragged coolie owners, barefoot or in sandals, their bare chests heaving and shaven heads bowed, were pulling loads of two soldier passengers and packs through the streets.

The massive Northwest and Northern Gates were ajar, swinging and creaking unguarded. I found the modern new railway station, a towering building with glass and white stone sides just outside the north city wall, had been destroyed by Nationalist demolition units. One of the walls of the station, which was deserted and littered, caved in as I approached. A few looters were still picking through the nearby Caltex oil depot and other warehouses, most of them already stripped and some afire. The waterfront was ablaze with fuel fires. A China Merchant Company freighter loaded with cloth was burning in the river port, set afire by retreating Nationalist soldiers. Across the river, Pukow lay silent, with no sign of the approaching Communist troops.

With my horn sounding constantly, driving at high speed to get by soldiers trying to flag me down so they could climb aboard my jeep, I turned, veered and twisted through the crowds on Chungshan Lu, back down to the Sun Yat-sen roundabout in the center of the chaotic city and out to the Ming Tomb Airfield, the inner field in the southeast district.

There was pandemonium on the field with dozens of C-47s and

C-46s of the Chinese Air Force and of the two Chinese airlines, CNAC and CATC, being loaded in a frenzy for quick takeoffs. In disbelief I watched a Nationalist general hoarsely shouting orders to soldiers to load his grand piano and other furniture aboard an air force plane. A line of legislators of the Legislative Yuan was boarding another plane, some of them wearing pith helmets for the southern climes and one or two carrying tennis racquets. "We shall come back," a bespectacled legislator said to me in an unconvincing voice. Soldiers were swinging their bayoneted rifles at sobbing inhabitants of the city trying to force or bribe their way aboard the airliners, which were taking on the families and possessions of senior Nationalist Army officers and officials. There were similar scenes at the airfield outside the east wall.

Philip Crowe, the chief of the ECA Mission in Nanking, who had suffered a heart attack, arrived at the Ming Tomb Airfield on a stretcher, escorted by Ronning, his close friend, and American officials who put him on an outgoing plane. A few planes still were landing on the airfield and from one of them emerged the Canadian Ambassador in high spirits. While visiting Shanghai, Davis had learned of the impending fall of Nanking. He rushed to Lunghua Airfield, scrambled on to a Chinese plane without a ticket and carrying his suitcase, and landed back at his post several hours before the Nanking Airport closed.

Before Li Tsung-jen and Premier Ho Ying-ch'in left the Ministry of Defense compound at about 9 A.M., George Yeh, the Acting Foreign Minister, telephoned Jacques Meyrier, the French Ambassador and doyen of the diplomatic corps, to tell him that the government was leaving and asking the chiefs of mission to follow it to Canton. Meyrier told him that the chiefs of mission, except for the Soviet Ambassador who already was in Canton, intended to remain in Nanking. The United States and the other Western governments, waiting to see how events in China would evolve, were leaving themselves the option of establishing official contacts with the Communists through their ambassadors in Nanking.

Diplomatic properties in the city had been unmolested by the looting mobs except for the unoccupied residence which had belonged to General Barr. The large house, situated south of the American Embassy compound in the northwest district of the city, had been demolished by looters who carried away doors, window sashes, plumbing fixtures and broke up the floors for firewood.

At dusk, the mood of the mobs turned ugly, sporadic shooting was heard in the city, and the foreigners, unprotected, waited apprehensively in the gathering darkness. Time bombs left by the Nationalists in ammunition and fuel dumps on the north and south banks of the river began exploding, causing spectacular fires that reddened the skies over the capital. Fire bells sounded constantly on the streets. Electricity and water services had been disrupted. Two battalions of Nationalist artillery from positions near Blue Dragon Hill in the southern suburb fired aimlessly over the city to the north bank, with the apparent mission of screening the withdrawal of troops through Tengshan, ten miles to the southeast.

In the large American Embassy compound, the young Foreign Service officers, Robert Anderson, Thomas Cory, Frank Kierman and Edward Anderberg, Jr., an attaché living with the Ambassador, patrolled the grounds with flashlights. There had been a platoon of Marines at the embassy, but thirty-eight of them had been flown to Shanghai on April 20 on the orders of Vice Admiral Oscar C. Badger, Commander of the West Pacific Fleet, to avoid incidents with the Communists. Six Marines were left behind as an internal embassy guard for the two hundred remaining personnel. The American Embassy, like the British and the French, had its own radio and was in touch with the United States Fleet and Washington. There was no longer any way for the embassy to extend protection to the some 280 American civilians scattered around Nanking. The Commonwealth missions had the protection of 150 armed Indians, many of them Sikhs, formerly employed by JUSMAG as police guards, who were organized as a security force by Sadar Pannikar, the Indian Ambassador.

In the afternoon, I had toured the old Chinese quarter, going down the narrow twisting streets. Mobs had broken into the grain shops, as distraught proprietors stood helplessly on the sidewalks watching, and good-naturedly were carrying off sacks of rice and flour. Noticing looters in one shop hauling off bags of rice but only one at a time, I asked one of them, an old bearded man, why he was not taking more. Grinning, showing his black stumps of teeth, the old man said: "Only one to a person." But by dark the appetites of the looters, swelled by soldier stragglers, had become insatiable. A mob wrecked the city museum, a former Japanese Shinto shrine, simply to use its walls for firewood. They attacked and stripped the abandoned police stations, small gray buildings surrounded by walls and barbed wire, making off with weapons. At the police commissioner's headquarters I found students of the Central

University carrying off rifles that had been stored there. "We need to defend our campus," a young student said, hoisting a rifle. A tot of about seven years, his split pants showing his behind, paraded before the police commissioner's headquarters as his amused father watched, carrying a bayonet and wearing a white police pith helmet that slipped over his eyes.

Shooting broke out as volunteer militia organized by the Emergency Peace Preservation Committee tried to restrain the mobs. There were some dead lying in the streets. Posters announcing the formation of the Committee and appealing to the population to preserve order had begun to appear on the walls of buildings in the afternoon. The proclamation of the Committee said:

Because of the military situation, government troops and other organizations have evacuated Nanking. During the transition period when the Communists have not yet entered the city, an Emergency Peace Preservation Committee is formed on behalf of the people to maintain security in Nanking prior to the peaceful takeover of the city. Beginning April 24 7 A.M., the Committee will start functioning with its office temporarily in the Nanking Hotel. It is hoped that the people in Nanking will make their joint effort to realize peace.

The proclamation was signed by General Ma Ching-yuan, a retired Nationalist Army commander, and Wu Yi-fang, the president of Ginling College for Women, a school supported, like Nanking University, with the help of American Protestant missionary organizations. Later in the night, when I saw Dr. Wu, she told me she learned of her appointment from one of the proclamation posters.

A security subcommittee was arming students and other volunteers with parts of policemen's uniforms and white arm bands and sending them out on patrols into the frightened city. A utilities subcommittee was trying to restore electric power and the water supply.

I picked up Bill Kuan, a young Chinese reporter who worked for Agence France Presse, and at 6 P.M. we drove out through the open unguarded East Gate to the military airfield. As we entered the field, the only guard at the gate was a youngster, about twelve years old, in army uniform, standing over two light machine guns on bipods. The wrecks of six planes were smoldering on the field, destroyed by the Nationalist Air Force before evacuation. Lights were burning in the hangars and control towers which loomed up ghost-like on the deserted field. The ammunition and fuel dumps and the runways were untouched. We found only one soldier on the airfield, a signal corps enlisted man who asked for a ride to the outer gate with his camp cot and bedroll. He said that after the air base commander took off in the afternoon, several Nationalist light Mosquito bombers had strafed the field without doing any damage. We dropped the signal corps man off at the gate. The boy guard was gone. The field, untouched by looters, was now completely deserted as we drove back to the East Gate.

The Ming Tomb Airfield, inside the walls, was ablaze with lights. The CNAC and CATC airline plane crews had stripped their installations of all movable equipment. The airfield installations, damaged only slightly by looters, were otherwise undisturbed. There was only one plane on the field, a United States Air Force C-47 transport, the embassy air attaché aircraft. Five volunteer militiamen were on guard. The radio and other parts were later taken from the air attaché plane, which was to be Ambassador Stuart's only means of leaving the capital.

Kuan and I decided to go to the Nanking Hotel in the center of the city to look for General Ma, the head of the Peace Preservation Committee. The streets were already empty as most of the population waited behind barred doors and windows. On the side streets, there was some shooting as militia opened fire on looters. As we drove down the well-lit but deserted Chungshan Lu, we were halted by a line of eight soldiers across the broad boulevard pointing their rifles at us. The soldiers wanted a ride and intended to get it. They were polite but firm. Their leader said the eight of them were the last Nationalist sentries on the Nanking river front and they had left their posts after dark. The soldiers, carrying packs as well as rifles, mounted the jeep, seating themselves on its hood, and hanging onto the steel frame of the canvas top and the rear. When we reached the Sun Yat-sen Circle, Kuan explained that we would have to turn off to the left to the Nanking Hotel. The soldiers got off the jeep reluctantly but without much persuasion. Kuan asked them where they were going. "Out the South Gate," their leader said. We watched the last of the Nationalist Army in Nanking walk down the road and disappear in the darkness.

In the Nanking Hotel, a dilapidated, filthy hostelry, flying the white flag of the Peace Preservation Committee, we found members of the Committee sitting in the dining room around small tables drinking tea and composing welcoming slogans for the Communists. The slogans were to be posted all over the city the next day and published in the newspapers. The hotel was the headquarters of the small security force which Ma had managed to assemble to look after the population of more than one million. He had found and drafted the remnants of a battalion of the Nanking garrison, some police units and the volunteers, a total of only a few hundred men. We were told that Ma was spending the night at the Cairo Hotel and we drove there.

In a dingy, small bedroom, painted pea green, of the seedy Cairo Hotel we found Ma, a weary, sixty-year-old man, charged with handing over the capital to the Communists. At midnight of April 22, Ma, a former divisional commander in the Nationalist Army, had been called from his bed by a telephone call from General Chang Yao-ming, the Nanking garrison commander. The garrison commander told Ma his troops were evacuating the capital immediately and asked him to take charge during the transition period. He promised to provide Ma with adequate police and other security detachments to maintain control of the city. Ma, a balding man, dressed in a black buttoned-up Sun Yat-sen tunic, bitterly recalled that conversation as he sat on the edge of his chair with his hands folded between his knees, shaking his head and repeating: "We don't have enough troops to protect the city against looters." Ma was concerned at the moment with getting enough men and vehicles to remove the fuel and bomb dumps from the Ming Tomb Airfield before daylight, when Nationalist bombers were expected to hit the city. The installations on the military airfield outside the wall which Kuan and I had toured at 7 P.M. had been blown up in a string of explosions beginning at 9 P.M. and were detonated by time bombs which had been ticking away as we roamed the field.

Ma had a strange assortment of people about him in the bedroom. There was a Nationalist colonel, in a snappy uniform, who had been ordered to remain behind for the city's surrender. A handsome girl dressed in a man's brown sweater over a khaki shirt with sleeves rolled up sat beside a spectacled young man. They were together and did not encourage questions. I assumed that they were of the Communist underground, whose plain-clothes agents were active in the city. Another of Ma's aides wore an unmarked wool olive-drab uniform, and the remaining member of the group was an elderly man whose odd costume attracted no special attention. He wore thick winter underwear of pinkish color, with a gray flannel coat over it, and bedroom slippers.

Ma said he had contacted the Communists by radio and told them that Nanking was ready to surrender without resistance. Communist troops had crossed the Yangtze at Shang Hsin Ho, about three miles from the city's Northwest Gate. The first landings had been made at 6 P.M., and several thousand troops were believed to have found enough boats to cross by midnight. The Communists were expected to march in at daybreak. Ma's concern tonight was to protect the population and the foreign diplomatic missions from the looting mobs and the city's public buildings and utilities from Nationalist saboteurs still operating in the capital.

Before word had been received of the landings at Shang Hsin Ho, Ma sent a Communist underground agent, who had contacted him after the Committee had been set up, across the river to Pukow to carry a surrender message to the Communists. He had been turned back by the violent explosions along the river front and the Nationalist artillery fire from Blue Dragon Hill. Ma, desperate to bring Communist forces into the turbulent city as soon as possible, now planned to make the try himself together with Ch'en Yu-kuang, the president of Nanking University, and Nu Cheng-yuan, a professor at Ginling College. "In the morning our Committee will try to send a delegation out through the Northwest Gate to Shang Hsin Ho to escort the Communists into the city," Ma said, as we left him.

Kuan and I went to the central telegraph office to file our dispatches. We pounded away at our portable typewriters as the excited clerks watched us curiously, chattering in their cubicles behind the counter. As we emerged from the telegraph office, we found a great fire was blazing along the Chungshan Lu. The Judicial Yuan, a large imposing yellow structure, was in flames. The building, one of the most impressive public edifices in the capital, was already a total loss, and furniture was being removed from adjacent houses by their owners fearing that the fire would spread. Speculating that the flames, which were casting a red glow against the clouds over the capital, might bring the Communists into the city more quickly, I drove slowly up the boulevard toward the Northwest Gate. It was 3:20 A.M.

As we crawled along the empty thoroughfare, there was a shout of "Halt" in Chinese. From each side of the road in the shrubbery under the plane trees, two soldiers with rifles aimed at us converged on the jeep. "Who are you and what are you doing?" one of the soldiers said, holding a flashlight on us. Kuan replied: "I am a correspondent of the French news agency, and he is from the American Associated Press." "American, American," the soldier exclaimed, shining his flashlight in my face and looking at me intently. "Do you know who we are? We are soldiers of the People's Liberation Army." They were Ch'en Yi's troops, the point on the first Communist column into Nanking. We were about one mile and a half from the Northwest Gate.

The Communist soldiers asked us to follow and took us about a hundred yards to a Communist officer leading a column of troops. The troops were obviously exhausted, carrying full packs and weapons and sweating in their yellowish-brown padded uniforms after a forced march. The officer was shouting to them, urging them to keep moving quickly into the city. These were not the troops who had been scheduled to march into the city in the morning. The fires in the city had brought them at forced march through the Northwest Gate. The officer questioned us impatiently, then ordered us back into the jeep and told us to drive back into the city. Slowly leading the column was a civilian jeep with six occupants, who were Communist officers and members of the Peace Preservation Committee. As we started up our jeep, the column moved past us. I pulled out from the side of the boulevard, came alongside of the leading jeep, which slowed for us, and I could see a well-dressed civilian who apparently was heading the Committee delegation. We then raced ahead, for the central telegraph office, past the burning Judicial Yuan. Twelve years later, at a dinner party in the Geneva villa of Ch'en Yi, who then had become Foreign Minister and was chief of the Chinese delegation to the Conference on Laos, I was to tell the burly, jovial marshal how his troops behaved that night while he exclaimed in delight.

In the telegraph office, Kuan and I flipped a coin to determine who would file first. He won and sent a three-word flash: "Reds take Nanking." My own sixty-six-word dispatch followed. Immediately after, Communist troops severed the land line between Nanking and Shanghai. When Kuan's flash reached the AFP desk in Paris, the editors waited for additional details, which did not come until morning when a radio transmission opened from Nanking. The delay denied Kuan a world beat on the fall of the Nationalist capital. My own lengthier dispatch went out immediately on the AP wires. By the time the sun came up over Purple Mountain, the Communists had occupied Chiang Kai-shek's capital.

CHAPTER 5

COMMUNIST OCCUPATION

At daybreak, I picked up Ronning in the Canadian Embassy compound, and we drove in my jeep to the Northwest Gate, where thousands of Communist troops in their yellow uniforms and flat peaked caps were entering the city. They sat in orderly lines on their bedrolls along the sidewalks, with their rifles tilted over their shoulders, listening to talks by political commissars and singing revolutionary songs. Crowds gathered to stare at them curiously. People from nearby houses brought hot water and tea for them to drink, pouring it into the cups and bowls which they carried on their belts. Nationalist stragglers, their weapons thrown away, passed by unnoticed.

Students from Nanking University and the other ten colleges and universities in the city came out, some riding in trucks, shouting welcoming slogans and cheering the entry of the soldiers. But they were ignored by the Communists, who silently brushed past them. These were the same students, six thousand of them, who three weeks earlier had courageously staged militant demonstrations in the city, demanding that the government make peace with the Communists. They had been attacked violently by Nationalist garrison troops, police, secret agents and the Kuomintang Youth Corps. Two had been killed and some hundred wounded. Yet the students, middle-class liberals, neatly dressed, serious young men and women, were not accepted by the Communists. They were trapped in the middle, among the most tragic victims of the civil war.

The Chinese liberals, of which the Nanking students were typical, had suffered only frustration when they tried to solve the basic problems of their society according to the democratic precepts they had learned in the missionary-supported educational institutions. Their education in the humanities and the sciences, taught in the Western tradition and political context, did not equip them for the monumental tasks of lifting the peasantry out of feudalism, nor did it school them to cope with Kuomintang warlord politics or the totalitarian challenge of the Communist Party. Hungering for an effective role in determining their country's destiny, they were compelled to make a choice of aligning themselves with a dictatorship of the right or one of the left.

In the center there stood only the Democratic League, which, together with other minor parties, ineffectually tried to offer a liberal third force to the country. Their members, together with the liberal students, were terrorized by the Thought Police controlled by Ch'en Li-fu and his brother, Ch'en Kuo-fu, the right-wing bosses of the Kuomintang Party, who were known as the "CC" clique. The Generalissimo depended on the Ch'en brothers to keep the liberals in line when they protested government dictatorship or corruption or agitated for an end to the civil war. Finally, the League was banned by the government on October 28, 1947. When the Communist Government was founded in Peking, the League, the Kuomintang Revolutionary Committee under Madame Sun Yat-sen and other splinter parties were tolerated as token ornaments of the coalition "People's Democratic Dictatorship." But power resided with the five million members of the Communist Party.

During the upheaval of the civil war, most liberal students chose the Communists, attracted by their asceticism and dedication, and repelled by the corruption and police brutality of the Kuomintang. Thousands went into the "Liberated Areas" to work for the Communist cause without any prior intellectual commitment to Marxism-Leninism. The students whom the Communist troops met on the morning of April 24 near the Northwest Gate had elected to remain in the Nationalist areas, to continue their schooling and to agitate for peace and good government from within. This was not enough to elicit the trust of the Communists. Several weeks after the Communist entry, I saw a column of thousands of students escorted by soldiers being marched down to the river to strengthen the dikes against the spring floods. The students were being indoctrinated not only through political lectures by army commissars but also by participation in manual labor, from which the classical tradition exempted intellectuals and to which they were not accustomed. The Party would be ready to greet those who passed the ideological tests.

The orderly entry of the Communist Army was marred by an incident at Stuart's residence. At 6:30 A.M. twelve peasant soldiers sightseeing around the big city chanced on the embassy, forced the night gatekeeper to open the iron gates, and several blundered into the Ambassador's bedroom, awakening the seventy-two-year-old envoy. "Who are you? What do you want?" the Ambassador shouted. The armed soldiers left muttering and returned with the others, one of them explaining that they were simply looking around and meant no harm. They left after Ed Anderberg, the Embassy Attaché, and Philip Fugh appeared. "Soon all this will belong to us," one of the soldiers told Fugh as the servants ushered them out the front door.

The incident was widely publicized after the embassy reported to Washington, making the Communists appear provocative and belligerent. The State Department ordered Brigadier General Robert Soule, the Military Attaché, to protest to the Communist military authorities, but Soule could find no one to receive his representations. The soldiers were later located by Communist officers and detained for further political indoctrination, according to a Party official.

On the eve of the Communist takeover, Stuart was surprised to receive instructions from the State Department ordering him to return to Washington. The Western ambassadors, in agreement, had earlier recommended to their governments that they remain in Nanking for an indefinite period after the Communists took over. The State Department quickly amended its instructions after the Communist entry, authorizing Stuart to remain until he was satisfied that the consulates and American nationals in the Communist-held areas were being satisfactorily cared for.

I, too, became involved in an incident with Communist soldiers at the Associated Press house. Upon my return from the Northwest Gate, three soldiers entered my office as I sat at a typewriter. They were accompanied by Liu, my number one servant. Pointedly addressing themselves to Liu, they asked what I did. "Oh, he sends messages to the United States," Liu said casually, not seeing he was arousing the ideological vigilance of our guests. "What does he say in these messages?" the spokesman asked suspiciously of Liu. My spirits sank as Liu replied: "He reports about everything." That did it. With fixed bayonets, the delegation marched out, and within a few minutes the house was surrounded by sentries. I could not leave, nor could my cook go to the market for food. Ronning, hearing of my plight, delivered food packages through the barbed-wire fence. I telephoned the USIS officer at the embassy and gave him a message to be sent to Fred Hampson, the AP Bureau Chief in Shanghai. The message, intended to describe my predicament, said: "Boy Scouts posted at front door." Hampson promptly included it in one of his dispatches. After two days the sentries vanished without explanation. Other incidents, almost always due to some misunderstanding, occurred at the French Embassy and other foreign properties.

In celebration of their victory, Communist soldiers climbed onto the façades and roofs of government buildings and Chiang Kai-shek's former office in the T'ai P'ing Palace to plant their red flags. Some of the Communist soldiers camped in the looted and stripped residences of the former Nationalist officials, bringing their small shaggy ponies into the houses or turning them out to graze on the lawns.

A proclamation signed by Ch'en Yi told government employees they could keep their jobs if they were not on the war criminal list. All property of Chiang Kai-shek was ordered confiscated. Foreign property and nationals were assured protection if they did not engage in espionage, shelter war criminals or otherwise "impair the interests of the Chinese people." The foreign missions were told to limit the use of automobiles on public streets to what was essential. (The American Embassy, which had 110 vehicles, was restricted to the use of five.) The American Embassy staff decided as a precautionary security measure to restrict their movements about the city and remain in the compound after dark. Embassies were ordered to register their radios and forbidden to use ciphers in telegrams sent through the commercial telegraph. A "South Yangtze Advance Headquarters" was established to maintain control of the city.

On the first afternoon, three Nationalist Mosquito bombers strafed the Ming Tomb Airfield, trying to detonate the fuel and ammunition dumps. They overshot the field on their strafing runs and wounded some children at play.

The only newspaper to appear, filled with laudatory articles welcoming the Communists, was the Catholic *Yi Shih Pao*. The official Communist New China News Agency began functioning, staffed by journalists who two days earlier had been working for the official Nationalist Central News Agency. About sixty political prisoners were released from jail, including a number of Chinese newsmen. Into the prison went the crippled former Mayor Teng Chieh, Shen Ching-cheng, director of the Nationalist Social Affairs Bureau, and Hsu Hsin-nung, director of the City Health Bureau. Teng was charged with trying to make off with the city funds that had been allocated as severance pay for the municipal employees.

Most of the shops in the city remained closed because of uncertainty as to what currency to accept. Those open sold goods only for silver dollars. Water and electric utilities were restored, but service was erratic.

The radio announced the fall of Taiyuan, the walled capital of Shansi Province which had been ruled continuously since 1911 by the warlord, Yen Hsi-shan. Marshal Yen, called the "model governor" by some, had run a prosperous quasi-independent province. He had built more than six hundred miles of excellent roads and two rail lines, also developing agriculture and the forests so that the province had become virtually self-sufficient in food. Behind the thirty-foot-thick walls of his capital, arsenals produced rifles, machine guns, light artillery and ammunition. When Communist troops swarmed into Shansi in the fall of 1948, the Marshal retreated into Taiyuan and a siege began. Yen's close associate, Chiang Kai-shek, began a massive airlift in civilian transports of about five thousand tons of rice a month to the airstrip within the city walls. Despite the airlift thousands starved in the besieged city. Desperately short of foreign exchange, the Chiang Government nevertheless spent U.S. $300,000 a day to sustain the airlift until the hopeless resistance ended April 24 after Yen flew to Canton. He succeeded Ho Ying-ch'in as Premier on June 2 and went promptly to Taiwan for a parley with his old ally, the Generalissimo.

Some of Ch'en Yi's troops remained in Nanking a few days as the bulk of the army wheeled to the east and thrust to Hangchow on the coast to cut off and envelop Shanghai. Liu Po-ch'eng was proclaimed chairman of the Nanking Military Control Commission and later named mayor. Not long after he assumed control of the city apprehensive Chinese businessmen were reassured by the legendary one-eyed Szechwanese General who met with them. "Members of the Communist Party announce unreservedly that we fight for Communism, that we plan eventually to materialize a Communist society," the General told them. "However, being believers in materialism we realize that the revolution in its present stage belongs to the new democracy. Under these conditions we should make friends with over 90 percent of the people and we oppose only the reactionaries who represent less than 10 percent."

Liu said that during the period of the "new democracy" the Communists wanted to concentrate on the development of production by promoting private as well as public enterprises, giving equal attention to capital and labor. In the past, he said, the Communists had espoused "erroneous policies of excessively high wages and excessively high income tax."

Liu's Control Commission administered the city through a secretariat and eight bureaus. These handled supplies, foreign affairs, real estate control, financial and economic affairs, military takeover, political takeover, cultural takeover and public security. The bureaus were largely staffed by former Nationalist employees who were content with the new regime. Many of them had indulged previously in graft simply because they could not feed their families on their fixed government salaries during a rampant inflation. The Communists had converted the old Nationalist gold yuan into new Communist People's banknotes. Although the general price index was rising gradually, the government employees and the population generally were able for the first time in years to buy basic commodities at fairly stable prices. As in other Communist cities, the prices of daily necessities were controlled by the Government Trading Corporation, dealing in such commodities as rice, flour, bean oil, pork, coarse cloth and fuel.

After the first weeks of occupation beggars disappeared from the streets, although there was considerable unemployment. Most shops reopened, but trade was slack. The Communists lifted the Kuomintang ban on dance halls. One did not hear from the people any more complaints of petty police corruption.

Beginning on April 28 Nationalist B-24 and B-25 bombers based on Formosa began wheeling over the city every few days, circling like enormous dark vultures over the river waterfront area where the city power plant, the waterworks, the railroad yards and the warehouses were situated. The bombers came in fairly low since the Communists had no antiaircraft other than 50-caliber machine guns whose range was limited. Many of the bombs, presumably aimed at the electrically operated ferry and the riverside plants, dropped into the Yangtze. It seemed almost as if the pilots were deliberately trying to avoid bombing their own people. Little damage was suffered in the first raids.

During May there was no radical change in the cultural life of Nanking. The Communists extended their controls gradually. They took over the National Central University, but the foreign-assisted private schools such as Nanking University and Ginling College operated under their former presidents with no changes in curricula. At Nanking University a new board was set up in which professors, instructors, administrative staff, students and campus workers were represented.

Students generally greeted the establishment of Communist power with great enthusiasm. They formed speaking teams which toured the city explaining the "new democracy" to the people. They sang Communist songs and performed the popular Yang Ko or rice-planting song dances on the streets. Each dancer, arms akimbo, would take three short steps forward and then three backward, with a kick often added as an extra flourish while cymbals and drums gave the beat. Couples would weave in and out under a bridge of arms. Communist soldiers taught the students the steps of the revolutionary reel, and newspapers published words of the songs. One popular song went:

> Reactionaries who exploit the people deserve to be cut into thousands of pieces.
> They totally ignore the afflictions of the common people and want only to be dictators.
> Big landlords, big warlords, big compradors, big families—all conspire together, all conspire together, all conspire together.
> And, therefore, we poor people suffer.

Another Yang Ko song was:

> Papa and Mama are poor and cannot send me to school.
> Others read and write while I am illiterate.
> We want to learn to read books, want existence; we want freedom.
> Let's all go to school together; let's all go to school together.
> Collective studying assures better results.

Some of the students petitioned school authorities to end the old learning, abolish examinations, and organize study groups to discuss the new democracy instead of requiring their attendance at formal classes. Enthusiasm waned somewhat at Nanking University after a Communist speaker told the students that under the new democracy there would be more rather than fewer examinations. The students were left uncertain as to how the Communists intended to fit them into the "new democracy."

When the dozen or more Nanking newspapers were ordered to

register to continue publishing, most were denied licenses. The Military Control Commission had informed the newspapers on May 16 that registration was required to "safeguard the freedom of press and speech of the people and strip the freedom of speech and press of the antirevolutionaries." The newspapers and periodicals were asked to submit one year's back copies with three copies of each issue since the Communist occupation of Nanking. The data sought from the registrants included a statement of past and present editorial policies, biographies of all staff members, and the past and present political beliefs, experiences and relationships with political parties and political organizations "of the publishers, shareholders, editors, correspondents and managerial staff." Only two newspapers survived, the *China Daily* and the *New China Daily*, both containing the same output of the official New China News Agency. A Communist bookstore opened and did a rushing business in the works of Mao Tse-tung.

Shanghai fell to the Communists on May 25 after the city had been encircled. Behind an enormous ditch and a ten-foot wall erected by thousands of civilians laboring under the command of the Shanghai garrison, the Nationalist defenders put up a brief face-saving resistance. T'ang En-po, the Nationalist Commander, pledged to turn Shanghai into "a second Stalingrad." Chiang Kai-shek flew into the port, spoke of "total victory within three years," and hastily departed. Ch'en Yi's troops thereafter paraded into, rather than stormed, Shanghai. They rounded up 100,000 passive Nationalist soldiers.

Rail, telegraph and telephone communication between Nanking and Shanghai resumed within a few days after the fall of the big port city. But the Nanking telegraph office declined, as it had for several weeks, to accept international telegrams. I sent my dispatches out by phone, mail or courier to the AP office in Shanghai, which retained international communication links. There was no attempt by the Communists to impose censorship on the few American and French correspondents who remained in the city. As coal began to come into Nanking from the Hwainan mines in Anhwei, the city began to enjoy steady electricity at night and a continuous municipal water supply for the first time in months.

In the diplomatic compounds life became very boring. The officers of the embassies had no diplomatic status as far as the Communists were concerned; and they were able to make only sparse and perfunctory government contacts. With their sources of information dried up, the diplomats had little to report to their home governments. The Communists did not intrude into the compounds, but the diplomats and the families who had declined to be evacuated before the fall of the capital were not permitted to go outside the city walls on the popular picnics to Lotus Lake and Purple Mountain. They were told by Communist officials that Kuomintang bandits had not yet been completely mopped up. "Charades at Jones after dinner," Stuart wrote in his diary on April 30. The diplomats lounged at the former American Officers Club, which was opened by the embassy to all the diplomatic missions.

The ambassadors and their ladies in the bar or the pool of the luxurious club, once the palace of the Japanese collaborator, President Wang Ching-wei, played bridge and talked endlessly of how and when they might go home. It was not Communist force that was preventing departure. The Nationalists had declared a blockade of the coast and bombed the port of Shanghai, and no ships or planes were calling there.

The other favorite topic was the servant problem. Some of the docile, usually punctilious Chinese servants, organized in a union by the Communists and emboldened by rules which made dismissal impossible without very large severance pay, began to make disconcerting money demands on their employers. As the torpid summer heat settled and spirits soured, Bob Anderson and Tom Cory organized huge "volleyball and gimlet parties" for the diplomatic corps in the spacious American Embassy compound. Romance flourished. Hank Lieberman, the *Times* correspondent, and Kay Martin, the Ambassador's secretary, were among those married by Stuart performing as a minister of the Church. Anderson became engaged to "Tati," the beautiful daughter of the Italian Ambassador, Dr. Sergio Fenoaltea. The nonstop parties in the confinement of the compounds dragged and became strained after a time. Several marriages broke up in open scandal. The gossip enlivened the cocktail party ennui.

In early May, Huang Hua arrived in Nanking to take charge of the Alien Affairs Bureau, which had been installed in the large red-brick compound of the former Nationalist Ministry of Foreign Affairs, and dealt with the diplomats and other foreigners. I had known Huang Hua well in Peking when he was personal secretary and press spokesman for General Yeh Chien-ying, the head of the Communist section of Executive Headquarters. The Headquarters, with American, Nationalist and Communist branches, had been set up by General Marshall as civil war mediator to implement the short-lived cease-fire agreement reached in

January 1946. It was Huang Hua who had arranged for my trip to Yenan in 1946.

Ronning, fluent in Chinese and acting on behalf of the diplomatic corps, was the first foreigner received by Huang Hua. He was told that the envoys were classified as "former diplomatists," since they had no official ties with the Revolutionary Military Commission then ruling in Peking, and they would not be entitled to the usual diplomatic privileges and immunities. Most of the contacts thereafter made with the office by the missions were through junior secretaries and always conducted in Chinese since the Communists declined to do business in any foreign language. Every conversation in the office was recorded in shorthand.

Huang Hua received me soon afterward. I was surprised to find him at his desk dressed in army uniform, rather than the civilian tunic he had worn in Peking, and deeply sunburned. He had been in the villages for some weeks working in the land reform movement after serving as head of the Alien Affairs Bureau in Tientsin. He was a short, trim man of thirty-nine, highly intelligent and quick in repartee. He spoke to me in Chinese, although we had previously always conversed in English, which he handled well. After a few minutes, Huang Hua became less formal, and he chatted with me in English, saying that I would be free to carry on my work as a correspondent. In June he was to arrange a trip for me to Shanghai, not an easy undertaking in the face of the bureaucratic confusion which existed in the security agencies during the first months of the Communist occupation of Nanking and Shanghai. There was some evidence that Huang Hua had been selected to go to Nanking because of an old association with the American Ambassador. Huang Hua had attended Yenching University in Peking in 1935 when Stuart was president. As head of Yenching's student council, Huang participated in the December 9 student demonstrations protesting against what they termed the inadequate national policies to resist Japanese encroachments on Chinese sovereignty and territory. His participation in the demonstration, for which he was jailed for a time, was one of the factors which led him to join the Communist Party. He was then called Wang Ju-mei, but he changed his name—as many new Communists did on joining the Party—to Huang Hua.

Stuart had renewed his old acquaintance with Huang Hua in 1946 during a visit to Peking. A few days after his arrival in Nanking, Huang Hua telephoned Philip Fugh, and they arranged to meet in the Alien

Affairs Bureau on May 6. Fugh spent an hour with Huang Hua and on leaving suggested that he make a personal call on his old university president.

At 8 P.M. on May 13, Huang Hua called on Stuart at his residence for a conversation lasting an hour and forty-five minutes. "May be the beginning of better understanding," Stuart noted in his diary without further comment.

Huang Hua raised the question of United States recognition of the Communist regime. The Ambassador wrote later in his published memoirs that he said in reply that "foreign countries could not do otherwise than continue to recognize the existent National Government as the Communist party itself had done; that when there emerged a new government which obviously had the support or at least the acceptance of the Chinese people, and gave evidence of its willingness and ability to maintain relations with other nations according to international standards, then the matter would naturally be discussed."

Fugh, whom I was to interview in Washington in 1971, also recalls that Huang Hua apologized for the intrusion of Communist soldiers into the Ambassador's bedroom on April 24, and for the first time raised the question of a visit by Stuart to Peking. "I am quite sure Mao Tse-tung and Chou En-lai would be very glad to see you," Huang Hua told the Ambassador. In Ottawa in 1971, when Huang Hua was serving as Ambassador to Canada, he told me that it was to be a personal visit by Stuart, in his capacity as the former president of Yenching, on his birthday, June 24. Yet it was obvious at that time that the Communist leadership, in a characteristically delicate Chinese manner, was seeking an opportunity for a general discussion with the American Ambassador of relations between the two countries. Stuart and Huang Hua notified their respective capitals of the results of this first contact.

Colonel John Dunning, the Air Attaché of the embassy, was permitted to inspect his plane, which had been under Communist guard at the Ming Tomb Airfield. He reported to Stuart that the plane could be repaired. It would be available if the Ambassador received permission from Washington to fly to Peking.

On May 17, Fugh again visited Huang Hua. Stuart, in his diary, reported that, "among other topics," Huang asked about the radio operating in the American Embassy, and Stuart's leadership of the diplomatic corps and his frequent visits to the British and French embassies. He also complained about four ships which the United States had given to the Nationalists. Stuart and Fugh went to tea on June 6 with Huang Hua, and another Communist official, K'o Yi, was present most of the time. Arrangements were being made for a visit by the Ambassador to Shanghai.

Stuart had asked the State Department for permission to go to Peking, but there had been no reply. On May 21, Stuart was informed by the Department that all the North Atlantic powers had endorsed its proposal for common action in dealing with the Communists. The Department had also impressed on its Atlantic partners "the disadvantages of initiating any moves toward recognition or giving the impression through statements by their officials that any approach by the Chinese Communists seeking recognition would be welcomed." At the same time, a controversy with the Chinese Communists involving American consular personnel was hardening attitudes in Washington toward Peking.

In Mukden, after the Communist occupation on November 1, 1948, a series of incidents had erupted involving Angus Ward, the American Consul General, and his staff. The Communists had leveled a series of charges against the consulate staff, all denied by Ward, which ranged from an accusation that a Chinese employee had been assaulted to a complaint that cesspools had not been properly emptied. Ward and four of his aides were arrested, confined for a time and harshly treated, and the consulate staff was not allowed to leave for home until December 1949. There was no question that local Communist authorities in Mukden, in the intoxication of their new power, had been excessively bureaucratic and violent in their reaction to any presumed slight by American diplomats. Yet it was highly dubious that the central authorities in Peking had deliberately provoked the incident, as was charged in the United States. The effect of the Mukden affair was to prejudice prospects of an understanding between Peking and Washington at a time when the Chinese Communists were cautiously appraising their relations with both the United States and the Soviet Union.

In Nanking, Peking and Shanghai, Communist officials dropped hints of their interest in economic cooperation with the West. Peking was well aware that in the dislocated, impoverished post–World War II world only the United States would be able to furnish what China required for speedy reconstruction. General Ch'en Yi, the Mayor of Shanghai and a member of the Central Committee, in an informal talk with his cultural and educational workers on June 5, stated that aid from any foreign nation—including the United States and Britain—would be welcome, provided it was offered on the basis of sovereign equality. Walter Sullivan, the *New York Times* correspondent in Shanghai, was told by an informant who was present that Ch'en Yi had said that material and technical help was needed to industrialize China and so prepare the country for the Socialist stage of its long-term revolution. He said the Soviet Union and its family of Communist nations, preoccupied with their own reconstruction, were unable to bear the burden of such help. Therefore, help would have to come from elsewhere, but he made clear that Peking would not go begging for help and would not accept it with "imperialist" conditions attached. Sullivan inquired of the foreign affairs section of the Shanghai Military Control Commission whether Ch'en Yi's remarks were considered confidential. The answer was no, that there was no objection to using them for publication. Sullivan speculated that they might have been allowed to slip out purposely as a trial balloon.

Stuart went to Shanghai on the overnight sleeper on June 11. There, Stuart met with three hundred students, members of the Yenching Association. Among them were some twenty Communists who urged him to go to Peking.

Four days later, Mao Tse-tung, in a speech in Peking to the Preparatory Committee of the New Political Consultative Conference, which was meeting to discuss formation of a government, made an overture for diplomatic relations:

We proclaim to the whole world that what we oppose is exclusively the imperialist system and its plots against the Chinese people. We are willing to discuss with any foreign government the establishment of diplomatic relations on the basis of the principles of equality, mutual benefit and mutual respect for territorial integrity and sovereignty, provided it is willing to sever relations with the Chinese reactionaries, stops conspiring with them or helping them and adopts an attitude of genuine, and not hypocritical, friendship towards People's China. The Chinese people wish to have friendly cooperation with the people of all countries and to resume and expand international trade in order to develop production and promote economic prosperity.

Meanwhile, Chiang Kai-shek dropped the pretense of retirement and reasserted his open control of the Nationalist Government in Canton by becoming Chairman of the Supreme Emergency Council, the central policy-making body of the Kuomintang.

Ambassador Stuart returned to Nanking to celebrate his birthday on

June 24, but without any news from Washington on his proposal that he go to Peking. "My seventy-third birthday made happy by flowers, telegrams, a few gifts," Stuart wrote in his diary. "Yenching students twenty to thirty came at 3:30 P.M."

Chou Yu-k'ang, an old friend of the American Ambassador, and a relative of Stephan Tsai, treasurer of Yenching University, returned to Nanking from a trip to Peking on June 26, and reported to Stuart on discussions there about his proposed visit. Chou had spoken to C. W. Luh, chancellor of Yenching University, and Tung Pi-wu, a high-ranking Communist leader. Chou said he had learned in Peking that Huang Hua had been assigned to Nanking specifically as a contact with the Ambassador. He quoted Mao Tse-tung as stating that Stuart "would be welcome as an old friend of many in the Chinese Communist Party."

Stuart wrote in his diary on June 28:

Philip called on Huang Hua telling him of a strangely phrased letter from C. W. Luh assuming that I was to visit Peiping. He [Huang Hua] said Mao and Chou would heartily welcome me but apparently confirmed this by another telegraphic exchange to this effect which he called in the P.M. to report. Huang Hua came to bring the message and stayed about one hour.

The next day, Stuart sent a dispatch to Washington discussing the pros and cons of his trip to Peking.

I was at work in the AP office on July 1 when J. C. Jao, the Chinese assistant, excitedly called my attention to a declaration being made on the Communist radio. It was a statement by Mao Tse-tung, marking the twenty-eighth anniversary of the founding of the Communist Party, which was to define the foreign policy line of China for the next decade. It shattered what prospects there were of an understanding with the United States; Mao proclaimed that China would "lean to the side" of the Soviet Union. He summed up his domestic and foreign policy as follows:

1. Internally, arouse the masses of the people. That is, unite the working class, the peasantry, the urban petty bourgeoisie and the national bourgeoisie, form a domestic united front under the leadership of the working class, and advance from this to the establishment of a state which is a people's democratic dictatorship under the leadership of the working class and based on the alliance of workers and peasants.

2. Externally, unite in a common struggle with those nations of the world which treat us as equals and unite with the peoples of all countries, that is, ally ourselves with the Soviet Union, with the People's Democracies and with the

proletariat and the broad masses of the people in all other countries, and form an international united front.

Then, almost as if he were reflecting a debate which had taken place in Peking among the Communist leaders, Mao Tse-tung posed a series of questions and provided the answers.

"You are leaning to one side?"
[Mao replied:] "Exactly . . . We are firmly convinced that in order to win victory and consolidate it we must lean to one side. . . . Sitting on the fence will not do, nor is there a third road."
"You are too irritating?"
"We are talking about how to deal with domestic and foreign reactionaries, the imperialists and their running dogs, not about how to deal with anyone else. . . . Either kill the tiger or be eaten by him—one or the other."
"We want to do business?"
"Quite right, business will be done. . . . When we have beaten the internal and external reactionaries by uniting all domestic and international forces, we shall be able to do business and establish diplomatic relations with all foreign countries on the basis of equality, mutual benefit and mutual respect for territorial integrity and sovereignty."
"Victory is possible even without international help?"
"This is a mistaken idea. In the epoch in which imperialism exists, it is impossible for a genuine people's revolution to win victory in any country without various forms of help from international revolutionary forces, and even if victory were won, it could not be consolidated."
"We need help from the British and U.S. Governments?"
"This, too, is a naïve idea in these times. Would the present rulers of Britain and the United States, who are imperialists, help a people's state? . . . Internationally, we belong to the side of the anti-imperialist front headed by the Soviet Union, and so we can turn only to this side for genuine and friendly help, not to the side of the imperialist front."   .

I telephoned Ronning at the Canadian Embassy to tell him of Mao Tse-tung's statement. There was a formal lunch in progress at the embassy, given by Ambassador Davis on the occasion of Dominion National Day, for the Commonwealth ambassadors and Stuart. Chester broke the news to them. It shocked Stuart, who had hoped that he would be able to visit Peking and reach some kind of an understanding between the Communists and the United States. He had waited more than a month for word from Washington on the Communist invitation. The next day, Stuart received a message from the State Department instructing him to decline the invitation to Peking, and Fugh called on Huang Hua to communicate the message.

Stuart was recalled to Washington by the State Department, but his departure was delayed by a dispute over the exit regulations. Foreigners were required to obtain a "shop guarantee" to assure payment of debts left unsettled by the departing person. The State Department, insisting on observance of diplomatic privileges, which the Communists did not recognize, demanded exemption from the regulation. After weeks of haggling, Huang Hua obtained an exemption for Stuart and also freedom from baggage inspection. On July 30 Fugh paid a farewell visit to Huang Hua and found him bitter against the United States. Recording the conversation in his diary, Stuart wrote:

Huang Hua said frankly they looked on U.S.A. as an enemy—the usual KMT aid—but more than that—in U.S.A. people were oppressed and knew it—would some day revolt—intellectuals aroused. Communist parties in all countries knew they would win—revealed an ignorance of U.S. and a bigotry surprising in one otherwise so intelligent and in many ways friendly—as to White Paper knew the main contexts—criticism of CKS—some of CP—chiefly against USSR —when Philip Fugh asked how he knew he said they had their ways.

(The China White Paper, "United States Relations with China— With Special Reference to the Period 1944–1949," was published by the State Department on August 2.)

Stuart left Nanking on August 2, 1949, on the embassy plane, going to Okinawa and then on to Washington. In Washington, the Ambassador's public comments were screened by the State Department. No public mention was made of his invitation to Peking.

The State Department announced on August 14 that the United States intended to retain its diplomatic relations with the Nationalist Government. Four days later, Mao Tse-tung published an article, "Farewell, Leighton Stuart!," in which he described the Ambassador as "a symbol of the complete defeat of the U.S. policy of aggression."

On November 30, aboard a train going from Cincinnati to Washington, Dr. Stuart suffered a severe stroke which incapacitated him until his death on September 19, 1962. He lived in Washington from 1950 until his death at the Chevy Chase home of Philip Fugh and his wife. In 1954 Stuart published his memoirs, *Fifty Years in China*. They appeared after the Korean War and at a time when Chiang Kai-shek had returned to favor in the United States. Because of Stuart's crippling illness, in writing his memoirs he obtained the help of a collaborator, Dr. Stanley K. Hornbeck, who retired from the State Department in 1947 after serving more than ten years as chief of the Far Eastern

Division. Dr. Hornbeck wrote the three concluding chapters in the book summing up Stuart's experiences and views after his return to the United States. These chapters dealt much more kindly with Chiang Kai-shek than the entries made in Dr. Stuart's 1949 personal diary notes. The book does not refer to the Communist invitation to Dr. Stuart to visit Peking, which has never been made public by the State Department. Stuart noted in the foreword to his book that Fugh, who assisted in its preparation, was "not responsible for the contents of the book; there are even some matters of substance regarding which his views and mine do not entirely coincide." When I spoke to Fugh in Washington in the fall of 1971, he was critical of the Stuart book and said it had omitted crucial facts. He believes that the invitation to Stuart to go to Peking was of momentous importance, and if accepted, could have changed the course of history in Asia. It was his impression that President Truman had vetoed the Stuart trip to Peking under pressure from the politically influential China Lobby, which was supporting Chiang Kai-shek. When I asked permission of the State Department to inspect the records of that period, my application was rejected.

Before Stuart left Nanking, I spoke to him about Mao's invitation. It was his view that he might have improved relations between Peking and Washington, and laid the foundation for the establishment of normal diplomatic ties when the Communist Government was formally proclaimed. But he also told me he held no hope for a radical alteration of Communist policy unless there was a basic change in the social philosophy of the leaders in Peking.

I did not believe then, nor do I believe as I write this account that Stuart or the Truman Administration could have influenced Mao Tse-tung to adopt a neutral position in the East-West struggle of that time. It is true that Mao's relations with Stalin were equivocal when he extended his invitation to Stuart. As late as December 1949, when he went to Moscow, Mao Tse-tung was not yet fully accepted into the Soviet camp. In his 1962 speech before the Eighth Central Committee he recalled: "Later on, I went to Moscow to conclude the Chinese-Soviet Treaty of Alliance and Mutual Assistance [February 14, 1950], which also involved a struggle. He [Stalin] did not want to sign it, but finally agreed after two months of negotiations. When did Stalin begin to have confidence in us? It began in the winter of 1950, during the Resist-America Aid-Korea Campaign. Stalin then believed we were not Yugoslavia and not Titoist."

Despite his problems with Stalin, Mao was profoundly committed to the international Communist movement. He doubted he could obtain aid from the United States on acceptable terms. Mao did not want the "missionary" type of aid which had been provided in the past by such Western Christian liberals as Leighton Stuart, their charitable organizations and their governments. Aid of this "missionary" character, extended always on condition that China accept Western forms of democracy and liberalism, had only been a palliative for the massive and deeply rooted disabilities of the more than half-billion Chinese. Mao was then seeking to carry through a fundamental social, economic and political revolution that would demolish forever the ossified feudal structure of his society so that a new, viable, independent nation could arise. His weapon to smash and purge the old society was his adapation of the tactics and philosophy of Marxism-Leninism. It was to the Soviet Union that he looked for economic help to build the new Communist China, which he knew the United States would not, for ideological reasons, help create.

This does not mean that the conversations which Mao and Chou En-lai sought with Stuart could not have led at least to the establishment of a channel of communication between Peking and Washington. For this reason alone, the Truman Administration should have eagerly accepted the invitation. Even in the absence of normal diplomatic relations, the Chinese usually have been disposed to maintain a channel for exchanges on critical issues. If Americans had continued to talk to the Chinese Communists, many of the misunderstandings and much of the agony in Asia over the next two decades might have been averted. It is conceivable that the entry of Chinese Communist "volunteers" into the Korean War might have been headed off. The United States might have been persuaded to see the wisdom of limiting its involvement in Indochina. During the 1950s American policy in Asia often was based on incomplete information and erroneous assessments of Chinese Communist intentions. In 1956, when Peking briefly became amenable to the return of American correspondents to China, the State Department refused to issue the necessary visas. Washington thus cut itself off from informal contacts as well as diplomatic relations with a government that controlled nearly one-fourth of the world's population.

In July 1949 the first Soviet military mission, headed by Colonel General Andrei V. Zhdanov, arrived in Peking. An artillery training school and a flying school were set up. It was not until 1950, however, that effective Soviet antiaircraft weapons, with Russian training crews, were installed on the roofs of buildings in Nanking. Subsequently, MIG fighters also arrived. After one or two Nationalist bombers were shot down, the raids ended.

But in August 1949 we were still subjected to daily air raids in Nanking. The Hsiakwan power plant was hit several times, and for days the population went without electricity or running water. People in the city began to grumble against the Communists. Taxes had been raised sharply, while the commercial life of the city withered. When the Communists took over the city, about twenty thousand checks had passed daily through the bank clearing center, but by August, as Nanking declined as a major administrative center, the number went down to two hundred. Floods along the Yangtze resulted in severe damage, causing the price of rice to go up sharply. The press complained of sabotage and assassination of Communist officials in the surrounding rural area by "Kuomintang bandits," who were said to belong to the Big Sword Association and the Heavenly Gate Association. Ideological strictures on the universities and other intellectual life tightened.

In schools, factories and municipal offices, the Communists instituted "reindoctrination courses" or formed "study groups" to discuss Maoist ideology.

Correspondents were permitted to observe one meeting of a study group held by the staff members of the Nanking power plant. Forty members, including ten women and an office boy, attended the first meeting held after working hours in an old building in the center of the city. Present as advisers were two uniformed representatives of the Nanking Military Control Commission and Kung, a labor union delegate who explained how study groups worked in the older "Liberated Areas." "Key persons," he said, "were appointed to collect material, outline discussions and make conclusions. Other individual members of the group then studied the materials in their spare time and brought their opinions back to a small meeting, with the chairman consolidating the ideas for discussion again at a larger group meeting.

"Now that we are liberated, we are masters," Kung said, "but to be masters is not an easy thing. We must qualify ourselves for our new position. We must study to improve our technical knowledge for the construction and industrialization of China, to clear out the evil influence of the Kuomintang regime and to indoctrinate ourselves in the principles of the 'New Democracy.' "

The chairman of the meeting was Chang Hung-kao, a thin, middle-aged man dressed in Western-style clothing, who was head of the plant's General Affairs Bureau.

"In the past we were working for the four rich families [Chiang, Soong, Kung, Ch'en] and an alliance of bureaucratic capital with foreign imperialism," Chang said. "Rich became richer, and poor and even middle class became poorer. Now it's different. So we must learn new things to prepare ourselves to participate in the reconstruction of the new China."

"I am a man over fifty and have studied abroad," said Chang Lan-ko, Deputy Chief Engineer, a graduate of Cornell. "Due to polite flattery by younger people, I considered myself sufficiently educated. I even read books sometimes, but this was motivated by the prospect of personal advancement. Now I study for a different purpose. I realize now that only through the advancement of the whole society is there a chance for individual advancement. It was individualism among other things that led to bribes, corruption and private influence in the Kuomintang regime."

One of the girls spoke up, as the Military Control Commission delegates sat silently: "As we are only newly liberated, there is still an evil influence on our way of life. The purpose of this study group must be to learn new principles so that we will change our conceptions about society and adapt ourselves to catch up with the advancing times."

Everyone attending the meeting signed his name in the recording book, and it was agreed to meet each Thursday.

The study and indoctrination meetings, into which virtually the entire population of the city was gradually drawn, were held more frequently as the months went on. Eventually, those attending were required to confess past sins and faulty ideological thinking, and to pass judgments on the thoughts and activities of friends, neighbors and business associates. As the re-education campaign became more intense and onerous, there was a change in the private attitudes of many liberals who had welcomed the Communists to the city.

The change was visible in the attitude of J. C. Jao, the Chinese news assistant in the AP office. A man in his late forties, Jao had been employed by Milks as an interpreter, translator and an occasional writer of short dispatches in his absence. Jao had taught at various universities in China and was the editor of the Tsingtao *Herald* before joining the AP. He was a graduate of my own school of journalism at the University of Missouri. A tall, spare man, Jao was somewhat reserved but an independent thinker and a political liberal. He had awaited the arrival of the Communists with evident apprehension. In the days immediately before the occupation he would not venture out of the AP house. I therefore was surprised on the morning after the Communist entry to find him in good spirits and hopeful about the future. Like many of his liberal friends, Jao was caught up in the talk of "liberation" and impressed by the good conduct of the Communist troops. His enthusiasm and optimism persisted for months. As the summer wore on, however, and the Communists began to tighten their controls, he quietly began to make sour observations. Bill Kuan, the AFP Chinese assistant, and his wife and Peter Liu, son of a Chinese official in the Nationalist mission in Tibet, who had worked with me for the International News Service, left for Peking to take teaching jobs in the Foreign Languages Institute. Jao did not look for a job in the Communist administration. When I left Nanking, leaving him in charge of the AP office, he distrusted the Communists. Some months later, he was brought into an indoctrination course and questioned about his background and ties with the Americans. He informed Fred Hampson, the AP Bureau Chief in Shanghai, that he was resisting taking a job with the Communists writing anti-American propaganda.

On February 21, 1951, the Peking Government promulgated a drastic decree on the "punishment of counterrevolutionary offenses." By then a purge had already begun in the countryside and urban areas. The people were spurred to denounce "counterrevolutionaries," and executions of the accused began to take place following mass trials. Those executed included former Nationalist officials, landlords and other gentry in the countryside believed hostile to the regime, businessmen accused of anti-state practices, intellectuals and others who had been associated with Westerners and were suspected of ideological opposition to the Communists. The Korean War thickened the atmosphere of fear, suspicion and denunciation.

In Shanghai, the *Liberation Daily* reported that J. C. Jao had been arrested in Nanking in a roundup of "counterrevolutionaries" in several cities. Although he was no longer employed by the AP, he was accused of having carried out "espionage activities" for the news agency. On May 5 the *Liberation Daily* announced that Communist firing squads had liquidated 376 "counterrevolutionaries" in Nanking, 293 in Shanghai and 50 in Hangchow. The Nanking and Hangchow executions were said to have taken place on April 29 following public trials attended by a total of 150,000 persons. The *Liberation Daily* report cited J. C. Jao as a typical "counterrevolutionary." Nothing was ever heard of Jao again.

The Communists never disclosed the total number of those executed in the nationwide purge, which continued into 1952. In October 1951 it was announced that the people's courts alone had tried 800,000 counterrevolutionaries during the first half of 1951. In a speech on June 26, 1957, Chou En-lai stated that 16.8 percent of the counterrevolutionaries put on trial had been sentenced to death, most of them before 1952. This would mean that at least 134,400 had been executed in the first six months of the purge. Jacques Guillermaz, the distinguished Sinologist, who served as French Military Attaché in Nanking during the civil war and later in Peking, estimated in his *La Chine populaire*, published in 1964, that a total of one to three million were executed. Other independent experts have made estimates ranging from hundreds of thousands to several million. The claim put forward by Nationalist officials on Taiwan that the figure was actually in excess of ten million has been dismissed as propagandistic.

After the departure of Ambassador Stuart from Nanking, the former capital shriveled as a news center. Foreigners restlessly waited for the opportunity to leave, and the AP asked me to proceed to Hong Kong when I could for reassignment. The opportunity came when the Nationalists announced that they would relax the coastal blockade to permit the American President liner *General W. H. Gordon* to call at Shanghai to pick up foreigners. Hundreds of foreign businessmen, plagued with labor difficulties, and others were clamoring to leave Shanghai. I traveled by train to Shanghai with the Canadian Ambassador, the British minister, L. H. Lamb, and other diplomats to board the *Gordon*, a wartime troop transport not yet completely converted to peacetime commerce. The white-capped Shanghai customs officials, the same as had worked under the Nationalists, passed us through, whispering friendly remarks. When a Communist officer watching over the proceedings heard me declare books, he stuck a hand into my trunk and came up with a copy of Mao Tse-tung's *Coalition Government* published in Yenan on local coarse yellow grass paper, "Where did you get this?" the Communist asked. "In Yenan in 1946." The officer looked at me intently, ordered my trunk closed and waved me and my baggage through without further formalities.

As the liner left the muddy brown waters of the Yangtze River's mouth and entered the blue waters of the East China Sea on September 25, one of the 1,219 foreign evacuees mounted a bulkhead on the deck and shouted, "We are liberated." I stood moodily at the rail watching the land recede and wondered when I would be able to go back to China.

CHAPTER

6

DEPARTURE

When the *General Gordon* slipped into the magnificent Victoria Harbor of Hong Kong, which in Chinese means "Fragrant Port," the whistles on the other vessels sounded in welcome to the first ship out of Shanghai since the fall of the port to the Communists. Having been utterly vulnerable because of an inadequate garrison when the Japanese seized Hong Kong in 1941, the British were taking more precautions as the Chinese Communists closed in. The aircraft carrier *Triumph* and the cruisers *Belfast* and *Jamaica* lay in the harbor of Hong Kong screened by destroyers and frigates. The colony they shielded embraced Hong Kong, an island with a hilly spine ten miles in length linked by ferry boats to the adjoining peninsula on the China mainland. Imperial China, intimidated by British naval guns, ceded the island in perpetuity to Britain under the 1842 Treaty of Nanking, and the tip of the adjacent peninsula, Kowloon, was ceded, also in perpetuity, under the 1860 Peking Convention. To provide a buffer, the British under the 1898 convention obtained a ninety-nine-year lease of the New Territories, a large fertile farming area which extended from Kowloon to the China border.

The Colony's garrison was now beefed up to about forty thousand service personnel, including such crack army units as the Royal Marine Commandos, the Argyll and Sutherland Highlanders, the Gurkhas and the King's Shropshire Light Infantry, backed by artillery, tanks and fighter planes. As the British awaited the arrival of the Communists at the border, they held their troops two miles back from the frontier in the New Territories while police squads manned the border. The British hoped the two-mile nonmilitary zone would minimize chances of shooting incidents.

The British were fearful of Communist fomenting of civil disturbances among the two million Chinese living in the Colony to provide a pretext for invasion of the Colony. There was an ugly mood in Wanchai, the Chinese slum district of Hong Kong, which was jammed with recently arrived refugees. Police and members of a four-thousand-man civilian reserve were holding antiriot exercises. The British were relying not only on military strength to restrain the Chinese Communists, but also on the hope that Peking, despite its denunciations of British imperialism, would want to leave Hong Kong undisturbed as a useful trading link to the Western world.

Tillman Durdin, the *New York Times* correspondent, an old friend who had been in Nanking up until 1948, was waiting for me on the dock. To celebrate our reunion, we went that night to a Chinese restaurant, where we met Ian Morrison, a *Times* of London correspondent, and Han Suyin, a Chinese doctor with a British passport, the widow of a Chinese general. I had become friendly with Morrison, a tall, good-looking, rather languid Englishman, in Nanking, where he sometimes joined us for picnics on Purple Mountain.

Morrison was an excellent correspondent, traveling widely through East Asia from his base in Singapore. I had not met Han Suyin before, but I knew that Ian had become attached to her. She was a slim, fine-featured young woman, born in China of a Belgian mother and a Chinese father. She was dressed in a vivid, luminous Chinese brocade dress. She and Ian looked exuberantly happy. It was the last time I was to see him. He went to cover the Korean War and was killed in August when his jeep ran over a mine. Han Suyin wrote a novel, *A Many Splendoured Thing*, about her life in Hong Kong with Ian, calling him Mark Elliot, and included excerpts of his eighteen letters from Korea. It was a good book, but like many of Ian's friends, I resented it because it bared the private emotions of a reserved man. It was common knowledge in the Far East that Ian was the hero of Han Suyin's novel. Many years later, when I reread *A Many Splendoured Thing*, I no longer felt that way. The book had preserved a remembrance of Ian's humanity, insights and grace. In one of Mark Elliot's letters from Korea, he observes: "And now, through loving you, the Koreans are much less strange to me than my own race."

Mao Tse-tung proclaimed the founding of the People's Republic of China on October 1, 1949, and in that month the Communist armies resumed their march south.

In the Communist general offensive across the Yangtze in April, Lin Piao had operated with the superb seasoned columns of his Fourth Field Army on the right flank of Liu Po-ch'eng. The Fourth Field Army plunged across the Yangtze into Central China, capturing Hankow, principal city of the Wuhan metropolitan area and capital of Lin Piao's native Hupei Province.

From Hankow, Lin marched down the trunk railroad toward Canton, the metropolis of South China. His columns slogged forward over roads flooded by the spring rains or jammed atop battered railway cars that inched forward as the torn-up tracks were repaired. Their flanks were harassed by the warlord guerrillas of the Tapieh Mountains, who fought anyone who infringed upon their fiefdoms.

As the Fourth Field Army sliced through the heart of China, Nationalist armies crumbled before it, sometimes because of Lin Piao's generalship or under the shock of his hard-fighting columns, but more often because of mass defections or the bungling of the opposing Kuomintang commanders. Only in Pai Ch'ung-hsi, the skilled and courageous Nationalist Commander of Central China, whom Chiang Kai-shek never counted among his personal retainers and therefore never fully trusted, did Lin find a worthy adversary. When Lin's troops marched into southern Hunan, Pai's divisions counterattacked and sent them reeling back to Changsha. However, once again the personal rivalries and jealousies of the other Kuomintang generals frustrated the Nationalists from exploiting a victory. Pai Ch'ung-hsi was not able to establish a stable defense line to shield South China.

In October, Lin's divisions, operating in tandem with the army of Liu Po-ch'eng, wheeled through Kwangtung and Kwangsi. Liu Po-ch'eng, after crossing the Yangtze and pausing in Nanking, had veered his army sharply to the coastal province of Fukien, then south through Kiangsi to join Lin Piao for the final roll-up of the Southeast. As the Communist armies advanced on Canton, Li Tsung-jen left for Chungking, where the capital would be until its fall to the Communists on November 30. Next the capital was moved to Chengtu, farther north in Szechwan, and eventually off the mainland of China to Taiwan on December 9. On December 5 the Acting President left for the United

States for medical care. After fifteen years in the United States he would go to Peking, where his old adversaries would welcome him.

From Hong Kong, on October 13, I reported the abandonment of Canton by Nationalist troops after getting through by telephone to some New Zealand Presbyterian missionaries stranded in the city. The Communists entered Canton two days later, but for some reason did not move on to the border of Hong Kong until December. Ahead of them fled Nationalist soldiers, who had thrown away their weapons and parts of their uniforms, and refugees—hungry, tattered men with bundles on their heads or on poles across their shoulders and women with babies on their backs—struggling overland and by junk and launch to slip into the crowded British Colony, which was trying to keep them out.

With the Communists at the border, the British taipans of Hong Kong, eager to resume trade with the mainland and ease pressure on the Colony, urged London to seek an accommodation with Peking. In January 1950 the British Government recognized the People's Republic and offered to establish diplomatic relations, but Mao Tse-tung did not agree to the opening of a diplomatic office in Peking under a chargé d'affaires until 1954. Before that, however, the Communists began using the facilities of the Colony, moving in banking and trade officials, political agents to penetrate Chinese unions, schools and other organizations, and representatives of the New China News Agency, among whom were undercover Foreign Ministry and other government officials.

Shortly after World War II, T. V. Soong, the brother of Madame Chiang Kai-shek, who was the president of the Bank of China and had exercised a freewheeling control over the corrupted finances of Nationalist China, began building a towering square edifice to house his bank's Hong Kong branch. Soong, with an effrontery that drew the ire of the British taipans, built his skyscraper several feet higher than the neighboring massive Hong Kong and Shanghai Bank building, which had been the tallest structure in the Colony. However, Soong was repaid for this twisting of the lion's tail when the employees of the bank defected to the Communists, and the British, of course, did not intervene. In the end the bankers from Peking set up shop in the spanking-new building, and eventually it became the headquarters for all Chinese Communist operations in the Colony.

When the Nationalist sympathizers in Hong Kong and the Communists began to joust with each other in a political and propaganda struggle for control of the Chinese community, the Governor, Sir Alexander Grantham, enunciated the don't-rock-the-boat edict by which the Colony hoped to survive, saying: "We cannot permit Hong Kong to be the battlefield for contending parties or ideologies. We are simple traders who want to get on with our daily round and common task. This may not be very noble, but at any rate it does not disturb others."

There was an interregnum during the Korean War when trade with the mainland was disrupted, but British pluck saw the crisis through, and the Colony prospered side by side with the Chinese dragon.

Soon after I reached Hong Kong, there was a letter from Audrey. We had been separated for eleven months, but her letter told me what I had hoped: our relationship was unchanged.

When the AP offered me leave if I would go to Fort Worth, Texas, to speak to a managing editors' convention, I agreed with alacrity and traveled a rather circuitous expense-account route to Texas via Vancouver, Canada, where Audrey was attending the University of British Columbia. She and I, one night after midnight, walked along an avenue in Vancouver and we agreed to be sensible and delay our marriage until she graduated. I took her home to her women's dormitory. Five hours later I climbed out of bed, mumbling "This is ridiculous." I took a taxi back to the dormitory and at 6:30 A.M. pounded on the door. A startled house mother in hair curlers summoned Audrey on my command. Audrey descended the stairs and agreed that it was ridiculous and that we should be married at once. She checked out of the university while I flew to Fort Worth to make my speech, and on November 10 we were married in Camrose, Alberta, in the home of her sister, Sylvia. The lead on an AP story reporting the marriage said: "One foreign correspondent is so confident that the Chinese Communists won't soon attempt an assault on Hong Kong that he is taking his bride back to that potential Far Eastern trouble spot." The story quoted me as saying that a frontal attack on the Colony was unlikely. In fact, when we arrived in Hong Kong some days later, the British were worried about the Communists spilling over the border into the Colony.

Audrey and I checked in at the flossy Gloucester Hotel, which we could not afford. It was situated in the downtown district of Hong Kong, where the big banks, office buildings and shops stood near the harbor. Above the business district towered the Peak, where terraces supported the palatial homes of the senior British officials, foreign businessmen and consular representatives and rich Chinese. Hong Kong commerce was booming with the influx from the mainland of wealthy Chinese, many of whom had paid fortunes to pilots or ship captains to bring them out of China with gold, jewels and priceless antiques. Foreign diplomats, businessmen and missionaries evacuated before the advancing Communist armies also swarmed through the Colony seeking to establish temporary offices or travel connections to America and Europe. Hotels, shops and streetwalkers did a rushing trade. Through the arcades of the Gloucester and past the majesty of the bronze lions before the Hong Kong and Shanghai Bank building, the pillar of British commerce, walked the slim girls in their narrow black slit skirts, swinging their handbags and smiling boldly at the sailors.

Hotel rooms were hard to get and rents astronomical so, near Christmastime, running out of money, we moved to a small Chinese hotel. Audrey had always had a tree at Christmas, so I went looking and found some that had been imported by a sharp Chinese merchant and were being sold at outrageous prices to Western sentimentalists. The tree I bought was too tall, of course, for our small room, and finally it stood bent against the ceiling half-blocking the entrance to the bathroom. I had to stoop beneath the branches to get into the bathroom; inevitably a Christmas decoration would go smashing to the floor, and I would hear Audrey sigh. On the second day, when we investigated why there was so much boisterous traffic in the corridors during the night, we learned we were living in a whorehouse. We fled, bearing our Christmas tree, to Sunning House, a more expensive but respectable Chinese hostelry.

At the end of January, I left Audrey in Hong Kong and flew in one of Chennault's CAT planes to the Kwangtung island of Hainan, which Lin Piao's troops were making ready to assault. Chinese and foreigners on the lush, green island, its 113,500-square-mile territory only 500 square miles smaller than Taiwan, were living in strange, uneasy seclusion. In Hoihow, the provincial capital, I stayed in the French Catholic Mission. Shortly after my arrival, the French Bishop Dominique Desperben led me to the flat roof of the mission. We looked over Hoihow, a dirty sprawling city of 250,000 people, many of them living in old two-story buildings made of mud and white plaster, across the narrow Hainan Strait to the Liuchow Peninsula on the mainland. We could see the Communist-held coast across the strait, which was only ten miles in width. As we watched, Nationalist Air Force planes and bombers based on Hainan whipped overhead, and we could see the puffs and hear the explosions of bombs falling on the coast. The fighters and bombers were also striking inland along the mountainous spine of Hainan where there were Communist guerrillas.

For more than twenty years, including the Japanese occupation of the island, which began in February 1939, the Chinese Communist guerrilla chieftain Feng Pai-chü had held the mountainous center of the island. His headquarters were situated somewhere in the Wuchih (Five Finger) Mountains, which rose to five thousand feet. Feng headed a government that administered a large part of the island, his officials working in villages only a few miles from some Nationalist Army camps. His troops, some twelve thousand of them, were divided into five lightly armed divisions.

Foreigners on the island told me that Feng had a wide following among the two and a half million peasants of the island because of his indoctrination program and land reforms. Communist influence was also strongly felt among the students in the Nationalist-controlled schools.

Since the spring the guerrillas, in anticipation of landings by Lin Piao's troops, had taken the offensive and expanded their control to a section of the southwestern coast. The Communists on the mainland were sending in agents and supplies on junks with great patched sails that silently slipped by the Nationalist Navy patrol boats in the night.

I went to the military headquarters to see General Hsueh Yueh (the "Little Tiger"), former Governor of Kwangtung. The General, an energetic man dressed in a flashy tailored American-style uniform, was the top commander. He complained that he was receiving only meager aid from Chiang Kai-shek. Hsueh Yueh was frantically trying to reorganize and train some 140,000 troops, about 80,000 of them first-line combat veterans, most of whom had been evacuated from the mainland. About forty bombers and fighters were based at the Hoihow Airport and at Sanya in the southern part of the island, both fields built by the Japanese and used in the war to strike at Allied positions in China and Southeast Asia. Nationalist gunboats were operating out of Hoihow and Yulin, the excellent natural port developed by the Japanese on the southern coast.

Amid all these martial preparations for mortal combat with the Communists, some three dozen foreigners were living fairly comfortably on the island, and they were determined to remain no matter what the outcome of the impending battle. Chennault's airline and an occasional steamer which called were their only links to the outside world.

CAT kept planes at its main base at Sanya on a standby basis for emergency evacuation in case of Communist invasion.

I went to call on the well-appointed garden compound of the American Presbyterian Mission in Hoihow, which seemed an oasis of efficiency and comfort amid the decay of the city. The failure of the Chinese to maintain the public works constructed by the Japanese had left the city with rutted roads and broken-down utilities. There were ten women and four men in the mission, the familiar sturdy, dedicated Protestant missionaries who doled out spoonfuls of material help and Christianity in a sea of misery. The mission supported a church, schools and a 186-bed hospital. With the Catholic missionaries, they helped to run a leprosarium where about 175 lepers lived, among them one foreigner, a man of German and Polish ancestry who was suffering the advanced stages of the disease. A French medical worker told me there were about three thousand lepers on Hainan.

"We sometimes watch the Nationalist planes bombing the Communists on the coast from the roof of our hospital," the Rev. David H. Thomas, executive secretary of the mission, a hearty businesslike man from Kansas City who lived in a compound house with his wife, told me. "But we don't intend to abandon our work because of the Communists. Our mission, which was founded in 1885 by Henry McClandis, was the first to bring Western medical practices to this island." The sixteen French and one Spanish priest of the Catholic Mission, and their Bishop, were no less bent on staying. The most elegant foreign residents of Hoihow were the French Consul, Hughes Jean de Dianous of Avignon, France, and his wife. His job was to report on Chinese activities that could affect French Indochina. He was now busy relaying pleas to Paris from the Nationalists for the right of passage through Indochina of the remnants of General Pai Ch'ung-hsi's army, which was penned by the Communists against the Indochina border. The Nationalist Air Force was making two flights a day from Hoihow to drop arms, ammunition and other supplies to these units, totaling some thirty thousand troops, which were in radio contact with Hainan. After their disastrous defeat in Kwangsi, these troops and thirty thousand others who had been evacuated to Hainan, were all that remained of Pai Ch'ung-hsi's 250,000-man army. Three months before, it had been the single most powerful force left to the Nationalists on the mainland.

The French Consul lived on a sliver of land separated from the Hoihow coast by a slender narrows. Once the sampan ferry to the island had been operated by boatmen dressed in blue and white uniforms, with their insignia reading "Sailors of the Consulate of Great France." In deference to the times, the uniforms had been dispensed with, but the cuisine and wine served in the fifty-two-year-old consulate, constructed of yellow lava stone from the island's extinct volcanoes, were no less aristocratic. On the same tiny island there was a warehouse of the British-owned Asiatic Petroleum Company, which the Nationalists seized after London recognized the new Peking Government.

The Governor of Hainan, Marshal Ch'en Chi-t'ang, agreed to receive me at Hoihow Airport. The fifty-eight-year-old Cantonese Marshal, a lively, outspoken man in a brown tunic and white Panama hat, sat with me on the veranda of the airport passenger shack looking out toward the Communist-held coast. He was awaiting the arrival of his young, pretty wife from Hong Kong.

The Governor complained angrily about the sparse assistance he was getting from Chiang Kai-shek on Taiwan. "We have not received the money or the supplies we need. Only some air force planes and navy ships have been sent to help us," the Governor said. In lieu of money from Taiwan, the Governor was turning out silver dollars at the provincial mint, but their silver content was diminishing rapidly. The Governor said that American aid should be divided equally between Taiwan and Hainan Island. "Hainan, with its vast resources, is potentially much richer than Taiwan," he said. "The mineral deposits have hardly been touched. The investment of private American capital will absolutely be welcomed."

The foreigners on the island were speculating that Chiang Kai-shek probably had already written off Hainan, one of the reasons being an old political feud with Ch'en Chi-t'ang. The Marshal had been the powerful Governor of Kwangtung from 1928 to 1936, when he was ousted by Chiang Kai-shek.

Ch'en Chi-t'ang assumed civil control of Hainan in April. He found that corrupt, inefficient Nationalist rule since the end of World War II had virtually wrecked the industrial foundation built by the Japanese. Of 170 factories erected by the Japanese, only about a dozen were operating. The port installations were a shambles, and steel rails of the new railroad had been hauled away. There was little left of the projects which the Japanese had initiated to develop the rich mineral deposits. Surveys had shown deposits of iron, tin, copper, manganese, lead, silver, coal, graphite, antimony, tungsten and crystal. Among the exportable agricultural products that the Japanese had begun to raise were rubber, pineapples, sugar cane, quinine, coffee and coconuts. Local Chinese leaders said that the island could support more than triple its population of 2.5 million.

Ch'en Chi-t'ang had energetically tried to salvage something from the wreckage he had found. Investing his own fortune, he repaired some roads, built a broadcasting station, two hospitals, a weaving mill and four schools. He also was re-equipping four divisions of the island garrison, paying them with dollars from the mint. The high-grade iron mines had been started up again with monthly production going from twelve thousand to fifty thousand tons, which were being exported through the port of Yulin.

I flew back to Hong Kong on February 2. The day before I left, the old French Bishop, dressed in his long black habit, mounted with me again to the roof of the mission. The sun, a huge, bright orange orb, was settling below the horizon on the mainland. Looking out toward the Communists on the coast, the Bishop tugged his long graying beard and said softly in French: "I have lived happily among the Chinese for thirty years, but now I am afraid."

The Communists came on April 17. The 119th and 120th Infantry Divisions of Lin Piao's army swarmed ashore from more than a hundred junks on the north coast, northwest of Limko. Other troops of the 121st and 125th Infantry Divisions, transported aboard some sixty junks, landed to the west of Hoihow. The Communist guerrillas struck from the interior. Hsueh Yueh's troops retreated south to Yulin, where some were evacuated to Taiwan. On April 21, having waited more than two decades, Feng Pai-chü was the unchallenged ruler of Hainan. Within two years all the foreigners were gone, except perhaps the lonely leper.

In Hong Kong, there were new travel orders from the AP. While in the United States, we had been assigned to open a new bureau in Peking as soon as the Communists would admit us. We thought that it would be only a matter of months. Although United States recognition of Peking did not seem an immediate prospect, neither was the United States embracing Chiang Kai-shek too closely. On December 23, 1949, a State Department policy paper was issued, saying that the Communist seizure of Taiwan was anticipated, and that American missions abroad should play down the importance of Taiwan to United States interests so as to minimize the damage to Washington's prestige. In January 1950 Dean Acheson, the Secretary of State, delineated the American "defense perimeter" without including Taiwan or Korea, thus signaling that neither was considered vital to American security. But on January 14, the Chinese Communists "requisitioned" a part of the grounds of the American Consulate General in Peking, the former military compound in which consular offices had been installed. Acheson promptly ordered withdrawal of remaining diplomatic personnel from the mainland and on January 18 said that the action in Peking made it clear that the Communists were not interested in American recognition. The AP then suggested that, since the Communists were ignoring my visa application, as they would for the next twenty years, I go to a funny little country whose name was sometimes mixed up by our editors in New York with Indonesia. It was Indochina. There was some kind of trouble in Vietnam and would I go there for a month? A few days after my return from Hainan, Audrey and I left for Saigon. We checked into the Continental Hotel, weary after our long flight, and had just sat down on the huge bed under a ceiling fan barely stirring the sultry air, when a shattering explosion ripped the square under our windows. We rushed to look. There, on the other side of the square in a one-story building, where one day the Caravelle Hotel would be built, was a café that had been blasted by a terrorist bomb. More than a score of Cyclo drivers, who pedaled bicycles that pushed ricksha seats ahead of them, were streaking away from the café in all directions. One of them had thrown the plastic bomb. French soldiers and sailors, dead and wounded, lay amid overturned tables and shattered glass inside the café and outside on the sidewalk terrace, where they had been sitting sipping drinks. A badly wounded soldier, clutching his groin, stumbled into the street. The war was on in the South in full fury. We stayed in French Indochina two years.

PART II

INDOCHINA
SEQUEL

CHAPTER 7

VIETNAM GENESIS

When we reached Saigon in early February 1950, Indochina had already been cohabiting with revolution, terrorism and the burning hatreds of colonial war for three years. In the struggle against Ho Chi Minh's Vietminh guerrillas in the jungles, mountains and on the great river deltas of Vietnam, the French Union forces had suffered 100,000 casualties, including 25,000 dead and captured. It was a war of surprise attacks on isolated French garrisons, of ambush and massacre, and ruthless retaliation employing the torch and napalm air attacks against suspected Vietminh-held villages. At night, the French remained in their fortified posts and the Vietminh became masters of the countryside. Millions of Vietnamese were uprooted in the merciless warfare, and thousands of refugees flooded into Saigon, Hanoi and the other French-held cities and towns. But it was a human tragedy hidden and forgotten by the world, overshadowed by the events in China and obscured by French press censorship. I was the first American correspondent to be stationed in Indochina covering the war against the Vietminh, and I was to be plagued for two years by French censorship and denial of information.

The sounds of battle in China were heard only faintly, and even as the final act in the Communist conquest of the mainland was drawing to its end I found in Saigon a strange disinterest in the Chinese civil war. It seemed far away and officials spoke of it with detachment. In the next months, the French would learn that the Communist victory in China and the presence of Mao Tse-tung's troops on the Indochina frontier would have a profound and militarily decisive impact on the war against the Vietminh. Unfortunately, after the French learned their Chinese lesson, they would never be able to convey its implications to American policy-makers. If they had, the United States might have been spared its own subsequent traumatic episode in Vietnam and fifty thousand dead.

Under the French, Saigon was a less safe place to live than during its second terrorist siege a decade later when the city was defended by Americans. Vietminh terrorists, the forerunners of the Vietcong, would throw an average of three or four plastic bombs each night into Saigon cafés crowded with French soldiers and sailors or into establishments that refused to pay taxes to the underground. Political assassinations would take place on the open verandas of cafés in the center of the city or on busy, crowded thoroughfares. In retaliation French agents would assassinate Vietminh suspects and dump their bodies on corner sidewalks as a warning to the underground to desist. At night, from the other side of the Saigon River, Vietminh guerrillas would lob mortar shells into the city.

Yet the French resisted transforming Saigon into a city of barred windows, barbed-wire barricades and antiseptic regulations upon which the American military command was to insist for the protection of its troops. Saigon remained a pleasant, vividly colored city of tree-lined streets and boulevards, with sidewalk cafés and restaurants serving superb food and wine. It was a metropolis of two million, including the twin Chinese city of Cholon. For most of the population the terrorist bomb explosions and gunshots were only muffled sounds in the distance or newspaper items. French Union soldiers in a melange of uniforms, many of them Foreign Legionnaires, African Senegalese, Moroccan Goumiers or French paratroopers, crowded the streets looking for women, bars, gambling, and they were rarely disappointed. The friendly opium-smoking Corsican who ran our hotel, the Continental, imported French prostitutes from Paris. There were lavishly furnished opium divans in Saigon and Hanoi whose patrons included prominent members of the French community who enjoyed occasional pipes without becoming addicted. They would recline on the couches taking perhaps ten pipes, thirty or forty less than the addicts, filled by young Vietnamese girls in white diaphanous dresses who were available to those male patrons whose sexual desires were not quenched by the suppressant effects of the opium. When Graham Greene, the English writer, first visited Vietnam, Audrey and I took him to his first opium den and watched his pale blue eyes light up as he absorbed detail which later went into his books.

About a dozen Americans were living in Saigon when we arrived, most of them in the small United States Consulate. The French had resisted American business inroads, and the bulk of the Americans in Indochina were about 120 missionaries, largely of the Christian and Missionary Alliance, with a much smaller number of Seventh-Day Adventists. The Alliance had founded a church of about fifty thousand members among the 28 million people of the three Indochinese states of Vietnam, Cambodia and Laos. Americans were popular with the Vietnamese, respected for their technological achievements and deemed anticolonialist because they had granted independence to the Philippines. Every American, however, was watched with suspicion by the French. United States agents had been in touch with Ho Chi Minh and other Vietnamese nationalists during and just after World War II, and the French remained convinced that the United States was intent on replacing them with an American presence in Indochina.

Within a few days after our arrival in Saigon, the United States recognized the French-sponsored Bao Dai Government for Vietnam. France had just granted limited autonomy within the French Union to Vietnam and the two associated Indochinese states, Laos and Cambodia. Galvanized by the Nationalist collapse in China, and determined to block any further march of Communism into Southeast Asia, the United States put aside its reservations about French colonial policies and agreed to support the dependent Vietnamese government headed by Bao Dai, the former Emperor of Annam (the central region of Vietnam), against the Vietminh. Almost immediately, the United States also began to assemble in Saigon the usual panoply of intervention: large diplomatic and information staffs, and economic and military aid missions. United States naval warships called at the port of Saigon as "a sign of friendship for Vietnam."

On February 9 Edmund A. Gullion, the newly appointed American Consul General in Saigon, arrived and delivered a formal note from President Truman proposing diplomatic relations. On February 25 the consulate was raised to a legation and Gullion was named Chargé d'Affaires, with the personal rank of Minister Counselor.

I called on Gullion not long after his arrival at his office in the small consulate building just off Rue Catinat. Gullion, a strikingly handsome, thirty-six-year-old bachelor, son of an army officer and a career diplomat, received me in a friendly but guarded manner. He told me frankly that he thought American correspondents who had covered the China civil war were defeatist in their attitudes toward the anti-Communist struggle in Asia. Vietnam was not China, he said, and the French Army was not the Chiang Kai-shek army, and the projections arrived at in Washington showed that with American material help the French-supported Bao Dai Government could bring about a military victory against the Vietminh. Most important, the French Army would be an effective weapon for the containment of China.

I left Gullion stunned by what I had heard. As I turned down the Rue Catinat and walked toward the Continental Hotel, I kept asking myself: "Didn't we learn anything in China?" We had poured thousands of tons of military equipment and hundreds of millions of dollars into supporting Chiang Kai-shek in his drive for a military victory over the Communists. Lacking an efficient government with a solid base of popular support, the Nationalist armies had crumbled before the Communists. Chiang Kai-shek had been defeated by a foe inferior in numbers and weapons, but backed by the peasantry, who saw in the Communists their economic and social salvation.

Now, against the advice of American intelligence agents in Indochina who knew the appeal of the Vietminh, the United States had decided to plunge into another Asian bog, seeking a military victory for a semicolonial government despised by the majority of the politically conscious Vietnamese intent upon winning independence from France.

The Bao Dai Government was generally looked upon as a "puppet regime," although many of its members had shown considerable courage in criticizing French policy. Bao Dai, the thirty-seven-year-old, French-educated heir to the "Dragon throne" of Annam, had been brought out of exile in Hong Kong by the French in 1948. The French were searching for a political response to the nationalist appeal of Ho Chi Minh. Bao Dai had served previously as the nominal Emperor of Annam under the French, continued on the throne during the Japanese occupation and abdicated to act as "High Counselor" to the short-lived Ho Chi Minh Government before escaping to an indolent existence in Hong Kong. On March 8, 1949, the French signed an agreement with Bao Dai which granted limited autonomy to Vietnam within the French Union. Bao Dai became the provisional Chief of State pending restoration of peace and the election of a constituent assembly to frame a constitution. The French retained direction of Vietnam's diplomacy and national defense. Vietnam, Cambodia and Laos were to be incorporated into an economic federation and their currency tied to the French franc. French business and cultural interests were assured special prerogatives. Frenchmen were to be tried before mixed courts according to French law and were to be given preference in the appointment of foreign advisers and technicians. The Vietnamese were given no official promise that the agreement would lead to full independence, and no provision was made for the eventual withdrawal of French troops from the country.

The agreement fell far short of the dramatic act of liberal statesmanship that might have placed Bao Dai's government on a solid political foundation and enabled him to attract support away from Ho Chi Minh. By failing to meet Vietnamese demands for a place in the French Union equivalent to that of a Dominion in the British Commonwealth, France lost the opportunity to ally herself with strong Vietnamese nationalist elements.

Bao Dai himself was a major weakness of the French-sponsored government—a stocky, fleshy man, whose passions were spent on a succession of women, carousing and tiger shooting. He passed much of his time in the mountain city of Dalat, while his wife, a Catholic, lived in France with their five children. By subordinating affairs of state to pleasure-seeking and acquiring a playboy reputation, he disappointed not only his French sponsors and American supporters but also the Vietnamese coterie surrounding him which was trying to restore the Annamese imperial dynasty. This was the man whom the Vietnamese in making their political choice compared with the ascetic professional Communist revolutionary, "Uncle Ho"—a slight, frail man with a wispy beard, then fifty-seven, who was to keep Vietnam aflame for the next two decades.

Ho Chi Minh ("The One Who Shines") was born in Annam, Central Vietnam, the son of a minor official. After leaving French-run schools, where teachers complained about his revolutionary politics and poor grades, he worked as a messboy on a French liner and in the kitchens of the Carlton Hotel in London. He visited New York, where he wrote about race problems for *La Race Noire*. In 1917 he preached anticolonialism in Paris to Indochinese conscripted for war service. Visiting the Soviet Union in 1920, Ho participated in the First Congress of the Peoples of the East, and two years later in the Conference of the Toilers of the Far East, sponsored by the Comintern, the Moscow-based international Communist organization. Working with Michael Borodin, the Comintern agent in Canton, Ho began laying the foundation for the Indochina Communist Party and assigned members of his youth organization to the Whampoa Military Academy, where future Chinese Nationalist and Communist leaders were being trained. In 1930, while in Hong Kong, Ho established the Indochina Communist Party, but he was imprisoned by the British for nearly two years on French instigation, while the apparatus of the Party was smashed. After three years in Moscow, Ho joined the Chinese Communist Eighth Route Army and in 1940 acted as Political Commissar of a Chinese Communist guerrilla training mission under General Yeh Chien-ying which was schooling Nationalists at Liuchow in South China's Kwangsi Province. He then organized the Vietnam Doc Lap Dong Minh, or Vietminh, the Revolutionary League for the Independence of Vietnam, and with Allied support based himself in the North Indochinese mountains to stage guerrilla raids against the Japanese. But in 1942, while crossing the border into China to make contact with Chinese and Vietnamese émigré groups, he was arrested by a Chinese warlord and imprisoned for thirteen months. During 1944 he operated in the North Vietnam jungles in contact with American agents of the Office of Strategic Services (OSS), from whom he solicited and received aid. With the Japanese defeat, the Vietminh were free to occupy Hanoi.

The Vietminh entered Hanoi triumphantly in August 1945 and proclaimed the "Democratic Republic of Vietnam," with Ho Chi Minh as President. But the Republic foundered quickly. In late September the French moved to retake possession of their colony. French troops released from Japanese internment by the British drove the Vietminh out of Saigon, and the fighting continued until the following year, when peace talks were initiated. Ho Chi Minh was welcomed to France to carry on negotiations, but they broke down. The Vietminh explanation was that the French refused to meet demands for qualified independence. The French contended that an agreement had in fact been signed recognizing the "Republic of Vietnam" as a free state with its own government, parliament, army and finance as part of the Indochina federation and within the French Union, but that negotiations to bring it into being had failed because of Communist intransigence. In any event, Vietminh troops attacked French positions on December 19, 1946, and all-out war exploded.

American Ambassador Leighton Stuart and Chou En-lai in 1946

Chiang Kai-shek and Ambassador Stuart. *George Silk, Life magazine*

Chiang Kai-shek leaving the Tomb of Sun Yat-sen outside Nanking before his final departure from his capital . *AP*

Fleeing from Nanking before the Communist advance. *Henri Cartier-Bresson, Magnum Archives*

Communist troops after their entry into Nanking. *Henri Cartier-Bresson*

Mao Tse-tung at a victory parade marking the defeat of the Nationalist regime

Ho Chi Minh. *The New York Times*

General Jean de Lattre de Tassigny, French High Commissioner of Indochina, 1951. *Europea*

At the entrance to the French Army post of Chi Ma on the China border: *(left to right)* Wilson Fielder of *Time* magazine; the French officer in command of the post; Carl Mydans of *Life* magazine; and the author. *Carl Mydans*

A French convoy on Route Coloniale No. 4. The mountains in the background are in China. *Carl Mydans*

Whatever the political character and intentions of the Communist leadership, the Vietminh attracted the support of a majority of the population for reasons that were largely nationalistic. Communists occupied the key posts in the Vietminh, but they were only a minority in the movement, probably not exceeding 30 percent. Unlike the Chinese Revolution, which was generated essentially by social and economic factors, the Vietminh insurgent movement was fueled mainly by nationalism, a reaction to ninety years of French colonial domination. The nationalist revolution in Vietnam was similar to the revolution in China in that the Communists were exploiting it as a vehicle to ride to power.

At the very moment that the United States had chosen to align itself with the Bao Dai regime, the Chinese Communist armies were making contact on the North Indochina frontier with the Vietminh and forming a liaison that would doom French power in Vietnam.

Six weeks before our arrival in Saigon, the advance columns of Lin Piao's Fourth Field Army, which had marched the length of China, reached the frontier of North Vietnam. Lin Piao's troops took up positions on December 14 opposite Mon Cay, the eastern anchor of a line of French forts along the North Indochina border.

In March, as the Chinese Communists extended their border control westward and the Vietminh began to hammer at the French border posts, Audrey and I flew to Hanoi, where the French headquarters for operations in the North was situated.

In Hanoi, we stayed at the Metropole Hotel beside a small, pleasant lake. The Metropole was a decaying French colonial hostelry, whose wine, high-ceilinged bedrooms and bathroom bidets were the principal remaining symbols of the French cultural heritage. In the bedrooms ceiling fans turned futilely over huge double beds encased in white mosquito netting. This netting spared Audrey and me injury a year later during an abortive Vietminh offensive on the Red River Delta toward Hanoi. We were asleep when an artillery blast shook loose a large section of the plaster. The heavy plaster struck the netting, which sagged to within an inch or two of our heads. More than twenty years later, the Metropole, currently called the Thong Nhat (Reunification) Hotel, remains the chief hostelry in Hanoi, mosquito netting, bidets and all.

Hanoi was a vigorous, bustling city in early 1950, lacking the sophistication, luxurious languor and brilliant tropical color of Saigon. The people were sturdier, more peasant-like in appearance, the women lacking the slender floating elegance of the Saigonnaise. The city itself had been built in the French provincial style, with wide boulevards and heavy ornate public buildings. The streets were crowded with French military trucks and Vietnamese pedaling bicycles or riding carts pulled by bullocks. The buildings, of crumbling yellow plaster, showed the scars of vicious street fighting between the French and Vietminh in 1946. As in Saigon, the municipal administration was largely French, even unto the policemen directing traffic at the main intersections.

Hanoi, more than Saigon, was feeling the pressure of the Chinese Communist descent on the border. I drove to Muong Dzuong, about ninety miles northeast of Hanoi, where 25,000 Chinese Nationalist troops who had fled across the border at Mon Cay before Lin Piao's advancing columns were interned by the French. At the encampment, I found the Nationalist troops in good condition. They had escaped with their excellent American equipment virtually intact. The French had confiscated their weapons. Although they had been defeated by the Communists, the Nationalists had swaggered into Vietnam making it plain that they regarded the country as something akin to the kitchen quarters of China.

Afraid of provoking the Chinese Communists, the French were resisting the pleas of General Pai Ch'ung-hsi's headquarters on Hainan Island that the interned troops be repatriated to his island fortress. The French also spurned Pai's request that some 30,000 of his troops, the remnants of his 200,000-man army, now penned up against the border, be allowed to pass through the French line of forts into Indochina for evacuation by sea to Hainan.

I had been told on Hainan by Chinese Nationalist officials that Pai had offered the use of his troops to the Bao Dai Government against the Vietminh. Although the Chinese Communists had already recognized the Ho Chi Minh Government, the French still hoped that they could persuade Peking to remain aloof from the Indochina fighting, and they declined Pai's offer. Two Nationalist ships with four hundred troops aboard were seized by the French and interned at Haiphong when they attempted to pass through French territorial waters.

Meanwhile, Lin Piao had established a Southeast China Command and had begun a systematic mop-up of regular Nationalist troops, guerrillas and bandits in the Kwangtung-Kwangsi border area. Liu Po-ch'eng swept west through Yunnan, whose Nationalist Governor, Lu Han, defected on December 11 like most of the Nationalist commanders in the west, and established a Southwest China Command. While Liu Po-ch'eng's forces pressed westward, in early March, one of his generals, Ch'en Keng, arrived in the Yunnanese capital, subordinated the turncoat Lu Han, and began rooting out the remaining Nationalist forces in the province contiguous to the Indochina frontier. By mid-April organized Nationalist resistance along the Indochina border had collapsed. Remnant Nationalist troops continued to cross into Indochina, where they were interned by the French. Eventually, the French, with American help, would quietly repatriate the Nationalist troops to Taiwan. Along the Indochina border, the Chinese Communists were systematically setting up their liaison with Vietminh units and Ho Chi Minh's secret jungle headquarters. The decisive battle of the French Indochina War, the struggle for control of the frontier, was impending.

When I returned to Hanoi from Muong Dzuong, I pressed the French headquarters for permission to visit the frontier. The French were hesitant. Two of their large convoys traveling along Route Coloniale No. 4, the main supply road serving the border posts, had just been ambushed, with heavy casualties. Two other American correspondents, both good friends, had meanwhile arrived in Hanoi with the same request. They were Carl Mydans, the *Life* photographer, a short, dynamic, compassionate man, wise in the ways of war, who had distinguished himself in covering World War II, and Wilson Fielder, a young, amiable *Time* magazine reporter who was based in Hong Kong.

General Marcel Alessandre, the French commander of the frontier forces, decided to take the three of us to Lang Son, the main border post. I left Audrey in Hanoi, and on March 23 we set forth for Lang Son. We traveled with General Alessandre and his staff in an old three-engined German Junker. The flight took one hour, twice the usual time, since the ceiling was low and we had to dodge through the mountain passes. A spit-and-polish Foreign Legion honor guard met us at the red-dirt strip at the base of a mountain, and we were taken to the residence of Colonel Jean Constans, the commanding officer of the Frontier Zone. Colonel Constans told us that his mission was to seal off the frontier and block the infiltration of Vietminh troops equipped with material obtained in China south to the Red River Delta and Hanoi.

French posts commanded the four traditional invasion and infiltration routes from China into Indochina. On the western flank, isolated and supplied largely by air, was Lao Kay. It dominated the partially

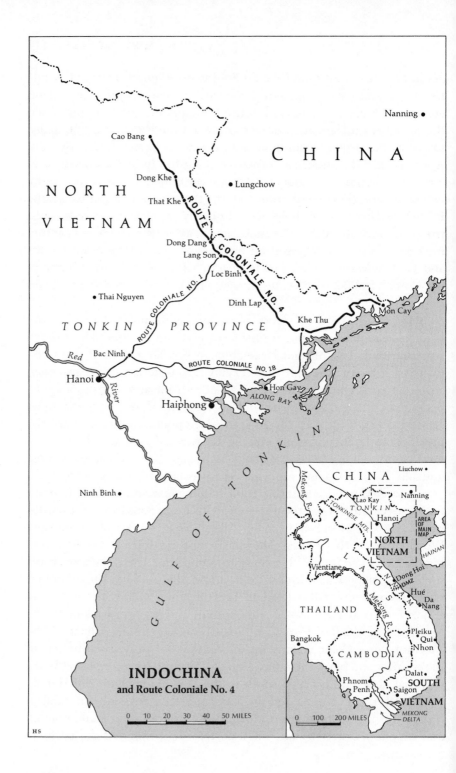

Nanning •

C H I N A

Cao Bang •

N O R T H

Dong Khe •

• Lungchow

That Khe •

ROUTE

V I E T N A M

Dong Dang •

COLONIALE

Lang Son •

Loc Binh •

NO. 4

• Thai Nguyen

Dinh Lap •

ROUTE COLONIALE NO. 1

Khe Thu •

Môn Cay •

T O N K I N   P R O V I N C E

Red

Bac Ninh •

ROUTE COLONIALE NO. 18

Hanoi •

River

Hon Gay

ALONG BAY

Haiphong •

G U L F   O F   T O N K I N

Ninh Binh •

Liuchow •

C H I N A

Lao Kay

Nanning

TONKIN

Mekong R.

TONKINESE MTS.

Hanoi

AREA
OF
MAIN
MAP

NORTH
VIETNAM

HAINAN

L A O S

Vientiane

Dong Hoi

DMZ

Mekong R.

Hué

Da
Nang

THAILAND

Pleiku

Qui
Nhon

Bangkok

C A M B O D I A

Dalat •

INDOCHINA
and Route Coloniale No. 4

Phnom
Penh

Saigon

SOUTH
VIETNAM

0   10   20   30   40   50 MILES

0   100   200 MILES

MEKONG
DELTA

H 5

demolished railway linking Kunming to Haiphong and a network of roads. The other three principal positions were linked by Route Coloniale No. 4, which had become known as the "Road of Death" because of a succession of bloody Vietminh ambushes. The highway bent along the China frontier for 150 miles from Mon Cay on the east coast through Lang Son to Cao Bang in the west. Lang Son was the major fortress and the headquarters town. Fifteen miles to the northwest of Lang Son lay the outpost of Dong Dang, directly opposite the mist-shrouded mountain pass of Nam Quan. This was the main invasion route. Traditionally, envoys traveling from Peking to the Indochinese capitals had come down the highway, now paralleled by a railroad, from Nanning, capital of Kwangsi, through the Nam Quan Pass to Lang Son, and then down what had become Route Coloniale No. 1 to Hanoi and Saigon. Lang Son itself was a pleasant town of ten thousand constructed in the French provincial style with wide streets and low yellow-brown houses. The first post was built about 1882 and lost briefly to Taiping rebels when they made a foray from China. In 1940 the Japanese had seized Lang Son, pouring two divisions through the Nam Quan Pass. When their truce with the French ended in 1945, the Japanese attacked again, massacring the French garrison of four hundred and executing the commander, General Lemonnière. The strong French fortifications around Lang Son were destroyed by the Japanese and never rebuilt apart from a thin line of posts which now screened the town from the Vietminh.

On our first night in Lang Son, we dined at the Foreign Legion officers club and listened to old songs of the Legion over endless rounds of cognac. Most of the officers, unlike the enlisted men, were French, but there was a tall, slim, erect lieutenant who turned out to be an American. He had been a captain in the United States Army during World War II. He was a freebooter, a lover of arms, uniforms and battle. His name was Robert Fleet, but he cautioned us against using it because of United States law banning service by Americans in foreign armies. He survived the debacle that came later on the frontier, and I saw him once again in Saigon. He eventually left Indochina disillusioned with the French, who never did entirely trust him, regardless of his proven ability as a soldier, because he was an American.

Two days later in a jeep, driven by Lieutenant André Wastin, a slight, dark, cocky French officer, and accompanied by a weapons carrier loaded with ten heavily armed Foreign Legionnaires, we set out for the China border. The Legionnaires were all German and received their commands in German. We followed a foot patrol that had been clearing the road of mines planted during the night by the Vietminh. The road twisted through the bare brown hills. It was ideal ambush country, and the debris of old clashes with the Vietminh were all about. There were lines of parallel trenches athwart the road, "piano keys" as they were called, dug by the Vietminh at night and filled in by French road clearers during the day.

When we turned off the road to head for Ban Chu, a post ten miles from the frontier, Lieutenant Wastin halted the jeep and said to us, "Gentlemen, you must now make a choice. Either our jeep goes ahead on the road, which is often mined by the Vietminh, or the Legionnaires go first in their truck. If we go first in the jeep and hit a mine, one or two of us may be killed or wounded, but the Legionnaires will be able to beat off the Vietminh who will attack after the mine explodes. However, if the Legionnaires go first and their truck hits the mine, we probably will be overwhelmed and killed by the Vietminh ambushers. Now take your choice—which goes first, the jeep or the truck?" We looked at each other and elected to go ahead with the jeep to the frontier.

From Ban Chu, we went to the post of Chi Ma. On the way, we passed a steady stream of Chinese coolies and merchants carrying food and other wares from China to sell the next day in the market in the nearby village of Loch Binh. This was a familiar scene in China along most of its borders. Regardless of war or how strictly guarded the frontiers were, Chinese peasants and merchants always found a way to get their merchandise to market.

On the border, the French outposts of Chi Ma and Pinquet faced two Chinese Communist-held strongposts, and between them was the village of Ai Diem. We walked down from Chi Ma through paddy fields and garden patches to within thirty or forty yards of the gate to the village, guarded by two Chinese Communist soldiers. Mydans photographed them, and one of the Communist soldiers looked us over with field glasses. I would not see another Chinese Communist soldier for fourteen years, until the day in 1964 when I visited the bridge at Lo Wu on the border between Hong Kong and China.

We returned to Lang Son that night. Mydans and Fielder were summoned to another assignment and flew out to Haiphong on March 27. I never saw Wilson Fielder again. He was killed during the Korean

War while covering the battle for Taejon. I waited in Lang Son for the weather to clear. A convoy was forming up for the dash eastward along Route No. 4. On the suggestion or a French officer, I sent a message to Audrey in Hanoi suggesting that she meet me at Hon Gay, south of the terminus of Route 4 on the beautiful Along Bay of the Gulf of Tonkin. I did not realize that I was launching her on a journey nearly as dangerous as the convoy run I was about to make.

In the drizzling morning mist that hangs over Lang Son during the rainy season, truck motors snarled as our convoy formed. A patrol of ten Goumiers, Moroccan mountain fighters of the French colonials, walked past the fog-shrouded vehicles. Led by a French sergeant, they moved out of the Lang Son outpost down R.C. No. 4. The red-clay road they walked on twisted for fifty miles southeast through the green foothills to Khe Thu. The convoy would have to reach Khe Thu before darkness that night.

R.C. No. 4 was a threadlike communications corridor vulnerable to attack at any time from the Vietminh, who moved easily in the adjacent country. Convoys used it going northwest from Lang Son but rarely. The thirty-six-mile run from Lang Son to That Khe was too hazardous for regular supply. Beyond That Khe, the remaining thirty-five miles to Cao Bang were controlled by the Vietminh and the road was impassable. Isolated Cao Bang was supplied by air. Our convoy was going southeast from Lang Son. The French battalions who held the forts along the way depended on it for supplies.

The Goumiers' patrol was the forward point for the detachment that was to clear the first six miles of road leading to Khe Thu. In a jeep mounting a light machine gun, the detachment commander, a French marine lieutenant, followed the patrol slowly. Behind him came two armored personnel carriers each mounting a 30- and a 50-caliber machine gun. The carriers sandwiched two truckloads of Foreign Legionnaires.

Covering the progress of the Goumiers, the machine guns were kept trained on the ridge that rose steeply on the left. The brown-skinned, bearded men, some with their soft-brimmed French campaign hats thrown back to show shaven heads, scrutinized the hillside, the paddy fields extending for a thousand yards to the foothills on the right, and searched the soggy road with its small wooden bridges for mines.

Three miles out of Lang Son, the detachment dropped off a section of twenty Legionnaires. The other section was dropped off two miles farther on. They climbed in four files toward the top of the ridge, alertly watching the underbrush on their flanks. They were among the sentries being posted on the foothills along the road to screen the convoy coming from Lang Son.

French posts all the way to Khe Thu were sending out similar security patrols. Some of the posts were only small brick blockhouses, each manned by about six native partisans. Others ranged from those with several watchtowers within a bamboo enclosure perched atop a hill to those like Dinh Lap, which was garrisoned with infantry, artillery and tank units. The posts themselves, when isolated at night, were favorite targets for Vietminh raids made in overwhelming strength.

The detachment moved forward another mile before meeting the tank patrol from Loc Binh, six miles away. The road was open. From Loc Binh, the radio signal went back to the convoy. The Vietminh were not on the road, and once again with the morning, R.C. No. 4 southeast from Lang Son belonged to the French.

It was 10:40 A.M. when the first element of our convoy rolled into Loc Binh, a small town of low, clay-plastered buildings and a gray stone Catholic church.

A truck carrying half a platoon of Legionnaires headed the convoy, followed by an armored radio vehicle. Traveling at two-hundred-yard intervals came thirty-three civilian and forty-five military trucks. There was a machine gun in every fifth military truck. Most of the convoy guards carried light automatic weapons. Another radio car and a truck loaded with Legionnaires brought up the rear of the column.

The convoy moved slowly on to Dinh Lap, the largest French post between Lang Son and Khe Thu. Here were stationed the intervention troops with their tanks and artillery units. When the radio trucks of a convoy signaled a Vietminh attack, or contact was lost, the intervention troops moved swiftly out of Dinh Lap to its assistance. The outlying posts also depended on help from Dinh Lap when they came under attack.

Southeast of Dinh Lap, the convoy passed from the land of the Thos, a people of Tibetan origin, into the Nung country where live some 300,000 mountaineers closely related to the Chinese. The foothills here were more densely covered with jungle foliage that crowded down to both sides of the road. It was ideal country for an ambush. The more dangerous leg of the journey to Khe Thu had begun.

The convoy commander, a cheerful, lean lieutenant of the Marines, lifted his camera from between the front seats of his jeep and looped the case strap around his neck. "The last time the Vietminh attacked," the lieutenant explained to me, "I had to leave the jeep and the Vietminh took my camera." He looked at the grenades in the glove compartment of the jeep and at the tommy gun which lay beside him, loaded and with safety off. I sat beside him with a carbine across my knees.

The lieutenant said that the Vietminh attacks on convoys along R.C. No. 4 were almost always alike. They came usually during the good weather between March and November. The point of attack along the road would be in one of the large gaps between posts. Hundreds of men could hide in the thick jungle growths covering the hills.

The convoy would know that it was under attack only after it had suffered its first casualties. From perfect concealment, the Vietminh would open fire with machine guns, other automatic weapons of which they had a plentiful supply, and rifles. When one truck was forced to halt, blocking the narrow road for the vehicles behind, anywhere from hundreds to several thousand Vietminh would swarm down on the convoy throwing grenades. Trucks would be burned. Many of the French wounded on the road would be killed. The Vietminh would then disappear quickly into the mountains, taking with them prisoners and captured matériel, especially weapons.

When a convoy came under attack, all the trucks immediately sped up and fire was returned on the move. If one truck was knocked out blocking the way, those behind took to the side of the road and tried to fight off the Vietminh while awaiting help. The Vietminh were generally already gone when the intervention troops arrived and the P-61 King Cobra fiAghter planes from the airstrip at Lang Son appeared overhead.

Looking at the terrain of North Indochina, I could see what the French officers had already told me—that it was impossible to pursue and root out guerrillas from the interior valleys and jungle-covered mountains. Only sixty miles southwest of Lang Son lay Thai Nguyen, the Vietminh military center and political capital, where hundreds of French prisoners were held. Among them were about five hundred French men, women and children, survivors who had been carried off from Hanoi as hostages by the Vietminh when fighting broke out there in December 1946.

When the French troops did locate Vietminh villages during operational sweeps into the mountains near their posts, the villages were usually deserted. The French left them burning, with the work water buffaloes shot dead on the rice fields.

At 5:10 P.M. the convoy commander and his rear radio truck halted at Na Peo, a French post, ten miles from the convoy's destination at Khe Thu. He dropped off a truck with motor trouble, the second to be left along the way. The radio operator tuned in clearly an English-language news broadcast of the Voice of America. Some of the Legionnaires gathered around to listen quietly. One German, a baker by trade, asked if it was possible after completing his enlistment in the Legion for him to settle in the United States.

The convoy escort was a typical cross section of the tough, well-disciplined Legionnaires serving along the frontier in Indochina. Over half of them were German war veterans who had signed up for the normal five-year enlistment either in France or in the French Zone of Germany. About one-fifth were French, and most of the others were Central Europeans who didn't want to go back to their countries behind the Iron Curtain.

The men in the convoy escort were dressed in the French field uniform for North Indochina: soft-brimmed campaign hat with one side turned up flat, fatigues, pistol belt, leggings and heavy shoes. Most carried automatic weapons or American carbines.

Several miles beyond Na Peo, the heavy bamboo jungle which came up to the sides of the road had been cleared away. The Vietminh had attacked a convoy here. Twenty-five had been killed, fifteen wounded and twenty men taken prisoner. Fourteen trucks were burned.

The last truck of the convoy rolled into Khe Thu at 6:10 P.M. Khe Thu was the big supply base for the frontier regiments. Small craft from Haiphong brought food, ammunition, medical supplies and the all-important *vin rouge* up through the Gulf of Tonkin to Khe Thu's tiny port on a narrow inlet. The convoy loaded with supplies was due to return to Lang Son the next day.

But that night the French tricolor flew at half-mast over Khe Thu. There had been a funeral for twelve. One was a French warrant officer who had come to Indochina four days before. They had died two days before in a Vietminh ambush of a small convoy eight miles south on Route No. 18. In the morning, a detachment would go out to reopen Route No. 18. I accompanied it.

The hills were steaming in a hot early morning sun, when our road-opening convoy moved out. A French major commanded the detachment of one section of Legionnaires and a full company of Nungs, men of the local region enlisted in the French colonials. They were to clear ten miles of road down to Tam Tri, a place on the Song Ba Che River where vehicles traveling on Route No. 18 were ferried across on a native barge. Another convoy under heavy Legionnaire escort was coming up from the south. The two convoys were to meet early in the afternoon at the river ferry point.

The Nungs went forward on foot shortly after the convoy left Khe Thu and turned down Route No. 18. They fanned out over the ridges and the paddy fields adjoining the road, where native farmers were at work, plowing with their water buffaloes. The Legionnaires followed on the road.

The leading patrol of Nungs reached the area where the convoy had been ambushed. A French lieutenant described it as a "classic ambush."

There had been thirty-five officers and men in four trucks traveling north. It was an engineering detail. They had just half-built a small brick blockhouse at Tam Tri on the ferry landing and were returning to Khe Thu.

The first truck, carrying a French lieutenant, warrant officer and sergeant and three Moroccan privates, headed the column. It was about two miles from the river and going through a road cut lined with bamboo jungle when the attack came. It was a complete surprise.

The Vietminh opened with one machine gun firing along the axis of the road and three other machine guns from the hillside rising on the left. Automatic weapon and rifle fire came from a force of over two hundred men concealed on the hillside. Everyone in the first truck was killed almost immediately.

The other three trucks stopped behind at intervals of 100, 200 and 500 yards. Two men who tried to fire the machine gun on the second truck were killed quickly one after the other. Several of the men in the second truck fell back to the next, where the defense centered. The Vietminh charged down onto the road. They were repulsed, but only after they had reached the first truck and collected the weapons of the dead. Six Nung partisans of a detachment of eight stationed in a tiny French post nearby were the first to come to the assistance of the convoy. Two were wounded by the Vietminh attackers. One of them dragged himself off without his rifle, but he took its bolt with him.

The Vietminh withdrew quickly when they heard trucks approaching with French reinforcements from Khe Thu. The Vietminh carried off about twenty of their own dead. In addition to the twelve men killed, three others of the French convoy had been wounded.

"That is all that happened," the lieutenant said. "That is all that ever happens."

The leading Nung patrol of our convoy walked out of the road cut and down the road curving to the river, where the unfinished French blockhouse, at Tam Tri, stood in the sun. Soon another convoy would go out to complete the work on the blockhouse.

I returned to Khe Thu to spend the night and the next morning with a French security escort drove to Hon Gay, anxious and wondering if Audrey was waiting there. It was March 29.

Audrey had received my message five days earlier saying that I hoped to be in Hon Gay on March 27. She had approached the French Information Service in Hanoi for help in getting to Hon Gay. Contrary to the advice I had received in Lang Son, she was strongly advised against making the trip. Vietminh guerrillas were operating along the sixty-five-mile road between Hanoi and Haiphong. The small river boats which plied between Haiphong and Hon Gay passed through country where the hills along the banks were controlled by the Vietminh. Determined, nevertheless, to go to Hon Gay, Audrey found a Vietnamese taxi driver in Hanoi whose fears about making the trip were assuaged with a wad of bills. Perched on the back seat of an old Citroën, Audrey, dressed in slacks, slender, all of twenty-one, with her blond braids piled atop her head, was driven at high speed to Haiphong by an apprehensive Vietnamese driver. She was then two months pregnant with our first child, Susan. The trip was made without incident, and Audrey checked into a French guest house run by a Frenchwoman. Sitting alone that night in a room of the decrepit villa, she heard American voices through the thin walls. She knocked on the door of the adjacent room and found Mydans and Fielder, who took her next morning to the river dock. The boat to Hon Gay was a native craft, less than thirty feet in length, pushed by a gasoline engine, and loaded with bags of rice, sixteen Vietnamese and a Frenchman carrying a submachine gun. The Vietnamese looked uneasily at her blond braids, a target that might draw fire from the Vietminh.

As the boat slipped out of Haiphong port and upriver, the Frenchman ordered Audrey down among the rice sacks. "Keep your blond head out of sight," he told her. For six hours, she crouched among the rice sacks. As the boat nosed through the narrow defiles, the French-man kept his machine gun trained on the cliffs towering above them. Then the boat entered the Along Bay, chugging through limpid waters afire with the intense colors of the sunset, winding through the bold rock formations. In Hon Gay at a French guest house fronting on the bay, Audrey waited for three days, not knowing I had been delayed by bad weather, and hearing rumors of a Vietminh ambush of a convoy—in fact the convoy that had preceded my own. That is where I found her, as I took the guest house steps two at a time. Together again, we walked along the shore of the bay, telling each other everything that had happened, while she tugged at my new black beard. We remained in Hon Gay for several days, boating on the magnificent bay among the strange natural rock protrusions that jutted out of the water like temple altars and idols carved by some forgotten race in a land now covered by the sea.

My observations on the journey along the frontier led to some jar-ring conclusions. In Saigon and Hanoi, American and French officials were saying that French troops had effectively sealed off the frontier except for small-scale infiltration by the Vietminh. In fact, the frontier was virtually open to the Vietminh, who controlled many of the roads by night, and the French positions were vulnerable and eventually might be overrun. Their lines of supply were already seriously im-periled. In the rainy season it would be difficult to supply or reinforce the more isolated posts if they came under heavy attack. It seemed to me the fate of the French frontier line was in the hands of the Chinese Communists, who were consolidating their positions along the Indo-china border. If they elected to provide the Vietminh with bases, train-ing, weapons and other supplies, the French frontier force was doomed. Once in control of the region, the Vietminh would have an excellent base area in which to prepare a massive descent onto the northern approaches to Hanoi. The balance in the war would swing decisively to the side of the Vietminh.

In March 1950 the French still had no positive indication of how the Chinese Communists would behave, although Peking had recognized Ho's Government on January 18. The Vietminh, with the toleration of both Chinese Nationalist commanders and Communist guerrillas, had been operating all along from sanctuaries in China. Their weapons, a melange of French, American, British and Japanese arms, had been seized in combat with the French or were being purchased from profes-

sional gun runners. The piasters being collected as taxes by the Vietminh underground in nominally French-held areas were traded in
Hong Kong and Bangkok for dollars that went to pay for guns and other
supplies that were smuggled in from China or landed on the coast.
Later, I was to learn that a number of French officials were involved
with racketeers in this traffic, which yielded millions of dollars in profit
for them and provided the Vietminh with weapons to kill French soldiers.

In mid-1950, instead of physically delivering their piasters to Hong
Kong in payment for weapons and other supplies, the Vietminh began
to hand the currency secretly to agents of a French syndicate operating
in Saigon. One of the agents was a senior Chinese employee of the Bank
of Indochina, a rich, politically influential institution, which had semi-
official status. The syndicate purchased these piasters at a cheap rate
and paid the Vietminh in Switzerland in hard currency, which the
guerrillas used to buy guns. It was a simpler procedure for the Vietminh
than smuggling currency to Hong Kong. As for the syndicate, it made
its profit by taking the piasters in Saigon to the official French Office of
Exchange. With the connivance of French bureaucrats, the syndicate
would receive authorization to remit the piasters at the official rate to
France. The official rate was so much more favorable than the buying
rate that the syndicate made a profit of about 100 percent over what
they had paid the Vietminh. I learned subsequently that information
about this traffic had been given to the French Government by one of
its intelligence agencies, Service de Documentation Extérieure et de
Contre Espionage (SDECE). No action was taken because the government feared a scandal that would damage it politically.

To escape censorship, I went to Bangkok to file my story. French
agents who trailed me searched my room at the Oriental Hotel and
apparently obtained details from a draft of my story which I had shred-
ded but left in a wastepaper basket. Upon my return to Saigon, my
French assistant, Max Clos, and I were called to the office of the Sûreté,
the French police agency. We found the Sûreté chief in a state of great
agitation, and to our astonishment, he began to plead for our understanding. He had assumed, incorrectly, that I knew his office was linked
with the piaster traffic. He told us that income from dealing in piasters
had been used by his office to pay agents, and he showed us records of
such payments to prominent personalities in Saigon. The Sûreté chief
accused his SDECE counterpart of attempting to ruin him and said that

the SDECE chief was obtaining funds by illegal sales of import licenses.

It was corruption of this kind that was not only undermining the war effort in Indochina but also having a cancerous effect on Metropolitan France.

From Hon Gay, Audrey and I returned to Saigon, but I was back in Lang Son on June 19 and found the military situation basically changed.

On the Chinese side, organized Nationalist resistance to the Communists had collapsed with the flight of General Chow Wei across the border on April 15 with sixty of his men. General Chow had operated in the Kwangsi region with about three thousand troops and had kept contact with Taiwan by radio. The Communists were now mopping up guerrilla bands, bandits and peasant dissidents.

At the time, no one on the border anticipated that there would be one more, final spasm of Chinese Nationalist military activity in South China. It was to be the consequence of an extraordinary episode involving the United States, and one in which I would have a role.

In the spring of 1951, I became aware of clandestine air movements through the airport of Saigon. Unmarked American-built transports were landing there, refueling under heavy guard and then taking off for an undisclosed destination. In June I learned that the planes were coming from Taiwan, and were under charter from Civil Air Transport (CAT), the airline now based on Taiwan operated by General Claire Chennault, whose pilots included a number who had flown in his World War II "Flying Tiger" squadron and others of the Fourteenth Air Force in China. The coordinating agency for the flights through Saigon was a "Sea Supply Company," with an office in Bangkok. The company, whose cable address was "Hatchet," represented itself as a commercial trading firm. In July, Audrey and I flew to Bangkok, where I discovered that Sea Supply was a cover for the covert operations of the Central Intelligence Agency. The unmarked CAT planes were landing on a strip in eastern Thailand and then apparently continuing on to Burma. We flew on to Rangoon.

In the diplomatic community in Rangoon, I began to piece together the incredible story. Three Chinese Nationalist Army columns, comprising some fifteen thousand men, had thrust about sixty-five miles into Yunnan Province from a refuge in northeast Burma. The columns had occupied a base area, about one hundred miles long, embracing the Kengma Airfield, about two hundred miles southwest of Kunming. Chinese Communist troops had counterattacked, and in a pincer maneuver were attempting to block the Nationalist supply corridor and line of retreat to the base in Burma.

The Nationalists were commanded by General Li Mi, who had escaped from the Communist encirclement in the final battle of Hwai-Hai. The CIA had flown Li Mi from Taiwan into northeast Burma, where he had reorganized the Nationalist Eighth Army, 93rd Division, and other units which had fled across the border before the Communist advance. Chiang Kai-shek had named Li Mi Governor of Yunnan. The transports, under charter to the CIA, flying via Indochina and Thailand, were bringing in arms, radio and other equipment, as well as food and funds for Li Mi. CIA liaison agents were operating with the Nationalists. The operation had begun the previous May, according to the best information available. The Korean War was on, and the operation was designed to harass the Chinese Communists.

In Rangoon, the government of Premier U Nu was in a state of alarm. It had appealed to the United States Ambassador, David McKendree Key, for help in getting Li Mi's forces out of Burma. The Burmese Army had proved ineffectual. U Nu was afraid that Li Mi's operations would provoke a Chinese Communist invasion of Burma or an internal Communist coup. Peking had declined to give U Nu assurances that this would not happen. The Burmese suspected American involvement in the Li Mi affair and were convinced, quite rightly, that the operation would have required at least tacit Washington sanction before it could be mounted. They had imposed a ban on the travel of American officials north of Mandalay or to the northeast frontier areas. The United States Ambassador repeatedly denied knowledge of any American involvement, although he undoubtedly suspected it. Technically, the State Department, except on the highest levels, was not aware of the CIA operation, and officers in the field were authorized to issue flat denials in response to inquiries. Apart from its CIA aspects, the staff of the United States Embassy spoke fully to me about Li Mi. They were incensed, considering the whole operation an act of folly from the United States standpoint. Relations with the neutralist Burmese Government were in a shambles. The Li Mi forays could have only nuisance value, and sooner or later the Communists would mass overwhelming force to crush his columns. Li Mi's troops would then be compelled to fall back into Burma, remaining a constant worry to the Rangoon Government and a provocation to the Chinese Communists. This, in fact, was the denouement of the affair.

The U Nu Government, afraid of stirring the Chinese, had suppressed news of the Li Mi operations. Not a line had appeared in the Rangoon papers. To evade the Rangoon censorship, I flew to Singapore to file my dispatch, which evoked a chorus of protests around the world on behalf of the Burmese but had little practical effect.

Ambassador Key returned to Washington and resigned, indignant over CIA operations in Rangoon. When the Eisenhower Administration came into office, the new Ambassador, William J. Sebald, was confronted by the same dilemma. He was assured by the State Department that the United States was not supporting Li Mi, and was compelled to reply in this vein to mounting Burmese protests. His own investigation in Southeast Asia soon revealed to him the degree of CIA complicity. Burma brought the matter before the United Nations in March 1953 and again in September. In November of that year, the evacuation to Taiwan of the Nationalist troops through Thailand commenced. However, despite the announcement in Taipei by Li Mi on May 30, 1954, that the Yunnan Anti-Communist and National Salvation Army had been dissolved, the evacuation dragged on for years, with repeated clashes between Burmese and remnant Nationalist troops. The sorry affair was protracted until the Kennedy Administration put an end to it by exerting strong pressure on Chiang Kai-shek to complete the withdrawal. By that time the Li Mi bungle had so embittered the Burmese that relations between Rangoon and Washington were still poisoned in 1972.

By June 1950, firmly established on the Indochina border, the Chinese Communists had initiated a major program of military aid to the Vietminh. Convoys carrying war matériel were crossing the border in the gaps in the French defense line northeast of Cao Bang, the western anchor on the R.C. No. 4 supply route, about sixty-five miles northwest of Lang Son.

On May 25 the Vietminh had attacked and taken the outpost of Dong Khe, employing for the first time a battery of five artillery pieces and antiaircraft machine guns, which damaged French King Cobra fighter planes intervening in support of the post. Only about 10 percent of the garrison of four hundred French-officered Moroccan and Vietnamese partisan troops escaped. Two days later, a French parachute battalion airlifted from Hanoi was dropped on Dong Khe and retook the post. The Vietminh operation was the opening blow of major operations against the frontier defense line.

The Chinese established major training centers for Vietminh officers and men at Nanning, and closer to the border at Lungchow and Chinghsi. The conversion of the Vietminh from guerrilla units to a regular army commenced on a major scale. In the next months, entire Vietminh units would cross into China and go into training centers with firing ranges and then return uniformed, equipped with field kits, and armed with automatic weapons, mortars and artillery. Much of their equipment and weapons was American matériel captured by the Chinese Communists from the Nationalists.

As the Vietminh gathered in strength around the French frontier posts, French officers told me privately that the defense line was becoming untenable. Some feared a debacle if the frontier force was not withdrawn to more defensible positions on the Red River Delta perimeter. But the order to fall back never came, presumably because of political considerations.

I was in Saigon when the Vietminh roll-up of the French frontier line began on September 16, and once again the blow fell on Dong Khe. Four Vietminh battalions, newly trained and outfitted in China, and supported by heavy mortars and artillery, struck from across the border at the outpost defended by two hundred Foreign Legionnaires. The Legionnaires fought gallantly, retreating foot by foot to the southern section of the citadel while French fighter planes and bombers flying through heavy mists hit the attackers. On the morning of September 18, when the French planes flew over once again, the firing had ended, the post was burning and the tricolor had disappeared from above the defense works.

The loss of Dong Khe placed the Vietminh athwart R.C. No. 4. Cao Bang, the big western anchor position, just to the northwest of Dong Khe, was thus isolated from the other French forts sited along the R.C. No. 4 highway twisting southeast through the hills for 160 miles to the coast. Belatedly, the French High Command recognized the precarious vulnerability of its frontier garrisons and began to plan the evacuation of Cao Bang.

The most decisive battle of the French Indochina War began on October 1 with a daring thirty-six-mile dash by French Union troops from the Red River Delta up through the rugged Tonkinese Mountains to seize Thai Nguyen, the principal political stronghold of the Vietminh. The action was a diversionary one as Vo Nguyen Giap, the Vietminh commander, was concentrating his forces for a devastating blow further north at the French frontier force. The French surprise operation was brilliantly executed. Two flanking columns and paratroopers dropped north of the city successfully enveloped the mountain communications center. It was an important psychological victory, but the French assault force did not seize the Vietminh political leaders in the hastily abandoned capital, nor did it dent or divert the Vietminh divisions from their target on the frontier.

On October 3 the French garrison of Cao Bang, 2,600 troops, including crack Foreign Legion and Moroccan troops, and 500 civilian men, abandoned the fortress and moved southeast on R.C. No. 4. Some 2,500 civilians, including all the women, children and sick, had already been evacuated by air in late September. The Cao Bang evacuation plan called for another relief force of 3,500 Moroccan troops commanded by Colonel Le Page to fight northwest up R.C. No. 4 from That Khe, retake Dong Khe, meet the Cao Bang garrison and then stage a joint withdrawal back to the haven of That Khe.

A trek of about thirty-five miles lay ahead of the Cao Bang garrison to the cover of the guns of That Khe. The withdrawal route lay along the red-clay R.C. No. 4, which twisted through the jungle-covered heights that dominated the road. The road had been the scene of so many fatal ambushes for French convoys that the supply run had been discontinued and Cao Bang was provisioned solely by air. The Vietminh had torn up the roadbed and blasted the wooden bridges along the way.

The Cao Bang garrison commander made a decision that was to doom his column. Apparently ignoring orders to destroy his heavy equipment and motor vehicles, and to make the dash to That Khe on foot, the garrison moved out on the road in trucks, with screening patrols on the flanks trudging over the hills. The trucks soon bogged down on the hacked-up road, and the column ran into a succession of ambushes. On the first day, the garrison only covered nine miles, losing the crucial advantage of surprise in the dash down R.C. No. 4 and giving the Vietminh time to concentrate their forces. When the garrison finally abandoned its trucks, artillery and other heavy equipment to move forward quickly, it was too late. The Le Page relief column, meanwhile, came under severe attack as it left That Khe and moved to the vicinity of Dong Khe. Heavily outnumbered, Le Page came under continuous Vietminh fire and assault as he held the road open for the

Cao Bang garrison battling its way toward them. The survivors of the two columns met in the hills around Dong Khe on October 5, and as they moved toward That Khe, Vietminh battalions in overwhelming force closed in from the hills. The French survivors, reinforced by three French paratrooper battalions, dropped into the battle in a final vain rescue effort, were overrun.

In Saigon, we had no idea of the predicament of the Cao Bang garrison and the Le Page relief column since the press had been told that the operation was going according to plan. On the night of October 9, we were called by the French headquarters to an extraordinary press conference and told of the disaster. At the same time, the Vietminh Radio proposed that the French Red Cross meet with the Vietminh to discuss humanitarian measures. At the bridge of Bascou, three miles northwest of That Khe, the Vietminh handed over to the French Red Cross the severely wounded survivors and the bodies of the dead, all that remained of the Cao Bang garrison and the Le Page column. More than six thousand men, including some of the finest units in the French Army, had been lost, together with enough equipment to outfit another Vietminh division.

Unnerved by the disaster at Dong Khe, the French command began a precipitant wholesale abandonment of the frontier. The garrisons of That Khe and the other small outposts were withdrawn under Vietminh attack to the main fort at Lang Son. On October 18 Lang Son was abandoned, the evacuation being undertaken so hastily, although the post was not under attack, that neither the military installations nor stockpiles or supplies were destroyed. As the Vietminh entered the post on October 20, French planes began bombing the fort and the depots to destroy the abandoned matériel.

In Saigon, the French communiqué declared:

> The withdrawal of the Lang Son garrison was not decided under the pressure of the enemy but in full cognizance of the necessity to recover certain units to reinforce the mobile reserves at the disposal of the High Command. It has been apparent for several months that the progress made by the enemy in augmenting his strength and armaments as well as the ability to maneuver required our forces to adapt new combat tactics based on the reconstitution of mobile units possessing strong firepower. The only means of constituting such mobile reserves is to regroup our battalions immobilized on the frontier. The severe reverse suffered at Dong Khe shows the necessity of this new plan of action, which is being rapidly implemented. No further withdrawal of our troops is foreseen.

Soon afterward, the last posts on the frontier, Lao Kay in the west, and Mon Cay, the eastern terminus, were evacuated. The French fell back on a 375-mile northern perimeter, with Hanoi, at its core, linked by a vulnerable sixty-mile communications corridor to the seaport of Haiphong. The perimeter embraced the delta of the Red and Black rivers, the rice bowl of the North and the home of most of Tonkin's nine million inhabitants. Within the perimeter the French controlled only about one-third of the villages. To the south, except for a two-hundred-mile sliver of territory hinged on Hué, the greater part of the Annamese coastal plain was occupied by the Vietminh. In Cochin China, which comprises the greater part of the Mekong River Delta, the French controlled the towns, but their hold on the countryside was as precarious as in the North.

The French headquarters in Saigon did not announce the evacuation of Lang Son until the morning of October 21. In the afternoon I went to the French military hospital to tell Audrey the news, the faces of the French soldiers I had come to know on the frontier parading in my mind. Our first child, Susan, had been born during the night as the hospital was shaken by artillery firing. The Vietminh had attacked an outpost on the perimeter defense near the hospital. French artillery immediately began to put down a protective barrage around the post. As Audrey was wheeled to the operating room for delivery, I walked beside her through the corridors. She could hear the rattle of small-arms fire. I heard Susan's first cries amid the burst of artillery shells. When she celebrated her twenty-first birthday, President Nixon announced that American troops in Vietnam were being reduced to a level of 184,000 men.

CHAPTER 8

CONTAINMENT

On October 14, 1950, as the French border posts toppled, I wrote that the Vietminh had "won control of the North Indochina frontier and ended French chances of winning a decisive military victory." Describing the loss of the frontier as "the turning point," I reported in a dispatch to the Associated Press:

Yielded to the Vietminh is a near impregnable mountainous base area with good transfrontier connections to supply sources and training centers in Red China. This means that the Ho Chi Minh regime now has the space and means of preparing a full-scale military offensive against the principal French strongholds located further south. The purely guerrilla phase of the war in Indochina has ended.

Thus the war was lost even before American power could make itself felt in Indochina. It was folly to assume that French soldiers and American military equipment transported thousands of miles could defeat Ho Chi Minh. Not only did he have an invulnerable base, together with a sanctuary and inexhaustible source of supply in adjoining China, but he was assured of the support of a majority of the population, which had rallied to his irresistible cry of *"Doc-lap!"*—"Independence!" It was a vain hope that the semi-independent regime of Bao Dai, client of France, could wean the population away from their "Uncle Ho." Lacking the means to achieve a total military victory, the French were confronted at best with the prospect of an endless war of attrition. The French people, already impatient with what they called "la sale guerre" ("the dirty war"), were much more likely to buckle than the Vietnamese, who were fighting for their land. Nevertheless, despite this

136

hopeless outlook as portrayed by observers on the ground at the end of 1950, the United States continued to rush into the Indochina involvement. Washington was not unaware of the bleak outlook for the French military effort in Indochina. As early as March 27, 1950, the National Security Council, taking note of possible Chinese assistance to the Vietminh, estimated that "it was doubtful that the French Expeditionary Forces, combined with Indochinese troops, could successfully contain Ho Chi Minh's forces should they be strengthened by either Chinese troops crossing the border, or by Communist-supplied arms and matériel in quantity." The secret memorandum, NSC 64, revealed in the Pentagon Papers, balanced this estimate against the need for the containment of Communism. It observed: "The threat of Communist aggression against Indochina is only one phase of anticipated Communist plans to seize all of Southeast Asia." It concluded with a statement of what came to be known as the "domino principle":

It is important to United States security interests that all practicable measures be taken to prevent further Communist expansion in Southeast Asia. Indochina is a key area of Southeast Asia and is under immediate threat.

The neighboring countries of Thailand and Burma could be expected to fall under Communist domination if Indochina were controlled by a Communist-dominated government. The balance of Southeast Asia would then be in grave hazard.

Six weeks later, President Truman initiated the U.S. assistance program with an allocation of $10 million for the year. The allocations mounted steadily to $1,063 million in the fiscal year 1954, the year of the final French collapse in Indochina.

The Truman Administration, accepting the "domino theory," discounted two counterarguments. First, Indochina was not a good place militarily or politically to take a stand against Communism or China. Second, United States prestige in most of Asia would slump as a consequence of American support of French colonialism in Indochina. Truman was reacting to the shock of postwar Stalinist expansionism in Eastern Europe and the Nationalist collapse in China before the Maoist tide. It was assumed that Communist China, like the Soviet Union, would be expansionist and intended to use Indochina as a springboard for seizing control of all Southeast Asia. When Chinese Communist "volunteers" entered the Korean War on October 25, 1950, the "National Intelligence Estimate," submitted to the President in December, was that large-scale Chinese intervention in Indochina was "impending." Priority was therefore given to propping up the French military campaign in Indochina. The French Union Army, made up of 130,000 troops, including a cadre of French soldiers, Foreign Legion units, African Colonials and 50,000 Indochinese volunteers, was seen as the most reliable force for the containment of China.

In Saigon, however, one of the State Department's leading exponents of this "military solution" began to have doubts.

I first heard the "domino theory" expounded by Gullion, the Minister Counselor in the U.S. Legation, during my initial meeting with him in Saigon in February 1950. Gullion continued to hold to the theory, but by early 1951 he conceded to me privately that he no longer believed in a French military solution of the Vietnam problem. He became a firm advocate of the need to establish quickly a truly independent viable Vietnamese Government that would rally popular support against the Vietminh. Unless this could be accomplished, he saw no way to contain Communism in Indochina. As the political and military situation deteriorated, Gullion became more open in his espousal of Vietnamese independence, and this brought him into sharp conflict not only with the French but also with his superior, the American Minister, Donald R. Heath, who arrived in Saigon on July 5, 1950.

Heath, a conservative career diplomat, was soon caught in the middle in a dispute between the French and Gullion, allied with Robert Blum, the head of the economic aid mission, over the issue of whether United States aid should be distributed directly to the Vietnamese or through the French. Gullion and Blum felt that aid should be of a type that would evoke a political response from the masses of the population and should go directly to the Vietnamese Government rather than be "reduced to a role of French-protected anonymity."

General Jean de Lattre de Tassigny, the French High Commissioner and Commander-in-Chief, who arrived in Saigon in December 1950, was adamantly opposed—like his predecessors—to direct aid to the Vietnamese. "Mr. Blum," he once told the American economic aid chief, "you are the most dangerous man in Indochina." General Francis G. Brink, the chief of the United States military aid group, complained to me that he was continually under French surveillance and so harassed by them that he found it difficult to do his job. He returned to Washington in a deep, deep depression and subsequently committed suicide.

De Lattre accused Gullion and other Americans of "fanning the fires" of extreme nationalism. "French traditionalism is vital here," he said. "No one can simply make a new nation overnight by giving out economic aid and arms alone." Although De Lattre told me before his departure at the end of 1951, when he was dying of cancer, that he was convinced that Ho Chi Minh would not be defeated unless a strong Vietnamese national army was mustered against him, the General would not approve of direct aid to the embryo Bao Dai army, nor did he allow its commanders much independence.

Once when I sent a dispatch reporting a curt French postponement of a direct American aid program, describing how the Vietnamese had been humiliated, De Lattre in a rage summoned me to the High Commissioner's palace. Two of his aides came to the door of my apartment at midnight and insisted that I accompany them. I found De Lattre waiting for me at the palace with the American Minister seated uneasily at his side. The latter had been subjected to a harangue about my dispatch. I was in no mood to take abuse from De Lattre since I was still smarting from a previous encounter in which the General had taken umbrage simply because I had interviewed Bao Dai and reported his nationalist sentiments. When De Lattre accused me of undermining the French position, I retorted sharply, and a shouting match ensued, with Heath perched nervously between us on a French-period divan. When I told De Lattre that I had stated the French position after exploring it thoroughly in conversation with a senior French official, he expressed disbelief. The next morning he grimly lined up his personal cabinet and asked each aide if they had spoken to me. His senior political adviser confessed to having given me a background briefing. De Lattre exploded in wrath. He habitually so terrified his subordinates that it was usually very difficult to elicit any information from them.

Despite our occasional altercations, I came to admire De Lattre. He was a brilliant soldier, an imperious man with a flair that made the French call him "le Roi Jean" and Americans call him the "French MacArthur." I was at his headquarters when in grief, but courageously and proudly, he received the news that his only child, Lieutenant Bernard de Lattre, had been killed by a Vietminh mortar burst while leading his platoon in the defense of Ninh Binh on the Red River Delta. Each year in Indochina the French were then losing in officers the equivalent of an entire class of St. Cyr, the French military academy.

De Lattre had an impossible task. While fighting a war already lost by the time he had arrived, he had to contend with a disillusioned, bitterly critical public at home, a government unwilling to give him needed reinforcements, and American critics whom he could not satisfy. There was a basic divergence and incompatibility in American and French interests in Indochina. De Lattre and his countrymen were fighting to preserve the French Union. Americans wanted only to defeat the Communists, even if the political price in advancing Vietnamese independence was the disappearance of the French presence in Indochina.

Gullion, Blum and their supporters in the American mission did not prevail on the aid issue or on other recommendations for rapid evolution of the Saigon Government to palpable independence. In Gullion's phrase, Washington lacked or was unwilling to apply its leverage. The U.S. Government retreated when the French hinted that they might withdraw entirely from the war, so unpopular at home, if Washington pressed too hard on the independence issue. In the State Department, the war in Indochina also was at times made secondary to European considerations. There was great reluctance to antagonize the French, who were being urged to join in creating a European Defense Community (EDC), a project which the French Parliament eventually rejected anyway.

Heath, the American Minister, was more solicitous of French interests and sensibilities than Gullion and also more the unquestioning executor of State Department policy in Indochina. As Gullion persisted on the independence issue, often infuriating the French, relations between the two men deteriorated to a point where Heath refused to allow his deputy to be privy to all the exchanges of messages between the legation and Washington.

This was the extraordinary situation in the American mission on October 19, 1951, when a young United States Congressman, Representative John F. Kennedy, Democrat of Massachusetts, arrived in Saigon on a ten-day private visit to acquaint himself with the situation in Indochina. He was accompanied by his younger brother Robert and sister Patricia.

In the House of Representatives, Kennedy had attacked the China policy of the Truman Administration in terms that displayed ignorance of what was transpiring in Asia. On January 25, 1949, as the Chinese Nationalist armies were collapsing as a consequence of their inept and corrupt leadership, the young Congressman delivered a prepared speech in which he said:

Mr. Speaker: Over this weekend we have learned the extent of the disaster that has befallen China and the United States. The responsibility for the failure of our foreign policy in the Far East rests squarely with the White House and the Department of State. The continued insistence that aid would not be forthcoming, unless a coalition government with the Communists were formed, was a crippling blow to the National Government.

So concerned were our diplomats and their advisers, the Lattimores and the Fairbanks, with the imperfection of the democratic system in China after twenty years of war and the tales of corruption in high places that they lost sight of our tremendous stake in non-Communist China. Our policy, in the words of the Premier of the National Government, Sun Fo, of vacillation, uncertainty, and confusion has reaped the whirlwind.

This House must now assume the responsibility of preventing the onrushing tide of Communism from engulfing all of Asia.

Kennedy's remarks were aimed at the China specialists in the State Department and two of the most distinguished Asian scholars in the United States, John King Fairbank and Owen Lattimore. His speech was among the preludes to the witch-hunting of Senator Joseph R. McCarthy, the Wisconsin Republican, and other politicians who generated and exploited the hysteria which attended the Communist conquest of the China mainland and the Korean War. In February 1950 McCarthy was to charge that China had been lost as a result of the plotting of Communist agents in the State Department. Later, he specifically named a number of the most respected China officers, together with Professor Lattimore, then of Johns Hopkins University. Professor Fairbank of Harvard University and Professor Lattimore, as well as the China officers of the State Department, were eventually exonerated of all charges of disloyalty, but only after years of suffering in the demagogic hunt for scapegoats. In his memoirs, Dean Acheson, who was Secretary of State in 1950 and also suffered the abuse of McCarthy, noted that Dr. Lattimore, who had been dubbed "the architect of our Far Eastern Policy" by the Senator, had never been connected with the State Department and that he had not known him.

Kennedy was on a "study" trip through the Middle East and Asia when he made the stopover in Indochina. I was at the Saigon Airport when his two-motored plane landed in brilliant sunshine and taxied to the tarmac, where senior French officials and embassy officers were waiting for him. I remember particularly how very boyish Robert Kennedy looked as he disembarked from the plane, ducked under a wing and smiled broadly as he followed his brother to the waiting line of officials. John Kennedy was then thirty-four and Robert was twenty-six. I was surprised when John Kennedy left the officials, walked across the tarmac to where I was standing with other correspondents and asked for me. Harold Milks, then the Associated Press correspondent in New Delhi, had told him of my familiarity with Indochina. Kennedy struck me as a handsome man, tall, hatless, with a shock of unruly brown hair and an engaging smile, but he was thin and did not seem well. While in Japan, he had taken sick and had been flown to a United States hospital in Okinawa, where he had become critically ill with an extremely high fever. When he recovered, he continued his "study" journey through Asia.

"I would like to have a talk with you," Kennedy said to me.

"All right," I replied, "I'll come to see you."

"No," he said, "I'll come to see you."

The next afternoon, at our apartment on Boulevard Charner, opposite the flower stalls in central Saigon, there was an unexpected knock at the door and Kennedy was there alone. "I'll only be a few minutes," he said, greeting Audrey and me as he came into our lounge, which served as living and dining room in the two-room apartment, and seated himself in an easy chair near the bamboo bar. He stayed more than two hours, asking questions about every aspect of the war. After hearing my pessimistic views on French prospects and American involvement, he remarked: "I'm going to talk about this when I get home. But it will give me trouble with some of my constituents." Then he rose, told Audrey she looked like a madonna out of a Botticelli painting, and walked down the long narrow flight of stairs to the street where an embassy car waited in front of the café on the ground floor. I did not see Kennedy again until June 4, 1961, when—as the new President of the United States— he emerged looking slightly shaken from the Soviet Embassy in Vienna with Nikita S. Khrushchev at his side after listening to a threatening harangue by the Soviet leader in his continuing effort to force the Western Allies out of Berlin.

Gullion had been at the airfield to greet Kennedy, whom he had met four years earlier in Washington while serving as special assistant to Dean Acheson. Kennedy saw more of Gullion than of anyone else in Saigon. He liked the personable, thirty-eight-year-old Embassy Counselor and was impressed by his views, especially on the need for creating a truly independent Vietnamese Government that would attract popular backing in the war against the Vietminh. Kennedy bristled at the pro-French line of the American Minister, Donald Heath, and enraged De Lattre to the degree that the French High Commissioner wrote letters to Heath and friends in Washington complaining about the Congressman's "impertinence."

Kennedy flew back to Washington, after completing his tour of Asia, with a better grasp of what was transpiring in that part of the world, and particularly in Southeast Asia. He had also found a rousing political issue in American support of French colonialism in Indochina that was to become the theme of a series of forceful speeches in the House and subsequently in the Senate.

In the month following his visit to Saigon, Kennedy asserted: "In Indochina we have allied ourselves to the desperate effort of the French regime to hang onto the remnants of an empire. There is no broad general support of the native Vietnam Government among the people of that area."

In June 1953, in a speech in the Senate, Kennedy was still hammering at the same theme:

Genuine independence as we understand it is lacking in Indochina. The Government of Vietnam, the state which is of the greatest importance in this area, lacks popular support, that the degree of military, civil, political and economic control maintained by the French goes well beyond what is necessary to fight a war. . . . It is because we want the war to be brought to a successful conclusion that we should insist on genuine independence. . . . Regardless of our united effort, it is a truism that the war can never be successful unless large numbers of the people of Vietnam are won over from their sullen neutrality and open hostility to it and fully support its successful conclusion. . . . I strongly believe that the French cannot succeed in Indochina without giving concessions necessary to make the native army a reliable and crusading force.

On May 7, 1954, when the French garrison at Dienbienphu fell in the final decisive battle of the war and delegates were already gathered in Geneva for a peace conference, President Eisenhower and his Secretary of State, John Foster Dulles, were still discussing a call for the French to grant "genuine freedom" to the Indochinese states. This was to be a precondition for United States military intervention to stem the Vietminh advance. However, the military situation in the Red River Delta deteriorated so rapidly that by June 15 Dulles informed the French that intervention was no longer feasible.

CHAPTER 9

EXIT THE FRENCH

Audrey and I, with a year-old daughter, left Saigon for home leave and reassignment to London in December 1951, but in mid-July 1954 I was at the Geneva Conference to cover the final spasm of the French Indochina War.

In Indochina, French Union forces were collapsing before the Vietminh onslaught. France itself, recoiling violently from the war in which French Union troops had suffered 172,000 casualties with probably 250,000 Vietnamese civilians killed, was in a state of near political anarchy. Pierre Mendès-France had become Premier on June 18 with the promise that he would end the war by July 20 or resign. In negotiating with the Vietminh at Geneva, and their principal allies, the Soviet Union and China, Mendès-France had little bargaining power other than the threat of United States military intervention. Indeed, as the Pentagon Papers reveal, the Eisenhower Administration successively considered an air strike by two hundred navy planes in support of the beleaguered French garrison at Dienbienphu, and then another plan for the intervention of U.S. naval and air forces together with limited ground forces for protection of bases they would be employing in operations against the Vietminh. Although all plans for intervention secretly were scrubbed by June 15, the possibility that United States forces would be committed was kept alive before the Communist delegations at Geneva to enhance Western negotiating strength. This tactic succeeded to the extent that Premier Chou En-lai, who headed the Chinese delegation, and Foreign Minister Vyacheslav M. Molotov, the chief of the Soviet delegation, became instrumental in persuading the Vietminh to compromise. Soviet and Chinese objectives at the Conference dovetailed, but did not always coincide with what the Vietminh were seeking.

The Russians were ready for a compromise settlement at Geneva that would avert the danger of a wider war directly involving the major powers. Molotov knew that the United States had consulted with Britain and France on "united action" in Indochina. If the United States intervened, there was the possibility that its forces would collide with the Chinese, and the Soviet Union would be expected to go to the aid of Peking, its ally. Nikita Khrushchev, then the Communist Party Secretary, was reported to have expressed apprehension that the United States might mount a nuclear strike in Indochina and touch off a world war.

China, its meager resources strained by the Korean War and intent now on internal economic tasks and other problems at home, was equally anxious to avoid a clash with the United States in Indochina. Peking's national interests at the Conference would be well served if the Vietminh were given control of Tonkin, which would provide a buffer zone for China, and if the agreement also excluded United States bases from Vietnam, Laos and Cambodia. By providing the arms which the Vietminh had used to defeat the French, China had already demonstrated its ideological dedication to furthering "wars of liberation."

In bargaining with Foreign Secretary Anthony Eden, head of the British delegation, and the French, Molotov and Chou En-lai struck many compromises. Eden played his role well. He was the ally of the United States, but he also impressed the Communist delegations by performing as the moderate statesman who was seeking concessions from them to deter Washington from military intervention.

The Communist delegations were not aware that American plans for intervention had been shelved a month earlier and that Dulles had signed a secret agreement with Mendès-France in Paris committing the United States to respect the terms of a proposed compromise pact with the Communists that would partition Vietnam. In response to a request by Mendès-France, the Eisenhower Administration sent General Walter Bedell Smith, the American delegation head who had been recalled, back to Geneva to take part in the Conference. In keeping with the understanding, Bedell Smith was not to become a party to the projected agreement with the Communists but merely signify the United States intention to respect it and not upset it by force.

The Conference was at this juncture on the morning of July 18, when the telephone in my hotel room shrilled. It was an official of the Chinese delegation, and he told me that Huang Hua would see me immediately. I had not seen Huang Hua since my departure from Nanking in September 1949. Huang Hua had gone in early 1950 to Shanghai, where he headed the Alien Affairs Bureau for three years. In January 1953 he was sent to Peking as a counselor of the Foreign Ministry, and in the fall of that year he was appointed the chief Chinese delegate to the negotiations at Panmunjom on arrangements for a convocation of a political conference on Korea to settle the problems left over by the war which had just ended. The Panmunjom negotiations lasted from late October until December 14, when the American delegate, Arthur H. Dean, walked out of a session complaining of Huang Hua's vitriolic denunciations of the United States. When the Korean negotiations were moved in April 14, 1954, to the forum of the Geneva Conference, Premier Chou En-lai took Huang Hua with him as an adviser and press spokesman. After the failure of the Korean negotiations, Huang Hua stayed on for the Indochina phase. It was during this period that I encountered him. My request to him for a meeting had gone unanswered until this morning, when his aide summoned me to Huang Hua's quarters. The circumstances were unusual, not only because of the short notice but also because the Chinese delegation had not previously granted an interview to an American newsman.

I found Huang Hua in his hotel, agitated and eager to talk. With him was another Chinese official who spoke excellent English and interpreted for Huang Hua on important points, although Huang's English was good. We talked for more than two hours. It soon became obvious that Huang Hua was both seeking information and anxious to use me as an intermediary to get a quick message to the American delegation before a crucial session of the Conference which had been called by Molotov for that afternoon.

Huang expressed his conviction that Bedell Smith had returned to Geneva to block an agreement. The Communist delegations were unaware, as was I, of the Paris secret agreement between Dulles and Mendès-France, and that Bedell Smith had been sent back at this time with instructions to accommodate to a settlement based on the partition of Vietnam. Huang Hua said that he believed Dulles had persuaded Mendès-France to stiffen Western terms so that they would be unacceptable to the Vietminh. The Chinese were now worried that the

United States was preparing for military intervention in Indochina. Once again, they felt their country faced the prospect of war with the United States, as in Korea, at a time when they wished to concentrate on the reconstruction of their own society. Like the Russians, they were fearful that this time the United States might employ nuclear weapons.

Huang Hua put a good part of the interview on the record and indicated plainly that he wanted this information conveyed to the American delegation before the afternoon meeting even if the medium was to be simply a dispatch to the Associated Press. In my dispatch I reported that the Chinese were prepared to sign an agreement, already approved in principle by Britain and France, based on the partition of Vietnam. Huang Hua said that a cease-fire agreement could be reached two days hence—when the deadline would expire for Mendès-France to either end the war or resign—if the Western powers would accept one "crucial" condition. "They must accept the barring of all foreign military bases from Indochina and keep the three member states out of any military bloc," Huang Hua said. "Refusal to join in such a guarantee could seriously deter a final settlement. On other important points in the negotiations we are in agreement or close to it. We are hopeful and we believe there is time to reach a settlement by July 20."

The Chinese knew that the United States and France were consulting on the organization of a Southeast Asia Treaty Organization (SEATO), and they were concerned that South Vietnam, Laos and Cambodia would be embraced in the security pact and become American base areas for possible future operations against China. "These efforts," Huang Hua said, "are a threat to any possible Indochina agreement. Success or failure of the Geneva Conference may depend on the attitude of the American delegation in this regard."

Huang Hua said the Chinese wanted the stamp of American approval on the agreement. "We believe that the U.S. as a member of the Conference should and is obligated to subscribe to and guarantee any settlement," he said. "Morally there is no reason for the U.S. to avoid this obligation." But significantly, in the light of the secret Dulles–Mendès-France understanding that the United States would only agree to "respect" the pact (of which we were both unaware), Huang Hua did not rule out an agreement if United States approval was not forthcoming.

I wrote and filed my dispatch quickly after my meeting with Huang Hua and at the same time gave a copy to the American delegation.

Bedell Smith and his deputies received it with an air of skepticism but privately were impressed and excited by its contents. To further authenticate the facts, they returned to me with a request that I identify the responsible Chinese Communist informant whom I had quoted as reflecting the views of Chou En-lai. I did not hesitate to do so, given the circumstances and the fact that Huang Hua had not stipulated that I not use his name.

Before the afternoon session of the Conference, Bedell Smith cabled the text of my dispatch to Dulles, noting that I had provided it in advance and that it "apparently represents official Chinese Communist position and was given Topping in order that we would become aware of it." Appended to the dispatch was this note from Bedell Smith:

The above seems to me extremely significant particularly in view of the fact that in my discussion with Eden last night he expressed pessimism which he said was now shared for the first time by Krishna Menon [the Indian delegate]. Latter had begun to feel, as I do, that Molotov wishes to force Mendès-France's resignation. Eden remarked that Molotov had now become the most difficult and intransigent member of Communist delegation. You will note obvious intention to place on shoulders of U.S. responsibility for failure of Geneva Conference and fall of French Government if this occurs.

Molotov is insisting on a meeting this afternoon which French and British are trying to make highly restricted as they are apprehensive of what may occur. If such a meeting is held and if demands are made for U.S. association in any agreement, I will simply say that in the event a reasonable settlement is arrived at which U.S. could "respect," U.S. will probably issue a unilateral statement of its own position. If question of participation Laos, Cambodia and Vietnam in security pact is raised, I will reply that this depends on outcome of conference.

Eden has already told Molotov that security pact is inevitable, that he himself favored it some time ago and that he would not (repeat not) withdraw from that position, but he made the mistake of saying that no consideration had been given to inclusion of Laos and Cambodia.

This final gambit is going to be extremely difficult to play and I do not (repeat not) now see the moves clearly. However, my opinion as expressed to you before leaving, i.e., that Molotov will gain more by bringing down Mendès Government than by a settlement, has grown stronger.

A second telegram to Dulles stated:

Topping has supplied in confidence following background information concerning his story on views of Chinese Communist delegation.

He stated his informant was Huang Hua, whom he has known for many years. Interview was at Huang's initiative, was called on short notice, and was conducted in extremely serious manner without propaganda harangues.

Topping said he had reported Huang's statement fully in his story but had obtained number of "visual impressions" during interview. When Huang spoke of possibility American bases in Indochina or anti-Communist pact in Southeast Asia, he became very agitated, his hands shook, and his usually excellent English broke down, forcing him to work through interpreter. Huang also spoke seriously and with apparent sincerity concerning his belief that I have returned to Geneva to prevent settlement. Topping believes Chinese Communists convinced Americans made deal with French during Paris talks on basis of which Mendès-France has raised price of settlement.*

When the Conference resumed that afternoon, the Communist delegations were forthcoming with further concessions that essentially brought the final agreement in line with the "seven points" accord reached by Dulles at Paris with Mendès-France and earlier with the British.

These "seven points" were:

1. Preservation of the integrity and independence of Laos and Cambodia, and assurance of Vietminh withdrawal from those countries.

2. Preservation of at least the southern half of Vietnam, and if possible an enclave in the Tonkin Delta, with the line of demarcation no farther south than one running generally west from Dong Hoi.

3. No restrictions on Laos, Cambodia or that part of Vietnam not taken over by the Vietminh that would "materially impair their capacity to maintain stable non-Communist regimes; and especially restrictions impairing their right to maintain adequate forces for internal security; to import arms and to employ foreign advisers."

4. No "political provisions which would risk loss of the retained area to Communist control."

5. No provision that would "exclude the possibility of the ultimate reunification of Vietnam by peaceful means."

6. Provision for "the peaceful and humane transfer, under international supervision, of those people desiring to be moved from one zone to another of Vietnam."

7. Provision for "effective machinery for international supervision of the agreement."

The "seven points" did not make any stipulations regarding the projected Western security pact. The Communist delegations left the conference table under the impression that they had wrung a major concession from the Western powers by the insertion of a clause in the

*From the Pentagon Papers.

final agreement signed on July 21 which barred the establishment of foreign bases in the three Indochinese states. Subsequently the ineffectual SEATO security pact was concluded on September 8, 1954, and a protocol eventually extended the treaty's protection to Cambodia, Laos and South Vietnam, but the American bases so vehemently opposed by the Chinese did not become a reality until United States military intervention in Vietnam in the 1960s.

The final agreement served Soviet objectives by averting an unwanted wider war in Asia that might have involved the Soviet Union. The Russians were also convinced that an agreement would encourage France to reject the American-backed European Defense Community (EDC), and when in fact this did happen, Moscow hailed it as a triumph of its diplomacy. The agreement further served the Chinese in the creation in North Vietnam of a buffer against attack from the south and the exclusion of American military bases from Indochina.

After the signing of the Geneva Accords, I attended a gay champagne celebration party given by the Chinese. Huang Hua greeted me warmly and introduced me to his colleagues as the author of the dispatch that had clarified the Chinese point of view.

However, Soviet and Chinese objectives were achieved at the sacrifice, at least immediately, of Vietminh interests. When Ho Chi Minh sent Pham Van Dong, his Foreign Minister, to the conference table at Geneva, he had already seized effective control of three-quarters of Vietnam and French forces holding the balance of the territory were rapidly collapsing. The price of victory had been perhaps a half-million casualties, and in applying the coup de grâce to France at Dienbienphu alone, his forces had lost 21,000 men. Now Ho was separated from the total victory sought in eight years of war only by the threat of American military intervention which induced the apprehension and wavering of his allies, the Soviet Union and China. In the course of the negotiations, the Vietminh had been persuaded to make a series of major concessions.

The Vietminh had insisted at first on immediate national elections under Vietnamese supervision, which would have certainly brought them political control over the entire country. Instead, they were compelled to accept a delay of two years and international supervision of elections. In the interim they were required to accept partition at the 17th Parallel instead, as they demanded, at the 13th Parallel, which conformed more closely to the existing military dispositions. Their efforts to get recognition of their Indochinese allies, the Pathet Lao in Laos and the Free Khmer in Cambodia, were frustrated.

The Vietminh no doubt had every reason to believe, as did Chou En-lai and Molotov, that all of Vietnam would fall to them within two years. In this sense, the Vietminh leadership was satisfied, although members of their delegation complained privately to me that they had been cheated and expressed doubt that the national elections would be held in 1956.

It may have been that Ho also underestimated the determination of Ngo Dinh Diem, who became Premier of the demoralized Bao Dai Government one month before the Geneva Accords and after the French, in June, had finally granted Vietnam full independence. With American help, Diem consolidated his regime in South Vietnam. When the time arrived for the national plebiscite on reunification stipulated in the Geneva Accords, Diem refused to go through with it. He said that a free vote was impossible in North Vietnam and complained about the presence of a Communist underground in the South. Further, he said his government was not bound by the Geneva Accords since it had not signed them.

The Pentagon Papers study contends that the "United States did not —as it is often alleged—connive with Diem to ignore the elections. U.S. State Department records indicate that Diem's refusal to be bound by the Geneva Accords and his opposition to pre-election consultations were at his own initiative." But the study also cites State Department cables and National Security Council memorandums indicating that the Eisenhower Administration wished to postpone the elections as long as possible and communicated its feelings to Diem.

Whatever may have been Ho's expectations, and those of his chief delegate at Geneva, Pham Van Dong, Premier of the present Hanoi Government, the 1954 experience profoundly affected the attitude of the North Vietnamese, who were to sit down once again, this time in Paris, with the Americans in May 1968 to negotiate an end to the war in which the United States had been a participant. Their disillusion-ment and feeling that they had been cheated of the fruits of victory in 1954 explains in part their stubbornness in negotiations and their insist-ence that the Vietnamese alone should determine future political ar-rangements in their country. It also explains the reluctance of the Soviet Union and of China to intervene to facilitate a settlement in response to requests by the United States, although the Vietnamese

Communists were once again dependent on their allies for military supplies.

In August 1971, when James Reston asked Chou En-lai if he was interested in mediating the struggle between the United States and the Vietnamese Communists, the Premier replied: "We don't want to be a mediator in any way. We were very badly taken in during the first Geneva Conference."

The Western Allies had every reason to be pleased in July 1954 by the conclusion of the Geneva Accords. Although the Diem Government insisted that it had been betrayed at Geneva, it was given sway over a territory more extensive than that controlled by the French military forces. France retained a measure of influence in the Indochinese states and the hope, still articulated by President Charles de Gaulle as late as 1966, that it would be able to perpetuate its economic and cultural heritage in the three states of Vietnam, Laos and Cambodia. Foreign Secretary Eden was credited with a diplomatic triumph and was rewarded by Chinese acceptance of a four-year-old bid to establish diplomatic relations with the exchange of chargés d'affaires in London and Peking.

Ostensibly, the Eisenhower Administration, which had declined to become a party to the Accords but agreed to "respect" them, should have been satisfied. The Accords were consonant with the "seven points" understanding arrived at between Dulles and Mendès-France on July 14. By this time the "domino theory," which held that the loss of a single country of Southeast Asia would put the whole region in Communist hands, had been modified. At a news conference on May 11, four days after the fall of Dienbienphu, Dulles said that "Southeast Asia could be secured even without perhaps Vietnam, Laos and Cambodia." He added that he did not want to underestimate the importance of these countries, but also he did not want to give the impression "if events that we could not control, and which we do not anticipate, should lead to their being lost that we would consider the whole situation hopeless." On May 20 the Joint Chiefs of Staff, in a memorandum to the Defense Department, had noted in a discussion of possible intervention: "From the point of view of the United States, with reference to the Far East as a whole, Indochina is devoid of decisive military objectives and the allocation of more than token U.S. armed forces to that area would be a serious diversion of limited U.S. capabilities."

Nevertheless, in meetings on August 8 and 12, the National Security

Council concluded that the Geneva settlement was a "disaster" that "completed a major forward stride of Communism which may lead to the loss of Southeast Asia." In June the Eisenhower Administration had already assigned a team of Americans under Colonel Edward G. Lansdale to begin secret operations against the Vietminh, and in the fall of 1954, in violation of the Geneva Accords, it carried out sabotage in North Vietnam. On August 20 President Eisenhower approved a National Security Council paper which laid down a threefold program for support of the Diem Government militarily. The United States would work with France only so far as necessary to build up indigenous forces able to provide internal security. Economically, the United States would begin giving aid directly to the Vietnamese, not, as before, through the French. The French were to be disassociated from the levers of command. Politically, the United States would work with Premier Diem, but would encourage him to broaden his government and establish more democratic institutions.

After these decisions, as an account in the Pentagon Papers commented: "American policy toward post-Geneva Vietnam was drawn." The commitment for the United States to assume the burden of defending South Vietnam was made, and President Eisenhower spelled it out directly in a letter to Diem in which he promised American support "to assist the Government of Vietnam in developing and maintaining a strong, viable state, capable of resisting attempted subversion or aggression through military means."

CHAPTER 10

KENNEDY AND INDOCHINA

When John F. Kennedy became President in 1961, I was posted in Moscow as a correspondent for the *New York Times*. I remember remarking that Kennedy's "study" tour of Asia and particularly his visit to Saigon in 1951 would help him to steer the United States clear of the pitfalls that had engulfed the French in Indochina. He had modified his attitude toward China and had retracted, privately and publicly, his remarks as a young Congressman in 1949 blaming scholars and State Department officials for the collapse of Nationalist China. Certainly, it appeared that he had grasped the motive power of nationalism in Asia and accepted that it was a more effective weapon than war planes and artillery. In 1954, when the Eisenhower Administration was contemplating American military intervention to bail out the French, Kennedy declared: "I am frankly of the belief that no amount of American military assistance can conquer . . . 'an enemy of the people' which has the sympathy and covert support of the people."

Nevertheless, only a week after he assumed the presidency, Kennedy approved a Counter-Insurgency Plan worked out over the previous eight months. It offered Diem financial support for a 20,000-man increase in the Vietnamese Army (ARVN), which then stood at 150,000, plus support for about half of the Civil Guard, the counterguerrilla auxiliary force. Kennedy was impelled to adopt the program because of the mounting crisis in Vietnam, attributed largely to the lack of popular support for the Diem Government and its military ineptitude. In return for the aid, Kennedy asked military and political reforms designed to rejuvenate the ARVN and rally the people to Diem. The projected American program was superseded in August by an even larger aid program to bring the ARVN to a strength of 200,000, although Diem had not carried out the requested reforms. By this time Kennedy was already swinging over from an emphasis on political to military solutions despite his earlier-stated view that victory in Vietnam was impossible without the sympathy and support of the people. On April 29 Kennedy had approved a hundred-man increase in the size of the American Military Assistance Advisory Group above the 685-man level permitted under the Geneva Accords. On May 11 he secretly authorized the deployment of four hundred Special Forces troops and the initiation of covert warfare against North Vietnam. In the thirty-four months he was in office, he increased the number of American support troops and military advisers to about sixteen thousand, sanctioning a combat role for them. The review of this period in the Pentagon Papers states that Kennedy's policies produced a "broad commitment" to Vietnam's defense, giving priority to the military aspects of the war over political reforms. His frustration with the failure of Diem to bring about reforms led to Kennedy's approval of the military coup d'état on November 1, 1963, that resulted in the assassination of Diem. The Pentagon study says that Washington did not originate the coup, nor did United States forces intervene, but it also adds: "Our complicity in [Diem's] overthrow heightened our responsibility and our commitment" in Vietnam. When Kennedy was killed in the same month as Diem, he had on his desk proposals for the commitment of American ground combat units to Vietnam although the United States had no assurance that the Saigon Government he was supporting had any more popular backing than the Bao Dai regime under the French.

In leading the United States deeper into the Vietnam bog, Kennedy had not simply turned his back on what he had learned in Saigon in 1951. When he became President, he found that the support given the French by the Truman Administration and the Eisenhower commitment to Diem had so entangled the United States and its prestige in Vietnam that quick extrication was impossible. Confronted by a Soviet challenge in Berlin and Laos, and Nikita Khrushchev's proclamation of support for "liberation wars" around the globe, Kennedy was unwilling to retreat from Vietnam, which had become a testing ground for American power and determination. Kennedy evidently was tortured by doubts as he was drawn deeper into Vietnam. Early in October 1961 he sent General Maxwell Taylor and Walt Rostow to Saigon on an exploratory mission. In *A Thousand Days*, Kennedy's biographer, Arthur Schlesinger, recalled the instructions he gave them: "Reminding them of his own visit to Indochina in 1951, [Kennedy] charged them to find out whether we were better off now than the French had been then—whether Vietnamese nationalism had turned irrevocably against us or still might serve as a basis for the fight against communism." The Taylor-Rostow report affirmed that a successful fight could be mounted against the Vietcong if the Diem Government was spurred by broadened American intervention, including the commitment of support troops. Throughout his Administration, Kennedy was misled by a succession of similar overly optimistic estimates by his senior advisers of United States capabilities in Vietnam, always appended to recommendations for escalation of American military intervention. The American intelligence community, which sometimes demurred, was not heeded.

For all of Kennedy's research into the French experience in Indochina—and Schlesinger recalls that he once set Jacqueline Bouvier, before their marriage, to translating French books about that country—Kennedy did not master the dynamics of change in Asia. Central to his failure in Vietnam, as to those of Johnson and Nixon after him, was his inability to apply the lessons of the French disaster in Indochina and the earlier American reverse in China.

In China, during the period 1946–49, the Communists rode to power astride an economic and social revolution that owed little of its popular appeal to Marxist-Leninist ideology. Truman tried to check it with a two-tiered policy. He bolstered the Nationalist Government with a massive infusion of military and economic aid. Second, he sought to pressure Chiang Kai-shek into instituting political, economic and military reforms that would make his government more effective and rally the people to its side. The White Paper is a record of the American failure.

In Saigon in 1951, Kennedy concluded correctly that Ho Chi Minh was riding to power on the back of anticolonial, nationalist revolution sustained by peasants who had slight interest in his Marxist-Leninist ideology. Kennedy thought he saw the way to take the leadership of this nationalist revolution away from Ho Chi Minh. Grant independence to the Bao Dai Government, help it become more efficient and democratic, and inevitably it would attract popular support. Ten years later, when the Saigon Government had become a client of the Kennedy

Administration, the situation differed only in that Bao Dai's successor, Ngo Dinh Diem, had nominally been granted full independence together with large-scale military and economic aid. What remained to be done was to encourage or compel Diem to carry out political, economic and military reforms so that his government would become more effective and democratic, and thus rally badly needed popular backing. Kennedy set out to do this, and encountered the same kind of resistance that led the United States finally to abandon Chiang Kai-shek on the China mainland. In 1963 Kennedy condoned the coup d'état against Diem to clear the way for reform. As late as 1971 President Nixon was not able, in the interest of political reform, to persuade President Nguyen Van Thieu to alter his arrangements for an election with only one candidate, himself. The Saigon Government remained an unpopular one.

China and Indochina should have taught American policy-makers that the dynamics of change in Asia are such that political and social movements and institutions must grow indigenously and that they rarely take permanent root as a consequence of foreign gifts, persuasion or transplants. Even when the transition from colonial status to independence is fairly orderly, as in the instances of Burma, the Philippines and Indonesia, a period of turmoil and change inevitably ensues as the political, social and economic order, freed of the artificial strictures of the colonizing power, adjusts to native forces.

The foreign presence is often counterproductive. In China, American aid tended to corrupt the government, and its close association with the United States undermined popular support since it was taken by some as evidence of neo-colonialism. In Vietnam, the same has been true. When I arrived in Saigon in 1950, one of a handful of Americans in the country, the United States was the most popular nation in the minds of the Vietnamese, hailed as the liberator of the Philippines. When I left in 1951, the United States ranked second only to France as the most hated nation, although Washington was pouring in many millions of dollars in aid, consumer goods as well as military supplies.

The Chinese Communists, who are committed to fostering world revolution, understand profoundly that foreign institutions cannot simply be grafted onto the body of another society. To be effective if not necessarily in respect of international propriety, the Chinese Communists do not render active support to a revolutionary movement in another country unless it has indigenous roots. This Maoist approach was articulated in Lin Piao's 1965 article "Long Live the Victory of People's War":

In order to make revolution and to fight a people's war and be victorious, it is important to adhere to the policy of self-reliance, rely on the strength of the masses in one's own country and prepare to carry on the fight independently even when material aid from outside is cut off. If one does not operate by one's own efforts, does not independently ponder and solve the problems of the revolution in one's own country, and does not rely on the strength of the masses but leans wholly on foreign aid—even though this be aid from Socialist countries which persist in revolution—no victory can be won, or be consolidated even if it is won.

In countries supported by Peking, Chinese advisers are few in number and maintain a low profile. Peking does not have military bases or any detachments of combat troops stationed abroad.

Gullion, Kennedy's mentor in Saigon in 1951, also never surrendered his belief that the United States could transform the Saigon Government. When he returned to Washington from Indochina, Gullion continued to advise Kennedy, who eventually appointed him Ambassador to the Congo after assuming the presidency. Gullion remained in touch with the Kennedy family after he left the Foreign Service to become dean of the Fletcher School of Law and Diplomacy at Tufts University. In February 1967 I visited Medford at Gullion's invitation to lecture at Fletcher. I found Gullion distressed because Robert Kennedy, whom Gullion had been advising on Vietnam, was moving away from him on the issue and was taking a more militant antiwar position. Gullion had remained a strong advocate of American support for the Saigon Government. On March 2, Robert Kennedy, the one with the boyish grin who had followed his elder brother onto the Saigon tarmac that afternoon in 1951, broke with the policies of the Kennedy and Johnson Administrations and joined those calling for American withdrawal from Vietnam. Appealing for an end to the bombing of North Vietnam and the opening of negotiations with the Vietnamese Communists, Kennedy declared: "Under the direction of the United Nations, and with an international presence gradually replacing American forces, we should move toward a final settlement which allows all major political elements in South Vietnam to participate in the choice of leadership and shape their future direction as a people."

Robert Kennedy had grasped the reality that eluded his brother. The war in Vietnam could be ended only if indigenous forces, without foreign interference, joined in determining the future of the country. He was also responding to a crisis in the United States which his brother might have anticipated if he had assessed the full measure of France's experience in Indochina. The United States was being torn by the antiwar movement in much the same way that France had been plunged into social and political dislocation by the movement against "la sale guerre."

The French military experience in Indochina should alone have dissuaded the Johnson Administration from becoming involved in a ground war there. If a position in Southeast Asia for the containment of China was required, the French Indochina War had revealed clearly that Vietnam was not the place to make a stand.

The French Union Army in Indochina, which included excellent volunteer Vietnamese troops, put into the field able, courageous fighters, who knew the countryside well. Yet I never met a French line officer who was convinced that France could win decisively against the Vietminh strategy of "protracted war," even if the army was heavily reinforced. Traveling through the jungles, mountains and great river deltas, one could see that it was impossible to halt infiltration from the sanctuary region in the North. These facts were reported then to the Truman Administration by the intelligence community when the American commitment was being broadened, but discounted by a National Security Council preoccupied with the global containment of Communism.

In December 1962 I was posted to Hong Kong by the *New York Times* as Chief Correspondent Southeast Asia, and as I shuttled regularly to Vietnam, I heard distressingly familiar talk in Saigon. Just as Gullion had assured me in February 1950 that the French Army was of a better caliber than that of Chiang Kai-shek and a military victory was feasible, now I heard a parallel theme. General William C. Westmoreland, the Deputy and later U.S. Commander Vietnam 1964–68, told me that with a proper logistical base American forces could do what the French had not been able to do. American firepower was greater and could defeat the Communists, the General said.

It was true, as United States military strength swelled to a peak of about 540,000 men after the commitment of ground troops in 1965, that a Communist victory on the pattern of 1954 became impossible. In the French Indochina War, the Paris Government had balked at sending draftees to Indochina, and French Union forces therefore had not exceeded about 150,000 soldiers, backed by native auxiliaries. In his northern sanctuary, Ho Chi Minh was able, with Chinese and Soviet aid, to train and equip enough divisions to sweep the limited French forces into the China Sea. But the difference ended there.

From 1965 on, American troops pressed their "search and destroy" sweeps against the Vietcong and North Vietnamese, just as the French had pursued their "nettoyage" campaigns against the Vietminh, without being able to defeat the "protracted war" strategy of Vo Nguyen Giap, the Communist commander. In 1972 Americans still were not able to halt the guerrilla infiltration from the northern sanctuary any more than could the French two decades earlier. By the end of 1971 more American bombs had been dropped on Indochina than the total weight of bombs unloaded in World War II. Yet the bombing went on. Western generals, whenever baffled and frustrated by the realities of revolution and geography in Asia, always seem to turn to the imponderables of air bombardment.

In China, the Nationalist Air Force, equipped with American fighters and bombers, proved ineffectual, although the Communists had neither planes nor significant antiaircraft. Apart from general inefficiency, the Nationalist pilots never seemed to find military targets whose destruction would impair or impede the fast-moving, lightly equipped Communist columns.

In 1947, on assignment from my post in Nanking, I visited Tokyo, and during an interview with General Douglas MacArthur, he questioned me about military developments in China. The General, leaning back in his chair, sucking on his corncob pipe and looking at the ceiling, did not seem to listen too closely. Then he observed that he had the solution for a Nationalist victory in the civil war. "Give Chiang Kai-shek five hundred bombers and maintain them," said the General, as I listened in bewilderment, recalling all the bombs that had furrowed empty fields in China.

The French had not much more luck with air power in Indochina, although their air force was much more efficient. When the French columns or supply convoys came under attack, the Vietminh would have melted into the countryside by the time the P-61 King Cobra fighters were streaking overhead. Often in attacks on French forts, the Vietminh, who usually attacked fixed positions at night, would drive in so close that it became impossible to strafe or bomb without risk of hitting friendly troops. In frustration, French planes would bomb or napalm suspected Vietminh villages, often striking only innocent civilians, just as their American successors did two decades later.

In February 1965, as the sustained bombing of North Vietnam began, I was in Saigon when a White House fact-finding mission arrived that included McGeorge Bundy, the Special Assistant to the President for National Security Affairs, John T. McNaughton, the Assistant Secretary of Defense, and Deputy Assistant Secretary of State Leonard Unger. On February 6 I lunched with the group at the home of Barry Zorthian, the public affairs officer of the American mission. I knew that they were in Saigon to discuss the proposal put forward by General Maxwell Taylor, the American Ambassador, with the concurrence of General Westmoreland, that regular bombing of the North commence. Our discussion at lunch was mainly whether "to bomb or not to bomb," but I was not aware until I read the Pentagon Papers in 1971 how far advanced the planning was. General Taylor, who, according to my observation, during his tenure as Ambassador lacked understanding of Vietnamese character and motivation, had urged the President, in the words of the Pentagon study, to break the will of Hanoi through bombing by inflicting "such pain or threat of pain upon the D.R.V. that it would be compelled to order a stand-down of Vietcong violence." At a White House meeting on September 7, 1964, a "general consensus" was reached that air attacks would probably have to begin early in the new year. In a memorandum, dated January 27, written by McNaughton and bearing the penciled concurrence of Robert S. McNamara, it was stated that the United States objective in South Vietnam was "not to 'help friend' but to contain China." Both officials favored initiating strikes against North Vietnam.

Over drinks before lunch in the lounge of Zorthian's villa, I was asked my views on the bombing question. I replied that it was doubtful that the bombing would be effective, and if it was undertaken at that time, when the Soviet Premier, Aleksei Kosygin, was visiting Hanoi, it would be dangerously provocative to the Russians and at a minimum Moscow would heavily increase their aid to the North Vietnamese. It was evident, however, that the Bundy mission was leaning to bombing. At lunch, I sat next to Bundy, and when I remarked that the United States might be confronted in Vietnam with the choice of withdrawal or acceptance of a protracted struggle similar to that of the British on the Northwest Frontier of India in the nineteenth century, Bundy replied testily: "We cannot do that."

That night in the early morning hours the telephone rang in my room at the Caravelle Hotel, awakening me. The Vietcong had attacked the United States military advisers' compound at Pleiku in the Central Highlands and an army helicopter base at Camp Holloway, four miles away. Nine Americans were killed and seventy-six wounded. Soon after dawn, I flew north on the only plane available to the hospital at Nha Trang, on the Central Coast, where the wounded were being brought. In touring the crowded wards of the hospital I spoke to the wounded, many of them badly hit by mortar fragments, and glimpsed the dying behind the white screens. As I emerged, I ran into General Westmoreland, accompanied by Bundy. They had been to Pleiku. The presidential adviser looked pale and shaken as he made the rounds of the hospital with Westmoreland. It was one thing to press the buttons of war from the White House, but another to see the blood on the ground. He had already spoken to President Johnson on the telephone, and a decision to stage a reprisal raid on North Vietnam had been taken. By 4 P.M. that afternoon, forty-nine U.S. Navy jets—A-4 Skyhawks and F-8 Crusaders from the Seventh Fleet carriers *U.S.S. Coral Sea* and *U.S.S. Hancock*—were bombing and rocketing the North Vietnamese barracks and staging areas at Dong Hoi, a guerrilla training garrison forty miles north of the 17th Parallel. Bundy flew back to Saigon, boarded the President's personal Boeing 707, Air Force One, and as the plane headed for Washington, sent a secret memorandum to Johnson, which in its introduction said:

We believe that the best available way of increasing our chance of success in Vietnam is the development and execution of a policy of sustained reprisal against North Vietnam—a policy in which air and naval action against the North is justified by and related to the whole Vietcong campaign of violence and terror in the South.

While we believe that the risks of such a policy are acceptable, we emphasize that its costs are real. It implies significant U.S. air losses even if no full air war is joined, and it seems likely that it would eventually require an extensive and costly effort against the whole air defense system of North Vietnam. U.S. casualties would be higher—and more visible to American feelings—than those sustained in the struggle in South Vietnam.

Yet measured against the costs of defeat in Vietnam, the program seems cheap. And even if it fails to turn the tide—as it may—the value of the effort seems to us to exceed its cost.

Bundy said that the object of the policy would not be to win an air war against Hanoi, but rather to influence the course of the struggle in the South by gradually forcing a decrease in the "VC terror." The French reprisal policy, which ranged from the demonstrative execution of VC agents to the bombing and burning of villages believed to be used as Vietminh bases, never worked. The United States was now to try it on a more massive scale.

The reprisal raid for Pleiku was code-named "Flaming Dart," and a heavier reprisal raid, "Flaming Dart II," came four days later, when the Vietcong attacked American barracks at Qui Nhon on the central coast.

In commenting on the reaction to Pleiku, the Pentagon Papers stated: "Though conceived and executed as a limited one-shot tit-for-tat reprisal, the drastic U.S. action, long on the military planners' drawing boards under the operational code name Flaming Dart, precipitated a rapidly moving sequence of events that transformed the character of the Vietnam war and the U.S. role in it."

In Saigon, after the second reprisal, I attended a cocktail party at the villa of an American general, and found the military jubilant about the adoption of the policy. "We have a surgical instrument, with which we can do precisely what we want to the North," Brigadier General William E. DePuy, the Deputy Chief of Staff, told me. Two days after "Flaming Dart II," President Johnson ordered commencement of "Operation Rolling Thunder," the sustained air war against North Vietnam. On April 1, recognizing that the bombing was not going to avert defeat of the South Vietnamese Army, which was being hacked to pieces by the Vietcong and their North Vietnamese cadres, the President ordered the commitment of American ground combat troops.

On March 31, 1968, recognizing that the North Vietnamese could not be defeated and to induce the North Vietnamese to negotiate, President Johnson ordered a halt to the bombing of North Vietnam, except in the area immediately north of the Demilitarized Zone. Essentially, Johnson accepted the terms first brought back by Ronning from Hanoi in March 1966, in the first of his two peace missions. On April 3 Johnson announced that Hanoi had agreed to meet with American representatives. In effect, the United States had concluded that short of an invasion of North Vietnam, which might bring Chinese and Soviet intervention, Hanoi could not be defeated militarily principally for two reasons, both of which also obtained in the French Indochina War. First, the Communists retained a sanctuary adjacent to the border of China in which they could constantly refit new troops, with Chinese and

Soviet equipment, and send them South to fight. Second, the revolutionary spirit of the Vietnamese Communists, regenerated in a nationalist reaction to the presence of United States forces, could not be broken. What Johnson perceived in 1968 had been evident in Indochina in 1950 when the French lost the northern frontier region to the Vietminh.

CHAPTER 11

THE CONTAINMENT MYTH

One week before President Johnson decided to use American ground troops for offensive action in South Vietnam, McNaughton addressed another memorandum to the Secretary of Defense on the "Proposed Course of Action," in which he stated U.S. aims as follows:

> 70%—to avoid a humiliating U.S. defeat (to our reputation as a guarantor).
> 20%—to keep SVN (and the adjacent) territory from Chinese hands.
> 10%—to permit the people of SVN to enjoy a better, freer way of life.
> ALSO—to emerge from crisis without unacceptable taint from methods used.
> NOT—to "help friend," although it would be hard to stay in if asked out.

Thus, in the space of fifteen years, as revealed in the Pentagon Papers, the rationale for United States intervention had evolved from one based totally on the containment of China, as the agent of world Communism, to an evaluation in which containment represented only 20 percent of motivation.

In 1950, even before the outbreak of the Korean War, American policy-makers, reacting to Stalinist expansionism in Eastern Europe and the fall of Nationalist China, had drawn a containment line extending from Europe through the Middle East and along the southern border of mainland China. While there was logic in the containment of the openly expansionist Stalinist state, the extension of the policy to Southeast Asia was a blunder that was to have disastrous consequences for the United States. In Europe, the United States, through the Marshall Plan and the North Atlantic Treaty Organization, had allied itself with resilient, democratic states to block the Soviet advance. In Southeast Asia,

165

the United States aligned itself with colonial France and the status quo in opposition to the nationalist revolution which had become the irresistible mainspring of change in Vietnam and throughout the region. Washington also wrongly assumed that Peking was only a tool of Moscow and would behave in Asia as Stalin had acted in Europe. The Americans best equipped to furnish the needed understanding of China and Asia, the elite China service officers of the State Department, and such scholars as John King Fairbank and Owen Lattimore, were already being made political scapegoats for the Chinese Communist victory on the mainland, an inevitable consequence of the revolutionary surge in China and the monumental ineptitude of Chiang Kai-shek's government. Their voices were no longer heard in Washington. In Asia, the Truman Administration stumbled into containment not only in reaction to the Stalinist challenge but also under the pressure of the McCarthy-spurred, anti-Communist hysteria infecting the United States in the early 1950s.

The history of the China containment policy bears reviewing. Some of the old myths which persist should be dispelled to enable Americans to weigh the merits of the new China policy as it evolves following the Nixon visit to Peking.

The simplistic projections, astonishing in retrospect, of the "domino theory," upon which the containment policy was based, were described in the secret policy paper, 124/2, issued by the National Security Council in June 1952. It stated:

Communist domination, by whatever means, of all Southeast Asia would seriously endanger in the short term, and critically endanger in the longer term, United States security interests.

a. The loss of any of the countries of Southeast Asia to Communist control as a consequence of overt or covert Chinese Communist aggression would have critical psychological, political and economic consequences. In the absence of effective and timely counteraction, the loss of any single country would probably lead to relatively swift submission to or an alignment with Communism by the remaining countries of this group. Furthermore, an alignment with Communism of the rest of Southeast Asia and India, and in the longer term, of the Middle East (with the probable exceptions of at least Pakistan and Turkey) would in all possibility progressively follow. Such widespread alignment would endanger the stability and security of Europe.

b. Communist control of all Southeast Asia would render the U.S. position in the Pacific off-shore island chain precarious and would seriously jeopardize fundamental U.S. security interests in the Far East.

c. Southeast Asia, especially Malaya and Indonesia, is the principal world source of natural rubber and tin, and a producer of petroleum and other strategically important commodities. The rice exports of Burma and Thailand are critically important to Malaya, Ceylon and Hong Kong and are of considerable significance to Japan and India, all important areas of free Asia.

  d. The loss of Southeast Asia, especially of Malaya and Indonesia, could result in such economic and political pressures in Japan as to make it extremely difficult to prevent Japan's eventual accommodation to Communism.

While this analysis as a whole would be rejected by most informed Americans in 1972 as hysterical, some of the underlying thinking persists in the United States because of assumptions about past Chinese behavior.

In Washington, China took on the face of a bellicose, expansionist power after the outbreak of the Korean War on June 25, 1950, and the entry on October 25 of Chinese "volunteers" into the conflict. Thereafter, American strategists assumed that Chinese troops would probably intervene in the French Indochina War. This was a questionable assumption in view of the events that led to the entry of Chinese troops into Korea.

According to Nikita Khrushchev, in the recollections *Khrushchev Remembers,* and considerable other evidence, the initiative for making the North Korean thrust across the 38th Parallel came from Kim Il Sung. The North Korean leader believed that the South Korean Army would crumble before his infantry and tanks, and that a revolutionary movement would ignite that would topple the Syngman Rhee Government. At the time, North Korea was a Soviet satellite, its armed forces having been equipped by Moscow. Kim Il Sung turned to Stalin for approval of the thrust into South Korea and got it. Relations between Peking and Pyongyang were not close. The Korean Communists who had been in Yenan and were oriented toward Mao Tse-tung had lost out in a power struggle to the pro-Soviet group within the ruling hierarchy. Nonetheless, Peking appears to have at least condoned the North Korean attack as an internal affair. The Chinese were also eager, even as they are today, to exclude American influence from Korea, one of their ancient tributary and buffer states.

There is no evidence that Peking intended to become directly involved in the Korean War. The Maoist regime was so preoccupied with the reconstruction of its economy, shattered by the civil war, and with preparations for an assault on Taiwan, the final refuge of Chiang Kai-shek's forces, that it gave relatively little attention at first to the Korean conflict. Ch'en Yi's Third Field Army was then engaged in amphibious training for a landing on Taiwan.

Peking, however, was to regret bitterly the outbreak of the Korean War. On June 27, two days after North Korea attacked, reversing his hands-off policy as regards Taiwan and further involvement in the Chinese civil war, President Truman decided to "neutralize" the Taiwan Strait by stationing units of the Seventh Fleet there, frustrating indefinitely Peking's plan to "liberate" the island. The eventual entry of Chinese troops into Korea was a costly undertaking which the impoverished Chinese could ill afford. The Russians compelled Peking to pay for all the Soviet supplies sent to support Chinese military operations. Mao's eldest son, Mao An-ying, was killed in combat in Korea.

Chinese troops did not intervene in Korea until United States forces under General Douglas MacArthur had crossed the 38th Parallel into North Korea and advanced toward the Yalu River, beyond which lay the Chinese industrial heartland in Manchuria, serviced by power plants on the Yalu. The Chinese were motivated in part by their deep suspicions of the intentions of General MacArthur, who had visited Taiwan on August 1 and in a joint communiqué with Chiang Kai-shek implied complete harmony of aims.

Successively, on September 25, September 30 and finally in a formal statement on October 3 by Premier Chou En-lai to K. M. Pannikar, the Indian Ambassador in Peking, China warned that it would intervene if United States troops crossed the 38th Parallel into North Korea. Pannikar in his book *In Two Chinas*, published in 1955, described his October 3 meeting with Chou En-lai at the Premier's residence in Peking:

Though the occasion was the most serious I could imagine, a midnight interview on questions affecting the peace of the world . . . Chou En-lai was as courteous and charming as ever and did not give the least impression of worry or nervousness or indeed of being in any particular hurry. He had the usual tea served and the first two minutes were spent in normal courtesies, apology for disturbing me at an unusual hour, etc. Then he came to the point. He thanked Pandit Nehru for what he had been doing in the cause of peace, and said no country's need for peace was greater than that of China, but there were occasions when peace could only be defended by determination to resist aggression. If the Americans crossed the 38th parallel China would be forced to intervene in Korea. Otherwise he was most anxious for a peaceful settlement, and generally accepted Pandit Nehru's approach to the question. I asked him whether he had already news of the Americans having crossed the borders. He replied in the affirmative but added that he did not know where they had crossed. I asked him whether China intended to intervene, if only the South Koreans crossed the parallel. He was emphatic: "The South Koreans did not matter but American intrusion into North Korea would encounter Chinese resistance."

Pannikar immediately relayed Chou En-lai's warning to New Delhi, whence it was forwarded to the State Department. On October 7 the U.S. 1st Cavalry Division crossed the parallel, and on October 25 the first Chinese "volunteers" went into action in Korea. As Allen S. Whiting points out in his comprehensive 1960 study for the RAND Corporation, *China Crosses the Yalu*, the "Chinese Communist intervention was initially cautious and limited." After the first contacts with U.S. forces the Chinese troops disengaged. The question arises: If MacArthur had not pressed his advance, would the Chinese Communists have attacked?

Whatever else may be said about the Chinese role in the Korean War, the charge does not stand up that Peking's intervention was a calculated act of aggression. Yet this was the popular conception in the United States in 1950 when the National Security Council classified China as bellicose and bent on subjugation of Southeast Asia. It was a conception that did not dissipate even after China withdrew its troops from North Korea in 1958. United States troops were still stationed in South Korea in 1972.

Two other events hardened the impression in the United States that China was an aggressor state. These were the Chinese Communist occupation of Tibet and the ousting of its traditional ruler, the Dalai Lama, in March 1959, and the Himalayan border war between China and India in 1962. The United States assumption that these two events confirmed the validity of the China containment policy deserves critical scrutiny.

In October 1949, with the founding of the People's Republic of China, Peking proclaimed its intention to "liberate" Tibet and troops began to move into the region one year later. The Dalai Lama appealed to the United Nations, hoping to gain international backing for its claim to independence. A Chinese Nationalist mission had been stationed in Lhasa until mid-1949, when it was expelled by the Tibetans as the Chiang Kai-shek armies collapsed before the Communists. The Chinese mission had been the symbol of traditional Chinese suzerainty over Tibet, but, in fact, the region had enjoyed virtual independence since

1911. The United Nations did not respond to the appeal of the Dalai Lama. Moscow supported Peking's right to reassert authority over Tibet and the Chinese Nationalists stood by the historical claim that Tibet was part of China. The United States in 1943 had told the British, who maintained trade ties and a military presence in Tibet:

> The Government of the United States has borne in mind the fact that the Chinese Government has long claimed suzerainty over Tibet and that the Chinese constitution lists Tibet among areas constituting the territory of the Republic of China. This Government has at no time raised a question regarding either of these claims.

The Dalai Lama elicited his principal support from India, which had inherited British interests in the Himalayan theocracy in 1947. But the Indian protests were rebuffed by Peking with a forceful reminder that Tibet was an integral part of China and would be defended as such.

In May 1951 Peking signed an agreement with the Tibetans, who had been cowed into submission by advancing Chinese Communist troops, granting regional autonomy to the government of the Dalai Lama but expanding its authority by assuming control over foreign affairs and the army. India recognized China's sovereignty over Tibet in a treaty signed at Peking on April 29, 1954, and two years later the Chinese set up a Preparatory Committee for the Tibetan Autonomous Region in Lhasa with the Dalai Lama as the chairman, and his political pro-Peking opponent, the Panchen Lama, as the deputy chairman. The Chinese adhered nominally to the agreement, although the actual Autonomous Region was not formally set up until 1965, but the Tibetans became increasingly restive as Chinese Communist Party cadres, technical experts and immigrants entered the region and expanded Peking's control.

In the border provinces, particularly the eastern Chamdo district, the Chinese carried out land reforms and tightened Communist administration. Thousands of Tibetans, including the Khamba guerrilla fighters, fled, many of them camping around Lhasa.

The Chinese influx finally sparked a series of revolts by the fierce Khamba tribesmen. The first revolt took place in the northeast in 1956 and gradually spilled, by 1959, into the central and southern region and finally engulfed Lhasa. On March 17 the Dalai Lama left Lhasa after his cabinet, the Kashag, had proclaimed Tibet to be independent.

This unexpected, and hopeless, gesture of the Tibetans had been sparked by a series of incidents between the resentful Khambas allied with other refugees camped around Lhasa and the large Chinese garrison stationed just outside the capital. The cry was raised that the Chinese were humiliating and threatening the person of the Dalai Lama. The Tibetan Army and armed Buddhist monks joined the Khambas in a futile attack on the Chinese Communist garrisons. Peking reacted swiftly. Chinese Communist troops in overwhelming strength swept through Tibet, putting down the revolt. Control of the government was handed over to the Panchen Lama as the Dalai Lama crossed into India at the end of the month and was given political asylum. Peking then took the frankly welcomed opportunity to carry out a purge of those who had led in resisting Sinicization and collectivization of Tibet, particularly in the lamaseries, whose monks were regarded by the Communists as the prime agents of counterrevolution.

The Dalai Lama, writing in his autobiography *My Land and My People* in 1962, reporting on the suppression of the rebellion, said: "Tens of thousands of our people have been killed, not only in military actions, but individually and deliberately." He charged that the "Chinese had destroyed hundreds of our monasteries, either by physically wrecking them, or by killing the lamas and sending the monks to labor camps, ordering monks under pain of death to break their vows of celibacy, and using the empty monastic buildings and temples as army barracks and stables."

The Chinese Communists accused the lamas of being corrupt parasites and counterrevolutionaries. The purge in Tibet was as ruthless as that carried out by the Chinese Communists against "counterrevolutionaries" and landlords accused of "crimes against the people" in China proper in 1951–52. Thousands of Tibetans fled as refugees into India, following the Dalai Lama. Years later, the Panchen Lama disappeared.

Although a great human tragedy had been suffered in Tibet, it was also evident that the Chinese Communists had dealt with what they considered to be an internal matter. Thus the Tibetan episode did not constitute a significant guide to what Peking's conduct might be in relations with foreign countries.

New Delhi acknowledged Peking's suzerainty over Tibet in 1954, but the Indians continued to regard the autonomous region as a strategic buffer and they retained religious and trade ties with Lhasa. The Communist repression in Tibet in 1959 shocked India and strained the personal rapport between Prime Minister Jawaharlal Nehru and

Premier Chou En-lai. Differences over the boundary line between the two countries, apparent for years in the discrepancies between Indian maps and those published by the Chinese Nationalists and later by the Communists, suddenly became explosive issues. China had never recognized the validity of the McMahon boundary line between the two countries drawn by the British in 1914 in agreement with the Tibetans. The Chinese Communists, nevertheless, declared their willingness to accept the McMahon line as the *de facto* border, but challenged what they insisted were Indian alterations of the line.

I was stationed at the time in Moscow, but at Christmas in 1961 and 1962 flew to India with my family, leaving behind the grayness and cold to enjoy the flowers and ideal climate in New Dehli. We stayed at the residence of Chester Ronning, who was then the Canadian High Commissioner to India. Chester was close to Nehru and General K. S. Thimayya, who had been Chief of the Army Staff until August 1959, when he resigned in a dispute with Krishna Menon, the Defense Minister. I had first met Thimayya in the Philippines. I was an army lieutenant and escorted him, then a dashing brigadier, more British than the British but openly hating the colonial Raj, on a tour of the Baguio area of northern Luzon. During my two month-long visits to New Delhi I became privy to the background of the unfolding border crisis.

The military confrontation along the border grew out of a quarrel over a stretch of uninhabited wasteland that India had not bothered to inspect for years. In October 1958 an Indian Army survey patrol reported that it had come across a good motor road traversing Aksai Chin in the eastern section of Ladakh in Kashmir. The road followed an old caravan route and had been built by the Chinese Communists as a military road linking the province of Sinkiang with Tibet. Construction of the road had begun in March 1956, and when it was finished nineteen months later, the achievement was recorded in the Peking press and was reported to New Delhi by the Indian Embassy. Two Indian patrols were sent out in July 1958 to investigate the Chinese project. One was captured and later released by the Chinese, while the other reported the existence of the new road to the Nehru Government in October. There was an exchange of notes between New Delhi and Peking, both sides laying claim to the Aksai Chin region. Nehru withheld information about the incident from Parliament until August 1959, when the country was already aroused about the events in Tibet.

In April 1960, Chou En-lai and his Foreign Minister, Ch'en Yi, flew to Delhi seeking a settlement of the Aksai Chin dispute. The Chinese contended that the border had never been properly defined and therefore general boundary negotiations were required. Chou En-lai was willing to accept the McMahon line, yielding a claim of about forty thousand square miles in the Northeast Frontier Agency (NEFA) of India, as represented for several decades on Chinese maps, if the Indians would surrender their claims in the west, including Aksai Chin. The Indians retorted that the boundary had been fixed in custom and tradition, and only "minor frontier rectifications" could be made. The Chinese then made an alternate proposal, urging maintenance of normal relations between the two countries and observance of the status quo pending a general settlement. The Chinese proposal was rejected.

The ensuing escalation toward the border war is described in detail in the thoroughly documented study *India's China War*, completed in 1971 by Neville Maxwell, the former South Asia correspondent of the *Times* of London, as a senior fellow at the London School of Oriental and African Studies. In 1961 the Indian Government put into effect its "forward policy," which meant that Indian patrols would begin to operate in territory occupied by the Chinese but claimed by New Delhi. Chinese positions were not to be attacked, but Indian patrols would penetrate areas between them. Partisan politics in the Indian Parliament and nationalist passions in the country combined to keep pressure on Nehru for a militant application of the policy, although it was opposed by the army, which felt it lacked the resources to implement it safely. A series of border clashes followed that led to the fatal encounter at Thag La ridge in the Northeast Frontier area.

On June 4, 1962, the Indians set up Dhola Post in territory that, according to their own army maps, was Chinese, and opposite a Chinese position on Thag La ridge. China did not move against the post for three months, but then shifted troops to positions dominating it in an effort to force an Indian withdrawal. The Indian Government decided to force the Chinese back to the northern side of Thag La ridge and began moving in reinforcements. The Indian troops were ordered on October 9 to envelop the Chinese positions by taking up positions on the crest of Thag La behind and overlooking the Chinese posts on the southern slope. An advance patrol of Punjabis moved out on the mission. On October 10, as the Indian troops continued to move forward, the Chinese attacked. When the Indians retreated, the Chinese held their fire, allowing the survivors to escape. The Chinese then buried the Indian dead with military honors as their comrades watched from the opposite positions.

The Indian build-up in the area continued, and on October 12 Nehru reiterated that his troops were expected to clear the Chinese off Thag La ridge. The army had ordered completion of the operation by November 1. Meanwhile, the Chinese did not conceal that they were preparing to react.

On the night of October 19–20, the Chinese troops attacked and overran the Indian positions. In the next month, three Chinese divisions, continuing the advance, shattered Indian defenses in NEFA and swiftly penetrated south, seemingly headed for the plains in a large-scale invasion. New Delhi panicked. Nehru appealed on November 20 to the United States to intervene with bomber and fighter strikes against the Chinese troops if they persisted in the advance. An American aircraft carrier was ordered into the Bay of Bengal, but the war abruptly ended in a totally unexpected way.

Chou En-lai summoned the Indian Chargé d'Affaires in Peking on the evening of November 20 and informed him that the Chinese would unilaterally cease fire at midnight. Beginning December 1, 1962, Chinese troops would withdraw to positions 20 kilometers behind the line of control in effect two years earlier. India was expected to do the same. Chou En-lai proposed that officials meet on the border to site local police posts, and arrange joint withdrawals and exchange of prisoners. The Chinese Premier offered to meet Nehru in Peking or New Delhi to discuss a settlement.

Nehru did not accept Chou's offer of a meeting, but the Chinese pulled back their troops nevertheless. India was humbled in the border war, and this suited Peking's purposes since there could be no question now where superior power resided in Asia. But the victor's terms were not that of an expansionist nation.

President Kennedy summed up the myopic American view of what had transpired when he wrote to Nehru: "You have displayed an impressive degree of forbearance and patience in dealing with the Chinese." The Kennedy Administration, meanwhile, went forward with the policy of containing China through intervention in Indochina. Two years later, when the Johnson Administration was ranking containment as only a 20 percent factor in its justification of the Indochina policy, American bombing of North Vietnam had already been extended up to the China border. Yet Peking, labeled an aggressive state by Washington since 1950, did not allow itself to be provoked into sending combat troops into Vietnam.

It would be as ridiculous to deny China's deep involvement in Southeast Asia as it would be to minimize United States concern about what happens in Latin America or Soviet preoccupation with Eastern Europe. Great powers always jealously guard their security and economic interests in smaller neighboring nations, often to the detriment of their sovereignty. During the 1960s the United States intervened militarily twice, in Cuba and the Dominican Republic, to oust regimes which Washington viewed as threats to regional security. To maintain its hegemony over Eastern Europe, Moscow brutally intervened in Hungary and Czechoslovakia, crushing independent-minded governments.

As a great power, China has no less a stake in Southeast Asia, looking upon the region as a security buffer and traditional zone of influence and trade, their Nan Yang, or Southern Ocean, as the Chinese historically have referred to Southeast Asia. During the Manchu or Ch'ing Dynasty (1644–1912), what constitutes modern Indochina, Thailand, Burma and Malaya were at times tributary nations to Peking. Their tenuous relations fluctuated according to the whims and fortunes of the imperial emperors of the "Middle Kingdom." The emperors in Peking were satisfied to accept token tribute from these nations without insisting on the posting of Chinese military garrisons or viceroys as the symbols of power. The tributaries were content, since for the price of a kowtow they enjoyed freedom from Chinese interference in their internal affairs and access to trade in the exotic wares of Cathay.

In its future relations with Southeast Asia, China is likely to revert to historic patterns of behavior. China is an immense, self-contained universe, one-fourth of humanity, with a strong sense of cultural, racial and, more recently, ideological oneness. Its government has been dedicated to consolidating its power within its historic boundaries, but shown no interest so far in expanding its territory beyond. China does not have military bases abroad, and professes to be opposed to acquiring any in the future.

The emperor in Peking has been replaced by Mao Tse-tung, and the imperial sway has been replaced by Maoism, a Sinicized adaptation of Marxism-Leninism, which the Chinese believe to be especially applicable to the solution of the problems of Asia. By demonstrating the success of the revolution in their own country, the Chinese hope to attract other societies to the principles of Maoism. As the nations of Southeast Asia once sent token tribute to the Manchu emperors, Mao anticipates that their societies will also one day defer to Peking as the ideological center of a new international Communist order.

Peking has not used its power to indiscriminately topple non-Communist regimes. While Peking has provided arms and propaganda support for the Burma Communist Party, whose main base of guerrilla operations adjoins the China frontier, Mao has chosen not to overthrow the government of General Ne Win. Instead, the Chinese have maintained relations with Ne Win, respecting his neutrality. During the Cultural Revolution, in the turbulent years 1967–68, relations deteriorated, but subsequently the Chinese resumed their aid program to Rangoon, and Ne Win was cordially received in Peking in August 1971 by Mao.

Better than any other major power, Peking understands that the peoples of Southeast Asia, stubborn in their nationalisms, tenaciously clinging to their ethnic and cultural identities, and blessed by geography favorable to defense against invasion, would fiercely resist any attempt by the Chinese Communists to impose direct hegemony.

The Vietnamese, who deferred to nominal Peking suzerainty until the French colonial conquest in 1883, retain a particularly guarded attitude toward the Chinese because of their proximity and because they alone in Southeast Asia have been subjected to Chinese colonization and occupation. In 111 B.C. the Vietnamese nation, situated in modern North Vietnam, was conquered by the armies of the Han Dynasty, and apart from sporadic revolts, remained a Chinese protectorate ruled by a governor and divided into military districts. After about a thousand years of subjugation, the Vietnamese succeeded in defeating their Chinese occupiers, reasserting their independence from A.D. 940. The Chinese left behind a strong cultural heritage, but also an inextinguishable memory of domination that hardened the nationalism of the Vietnamese and made them determined to resist reassertion of Chinese authority over them.

In 1950, as the Chinese Communists reached the border of Indochina, Ho Chi Minh turned to them for help against the French and their American supporters. But earlier, between October 1945 and February 1946, he had sent at least eight communications to President Truman and the Secretary of State appealing for help against French colonialism. His letters were spurned because it was assumed that, as a Communist, Ho Chi Minh would allow his country to be used as a satellite by Stalin, although the Vietnamese leader had endured extraordinary hardships in fighting for independence. As for Ho Chi Minh's attitude toward Chinese domination, once in 1946, in an outburst of anger, he revealed his underlying feelings. At the end of World War II, Chinese Nationalist troops, many of them under the command of generals who were unabashed warlords, descended on famine-stricken North Vietnam, systematically looting the country. In desperation, unable to get help from the Soviet Union or elsewhere, Ho entered into an agreement with the French, accepting their military presence in North Vietnam for five years in return for a loose promise that the DRV would become "a Free State within the French Union." When Ho was criticized for making the agreement by a pro-Chinese group in his Laodang or Workers Party, he retorted:

You fools! Don't you realize what it means if the Chinese stay? Don't you remember your history? The last time the Chinese came, they stayed one thousand years!

The French are foreigners. They are weak. Colonialism is dying out. Nothing will be able to withstand world pressure for independence. They may stay for a while, but they will have to go because the white man is finished in Asia. But if the Chinese stay now, they will never leave.

As for me, I prefer to smell French shit for five years, rather than Chinese shit for the rest of my life.

Ho was then speaking in reference to the Chinese Nationalist incursion into North Vietnam, but he was also, like his present-day successors in Hanoi, adamant in opposing any Chinese long-term presence. When I visited Lang Son on the North Indochina border in March 1950, French officers insisted that there was no evidence of Chinese Communist aid to the Vietminh. On May 1 President Truman approved $10 million for urgent military assistance to the French forces. It was not until June, when I visited Lang Son again, that the same French officers told me they had reliable evidence of the commencement of Chinese Communist military aid. Subsequently, there were reports that Chinese technical specialists had been serving with the Vietminh, but the presence of Chinese combat units was never confirmed in operations during the French Indochina War.

When the American bombing of North Vietnam was at its height in the 1965–68 period, Chinese railway engineer troops, perhaps as many as fifty thousand, were invited into the country to help repair the disrupted communication lines. The Johnson Administration, fully aware of the entry of the Chinese troops, concealed the information, perhaps fearing that it would alarm American public opinion. When I reported the facts from Hong Kong in 1966, the State Department reprimanded its Consulate General in Hong Kong, mistakenly accusing the staff of having leaked the information to me. When the sustained American bombing of North Vietnam ended, the Chinese withdrew, leaving behind about a battalion of railway engineers to coordinate traffic with China.

From the early 1960s the Vietnamese have exploited the Sino-Soviet ideological split, delicately balancing Peking against Moscow, taking aid from both and orders from neither. The same balancing act has been performed by the Kim Il Sung regime in North Korea and also by the large Indonesian Communist Party (PKI), before it was wiped out in the 1965 right-wing army purge. In early 1965, shortly before he went underground in Indonesia and was killed in the purge, D. M. Aidit, chairman of the Indonesian Communist Party, told me that he was opposed to the establishment of any world body of Communist parties under the aegis either of Moscow or of Peking. "I am not for a world organization with leaders and conferences," Aidit said. "With such an organization, if we wanted to do something in Indonesia, we would have to consult. We know better what has to be done in Indonesia."

One of the more inexplicable aspects of American policy in Asia during the 1960s was the disinclination to take cognizance of the Sino-Soviet dispute. By 1960 Soviet military and economic aid to China had been terminated, Soviet technicians had been withdrawn, the ideological polemics between Moscow and Peking had become vituperative, and the international Communist movement had been fragmented. The containment policy in Asia had evolved from a theory that there existed a world-wide Communist expansionist conspiracy, with Moscow as its center. Although the conspiracy, if it ever existed, was now obviously undone, United States policy in Asia remained unchanged. As late as January 1962, in a secret memorandum to the Secretary of Defense, the Joint Chiefs of Staff referred to the strategic advantages that would accrue to the *"Sino-Soviet Bloc"* if the United States did not broaden its intervention in Indochina. It was not until the advent of the Nixon Administration in 1969 that the momentous implications of the Sino-Soviet split began to be factored seriously into American policy-making.

In 1972, with the United States withdrawing from Indochina, the

big-power confrontation in Southeast Asia increasingly became one
between China and the Soviet Union as they tilted for political influence in Burma, North Vietnam, Laos and Cambodia. These nations
balanced one Communist giant against the other. The problems of the
Southeast Asian leaders in playing the dangerous, intricate, often tragic
game of big-power politics were illustrated by the misfortunes of Prince
Sihanouk of Cambodia.

I first interviewed Sihanouk in May 1950 in his Phnom Penh palace,
an improbable fairy-tale cluster of yellow edifices with tall spires and
roofs inlaid with colored tiles styled in the architecture of the ancient
Khmers. It was before he abdicated as King, taking the title of Prince,
so that he could assume a broader political role. Sihanouk was a hero
and father figure to his people as he struggled against French colonialism and resisted the infiltration from Vietnam of the Vietminh, who
were allied with the Cambodian Issarak dissidents. Attired in a Western
white linen suit, the twenty-eight-year-old, French-educated monarch,
a short dynamic man with dark curly hair and brown eyes, received
Audrey and me in his luxurious private apartments. He told us that Ho
Chi Minh's Vietminh, if they were victorious in Vietnam, eventually
would bring about a puppet regime in Cambodia.

During the next two decades, Sihanouk alternately juggled and
played off the contending ambitions of the French, Americans, Russians, Chinese and Vietnamese while striving to keep his country intact,
neutral and free of war.

Vietnamese Communist infiltration became a critical problem again
for Sihanouk after 1960 as the war in Vietnam intensified. Initially,
Sihanouk resisted it. But when heavily armed North Vietnamese and
Vietcong units established bases in his frontier area to counter the
American build-up in South Vietnam, Sihanouk's weak army could not
cope with them. By his private admission in 1971, he winked at the
presence of the Vietnamese Communists, although publicly he insisted
vigorously that they were not there. Sihanouk feared that acknowledgment of the existence of the Communist bases would bring a massive
American and South Vietnamese military drive into his country. Disin-
genuously, Sihanouk invited me in October 1965 to visit Cambodia and
challenged me to find the Communist troops and bases which the
American military in Saigon had reported to be operating in the Cambodian frontier region.

In Phnom Penh the British and French military attachés told me that they had failed in many investigations to confirm that the Communist bases existed, and they had concluded that the country was not a major Vietcong sanctuary or route for the delivery of military equipment and supplies to South Vietnam. The attachés told me of areas in which there was possible Vietcong or North Vietnamese activity. Accompanied by General Lon Nol, then the Cambodian Defense Minister, I toured the frontier areas by helicopter and jeep. I made two unscheduled visits by foot through dense jungle to the most sensitive points on the Vietnam frontier, where no Western observers had been allowed to go in years. All I stumbled into were Cambodian villages and army posts which had been strafed by American and South Vietnamese planes. In my dispatch to the *New York Times*, I noted, however, that "there are some remote jungle areas of the Cambodian-Vietnam border that are impossible to check for Vietcong activity." Without doubt, in retrospect, one can say that the Communists were operating in those areas. In the late 1960s, as the Communists made bolder use of the Cambodian sanctuary, United States and South Vietnamese ground and air forays were launched into the frontier region against the bases. Sihanouk reacted by drifting politically from a neutral position closer to Hanoi, Peking and Moscow. Still, at the end of two decades of rule over Cambodia, he had succeeded in what no Vietnamese or Laotian leader had been able to do. He had managed to shield his people from large-scale warfare.

In March 1970, while Sihanouk was abroad on a trip to Moscow and Peking, Lon Nol, who had become Prime Minister, staged a coup d'état and ousted him as Chief of State. Lon Nol, confident of American support and in touch with the United States Embassy in Phnom Penh, cited Sihanouk's toleration of the Vietnamese Communist bases as one of the reasons for the coup. The following month, United States and South Vietnamese troops invaded Cambodia. Ostensibly, the invasion was mounted to wipe out the Communist bases in the frontier region, but the result confirmed the remark made by Sihanouk in 1965 when he said: "Where there are American troops, the Communists gather like red ants around sugar." By 1972 the North Vietnamese and Vietcong had recruited an estimated eight thousand Cambodians as Khmer Rouge, and were operating over most of the country rather than only in the frontier region. Four Vietnamese Communist divisions continued to base along the Vietnam border. United States troops had been withdrawn, except for a military aid and advisory group assigned to the

Lon Nol Government, but American war planes were bombing in support of South Vietnamese troops, who alternated between fruitlessly chasing the Communists and pilfering Cambodian villages.

Sihanouk was at the Moscow Airport en route to Peking on March 18, 1970, when Soviet Premier Kosygin told him that he had been deposed. When the Cambodian leader arrived in Peking, Chou En-lai was waiting for him with a pledge of Chinese support if he would commit himself "to fight to the end." Sihanouk agreed. On March 21 Premier Pham Van Dong of North Vietnam flew to Peking to meet with Sihanouk, who for the first time asked for Hanoi's intervention in his country. Secretly, an alliance was worked out providing for two thousand North Vietnamese advisers to be assigned to train pro-Sihanouk guerrillas, including the Khmer Rouge, use of Hanoi's supply network to bring in Chinese arms, and joint Cambodian–North Vietnamese military operations. Later, Sihanouk told Wilfred Burchett, the leftist Australian journalist, that Pham Van Dong, with Chou En-lai's cognizance, had given him an assurance that after victory Cambodia would be "independent, neutral and free of any Vietnamese presence." When I learned of this accord, I thought back twenty years to the time when young Sihanouk had told me that if Ho Chi Minh triumphed in Vietnam, the Communists would set up a puppet regime in his capital.

In Peking, where Sihanouk was living when I visited the Chinese capital in May 1971, the Cambodian leader had set up in exile a Royal Government of National Union, and a political organization, the United National Front, which included the Communists and Socialists. The government had been recognized by China and North Vietnam, as well as the other Asian states and revolutionary movements, but not by the Soviet Union. Resentful of Sihanouk's close tie with the Chinese, Moscow continued to maintain its embassy in Phnom Penh. When the Front triumphed, Sihanouk told visitors in Peking, he expected to return to Phnom Penh long enough to consolidate the new government. The Front guerrillas, aided by the Vietnamese Communists, were then steadily expanding their control of the countryside while Lon Nol's forces were confined largely to the towns and cities. But Sihanouk also said he was under no illusions as to the dominant power of the Communists within the Front, and he saw only a limited political future for himself. In March 1972 Lon Nol dissolved the parliament in Phnom Penh, and appointed himself Chief of State and dictator.

The Cambodian people, drawn into the vortex of big-power politics, much of their country wasted by war, and their pleasant capital repeatedly rocketed by Communist guerrillas, had become less interested in political choice than in simply securing peace and ending foreign intervention. It was my view that the United States in all conscience was obliged to terminate its armed intervention without delay, offering also to suspend shipments of military equipment to the Lon Nol Government and arrange the withdrawal of South Vietnamese troops in return for evacuation of Vietnamese Communist forces and the restoration of the neutral status of Cambodia.

In February 1972, in a joint communiqué at the conclusion of President Nixon's visit to China, the United States declared its intention to withdraw from Indochina in these terms:

The United States stressed that the peoples of Indochina should be allowed to determine their destiny without outside intervention; its constant primary objective has been a negotiated solution; the eight-point proposal put forward by the Republic of Vietnam and the United States on January 27, 1972, represents a basis for the attainment of that objective; in the absence of a negotiated settlement, the United States envisages the ultimate withdrawal of all U.S. forces from the region consistent with the aim of self-determination for each country of Indochina.

After stating that: "All foreign troops should be withdrawn to their own countries," the Chinese side expressed in the communiqué its support of the seven-point proposal of the Provisional Revolutionary Government (Vietcong). The failure to effect a compromise between the American-supported peace plan and the Vietcong proposal led to interruption on March 23, 1972, of the Paris negotiations which had been in progress for three years among the representatives of the United States, North Vietnam, South Vietnam and the Vietcong.

The plan backed by the United States and South Vietnam provided for a total withdrawal of all U.S. forces from South Vietnam within six months of an agreement, which would include a general cease-fire. Within six months of an agreement there would be a presidential election under international supervision in which all political forces in South Vietnam could participate. One month before the election, the incumbent President and Vice President of South Vietnam would resign. The Vietcong proposal called for the immediate cessation of all United States military activities in Vietnam, and unconditional withdrawal of all American personnel and war matériel. It also demanded

the immediate resignation of President Nguyen Van Thieu, disband-
ment of his "machine of oppression and constraint" and end of the
pacification campaign. The Vietcong would then discuss with the Saigon administration the formation of "a three-segment government of
national accord" to organize elections for a constituent assembly that
would frame a constitution and set up a government.

In my opinion, the American plan would perpetuate intervention
through foreign supervision of an unworkable political process and
truce arrangement. As for the Vietcong proposal, it was an effort, using
American prisoners of war as bargaining counters, to compel Washington to dismantle the Saigon Government so that a Communist-con-
trolled administration could be brought into being quickly.

The experience of the last two decades in Indochina should dictate
to Washington that it end its armed intervention in Vietnam and withdraw all troops as soon as possible without trying to impose any kind of
political process or settlement on any party in the civil war. Having
abrogated the 1954 Geneva Accords, the United States has no right to
insist that North Vietnam not involve itself in the affairs of the South.
It would be naïve to believe in any case that any political arrangement
will endure that does not reflect the real and evolving balance of indigenous forces in the country as a whole. The United States should also offer
to terminate its shipment of military equipment to South Vietnam if
China and the Soviet Union will agree to a similar embargo on aid to
North Vietnam and the Vietcong.

In Laos, the United States has a responsibility to continue to assist
the Vientiane Government, which has been embattled against the pro-
Communist Pathet Lao, until the 1962 Geneva Agreement is implemented. The agreement, signed by the Laotian parties, the United
States and twelve other governments, provided for a neutralist coalition
government of the rightists, centrists and Pathet Lao. North Vietnam,
which is allied to the Pathet Lao, has violated the agreement by stationing thousands of its troops in eastern Laos to guard and service a seg-
ment of the Ho Chi Minh Trail, its supply corridor to South Vietnam.
By bombing eastern Laos and in interdiction operations employing the
Central Intelligence Agency, the United States also has violated the
agreement. The end of the war in Vietnam might open an avenue to
a settlement based on the 1962 accord, since Hanoi would no longer
feel the necessity to use the country as a supply corridor.

The American purpose in Southeast Asia should be the restoration of peace and respect for borders, and the fostering of a community of independent, self-determining and viable societies. The presence of American troops or bases will not help in the attainment of such an order. The white man's colonialism and his bombs have reduced to zero the tolerance of most Asians for any of his uniformed emissaries. There may be a role for American naval and air power, based on aircraft carriers and the island chain off the Asian mainland, in deterring external aggression against nations of the region, particularly Thailand, an ally. As a Pacific nation, and a world power, the United States has a responsibility in concert with the United Nations and other governments to maintain international security. But the Indochina experience should have convinced the American people of the immorality and futility of interference in the internal affairs of another nation.

The United States can make its best contribution toward sustaining the independence and viability of Southeast Asian nations by assisting in their economic reconstruction, but not in the main through bilateral aid programs. Inevitably, political strings become attached to bilateral arrangements, and the presence of large American aid missions tends to corrupt both the dispensers and the recipients of the largess. The most sensible means is through multilateral channels, such as the United Nations and the Asian Development Bank. Loans can be extended by these agencies according to criteria that relate to performance and permit the helped society to retain its self-respect.

The era of static containment is ending amid devastation and vast human suffering. This tragic heritage makes it incumbent upon the United States to exercise its power more wisely, tolerantly and generously.

PART III

CHINA
UNDER
MAO

CHAPTER *12*

CHINA-WATCHING

In December 1963 we were back in Hong Kong, which was to be my base for three years as Chief Correspondent Southeast Asia for the *Times.* I had returned to Asia after three years in Moscow for the *Times* and a three-month breather at home. On my last day in the New York office, I was at lunch with the Publisher, Arthur (Punch) O. Sulzberger, in his dining room on the fourteenth floor when Clifton Daniel, then Assistant Managing Editor, was called to the telephone, and returned to say: "The President has been shot." We did not have a complete obituary for the young President, John F. Kennedy, and when I went to the news room on the third floor, I was drafted to write the section devoted to a review of his foreign policy. I was sitting next to Homer Bigart, who was writing the domestic policy review, on the front re-write bank when Daniel came up to us and said: "He is dead." Between 2 and 6:30 P.M. Bigart and I wrote a page of the *Times,* grateful for the total preoccupation, and then we walked out to Times Square, where the lights had been dimmed in deference to the dead President. We walked to Bleeck's on Fortieth Street, the favorite bar of the staffers of the old *Herald Tribune,* where we talked about Kennedy, and I told Homer about the day he came to Saigon. It seemed such a long time ago. I spent the night at the Astor Hotel, lying awake welcoming the dawn, and then I left for Hong Kong. Audrey and the girls followed, going through Europe and the Middle East, stopping off in Cairo to canter joyfully around the pyramids atop camels and horses.

In Hong Kong, we lived in more elegant fashion than in the Chinese hotel of thirteen years ago. We had a hillside apartment, four split-level

187

floors, with two balconies, looking out high over the magnificence of Repulse Bay. On some evenings, as the pink flush of the descending sun illuminated the clear waters, our red-sailed Chinese junk, the *Valhalla*, would be brought close to the beach by Ah Liang, the boat boy, and we would go out in the fresh evening to picnic on fried chicken and chilled Portuguese rosé imported from Macao. Often our friends, Dr. Tony Dawson-Grove, and his wife, Diane, long-time residents of Hong Kong, would bring their speedboat and we would ski, swinging wide away from the wake, the single ski leaving long ripples in the limpid water. Hong Kong had become crowded. The two million of 1950 had increased to 3.7 million, as the Colony continued not only as an entrepôt but also a great industrial center. The beaches had become crowded; even Big Wave, beyond Wanchai Gap at the end of the island, became overrun, and so we sailed to the tiny deserted islands far offshore, anchored and swam to the white beaches, snorkled among the brilliantly hued rocks, and water-skied until it was time for the voyage home in the sunset, with the wind bending the sails or pushed by the junk's two outboard motors.

Audrey loved the *Valhalla*, which she named after the valley settlement in northern Alberta, which her pastor grandfather had opened in the early 1900s after driving through the wilderness with her father and his brother Nelius walking beside the covered wagon. She had found the *Valhalla*'s graceful thirty-three-foot hull in a small shipyard near Aberdeen Bay and tenderly hovered over the Chinese carpenters as they completed the construction and sold it to us for $5,000. From the prow of a huge junk wrecked and cast up on the shore by a typhoon, she took a phoenix, dragon and other good-luck carvings, and adorned the *Valhalla*. Eyes cast down into the waters were painted on the bow in traditional style so the *Valhalla* would see the dangers of the deep, and we launched her, to the high amusement of the Chinese builders, with a bottle of French champagne.

I spent only half my time in Hong Kong China-watching, and the balance covering the war in Vietnam and other countries of Southeast Asia. I was usually away three weeks or a month at a time. Then, eager for reunion with Audrey and the girls, I would be flying into Hong Kong, looking down at the sailing junks scooting before the wind and the freighters plying through the vivid blue-green waters in and out of the great harbor, and then impatiently enduring the long landing approach winding through the scrub-covered hills to Kai Tak Airport.

Audrey would be waiting at home, never revealing the loneliness. We would sit in the wicker swing chairs, drinks in hand, looking out to the faintly visible islands belonging to mainland China, and she would listen to me rage about the war. Then we would go out on the junk, the days would slip by, and it would be time to go again.

In appearance most of Hong Kong had changed considerably since 1950. New luxury apartment houses marched row-on-row on the Peak-side, overlooking the harbor, enhancing the skyline at the cost of the old charm. The Gloucester had become a seedy office building, and the big hotels were the Hong Kong Hilton and the luxurious Mandarin, owned by British and Chinese interests. New shops had mushroomed in incredible profusion on the island, and in largely Chinese Kowloon, to serve some one-half million tourists pouring into the Colony each year. The most important spurt had been in industry, transforming the Colony into a competitor with Japan. The talented, industrious, refugee manpower and flight capital from the mainland fueled a boom, and from more than eight thousand factories poured goods destined not only for the cheap shops of Southeast Asia but also for Western markets —rich silken brocades, sequined dresses and suits and other fine goods for the haute couture departments of stores such as Harrods in London and New York's Lord & Taylor. More than 41 percent of the Colony's total labor force, or 147,000 workers, were employed in the artistic, innovative textile and garment industry.

But the exotic in Hong Kong was in retreat, and Audrey and I, hungry for old China, went in search of it. Audrey was editing, writing and taking photos for the *Mandarin* magazine, a small glossy quality periodical, which the hotel distributed all over the world. With cameras and notebooks, we went into the New Territories, where the peasants, wearing their conical straw hats, guided their plows behind water buffaloes in the lush rice fields as their brethren did on the other side of the border. Amid the green hills of Dragon Boat Bay on High Island, one of the 235 small outlying islands included in the New Territories lease, there were the Hakka people, wearing the large straw hats rimmed with black cloth which had been worn by their ancestors when they emigrated from Kwangtung on the mainland centuries ago. In the harbor of Aberdeen and in the Yau Ma Tei typhoon shelter in Victoria Harbor there were the Dragon People, descendants of the fishermen-pirates who had dominated the island before the British, now living crowded on the floating sampans and junks. These people kept alive the traditional festivals and spirit worship. The camera-draped tourists swarming through Hong Kong and Kowloon, pinioned in the fitting rooms of a twenty-four-hour tailor or lured into the shops of the makers of ancient curios, rarely became privy to this ancient world of Her Majesty's Crown Colony.

Hong Kong had not changed in other ways. It was still an anachronism in a world in which other vestiges of colonialism were fast dying. Culturally, apart from Chinese influences, Hong Kong had remained a desert for a century, offering its population no other Western arts than those associated with making money. Hong Kong University provided graduates for the civil service. Chinese University, founded as an afterthought in 1964, gave the Colony its first facilities for serious Chinese scholarship. There were a few more Chinese members in the staid British Hong Kong Club, but none in the Royal Hong Kong Golf Club in Fanling, New Territories, from whose links you could drive a golf ball into China. The British ladies gave elegant charity balls on behalf of the refugees who lived in clusters of shacks on the hillside, but the government still did not provide universal free education or comprehensive welfare benefits for the Chinese who comprised 99 percent of the population. In fairness, guaranteeing such public aid was probably economically impossible, given the massive refugee population. The British barred refugee entry; but once an escapee eluded guards on both sides of the frontier, and made his way to a registry office in the Colony, he was granted asylum and residence papers.

The anomaly of the existence of this foreign appendage was not lost on Communist China, and the Colony lived by the sufferance of Peking. The Colony was now indefensible, and for economy reasons the garrison had been cut back sharply. Hong Kong might be a jewel in the Crown, but in terms of costs London found it a pain in the exchequer.

Mainland China supplies by pipe about one-fourth of the Colony's water, vital in time of drought when its own reservoirs dry up. About one-third of the food comes from the mainland. If Peking desired to cause the economy of Hong Kong to collapse, it could cut off these supplies, suspend trade, cut rail and water communication, and the capital on which the economy depends would flee. Hong Kong entrepreneurs, always sensitive to the shifting tides of politics, usually invest with the intention of regaining their capital in addition to profits in about five years.

No business firm looks beyond 1997, when the New Territories will revert under the 1898 lease to China and the Colony will shrink to Kowloon and the island, an expensive spit of real estate that probably will be impossible to sustain. The businesses counted, as does the colonial government, on the tolerance of Peking as long as Communist China continued to earn more than U.S. $500 million in hard currency or about 40 percent of its annual intake of fully convertible foreign exchange through Hong Kong. The time of danger comes when political upheaval within China causes these dollar considerations to be put aside and disorder begins to spill across the border. In early 1966 the China-watchers in Hong Kong, myself among them, began to sense that once again there were fateful stirrings in mainland China that would have implications not only for Hong Kong but for the whole world. It was not known then, even to the top leadership of the Chinese Communist Government, that the faint rumblings presaged one of the most momentous events in modern Chinese history, the Great Proletarian Cultural Revolution.

Barred from the People's Republic of China by Peking, American newsmen found Hong Kong to be the best observation post for reporting on the mainland. China-watching was one of the Colony's major industries, although the British never ceased to be nervous that Peking would one day retaliate against the activities of the agglomeration of diplomats, military attachés, intelligence agents, propagandists and writers hunting and correlating information about the secretive colossus. Those governments, such as Britain, France and India, which had embassies in Peking enjoyed the advantage of visual reporting by their diplomats in the Chinese capital. But all depended on the Hong Kong information mill. Western diplomats in Peking could do little traveling, had only infrequent contact with Chinese officials and lacked the large translation staffs needed to pan the Chinese press for nuggets of information. More information went up to Peking in the diplomatic bags from Hong Kong than came down from the embassies.

The United States Consulate, so called but in fact larger than most embassies because of its China-watching Political Section, managed to collect a considerable amount of information. In addition to the central Chinese press, whose articles were distributed abroad by the New China News Agency and broadcast by Peking Radio, the consulate could buy provincial newspapers and magazines forbidden for export but smuggled out to Hong Kong. Refugees, who came in the hundreds every month, and travelers provided information. Embassies, consulates and

Central Intelligence Agency offices all over the world reported on the movement of Chinese officials, ships and planes. Electronic stations monitored mainland radios. Information also came from the high-flying U-2 reconnaissance planes, financed by the CIA and piloted by Chinese Air Force personnel based in Taiwan, as well as pilotless plane and satellite cameras. The daily ration of information sooner or later filtered out among all the China-watchers. The difference in the quality of a China-watcher lay in the skill of his correlation and analysis, and sheer sensing of what was going on in the great sprawling mainland.

My office was in an apartment on MacDonald Road, just up the hill from the elaborate, modernistic consulate. I shared it with the permanent *New York Times* Hong Kong correspondent, Ian Stewart, a personable New Zealander, who had lived for many years in the Colony with his wife, Truus, a sophisticated, attractive Chinese born in Indonesia, and two sons. Ian and I had individual offices, another was given over to clacking news agency teleprinters, the most important being the English-language New China News Agency report from Peking, and a Chinese secretary presided over the reception room. One or the other of us would check the New China News Agency printer for important occurrences periodically from 9 A.M. to midnight. During the night, a Reuters news agency monitor would telephone us if an important break developed. With a thirteen-hour lead time in New York, we were often out of bed and writing for the first edition at three or four in the morning.

In the detective work of China-watching my three years in Moscow were of inestimable value, as well as my previous China experience. The Chinese Communists patterned their press on the Soviet, using the same Marxist-Leninist jargon and signaling to the faithful in a way similar to the Russians' when they wanted to ascribe a particular degree of importance to some statement or news report. As in *Pravda*, the Soviet Party organ, the ascending order of importance in *Jen Min Jih Pao* of a statement could be estimated according to whether it was contained in a news article; a commentary, signed "Commentator," denoting a top Party official; or a front-page editorial. The summary of a statement reprinted from the foreign Communist press placed in juxtaposition with the original article often revealed what the Party disapproved of or wanted to emphasize. The repeated omission of a name from lists of guests at a reception or a change in the order of their mention was often the first hint of a purge or a reshuffle in the hierarchy. Since all this was a code meant to be understood by the Party bureaucracy all over the country, the China-watcher who read the signals correctly could detect the first seismic tremors of a political earthquake.

CHAPTER 13

THE CULTURAL REVOLUTION

In February 1966 I reported in a dispatch to the *Times* that the Chinese Communist leadership seemed to be "laboring under a severe strain and there appeared to be an atmosphere of uncertainty in Peking." The last reported official appearance of Mao Tse-tung had been on November 26, 1965. It was not known then that Mao, the Party Chairman, was in Shanghai, planning a counterattack against top Communist leaders of the government and Party, who had been undermining his ideological program.

The opposition to Mao was rooted in the upheaval that stemmed from his radical 1958–59 policies of the Great Leap Forward and the communes. These policies had been an expression of Mao's belief that the masses through "Socialist education" could be spurred ideologically to a "high tide" of endeavor that would overcome any problem of national construction. In the Great Leap Forward, pressing to bring about quickly the industrialization required for the realization of Communism, a gigantic home-factory effort was launched which drafted virtually the entire adult population, on a full- or part-time basis, into industrial production. By October 1958, 600,000 backyard furnaces for the production of iron and steel were reported built. As the people, responding to the exhortations of the Party, plunged into frenetic day and night labor, the steel target was progressively raised from 6.2 million metric tons in February 1958 to 10.7 million in August. Successive quota boosts were also proclaimed in coal, electricity and other key fields. The New China News Agency projected a general industrial production increase for the year of 33 percent. At the same time, an

194

intensive program of collectivization of agriculture was put into effect with the organization of communes.

The poorer peasants who had rallied to the Communists in response to their cry "Land to the tillers!" enjoyed the benefits of land redistribution up until 1952. The Communists then began to put into effect, stage by stage, the organization of cooperatives and state buying of grain that ended individual farming. In the Great Leap Forward the peasant cooperatives were merged by 1959 into 24,000 giant farm units, mobilizing 99 percent of the peasantry. Each commune, pooling land, houses, agricultural implements and farm animals, comprised on the average a unit of about ten thousand acres worked by five thousand households. The commune work force, organized into brigades and component production teams, was intended to reap benefits from a mass approach to production and such land improvement projects as water conservation. There were also some urban communes set up around factories.

At the end of 1958, the regime announced statistics that reflected fantastic production increases. Iron and steel output had doubled, while electricity was up 40 percent and oil by 50 percent. Agricultural production was said to be twice that of 1957. On the surface, Mao had succeeded in putting China, powered by the locomotive of Socialist ideology, on the rails to an earlier attainment of Communism.

However, as the results of the Great Leap Forward were examined more closely, disillusionment set in during 1959.

The population was emotionally and physically spent. In industry, it was found that quality standards had declined sharply. Three million tons of steel produced in 1958 were declared unusable in industry. Many of the backyard furnaces were abandoned. In agriculture, production statistics were scaled down, and it became apparent that serious dislocations had developed because of the forced pace of collectivization. With industrial and agricultural production declining, the Party ordered a retreat. The Second Five-Year Plan was apparently scrapped.

In my subsequent tour of China, I was to hear convincing testimony from local managers and officials to indicate that the "Leap" had resulted in some long-term gains. The plunge into accelerated industrialization and the policy of learning by trial and error initiated worthwhile construction and industrial projects in areas that otherwise might have been bypassed by central planners. Also, the agricultural communes were brought into being sooner. In 1959, however, there was no doubt that the rhythm of production had been seriously disrupted by Mao's overly ambitious "Leap."

The move to repair the damage strengthened the position of the more pragmatic officials, who had become increasingly impatient with the revolutionary romanticism of the aging Mao. Among these opposition officials, whom I shall call pragmatists for want of a more precise description, was Liu Shao-ch'i, sixty-one, a brilliant theoretician and Party organization man who became Chief of State in 1959 after Mao was nudged out the year before, ostensibly to devote himself as the Party Chairman to more theoretical pursuits. Liu, for more than two decades second to Mao in the hierarchy, gradually consolidated his control over the state apparatus and, with the help of Teng Hsiao-p'ing, General Secretary of the Party, over the Party bureaucracy.

Mao was subjected to subtle attacks by the pragmatists, who suggested that he had become senile and that his revolutionary credo was no substitute for the modern statecraft needed to run China. On June 16, 1959, the Party organ, *People's Daily*, published an article entitled "Hai Jui Scolds the Emperor," in which a mandarin of the sixteenth-century Ming court tells Emperor Chia-ching: "For a long time the nation has not been satisfied with you. All officials, in and out of the capital, know that your mind is not right, that you are too arbitrary, that you are perverse. You think that you alone are right. You refuse to accept criticism and your mistakes are many." The article, written under a pseudonym by Wu Han, Deputy Mayor of Peking, was recognized by many as a bold attack on Mao.

Two months later, a frontal assault was made on Mao at a Central Committee meeting in Lushan, by P'eng Te-huai, the Minister of Defense. His supporters, later to be denounced as a "rightist group," complained that the agricultural communes had been set up "too soon and too fast and they had gone wrong." The dissidence at Lushan was also an expression of deep-seated dissatisfaction among the military. Within the revolutionary army, a new professional army corps had arisen. It had become impatient with Mao's political controls on the army and resentful of his ideological split with the Soviet Union, which had choked off the country's only source of modern weapons and know-how in the development of a nuclear-missile arsenal. Mao struck back by firing P'eng Te-huai, and his supporter, Huang K'o-ch'eng, the army Chief of Staff. In place of P'eng Te-huai Mao appointed as Defense Minister Lin Piao, who accepted his "man over weapons" thesis and declared that the Thought of Mao Tse-tung was a "spiritual atom bomb," mightier than the modern weaponry which could be supplied by the Soviet revisionists. In September 1971, when Defense Minister Lin Piao and his close collaborator, Huang Yung-sheng, the Chief of Staff, were to disappear, there were parallels between this apparent new purge and the firing of P'eng Te-huai and Huang K'o-ch'eng.

In 1959 the pragmatists were not yet a closely knit opposition group and Liu Shao-ch'i did not stand up openly for P'eng Te-huai. However, in January 1961 the Wu Han article reappeared in *Peking Literature and Art* in the form of an historical play, *Hai Jui Dismissed from Office*. The play criticized Emperor Chia-ching for having dismissed Hai Jui for telling him unpleasant truths. To the members of the Party, it was plain that the Emperor was Mao Tse-tung and Hai Jui was P'eng Te-huai.

In Hong Kong, there had been intense interest in the Hai Jui works. Many speculated that the article had been an attack on Mao. The emerging struggle manifested itself also in other conflicting statements about economic policy, the role of the cadres (which was the inclusive description of Party and state officials), and "Socialist education." But all this was obscured by the surface adulation of Mao and his ideology. The Mao cult had become so much a part of the Chinese Communist mystique that the latter-day critics of the Party Chairman felt compelled to pay almost as much obeisance publicly as Mao's true supporters.

Mao initiated his historic open attack on his detractors on November 10, 1965, with the publication in the Shanghai newspaper *Wen Hui Pao* of an article denouncing Wu Han as the author of *Hai Jui Dismissed from Office.* The writer was Yao Wen-yuan, a young literary critic who had worked with Mao's wife, Chiang Ch'ing, in her campaign to bend literature and the performing arts to a more radical emphasis on the class struggle. Yao, who was to climb rapidly to membership in the Politburo, had been used by Mao in 1957 to reprimand publicly *Wen Hui Pao* for publishing "bourgeois rightist" criticism of the Party leadership. In his attack on Wu Han, Yao accused the Deputy Mayor of Peking of being a dangerous class enemy who had distorted history. Wu was lumped together in a "Three Village Black Gang" with Teng T'o, secretary of the Peking Municipal Committee and Liao Mo-sha, another senior member of the same committee, the two having also written transparent parodies of Mao. The trio was charged also with seeking to block the program to heighten the class consciousness of the masses and school them in the need for a continuation of class struggle. In this seemingly theoretical debate about an historical play, Mao was laying the groundwork for the massive purge that would engulf Chief of State Liu Shao-ch'i in the Great Proletarian Cultural Revolution.

Liu was in a strong position at this juncture. He controlled the Party organization and much of the government apparatus, and his adherents were in charge of much of the media. Most of the intellectuals, including artists, literary writers, educators and scientists, were weary of the strict Maoist ideological strictures. On his side, Mao had his enormous personal prestige with the bulk of the population, the backing of the army, controlled largely by Defense Minister Lin Piao, his "closest comrade," although the subsequent purge of Lo Jui-ch'ing, the Chief of Staff, suggests that Liu's influence had penetrated there as well. Around Mao were also grouped the Party radicals who feared that China's revolution was decaying and following a "right opportunist" line that would lead to Soviet revisionism and revival of forms of capitalism. The durable Premier, Chou En-lai, one of Mao's closest comrades, also stood with him ready to pick up the reins of government leadership from the oppositionist Chief of State.

The power struggle often tended to blur the issues. In fact, despite the charges of the Maoists, the pragmatists and the Maoists shared a common vision of a Communist society for China. The quarrel was concerned more with methods of getting there and rival personal ambitions. The Maoists, fearing the creation of a new privileged bureaucracy and elite similar to that which had developed in the Soviet Union, summoned the lower-middle-income and poor peasants and workers to mass action to maintain the advance toward a classless society. They insisted on "Politics in command." When the Party bureaucrats, managers and technicians demanded a more orderly development of industry, the Maoists retorted that redness was more important than expertness. The pragmatists wished to utilize material incentives as a spur to production, but the Maoists saw bonuses and other material rewards as corrupting capitalist tendencies and insisted that workers and peasants could be inspired to greater efforts through Socialist education. In the arts, the pragmatists accepted the classics and were tolerant of some deviation from ideological strictures, but the Maoists viewed culture as a tool that should be devoted totally to "Socialist education" of the masses.

In foreign policy, it was more difficult to detect differences. The

Maoists were pressing for an intensification of the polemical ideological attacks on the Soviet Union in the competition for leadership of the international Communist movement. Among the pragmatists, there was evidence of a desire to ease tensions with the Soviet Union, leading perhaps to a renewal of economic and technical cooperation, and a united front in support of the Vietnamese Communists against the United States. Both the pragmatists and the Maoists seemed firmly committed to the concept of world revolution and support of "liberation movements."

As the Maoists arrayed themselves for a showdown battle, Liu made a fatal tactical error. On March 26, 1966, he left Peking on a scheduled state visit to Pakistan and Afghanistan. The Maoists moved in on Liu's power base in Peking.

On May 3 the New China News Agency broadcast an editorial from the army newspaper, *Chiehfang Chün*, calling for vigilance against "anti-Party, anti-Socialist" intellectuals. The substance of the editorial and its terminology convinced me that a major purge had been launched, and I cabled a dispatch saying: "A widespread cultural purge with clearly stated political overtones is under way within the Chinese Communist Party." I also reported that the agency had distributed the text of a speech by Premier Chou En-lai, made April 30 in Peking, in which he stated: "A Socialist cultural revolution of great historic significance is being launched in our country. This is a fierce and protracted struggle as to who will win, the proletariat or bougeoisie, in the ideological field." Calling for the eradication of bourgeois ideology from all fields, the Premier declared: "This is a key question in the development in depth of our Socialist revolution at the present stage, a question concerning the situation as a whole and a matter of the first magnitude affecting the destiny and future of our Party and country." (Chou later recalled that the Cultural Revolution was definitively launched on May 16.)

The next morning, I was stunned to receive a casual message from the New York Foreign Desk saying that my story had been held over for lack of space. In great agitation, I telephoned the editor on duty and told him that my dispatch signaled the onset of momentous events on the mainland. He consulted with Harrison Salisbury, then Assistant Managing Editor and an expert on Communist affairs, who immediately saw the significance of the dispatch, and it was on the front page the next day. Meanwhile, the Maoists closed in on the "Black Gang" trio, members of the Peking Municipal Committee. On May 9 they were publicly denounced. In reporting this event, I speculated that P'eng Chen, Mayor of Peking and a member of the ruling Party Politburo, had been purged. He had not been mentioned in the press since March 29, when he went to Peking Airport for a farewell ceremony for Kenji Miyamato, General Secretary of the Japanese Communist Party. On June 3 the ouster of P'eng Chen was announced, and a purge swiftly followed of key officials of his Municipal Committee, the president of Peking University, Lu P'ing, and the staffs of the central and municipal media in the capital. The Maoists now turned their attention to the rest of the country, where Liu's men still exercised firm control.

In early June, I experienced the frustration, as a China-watcher, of taking my wife to the Kowloon railway station and putting her on the train for Canton while I stayed behind to report on mainland developments. Audrey, a Canadian citizen, had obtained a three-week tourist visa for a tour of seven cities and, as it turned out, with no objections from the Chinese to her working as a writer and photographer for the *New York Times Magazine*. Strangely, it was the Russians who had converted Audrey into a magazine writer and photographer. In London and Berlin she had studied sculpting, and exhibited in the two cities. On arriving in Moscow, she found she had no place to work in our crowded apartment and no chance to get a studio. When a sympathetic Soviet sculptor invited her to use his, the secret police warned him off. In frustration, she became a successful free-lancer for the *Times Magazine* and other publications. Now, draped in cameras, she bade me farewell with a pixy grin and sallied off to China just as the Cultural Revolution was getting under way.

She saw the first evidence of it in Nanking in mid-June when a visit to the university was canceled. The radio announced that K'uang Yaming, the rector, had been purged because of his "ignoble and villainous" conspiracy to "suppress the revolutionary movement" in the university. It was June 16 and the Cultural Revolution was spreading to the provinces. By the end of the month giant processions of young demonstrators with cymbals and gongs sounding and fireworks exploding were parading in Peking before the Central Committee Building shouting "Long Live Mao!" Audrey stood opposite, before the International Club, photographing the turbulence about her. Her Chinese guides had been too frightened to accompany her, and she worked alone, drawing curious stares from the excited demonstrators.

Neither Audrey's tour group, her guides nor the marchers themselves knew precisely what Mao was setting in motion. Within a few
days, the government began canceling visas of tourists, businessmen
and other foreigners. The gates to the country were slammed shut as
the mainland braced for an internal upheaval. Except for diplomats,
businessmen who subsequently were admitted to Canton for the semiannual Trade Fair, and a trickle of other visitors, the mainland was to
remain virtually closed to foreigners for the next four years.

Mao reappeared in Peking on July 18, with the capital now securely
under the control of the Maoists, and the Eleventh Plenum of the
Central Committee was summoned into session on August 1 to give
formal approval to the Cultural Revolution. Liu attended the closed
meeting, at which he was criticized. Isolated, Liu rapidly lost all influence thereafter in the central organs of the Party, although he was not
ousted from all Party and government posts until the Central Committee Plenum of October 1968. Lin Piao was referred to by Mao as "my
closest comrade-in-arms," thus consolidating Lin's position as No. 2 and
next in line of succession. But Mao still was confronted by pragmatic
Party and government cadres all over the country, who were opposed
to his radical ideology, and loyal to Liu and his Party manager, Teng
Hsiao-p'ing, the General Secretary. To smash the cadres or bureaucrats
of the Party government, Mao turned to the youth to carry out the
Cultural Revolution in the provinces. Young "shock forces" formed in
Peking were quickly emulated all over the country. Mao wrote the first
"big-character" wall poster on August 5, "BOMB THE HEADQUARTERS,"
a call for militant demonstrations against his opponents in Peking. Hundreds of thousands of the "big-character" wall posters were to be pla-
carded throughout the country as the Cultural Revolution picked up
momentum. On August 17, at a mass meeting in Peking's T'ien-an-men
Square, Mao received the red arm band of a middle-school group associated with Tsinghua University, which bore the name in gold characters "Hung Wei Ping"—"Red Guard." It was a highly militant group,
which had denounced and humiliated members of the Tsinghua faculty
who had been branded as too moderate in their revolutionary outlook
or influenced by Chinese classical or foreign ideas. Thus Mao designated
the name and shaped the tactics of the diverse youth groups which
were forming in middle or secondary schools and colleges all over the
country. Millions of Red Guards rallied to Mao, about nine million were
received by him in Peking, and all went forth fanatically to do ideologi-

cal battle. A paroxysm of demonstrations, emotion, violence and conflict seized China, as the Red Guards collided with bureaucrats, industrial and farm managers, educators and all others who would not give total precedence to Maoist revolutionary ideology. At the end of August, we left Hong Kong for Bonn briefly and then New York, where I became Foreign Editor in mid-September. Like the rest of the world, I was to watch for the next five years in wonderment as China was convulsed and then, suddenly, tranquil on the surface. When I left New York on May 16, 1971, and flew back to China, I wondered what I would find beneath that appearance of tranquillity. I would soon learn that the Cultural Revolution was not yet ended.

CHAPTER 14

RETURN TO HONG KONG

Takashi Oka, the *Times* correspondent in Tokyo, was waiting for me when my Northwest Airlines jet landed at Haneda Airport at 9 P.M. after the seventeen-hour flight from New York, with a refueling stop in Anchorage, Alaska. I was weary but eager to talk, and we went to the rooftop lounge of the airport hotel, where I was to spend the night, looked out over the enormous Haneda complex and, over drinks, discussed the re-emergence of Japan as a great power. Pentagon officials were prodding the Japanese Government to assume larger defense responsibility in the region as the United States military presence diminished, while China was violently denouncing what it called a revival of Japanese militarism. Oka, an American citizen of Japanese ancestry, was a perceptive, well-informed reporter, and I valued his opinions. I had first come to know him in Hong Kong and Vietnam when he was working for the *Christian Science Monitor,* and later lured him to the *Times* when he was posted in Moscow. Tak expressed doubt that Washington would be able to move Japan into a major military role. "The Japanese have nothing to gain," he said. Japan wanted to continue her rapid economic expansion, which had been made possible by freedom from large military spending. In any case, Japanese public opinion would not stand for it. The Sato Government was under strong pressure to improve relations with China. Since Premier Chou En-lai had inaugurated his Ping-Pong flirtation with Washington a month before, the Tokyo Government had become extremely nervous. Because of United States pressure, and its large economic stake in Taiwan, a Japanese colony for fifty years until the restoration to China after

World War II, the government had maintained diplomatic ties with the Chiang Kai-shek Government at the expense of good relations with Peking.

Oka bid me farewell in the lounge, and I congratulated myself again at having snared him for the *Times* staff, not knowing that the shy man was in the process of being lured back to the *Monitor* for a choice post as roving correspondent based in Paris. The fortunes of war and the foibles of men! In my room, I telephoned for a massage, standard service in Japanese hotels, and a masseuse, a young muscular woman in a white smock weary after pummeling bodies all day, soon appeared and gave me an expert rubdown. I dropped off to five fitful hours of sleep, my brain seething with thoughts of China.

At nine the next morning, I took off for Hong Kong, and at 1 P.M. the Japan Airlines jet was skimming over the whitewashed Chinese tenement slums at the edge of Kai Tak Airport and rolled to a halt in the hot sun before the modern terminal. Ah Sun, the rotund, versatile, Shanghai-born Chinese chauffeur who had served generations of *Times* correspondents in Hong Kong, was waiting, and we moved slowly through the clutter of Kowloon streets to the car ferry that took us across to the Hong Kong side. The Colony was unchanged except in that there was more of everything: apartment houses, although rents had soared to as much as U.S. $1,200 monthly for a good, average flat; office buildings; shops; traffic; and tourists, one million being awaited in the next year. In the neon-splattered nightclubs of Wanchai, the Chinese bar girls had shed their tight cheongsams with short slit skirts for hot pants to delight the sailors of the U.S. Seventh Fleet as they danced to the rock music of the jukeboxes. Apart from some bad months in 1967 when the militancy of the Cultural Revolution spilled over into Hong Kong in serious rioting, the Colony had enjoyed a continuous boom.

I checked into the British-Chinese-owned Mandarin Hotel, a superb oasis, providing the amenities of the West and the luxuries of the East, and telephoned Ian Stewart at the *Times* office. It was Tuesday, May 18, 1971, and if I was to enter China as scheduled on the following Thursday, it was required that I go that afternoon to the office of the China Travel Service, the Chinese Communist Government tourist agency, which makes all arrangements for visits to the mainland. Stewart led me down a crowded shopping street in Kowloon to a building adjacent to a bar. We climbed a narrow flight of stairs and entered a large room, with incongruous banners such as "DEFEAT THE U.S. AGGRESSORS AND

THEIR RUNNING DOGS" nailed above the long business counters. I was introduced to the manager, a polite Chinese who told me with a sigh that his clerical staff was inundated since the advent of Ping-Pongism with visa applications from Americans. He complained about a *Newsweek* article, which he showed me with poorly concealed pride, giving the name and address of his office, as a place to apply. Actually, until Peking agreed to accept American tourists, such visa applications had to go for processing to a Chinese Consulate or Embassy subject to approval by the Foreign Ministry in Peking. The manager knew of my coming and, after inspecting my visa, said he would telephone Canton to make all arrangements. He issued me the usual railway travel voucher which would take me from the border to Canton.

I dined that night with Tillman Durdin, who was now the correspondent in charge of the Hong Kong Bureau. Till and his wife, Peggy, who had been born in China and, like her husband, was a respected writer on Asia, were close friends, the godparents of Susan, our Saigon-born daughter. I first met them in 1947 in Nanking, where we shared a house with Henry Lieberman, now Director of Science and Education News for the *Times*, who had been instrumental in bringing me to the staff of the paper in 1959. The three befriended me and initiated me into the maze of Chinese Nationalist politics. Till, a lean, introspective Texan, now sixty-four, had spent thirty-seven years in Asia, largely in China, knew Chinese Communist officials well before his departure from the mainland in 1948. When John Roderick of the AP and John Rich of NBC were granted the first visas to American newsmen to enter China with the American table tennis team, Till was in Ceylon covering the uprising of young leftists, and it was a week before he picked up his visa, which had been available in Hong Kong. Till spent three weeks in China. His copy won wide praise, but he left China dissatisfied, feeling that his reporting opportunities had been too restricted, since he was compelled to travel with other correspondents on a prearranged itinerary. By the time I arrived in Peking, the Chinese, perhaps sensitive to the criticism, had eased the restrictions.

Durdin drove me out along the winding road dug out of the stony hillsides, to the Repulse Bay Hotel, a large old colonial-style hotel, where we had dinner with Peggy and June Shaplen, the wife of Bob Shaplen, the *New Yorker* correspondent, an old friend from China days, who wrote the classic book on Vietnam, *The Lost Revolution*. As I walked up the stairs to the broad veranda overlooking the bay, where we were to have dinner, I glanced up the dark cliffs to Repulse Bay Towers, to the balcony of our old apartment, and thought of our evenings before we left Hong Kong in 1966, when Audrey and I would watch the sunset, sitting in the wicker swing chairs as Charley, our white cockatoo, would raise his yellow crest and stagger along the flat balcony railing after nibbling the olives in the drained martini glasses. When we looked at the distant hills of China, we always speculated when we would return.

Peggy was her affectionate elegant self, her graying hair swept up and her Chinese jewelry sparkling. With Audrey, she had traveled to Peking to join Till and stayed a week there, but it had not been a particularly happy experience. Peggy, who speaks colloquial Chinese, complained that ordinary Chinese had been afraid to talk to her. I remembered in the old China how she loved to gossip and laugh with the Chinese. "Only once, in a park, when I said hello to a child who was with an army officer," she said, telling of her trip to Peking, "did someone speak to me."

As Till drove me back to the Mandarin, I thought of the old days in China and the many foreigners who had dwelt there so happily. We had lived in China so exquisitely, savoring the luxury of superb servants and marvelous food. How lovely were the old houses in Peking with their cobbled courtyards and oval moon gates! There was the excitement, too, of being privy, as were most of the privileged foreigners, to the Chinese political intrigue and witness to the unending spectacle. There would be no going back to that kind of life, even for those old China hands who joked and drank ganbei, bottoms up, with the Communist leaders in Yenan. For some, the gates were barred. I counted myself fortunate to have dipped into the old life before revolution washed over China. Yet I was lucky, too, not to have enjoyed it so long as to have become burdened with unbearable nostalgia.

The next morning, Till and I called in at the consulate for a background briefing, which I had requested with Robert W. Drexler, the Chief of the Political Section. Drexler had not lived in China as so many American China specialists had, nor served in the Soviet Union, but he was well informed and obviously a perceptive political observer. It was not apparent to me then, as it was some six weeks later, when I talked again to Drexler, as well as to his chief, the Consul General David L. Osborn, how wide of the mark China-watchers, including myself, could be. On my return, I would realize that the China-watchers, apart from being late in appreciating developments in Peking, lacked a feel of the country and the people essential to precise political and economic analysis. No matter how much information would be fed into computers or documents read, there could be no substitute for direct contacts and observation. I was to change some of my own assumptions made as a China-watcher and become even more convinced that United States diplomatic exchanges with Peking were indispensable if for no other reason than their importance in formulating a rational policy toward China.

During the day, the China Travel Service manager had telephoned to say I was awaited in Canton, and Thursday morning, carrying a typewriter and dispatch case, I left the Mandarin followed by a porter handling my large suitcase. The station of the Canton-Kowloon Railway, the only link between the Colony and the mainland, is situated in Kowloon near the quay. The simplest way to get there is to take the ten-minute ride on the Star Ferry across Victoria Harbor. The Mandarin doorman, a towering Sikh wearing a white turban and a red uniform with gold epaulets, summoned one of the cluster of waiting street baggage carriers to haul my suitcase the short distance to the foot ferry and across to Kowloon. "Coolie," he said to the ragged Chinese, "take the master's bag to the ferry." The porter put the heavy bag on his shoulder, and I followed him to the ferry and then to the China Travel office in the railway station, where he put the suitcase down and waited for me to pay him. The China Travel clerk, in a tiny office decorated with a portrait of Mao, greeted me and said: "My colleague will take your bag." A China Travel porter, dressed in a neat blue uniform, took the suitcase from the man called "coolie" by the Mandarin doorman. As they stood there side by side, I saw in them the contrast between the new and the old order.

Boarding the British train for the border, in a coach cooled by overhead fans, I found my travel companions, a group of foreigners bound for Peking. Two of them, Derek March and Gordon Barrass, were diplomats returning from leave to what was officially designated the British Office, so called because the mission had not been raised to embassy status despite the establishment of diplomatic relations between Britain and China in 1954. The Chinese, complaining about British policies, particularly London's insistence on retaining a consulate on Taiwan, had declined to exchange ambassadors, leaving the office in Peking under a chargé d'affaires. It was not until March 1972 that the office was raised to embassy status after Britain closed its consulate on Taiwan and acknowledged that the island was a province of China. March, a lively, alert man, was commercial secretary. Barrass, a pleasant young Englishman who had learned Chinese in Hong Kong, was a political officer. He was accompanied by his American-born wife, Alice. The others were an Indian diplomatic courier accompanying the schoolboy son of the Indian Chargé d'Affaires, B. C. Mishra, who was joining his parents during his summer vacation, and a woman clerk of the Canadian Embassy. The British diplomats were in shirt sleeves, and Alice wore slacks. Dress for everyone in China, including foreigners, is casual, and soon I doffed my coat and tie.

I spent most of my time during the hour-long trip through the New Territories to the border talking to Gordon and Alice Barrass, who were in good spirits after their semiannual leave in Hong Kong. Since the Cultural Revolution the Chinese had allowed diplomats little travel within the country, restricting them largely to Peking and its environs. To make the confining life more bearable, most diplomatic missions sent their staffs out of the country to Hong Kong or other cities periodically. Of late, the Chinese had been relaxing restrictions, but Peking still was not considered a fun post.

Chatting about their life in Peking during the past year, Alice, an attractive, auburn-haired woman with a dry wit, laconically said, "Women can always take French-language lessons in Peking. Most of them find life pretty boring. At parties, the men bunch up to exchange information about China and there is little other talk." In the United States, Alice had worked for the Federal Reserve Bank and later in London for the *Economist* magazine. As the wife of a diplomat, she could not work as a journalist for her old employer, but she obviously enjoyed the China-watching game.

The train jolted to a halt at the border station of Lo Wu. A platoon of porters came aboard to get our baggage, and we were led into a shed to clear British customs. A narrow railway bridge over a thin, muddy, desultory river separated Lo Wu from Shum Chun, the station on the Chinese side. Atop the bare hills about us, British observation posts faced out on China. The British Union Jack hung limply in the humid air matched on the other side by the red flag with yellow stars of the People's Republic of China. Local peasants carrying vegetables and live chickens in straw cages and other farm products at the ends of poles across their shoulders seemed to be passing back and forth over the bridge without more than an exchange of nods with the guards. Then a China Travel Service guide gathered up the foreigners. Our baggage was placed on a trundle. Single file, we were led over the planks of the bridge, past three impassive soldiers in baggy olive-drab uniforms, red tabs on their collars and wearing caps with the red star insignia, who stood athwart the center of the bridge. They were men of the People's Liberation Army (PLA). We were in China.

CHAPTER 15

SHUM CHUN

Just beyond the bridge, there were open-sided sheds where, at wooden tables, soldiers of the PLA's Public Security Force were interrogating Chinese travelers. Soldiers in columns of two, with cartridge belts, holstered pistols affixed, marched from one installation to another, and to the nearby village of Shum Chun, a huddle of small white houses. The Public Security guards at the bridge had been armed with submachine guns, rifles and pistols of Soviet design but made in China. Apart from these frontier guards and those at the entrances to army compounds or sentries at public buildings in various cities, the thousands of PLA men I was to see in China went unarmed. My request to visit a PLA unit was ignored, and I never saw an armed column in the thousands of miles I was to travel by car, train and plane. PLA combat divisions are concentrated at strategic points facing the frontiers of the Soviet Union and Southeast Asia, and in the coastal provinces opposite Taiwan. The army garrisons in or near the cities make no demonstrative show of force. If the municipal street police carry pistols, they are concealed beneath their tunics. Force in China is implied and is not used unless persuasion fails.

We were escorted into a long, two-story customs building, up the stairs to a small waiting room, where we filled out customs declarations and were called in turn for baggage inspection. A stocky, round-faced woman, in the green uniform of the customs, examined the contents of my baggage and the currency in my billfold. Her eyes widened when she saw some four hundred rolls of raw film, which I had declared, explaining that I was taking it to my photographer wife. She waved my baggage through, but before I left the building came to me and said, "As for your film, my comrade superior has made a special exception, and it is passed."

I had brought in more than a thousand American dollars, in five hundred Hong Kong dollar notes and American Express traveler's checks. The Chinese were beginning to accept American currency and traveler's checks, but reluctantly and only at some exchange offices. They preferred to deal in Hong Kong dollars, which were six to one American dollar. Thinking I would get all the money-changing over at once, I surrendered all my Hong Kong currency to the two cashiers at the exchange cubicle in the customs building. To my dismay, the cashiers handed me an enormous stack of bills. This was how I discovered that the largest bill in Chinese currency is a ten-yuan note. The yuan was exchanged at about 2.4 to the American dollar. The cashiers, smiling, allowed me to retrieve most of my five hundred Hong Kong dollar notes, which subsequently I had no difficulty exchanging quickly in hotels and airports. Chinese currency, incidentally, has remained stable. Officials tell you with pride that China has no internal or external government debt.

After clearing customs, our party was taken into a private waiting room furnished with square, heavy chairs, sofas covered with white cotton lace antimacassars and round traditional Chinese tables. Jasmine tea was served, and we waited for lunch before boarding the train for the long afternoon ride to Canton.

Derek, quite excited, noticed that a scroll landscape painting had replaced a propaganda banner on the wall above one of the sofas, which he had seen two months earlier on his way to Hong Kong. In China, the foreigner gets his first clues of a shift in the regime's policies from tiny changes in the order of things, and so the party proceeded to analyze the implications of Derek's discovery.

Alice pronounced the scroll to be a copy of a painting of Hsu Pei-hung, who had died in the 1950s and had been a contemporary of Ch'i Pai-shih, the most famous of the moderns. Only a few months ago, copies of works done prior to 1965 had begun to reappear in the shops. Classics had been banned in 1966 at the start of the Cultural Revolution as part of the campaign against all manifestations of old bourgeois thinking. Only Socialist realism, poster-type art, emphasizing the themes of Maoist ideology, depicting heroic embattled figures of peasants, workers and soldiers, was allowed public display or sale. The art galleries and museums were still closed. Now presaging a slight thaw in the arts, reproductions of the classic paintings and copies of old stone rubbings had been seen in a few shops in Canton, Shanghai, Peking and Tientsin. In Friendship Shops, which were reserved for foreigners to facilitate foreign exchange earnings, some antique originals were being sold at very stiff prices. The Communists were carefully husbanding their artistic treasures after decades during which a steady stream of antiques had gone to embellish the museums and homes of the well-to-do all over the world. They still hoped to regain the vast priceless trove of art which the Chinese Nationalists had carried off to Taiwan during their retreat from the mainland in 1949 and was now exhibited in a museum in Taipei or stored in underground shelters. Alice said the last Ch'i Pai-shih to be sold by the Communists went in January 1970. Abroad the Chinese were offering to dealers reproductions of paintings, figurines and furniture with only a small sweetening of genuine antiques in each order. The contradiction between the restrictive policy of displaying classical art and the state's concern for its preservation suggested that the people would someday, perhaps soon, be allowed to enjoy fully their cultural heritage once the Party was convinced that ideologically they were committed to the Maoist future rather than to the glories of the past.

Barrass remarked that he had noted during the past several months less propaganda adulation of Mao and his works, and fewer banners in English denouncing the United States, although the Chinese versions often remained in place. This surprised me because I had already found the force and repetitiveness of the propaganda to be staggering. Shum Chun and the surrounding area was bedecked with posters and banners proclaiming Mao quotations, every wall seemed to bear his portrait, and every Chinese in sight wore a large button displaying the Chairman's countenance. On the station platforms, the clenched fists of revolutionaries importuned the innocent traveler, and I ran headlong into a large billboard which shouted in Chinese and English above Mao's signature: "PEOPLE OF THE WORLD, UNITE AND DEFEAT THE U.S. AGGRESSORS AND ALL THEIR RUNNING DOGS!" This exhortation, issued by Mao on May 20, 1970, as a call for a united front against the United States, particularly in support of the Indochinese Communists, is the most frequently seen anti-American slogan. I soon discovered, however, that the Chinese tended to concentrate their propaganda on international themes in places where it would be seen by foreigners, specifically at airports, railway stations and hotels used by visitors, and especially in the more international cities of Canton and Peking. Away from the transit points, and in other cities and the countryside, the propaganda slogans grew more sparse and were more concerned with production and domestic ideological problems.

The corridors of the customs building were reverberating with the strident heroic music of the Communist Party, blaring from loudspeakers. I now heard for the first of many times, in public buildings, on trains, planes and in airports, and from loudspeakers on city squares, the strains of "Sailing the Seas Depends on the Helmsman," the helmsman being Mao.

> You cannot sail the seas
> Without a helmsman.
> You cannot make a revolution
> Without the thought of Mao Tse-tung.

I stepped into the corridor from our waiting room and found the men's room, inscribed in Chinese and with the English legend "Gents," and on my return noticed that in the opposite waiting room a Japanese delegation was being given a lecture by a Chinese. Already they were wearing Mao buttons. The revolutionary songs were being piped into the waiting rooms along the corridor, but in my own, where my companions were dozing after an excellent Chinese lunch, someone had found the switch to turn off the music.

Gratefully, in the early afternoon, we clambered aboard the Chinese train, air-conditioned and cleaner than the British train, a comparison that the Chinese no doubt were intent on making. The brilliant foliage of the flamboyant trees and bougainvillaea in the vicinity of the Shum Chun station slipped away, a young Chinese train stewardess welcomed us with smiles and mugs of green tea, and soon we were looking at the magnificent green hues of terraced rice fields. It was lusher country than the New Territories, but the farmers in their huge straw hats, maneuvering their plows behind water buffaloes through the flooded paddies, did not seem much different. An occasional red banner fluttered in the fields, catching the eye. I stared out the train window during most of the eighty-mile trip, increasingly conscious that at last I was back in China, once saying softly to myself, "China, China," and after two hours the train pulled into the bustling, clanging station in the eastern district of Canton.

CHAPTER 16

CANTON

On the broad concrete station platform, we were met by a plethora of guides from the omnipresent China Travel Service. My fellow was Chu Ha-chu, a slightly built man who spoke passable English. I did not find many good English-speakers in China, which surprised me since the language superseded Russian as the principal foreign language taught in schools after the open ideological split with Moscow in 1960. One of the problems found by the Chinese in caring for a large influx of foreigners was the provision of interpreter-guides, since apparently the excellent Foreign Languages Institute in Peking could not turn out qualified graduates fast enough to meet the demand. Chu was somewhat stiff in manner, but warmed up considerably before the end of my visit when he learned that I was considered an "old friend of China," not simply a monopoly-capitalist American journalist.

There was a porter who placed my bags on a trundle, and after taking my passport Chu led me into the large station. Every foreigner traveling within China must carry in his passport an internal visa specifying his itinerary. The visa is usually issued by the Foreign Affairs Bureau of the municipality and is obtained through China Travel. It is inspected by officials upon your arrival and departure from railway stations, airports and at highway checkpoints when you travel by car. The system enables the authorities to trace the movements of foreigners and locate them easily since they transit through specially designated hotels staffed by China Travel. There are other arrangements for Chinese citizens, who are also required to obtain permits if they wish to travel. After showing my passport at the checkpoint, Chu led me to a car chauffeured by another China Travel man. The porter was paid for his service the fixed fee of a few cents, and he handed me a chit for the payment. The chit system is ubiquitous in China, requiring you to collect bits of paper, either printed or written out, for the smallest purchase or payment to taxi drivers or other service workers. There is no tipping in China, and unlike the Soviet Union where the regulations barring tipping are winked at, Chinese are puzzled and affronted if extra payment is offered. Our car was a British Austin-Healey, an immaculately kept sedan probably manufactured in the mid-sixties. The Chinese produce trucks, but only a relatively small number of passenger cars, which like the few imported are reserved for essential official use. The cars are maintained painstakingly and overhauled at special refitting plants.

Driving to the hotel, the Tung Fang in the northern district of Canton, was a jolt to my memories of the city as it had been during the civil war in the late forties. Then the avenues and streets had been jammed with traffic, a clutter of American-made military trucks and jeeps of the Chinese Nationalist Army, the black- and khaki-colored Fords and Chevrolets of the American diplomats and military advisory groups, the luxury cars of the foreign businessmen, Chinese officials and millionaires, swarming rickshas pulled by trotting coolies, and the peasant carts loaded with farm produce hauled by scrubby-looking horses. The din had always been overpowering, honking horns threatening pedestrians and ricksha men, and shouted curses exchanged among drivers and the helpless traffic gendarmes. Now there were only a few cars and trucks on the streets, honking as always, but threading quickly through a great procession of bicyclists. Apart from those using buses, some diesel-engined and others powered by overhead electric lines, just about everyone seemed to be pedaling bicycles. The rickshas were gone, but there were still the pedicabs, similar conveyances pulled by a driver on a bicycle instead of a running man. The traffic moved smoothly and relatively quietly, easily controlled by police, dressed in green tunics and blue pants. Several times we passed teen-age youngsters, wearing red arm bands, assisting in traffic control and at pedestrian crossings.

The Tung Fang Hotel was a cavernous building in the square ponderous style of Soviet architecture, leavened only by the luxuriant gardens and parkland at the sides and rear. The dark lobbies on the ground floor were given over to reception desks, an ornate sitting room, shops, a cable and post office, and, over an arched passageway, an enormous restaurant. In the restaurant, a scattering of foreigners patiently waited to be served by waiters, whom they addressed as "T'ung Chih," or "Comrade," not crying "Boy!" as in the old days. The second floor was also given over to service offices; then five vast floors of rooms, and on the eighth floor a large dining room and reception chambers. In the Soviet manner, each floor had its desk with attendants who ministered to the needs of the guests. The rooms, each with bath and telephone, were stark but adequate. With a good connection, a telephone call could be put through to Hong Kong fairly quickly. The hotel had been built with the advice, dubious in quality, of the Russians after 1949. Among the portraits of Mao and the red banners inscribed with political slogans in the lobby was a large portrait of Stalin, a sight familiar in the Sovet Union before Nikita Khrushchev, a revisionist scoundrel in the Chinese political lexicon, instituted destalinization there and the countless likenesses of the Soviet dictator had come down. There were similarities between the Stalin cult and the adoration in China of Mao, and in my notebook I wrote: "How long will the Mao cult last after the death of the 77-year-old Great Helmsman?"

The month-long spring session of the Canton Trade Fair had just ended, and the some three thousand foreign businessmen who attended had decamped for home until October, when the fall buying and selling spurt would take place. Many of them had stayed in the hotel, which was now strangely still and nearly empty.

I threw my baggage into the room, and declining Chu's suggestion —oft expressed by Travel Service guides with the words "Please take a rest"—insisted on sortieing out into the city. We drove south from the hotel down Liberation Avenue, which divides the eastern and western districts, toward the International Trade Fair complex, centered around the huge exhibition hall, now overshadowed by the new adjacent twenty-seven-story Canton Hotel, the tallest building in the city. Only a few hundred yards away were the quays of the Pearl River, which flows through the city. Downtown Canton snuggles into a bend on the northern bank of the river, while the main industrial districts lie beyond the southern bank. Canton, whose Chinese name is Kwangchow, was always a raucous, violent, unbeautiful city of political intrigue and passion, which historians call the cradle of the Chinese Revolution. Sun Yat-sen, the father of the Revolution, which had its origins in the revolt against the Manchu Dynasty in 1911, organized the

Kuomintang in Canton, which also embraced the Communists for a time. One of his disciples was a young general named Chiang Kai-shek, whom he made Superintendent of Whampoa Military Academy outside of Canton. A young Communist, Chou En-lai, was deputy chief of Whampoa's Political Education Department. One of the students of the fourth class at Whampoa was Lin Piao. In 1926 when Chiang launched his Northern Expedition against the warlords to unify China, a young Communist, Mao Tse-tung, was leading the Peasant Movement Training Institute. In 1927 the Communists tried to seize power in Canton but were virtually wiped out by the Nationalists.

We drove by the Peasant Institute, now a Maoist shrine, past the memorials to Sun Yat-sen, but there was no mention of Chiang Kai-shek. Our car crossed the Pearl River over the Haichu Bridge, rebuilt in 1952, and I remembered reporting on October 14, 1949, that the withdrawing Nationalist troops had blown it up. The demolition charges had sent steel splinters flying underneath into the closely packed sampans and junks of fishermen and haulers of goods who lived along the southern bank, killing and maiming many of the boat people. The sampans were gone now, and Chu told me proudly the boat people had been moved into apartment houses not far from the river bank. Some of them still worked on the water, but they joined the fishing junks farther downriver.

The Cantonese are a deft, intelligent people, but also acquisitive and aggressive, and it seemed to me that whenever there was upheaval in China, its manifestations in Canton were more violent. Perhaps the impression arose from Canton's proximity to Hong Kong so that the sounds of conflict were heard more clearly than from other parts of China, or because of the vivid tales of refugees who each month slipped by the hundreds or thousands into the British Colony. I remembered the stories from Canton during the 1951 nationwide purge of "counterrevolutionaries." One day, a trial of twenty-three "sample counterrevolutionaries" was broadcast by Canton Radio. "This is a time of an eye for an eye, a tooth for a tooth," Huang Yeh-ping, chief of the military tribunal, told ten thousand spectators gathered before the Dr. Sun Yat-sen Memorial Hall. "Spit on them, bite them, beat them!" one voice shouted into the microphone. Then the crowd passed judgment: "Kai Sha! Kai Sha!"—"They should be killed!" The twenty-three, including Yao Pao-hsien, former Director of Education in the Canton Municipal Government, were paraded through the streets and at the Liu Hua

Chiao (Floating Blossom Bridge) were made to kneel and then shot in the backs of their heads.

We drove along the south bank, over the graceful arched People's Bridge to the northern bank and then on to Shameen Island, a famous spit of land, about a half-mile long and four hundred yards wide, separated from the north bank by a narrow canal. This was once the French and British concession, where until the 1930s Chinese could not enter without foreign permission. Until shortly before the fall of the city to the Communists, Shameen was the enclave of the British, French and American consulates. The diplomatic community had been enlarged by embassy missions, including those of the United States and the Soviet Union, which followed the Nationalist Government to Canton in February 1949 as Mao's armies closed on Nanking. Then, carefully tended flower beds ran the length of the island, flanked by stone walks lined with great spreading banyan trees under which Chinese amahs pushing high-wheeled baby prams paused to gossip. Behind the banyan trees there were rows of palatial residences of diplomats, foreign oil and trading merchants and wealthy Chinese. On the broad shaded verandas, Chinese servants in immaculate white jackets over black pants served gin and tonic to masters in crisp seersucker and whites, who chatted easily about the turbulence, corruption and incredible misery that engulfed the city beyond the canal.

I left the car parked at the eastern end of the island and began to walk, with Chu silently trailing after me. The great houses were now scrubby living quarters for Chinese worker families, and laundry hung from the windows across the yards. Some of the former diplomatic buildings had become Chinese offices, but what had been the American Consulate was barred and empty. The gates of Anglican and Catholic churches were shut. The fences sagged around the tennis courts, and youngsters in blue tunics played volleyball on the clay courts. Chinese residents lounged on the benches along the walk fronting the harbor and looked at me curiously but with not unfriendly eyes. The foreigners were gone from Shameen. Looking back on the colonial past, beginning when the British and French first surveyed what was a mud flat in the mid-nineteenth century, it was hard to find cause to shed tears that Shameen was Chinese once again. The only foreign consulates in Canton or Shanghai now are those of North Vietnam and Poland, whose merchantmen carry much of the trade between Eastern Europe and China. The Communists have dredged Canton's Whampoa Harbor so that ships up to ten thousand tons can reach the river port from the South China Sea.

Impatient to walk the streets of the city, I left the car parked on Shameen and strode across the eastern bridge to Liu Er San Lu. Dusk crept over the city as I walked among the people hurrying home from work or shopping, and I looked eagerly at the faces and dress of the men and women of the new China.

In dress there was a disappointing dull sameness: white, blue or gray shirts or blouses worn over unpressed blue trousers, and sandals or rubber-soled shoes with blue canvas tops resembling tennis sneakers. The women wore their hair short or in braids and no makeup. Yet what struck me immediately, as it was to strike me throughout my travels in China, was the obvious good health and fit condition of the people. Gone were the emaciated faces, the trachoma-laden eyes, the facial sores which had once horrified me. The younger people flashed smiles which showed good white teeth instead of gaps and blackened stumps. Not only had a political revolution taken place, but over the past two decades a revolution in health had made the Chinese sturdier and bigger in stature. Life on the sidewalks was no longer a jumble of shoving, gesticulating, arguing, laughing Chinese women carrying fat snotty babies on their backs as they haggled with peddlers. The people were more passive, self-contained and dignified. At rush hour they pressed into the blue buses firmly but in good order.

Fascinated by this spectacle of the new Maoist man, I went through the Nanfang Department Store and hurried up the street to the Aich'ün (Love the Masses) Hotel, where I had stayed during a visit in February 1949 shortly after Premier Sun Fo had flown in from Nanking. The hotel, which was then the Oikwan, is a fourteen-story structure, the tallest building in the city before the erection of the Canton Hotel, and stands on the river front or the Bund, as the foreigners called the quayside. The Aich'ün, a narrow triangular structure resembling some-what the former *New York Times* Building in Times Square, was the city's best hotel, and in 1949 it was packed with rich Chinese fleeing before the advancing Communist armies, foreigners who had left their businesses, missionaries who had evacuated their churches and di-plomats following a disintegrating government. At the bar, officers of the U.S. Military Assistance Advisory Group, which had finally folded in despair, who were waiting to go home, told tales of corrupt National-ist generals who would not take advice, and paid astronomical prices for martinis in wads of Nationalist currency. The government's "gold yuan" was then selling at more than a thousand to the American dollar and dropping value almost hourly. On the tenth floor, young American diplomats talked bitterly about the hypocrisy and hopelessness of supporting Chiang Kai-shek. On the sixth lived Russian diplomats who had trailed after Premier Sun Fo for protocol reasons, now celebrated his misfortunes, and waited to go to Peking as soon as the Communists formally established their government there. They decamped for Peking in October.

I walked past the big foreign-style buildings on the Bund which had once housed the great British and French banks and trading houses, and were now Chinese offices. With a start, I realized that the swarms of beggars had disappeared and that the wasted opium addicts, who had once sat propped against the walls or in the doorways of the dirty-white, jerry-built Chinese structures in the shadow of the banks, were also gone. Not much new construction was in evidence, but the buildings were in good repair. The streets and sidewalks were swept clean. I remembered one night coming out of the hotel late to file a dispatch, and finding under the yellow street lights enormous rats feeding on the garbage scattered in the gutters. I retreated, wondering how the ricksha men and the beggars, wrapped in rags and sacking against the February cold and damp, could sleep in the doorways without fear of the prowling rats.

Since 1949 Canton's population had grown from an estimated 1.5 million to about three million, but the press of people and traffic in downtown Canton did not seem as great as before. Most of the housing construction and industrial expansion had been in the suburbs. Chu, weary of pursuing me and longing for his evening meal, led me back to the Nanfang Department Store building, where our car with its China Travel chauffeur waited for us.

Chu gratefully said goodbye at the Tung Fang and said he would be back early in the morning to take me to the Trade Fair exhibition hall, which was being especially reopened for my inspection. I returned to my room, quickly wrote a dispatch which I filed from the cable desk in the lobby, and declined an invitation from the Barrass' to dine in a restaurant in the city. Then, intent on seeing Canton by night, I went out onto Liberation Avenue, hailed a pedicab and soon was merrily wheeling back downtown. My objective was T'ai P'ing Lu, recalled as a neon-splashed avenue, lined with four- or five-story buildings with arcades that sheltered bars with jukeboxes playing "Rum Boogie," steaming restaurants and shops cluttered with junk goods from all the world.

I clambered out of the pedicab at the foot of T'ai P'ing Lu, suddenly disappointed at how dark and drab the city looked. The neon advertising signs no longer blinked on behalf of beer and stylish gents' suits along the river front. I walked up T'ai P'ing Lu and missed the clack-clack of the mah-jongg tiles of the gambling-addicted Cantonese which used to sound from the upper stories of the white-plastered buildings. Gambling is forbidden in the People's Republic. The bars and the taxi dancers had vanished. Gone also were the brothels where round-faced girls with flashing eyes and chattering, birdlike voices insisted to rough seamen on the civility of sipping tea ceremoniously before sex was dispensed. Glancing into a restaurant, where the round tables were covered with small spicy-looking dishes and tall bottles of local beer, I was reassured by the unrestrained laughter and shouted conviviality that the Cantonese zest for sensual pleasure was still there.

The department stores and other regular shops had closed at 9 P.M., and people were shopping at tiny open-front cubicles tucked into shacklike or two-story buildings, for tobacco wares, fruits, rice and vegetables. I stopped at one such cubicle where an old man, whiskers at his chin and an apron tucked around him, presided, with the help of a shaven-headed grandson, over tubs of prepared rice, noodles, shrimp and steaming soups. His dark leathery features crinkled into a grin that showed a silver tooth when I asked for noodle soup and, bowl lifted to my chin, scooped in the delicious contents with wooden chopsticks. He nodded politely and looked at me with unabashed curiosity when I told him in my fragmentary Peking Mandarin that I was an American journalist. Cantonese is another language, but Mandarin had been taught for many years in all the schools, and is understood by most people in the big cities.

"Americans have not been here for many years," he said, as his grandson's eyes became round and his other customers crowded closer to scrutinize this foreign creature. Because of the semiannual influx of foreigners for the Trade Fair, the Cantonese have become fairly blasé about their presence—but an American!

"Are things good or bad now?" I asked the old man.

"Very good now. But several years ago we shopkeepers suffered very much." And he shook his head and turned to ladle rice into a customer's pot.

I understood his complaint. Most of the cubicle shops were businesses owned by the men who tended them in cooperation with the state supply enterprises. They were tolerated as useful, temporary evils in an economy otherwise almost entirely state-owned. These private traders were not permitted to hire help and therefore their shops were family run. Prices were fixed as in the state shops and supplies purchased from the state, which shared in the profits. In 1966 these petty merchants as well as other sections of the population became the targets of the Red Guards.

When nearly one million students marched on August 18, 1966, in Peking's T'ien-an-men Square, and saw Mao accept an arm band of the Tsinghua Red Guards, they also heard a call to action that would inflame the youth of the country. Until that day, the youth, stirred by Maoist rhetoric urging them to make revolution, had been busy holding demonstrations, putting up wall posters and denouncing the bourgeois "monsters and ghosts" who had infiltrated into important Party posts and were betraying the Great Leader's ideology. But there was a vagueness about the action program; the top shadowy opposition Party figures had not yet been named. Liu Shao-ch'i still shared the rostrum in T'ien-an-men Square with Mao, although he had been secretly criticized within high Party councils. It was not until the end of the year that Liu was to be castigated by the students as "China's Khrushchev," and not until April 1967 that he was finally purged and placed under house arrest. However, at the August 18 rally Lin Piao gave the impatient students immediate targets when he instructed them to sweep away the "Four Olds"—old things, old ideas, old customs and old habits— which do not conform to Socialist society. Within a matter of days squads of Red Guards roamed the cities destroying what they thought were vestiges of the old culture, bourgeois or foreign. In Canton the privately owned little shops and stands were closed or smashed and denounced as anti-Socialist. Buddhist temples and Christian churches were closed and defaced, prerevolutionary historical monuments were smashed, the homes of Black Elements—former landlords or other so-called bourgeois families—were sacked. Overseas Chinese were stripped on the streets of foreign-made clothing and humiliated.

In Peking, as in other cities, on the college campuses faculty members were paraded with dunce caps, women with long hair were shaved. In Shanghai the apartments of elderly couples were broken into, their precious antiques hauled into the streets and burned. Suicides of the elderly became common.

This violent, destructive fever, surface manifestations of professed revolutionary ideology and an underlying power struggle, tortured China, subsiding and then raging again for the next two years. Before the end of 1966 millions of Red Guards had toured the country, invited by Mao to Peking, shouting slogans and "exchanging revolutionary experiences," and some nine million paraded before him in T'ien-an-men Square. By early 1967 the Red Guards had paralyzed the Communist Party apparatus by detaining the opposition bureaucrats or occupying their offices, and the army gradually took over administration of the provinces, laying the groundwork for a new form of Maoist revolutionary control. The army protected vital factories and utilities as rival coalitions of students, workers and cadres or officials, all waving the red Maoist flag, became locked in violent combat.

Canton, following its tradition of being at the center of revolutionary upheaval, was a focal point for this internecine collision among the Maoist factions. In early 1967 two broad rival coalitions had formed, the radical Red Flag and the relatively conservative East Wind. Fighting with iron bars, staves and arms looted from army arsenals, the factions engaged in pitched battles, with thousands wounded or killed. Rail traffic and city services were disrupted, while theft and other crimes flourished. The radicals, encouraged by leftist Maoist leaders in Peking, who felt the Red Flag faction was pressing the struggle more militantly, nevertheless encountered resistance from the Canton Military Command. Emboldened by backing in Peking, the radicals repeatedly raided installations of the Canton garrison. Finally, in August, as clashes between the army and radical revolutionaries spread in Canton and elsewhere in the country, Mao, touring five affected provinces, authorized a military clampdown, and the army gradually brought about order, although sporadic outbreaks continued into 1968.

In Peking I was to get a better appreciation of the extent to which the Red Guards had performed as puppets responding to strings pulled in the capital by the contending personalities that surrounded Mao. A purge of leftists blamed for many of the excesses was still in progress when I arrived in the capital at the end of May 1971.

It was well after midnight when I left T'ai P'ing Lu. The lights from the cubicle shops still shone brightly into the darkness. They remained open to serve workers on late shifts and the peasants whose horse-drawn carts were rattling in the empty streets as they brought farm produce into the city to feed its masses. As a pedicab man pedaled me back to the hotel, I realized that Canton had become a truly Chinese city. The neon lights and other glitter, the foreign cars, the bars and taxi dancers wearing crimson American lipstick, which had so titillated me and the other foreigners, had been part of the China coast colonial trading past. Canton and the other great coastal industrial cities, such as Shanghai and Tientsin, have discarded their foreign ornaments, emptied their shops of imported trinkets, and taken on the character of China, integrating closely for the first time with the economy of the country as a whole.

Chu picked me up at the hotel the next morning, and we drove to the Trade Fair complex, which had just enjoyed its biggest influx of traders and sightseers. During the session, the twenty-ninth, about 16,-000 traders and sightseers from 95 countries had toured the exhibition center, housed in a nine-story structure with enormous halls, and a smaller five-story building. The biggest contingent of businessmen had come from Japan, 1,500, about 400 more than last year; about 100 Australians; a similar number of Britons; some 80 traders from Canada, whose business with China was expanding quickly after the establishment of diplomatic ties; and many from West Germany, Sweden, Switzerland, Italy and other European countries. The largest contingent of traders, as always, were overseas Chinese from Hong Kong, the nearby Portuguese colony of Macao and the Southeast Asian countries. Although many of these businessmen came from countries which have no diplomatic relations with Peking, but do a thriving business nevertheless, there were no Americans. Since President Truman had imposed an embargo on trade with China at the time of the Korean War, American businessmen had been barred from the country. Later, in Peking, I asked Chou En-lai, in view of the admission of American newsmen and the termination of trade restrictions on the export of nonstrategic goods and the abolition of the ban on imports by President Nixon, whether American businessmen would soon be admitted to the Fair. He replied: "If American businessmen make a request to visit the Fair, which meets twice a year, the Chinese Government will be willing to consider this matter." In Chinese parlance, the nature of his reply was encouraging. American businessmen were admitted to the spring 1972 Fair.

Trade with China has always been entangled with political and ideological considerations. In 1842 British warships blasted open Canton to trade after the Ch'ing Emperor had closed it in retaliation for the opium traffic carried on largely by the British. Jardine, Matheson & Company, the East India Company and the British Government itself, with some help from American traders, had sold the Chinese enough opium by 1838 that it was said that nine out of every ten inhabitants of Kwangtung Province, of which Canton is the capital, were addicted. When the Emperor was compelled to yield in the Opium War, he agreed to the restoration of trade but sought to restrict foreigners to some areas of Canton.

After the Chinese Communists conquered the mainland in 1950, they showed no great interest in foreign trade as they went about consolidating their hold on the country. In 1957, when Peking was ready to pursue trade vigorously, the Canton Trade Fair was founded. Again, as in the Ch'ing days, demonstrating that the Chinese Communists have not broken entirely with past custom, the foreigners came at specified intervals—April 15 to May 15 and October 15 to November 15—stayed at designated hotels, and spent most of their working days in the Trade Center complex. Most of China's foreign trade contracts are arranged at the Fair. Normally, only official trade delegations and businessmen concluding very large contracts for large amounts of goods or complete plants are welcomed to Peking and Shanghai. Mao is better equipped than his Ch'ing predecessor to cope with foreign traders. The British are once more, sans guns or opium chests, ever so politely seeking to catch up with the Japanese and West Germany in the China trade. John R. Keswick, a director of Jardine, Matheson & Company, that company so well known to the Ch'ing Emperor, is a regular guest at the Fair. He is the most active proponent of business with China and heads the Sino-British Trade Council. "The doors are open for us to enter in order to participate in an advancing prosperity," he says.

Japanese businessmen, in their eagerness to trade during the most militant phase of the Cultural Revolution in 1968, dutifully donned Mao buttons, participated in Maoist readings before negotiations, sang songs in praise of "the Great Helmsman," and signed statements denouncing their own government's politics. Other foreign businessmen, less pliant than the Japanese, were sometimes awakened early in the morning, in their rooms at the Tung Fang, by Red Guards and compelled to listen to readings from Mao. During the severe factional fighting in Canton in the fall of 1967, the Fair was postponed for one month and then opened under heavy army protection, with restrictions on the movements of foreigners.

We entered the main exhibition building through a large courtyard in which were parked an array of tractors, trucks and farm machinery, including harvesters ranging up to giant sizes. Except for a few items, they were not for sale, but on display to demonstrate China's "Socialist construction." China is seriously short of machinery and vehicles of almost every sort, and their output is quickly consumed by the domestic economy. Great red banners rimmed the courtyard, one of them quoting Mao: "Revolution is the main trend in the world today!"

Chang Te-shen, vice chairman of the Trade Fair, a tall, thin man with close-cropped hair, received me in a large reception room. We sat on a sofa before a table spread with several brands of Chinese cigarettes and cups of jasmine tea. A smiling young lady with a thermos jug hovered in the background, solicitously keeping the cups filled.

Chang assured me that the Chinese were ready to do business with all comers on a basis of "equality and mutual benefit. It is imperative that we export." Chinese exports had exceeded imports, he said, in the transactions concluded at the Fair. Textiles headed the list of Chinese sales, followed by meat and other animal products, agricultural products, manufactured goods and handicrafts. About one hundred new Chinese items had been added to the exhibition since the previous Fair. "We bought chemicals, steel and machine tools," Chang said, with Japan, West Germany and Canada getting most of this business.

Chang took me on a tour of the empty exhibition halls, showing me lovely silks and carpets made in the great tradition of China, as well as a new line of attractive textiles in wool, cotton and artificial fibers, and inexpensive cloths which were obviously meant to compete in Southeast Asia and other low-rice markets with goods from Japan, Hong Kong and India. There were lovely colorful blankets and yarn from new factories in Tibet. "We have products on display from every province and region except the province of Taiwan," Chang said. He showed me what was described as advanced machinery and indigenous machinery, the latter being manufactured by workers or peasants who were not specialists but produced to meet their immediate local needs. The advanced machinery, which included digital computers and electronics equipment, obviously lagged behind what was being produced in Japan or the West, but was displayed out of pride in Chinese industrial development.

This equipment, all examples of "Socialist construction," constituted a good part of some thirty thousand items on exhibit. China has limited quantities of such valuable metals as antimony, tungsten and wolfram to export. In general, looking over the goods offered for sale—such farm products as hides and nuts, such light-industry items as tableware and thermos jugs, as well as textiles—and given the limited foreign exchange available to Peking, it is obvious that trade opportunities for the United States are limited. Many of the rumors about the vastness of the China market are a myth. The Chinese have no great need to buy from the United States since they can get most of the advanced equipment and know-how at cheaper prices from Japan, partly because of the lower cost of transport. After their experience with the Russians in 1960, when as a consequence of the ideological dispute the Russians cut off technical aid, and trade dried up, the Chinese are avoiding dependence on any one foreign source. They are spreading their trade around, with West European nations scrambling for a share, and so far have declined foreign assistance. The pattern of their trade and the potential for the United States can be seen from the 1970 statistics.

China's total trade volume, balanced between exports and imports, was U.S. $4.25 billion, with $3.38 billion carried on with the non-Communist countries. Trade with Japan was the greatest, $823 million, of which $569 million represented imports, and $254 million exports. It is significant that Japan's total trade with Taiwan was $951 million, exceeding the total of its business with China. Japan's trade with the United States alone totaled $11.5 billion.

China imports from West Germany were $254 million, and her exports were $85 million, while Britain lagged, with only $188 million in exports to China and imports of $81 million.

The importance of Hong Kong to China, and the motivation behind Peking's tolerance of the Colony, is illustrated in trade figures, which show $359 million in exports to and only $85 million in imports from Hong Kong. Peking's exports to the Colony, largely food and materials for re-export, finance a good part of its foreign trade.

It has been estimated by Robert F. Dernberger of the University of Michigan that if the United States should bestir itself energetically to capture the same relative share of China's business as it enjoyed during the peak period in the 1920s, it would amount to less than 0.5 percent of total U.S. foreign trade by the year 1980. This would be around $1.27

billion as compared with American trade of $1.04 billion with Taiwan in 1970.

Negotiations are conducted at the Fair by representatives of state trade corporations, who arrive in Canton with a shopping or selling list approved by the Ministry of Foreign Trade. There is hard bargaining with foreign businessmen, who are often at a disadvantage because of the lack of good private communication links with their home offices. Contract terms are often sticky by Western standards, but the Chinese pay promptly.

In general, the experience of foreign businessmen in Canton has been that the Chinese traders give priority to economic over political considerations. Thus Japanese and West Germans often get the nod over their British competitors, although Britain is the only one of the three exporting countries to have diplomatic relations with Peking. An exception seemed to have developed in 1971 when Peking became irritated with the Australian Government of Prime Minister William McMahon because of its ties with the Chiang Kai-shek regime on Taiwan. The large annual wheat imports from Australia were canceled, and Peking turned to Canada, buying 2.5 million tons of wheat although Australian wheat was cheaper. China has been importing wheat to make up a deficit in food production, to stockpile and to replace rice, which is exported at a profit.

Along with the wares at the Fair, foreign businessmen get a heavy dose of Maoist ideology. Large portraits and statues of Mao loom over every section of the exhibition, and the entire eighth floor is given over to Maoist literature. Chang took me quickly by a large photo of a demonstration in the United States said to be denouncing Nixon and the Vietnam war. It was time to go and we drove back to the hotel, where Chu became the purveyor of good news. The Ronning party had arrived from the interior in Shanghai and was now on the way by train to Hangchow, the resort city where I would meet Audrey on her birthday. It had all been arranged. The plane to Peking would break its regularly scheduled nonstop flight to the capital to let me disembark in Hangchow. Chu was impressed, and his frozen demeanor melted. The plot of the Chinese Embassy in Ottawa on behalf of sentiment had hatched.

I was in high spirits as our Shum Chun party, reunited, left the hotel in the afternoon for the Canton Airport. We drove north on a good road lined with thousands of saplings planted at spaced intervals through vivid green fields of rice and vegetable communes to the glistening new airport terminal. Entering the spacious lobby, which was nearly empty except for two or three passengers and the attendants behind the baggage check-in counter at the right, we stood beneath a massive white plaster statue of Mao which faced a large mural above the entrance depicting Mao with people of the national minorities in their gay native costumes. Air travel is cheap in China. A ticket to Peking, which lies nearly twelve hundred miles north, was only $36. I walked across the long waiting lounge to the balcony overlooking the airport and was surprised to see only one plane on the runways, a British Vickers Viscount propjet of the national airline, the Civil Aviation Administration, which was to take me to Hangchow. At the far ends of the airport, I could see other aircraft parked. The scene was close to typical of other airports in China, with the exception of Peking, which has more traffic, but sparse in comparison with any other major capital. Travel on the national airline, which relies mainly on Viscounts and Soviet Ilyushin-18s, another turbojet aircraft, for trunk line flights, is light, and quite often the thinly scheduled flights are not fully booked. The only international flight into Canton was that of Pakistan International Airlines, which flies an American-built Boeing 707 twice a week into the southern capital and then on to Shanghai.

In the waiting lounge, passengers were being entertained by eight girls dressed in green uniforms over blue pants and field caps, who danced across a small stage waving red flags and singing revolutionary songs. They returned for a finale, waving the omnipresent little red book of the quotations of Chairman Mao, and danced off the stage with a last shout, "Long Live Chairman Mao!"

I was not yet fully numb to the visual evidence of the Mao cult and was beginning to find the unending array of portraits, statues, the works of Mao in a dozen languages displayed for the taking in hotels and airports oppressive. Mao had ordered a thinning out of the icons devoted to him, but I was not aware of the new policy or that it was being implemented. One wall of the airport covered with Mao's calligraphy in white on red with an English translation was pleasanter to read because it was one of his poems, entitled "Snow":

> This is the scene in that northern land;
> A hundred leagues are sealed with ice,
> A thousand leagues of whirling snow
> On either side of the great wall

One vastness is all you see
From end to end of the great river
The rushing torrent is frozen and lost
The mountains dance like silver snakes
The highlands roll like waxen elephants,
As if they sought to vie with heaven in their height;
And on a sunny day
You will see a red dress thrown over the white
Enchantingly lovely!

Such great beauty like this in all our landscape had caused
    unnumbered heroes to bow in homage
But alas these heroes!—Ch'en Shih Huang and Han Wu Ti were
    rather lacking in culture;
Rather lacking in literary talent
Were the emperors Tang Tai-tsung and Sung Tai-tsu;
And Genghis Khan
Beloved son of heaven for a day,
Only knew how to bend his bow at the golden eagle
Now they are all past and gone:
To find men truly great and noble
We must look here in the present.

CHAPTER 17

HANGCHOW

The plane wheeled over Hangchow Bay, which flows into the East China Sea, and I looked down on the beautiful garden city on the east shore of the great West Lake. Hangchow, a city of 720,000 population, lies about a hundred miles southwest of Shanghai, on the north bank of the Tsientang River, which empties into nearby Hangchow Bay. It is the capital of Chekiang Province. We glided to a smooth landing, and at the foot of the ramp Audrey was waiting for me. Dressed in a red gingham shirt and blue jeans, draped in cameras, she was brown, slim and as ever beautiful and eternally youthful. Her blue eyes danced as she sang out with her familiar "Hi, Top!" and I embraced her whispering "Happy birthday." In the terminal, she introduced me to Yu Changching, a twenty-nine-year-old interpreter of the China Travel Service who had been sent by the Foreign Ministry from Peking to meet me. During most of my five-week tour of China, Yu, a tall, lean, bespectacled bachelor, accompanied Audrey and me as our guide and as a congenial valued companion. Other foreigners were sometimes not so fortunate with their assigned guides.

I noticed that Yu was wearing a Canadian red maple leaf insignia on his white shirt beside his Mao button. Audrey caught me looking at the maple leaf and said laughing, "I thought I would stake him out before you did." "Canadian chauvinist—first my children and now Mr. Yu," I retorted, and told Yu of the time in Moscow when we had picnicked outside the city beside the river and our daughters had climbed a huge pile of sand left on the bank by a barge. The four young pioneers stuck a pole atop the towering mound. When they returned, I asked them

231

what they had done. Susan, spokesman for the four, holders of American passports all, declared, "We claimed it and all the land around for Canada, just like Mummy said we should." Appreciative of Canada's recognition of Peking and always somewhat dubious of American intentions, Yu would side with Audrey in the clash of nationalities and continued to wear his maple leaf.

Yu, or Hsiao Yu, a diminutive meaning "young" or "little Yu," as his friends called him, was born and educated in Peking. An outstanding student, he was sent to London in 1965 to study English, which he did for a year, living in the home of an English doctor. Then he enrolled in the London School of Economics, but could remain for only three months. When the Cultural Revolution entered a convulsive stage in 1967, Chinese diplomats and students, Yu among them, were summoned home to be screened and re-educated ideologically after their exposure to foreign ideas. Most of the students were doing graduate studies, and the recall meant disruption of their careers. But once, when Yu broke with his practice of shunning discussion of himself, he recalled: "I wanted to participate in the Cultural Revolution. When I returned to Peking, I wrote big-character posters denouncing Liu Shaoch'i." In 1969 he was sent south with other intellectuals to a rice commune in Kwangtung Province to labor in the fields. The assignment was in keeping with Mao's policy of re-educating the intellectuals and officials through manual labor, which he said would reunite them with the masses and give them a better understanding of the peasants and workers. "It was hard at first," Yu recalled. "We had never planted rice and the work was hard. But we learned and after several months we became friends with the peasants." Having won the approval of the peasants and Party officials of the commune, Yu was called back to Peking to work as an interpreter. He was a diligent student of Mao, reading his works every morning, and often thoughtfully discussing with us some new insight. As our interpreter it was his job to make available to us the ideological spectrum of the Communist Party as a frame of reference for looking at China. However, he never came between us and what we chose to look at, and the Chinese which I retained from my earlier days in the country told me that he interpreted faithfully, even when he was embarrassed by our questions or answers.

I joined the Ronning party in the Hangchow Hotel, a large comfortable hotel with spacious, high-ceilinged rooms fronting on the ethereal West Lake. Beyond the lake, on whose waters glided gondola-like pleasure boats, rose the green terraced hills of the tea-raising communes. In secluded sections of the lake's nine-mile-long wooded shore were perched vacation retreats of Mao and other Chinese leaders. There were also convalescent and nursing homes for workers around the lake. Families strolled in the West Lake Park, and in the Hua Kang fish lagoon beside the Pavilion of Calm Lake and Autumn Moon they fed the foot-long red carp that swarmed to the surface lunging for bread crumbs. Along the blacktop walks, columns of Red Guards, teen-aged smiling boys and girls, members of a now tamed youth organization, paraded in cadence on what seemed to be physical training marches. As our car arrived at the hotel, a long column of elementary school children stepped by, two by two, following a serious-faced boy carrying a portrait of Mao. Processions of this kind, usually en route to a meeting, are frequent sights in the cities and villages.

Hangchow remains a mecca for pleasure-seekers, as it was in the thirteenth century when that energetic tourist, Marco Polo, remarked after a night on the town: "Where so many pleasures may be found . . . one fancies himself in Paradise."

Hangchow under Communism offers simpler pleasures than the frolics on West Lake boats with beauteous concubines popular in the days when the city was capital to the Southern Sung Dynasty. Today Hangchow is no longer a playground solely for rich Chinese or foreigners. At the Hangchow Hotel, foreigners are seen only when an official delegation passes through or diplomats get permission to come down from Peking. Today the mainstream of visitors consists of workers or peasants bused into Hangchow on organized tours. Family groups travel on the comfortable trains from Shanghai and other nearby cities. While Hangchow provides the proletariat with only such puritan pastimes as boating and industrial exhibits in the cultural parks, they gain some relief from the ideological bombardment common to life in the other big coastal cities. There are far fewer propaganda posters and the public loudspeakers speak more softly, perhaps in deference to the imperious tranquillity of West Lake.

In our room, over large cold bottles of excellent Shanghai beer, while Ronning and Audrey's sister, Sylvia, were out visiting a silk factory, Audrey, sprawled in a deep square wicker chair, full of joy and excitement, told of their trip to Fancheng, her father's birthplace.

From Wuhan, the great tri-city metropolis of Central China in the Yangtze River valley, they had gone by overnight train to Fancheng in the rich agricultural country of Hupei Province. "Fancheng is three hundred miles up the Han River, as Dad describes it from the days when he used to travel on the big sailing junks," she said. "In 1927, when the British Consul ordered the family out with the other missionaries because of the fighting with the revolutionaries, Dad, Mum and Sylvia and Meme and Alton, who were babies, sailed down the river through the pirate junks.

"When we got to Fancheng, all the town dignitaries were out at the railway station, and hundreds of staring Chinese. We were the first foreigners to come to Fancheng in about twenty years," Audrey said, pouring herself more beer. "Dad was flabbergasted at what he found as we toured the place."

Audrey's grandparents, Halvor and Hannah Ronning, Americans of Norwegian extraction, among the first Lutheran missionaries to go to China, went to Fancheng in 1890 and there founded a church and established the middle school, one for boys and one for girls. Audrey's father was born there in 1894 and lived in the town for thirteen years. After the death of Hannah in 1907, he left with his father to settle in northern Alberta. In 1922 he returned to teach in the school founded by his father.

"Dad said," Audrey continued, "that the houses in the area were clusters of mud surrounded by mud walls. Every village had a watchtower and guards on constant duty to guard against robbers and soldiers who would loot the villages. Now the watchtowers are gone, and many of the houses are of brick. Everything was really beautifully clean."

Fancheng had grown from a town with a population of less than 40,000 to 189,000, with a spanking-new cotton textile mill built since the Communist Revolution and other industry rising nearby. Dikes had been erected along the Han River to bring water into the fields and keep back the floods, which Ronning recalled terrorized the people. In 1938 three thousand people died in a single flood.

"They put us up in a nice guest house, used ordinarily for meetings. The bedrooms had been fixed up with bamboo furniture and embroidered spreads on the double beds. There was a john that works just about like the one we've got at home. Above the toilet was a tank marked 'super flush' in English. When you pulled the chain, nothing happened, but then it would explode a few minutes later and keep going. Sylvia and I would hear it all night."

Audrey and I left our room and sauntered out of the Hangchow

Hotel, crossed the wide veranda and its gardens, and went through the gate guarded by a soldier and across the road to the shore of the West Lake. We strolled along the walk at the water's edge and then sat on a bench. A slight haze over the lake in the distance gave the scene the appearance of a painting from an old scroll, and Audrey remarked that it was dreamlike.

"Dad said that about the only thing unchanged in Fancheng," Audrey continued, "were the junks of the Han. We watched the families of the boat people get into harness and help pull the boats when they were sailing upriver just as they did when he was a boy."

She suddenly grew more pensive. "They took us into the old mission compound, and we came face to face with the tombstone of Hannah Roren Ronning in the courtyard, with her name still clearly inscribed. Tombstones of the other missionaries who died in Fancheng also stood in the compound. It was an emotional moment for us, and we left the others to stand alone under a little grove of trees outside the compound. Soldiers are now living in the old Ronning house. The school is still operating, but much larger, about eight thousand students compared with about two hundred in 1927."

Chester's old friends told him that some of the older people in town still meet once in a while in the guest room of the Lutheran church, which otherwise stands empty and unused.

The story of the demise of the Fancheng Lutheran Mission is, in a sense, the history of the foreign missionary movement in China. There remained a memory of humanitarian service and evidence of the substantial contribution to education, but the religious heritage of a century's work has virtually disappeared. Chester recalled, however, that in his father's mission school many young Chinese, through education, were inspired, as in other missionary middle schools and colleges, to join the Chinese revolutionary movement.

According to official statistics, there are two million Chinese enrolled in the Catholic Patriotic Association, a religious organization which appoints its own bishops and does not defer to the Vatican or the Pope. In central Peking there is a Church of the Immaculate Virgin where a Latin Mass is celebrated by the Rev. Wang Ki-ting, who has the title of vicar-general and assistant to the Bishop of Peking. Foreigners are usually barred from entering the church, as they were at Christmas of 1971, but the previous month two Italian officials, accompanied by Mrs. Vada Princigalli, the correspondent in Peking of the Italian news agency Ansa, were allowed to attend Mass. Rev. Wang, who wears a clerical collar with his Chinese tunic, told them that many missionaries in the last century had "aroused the resistance of the people through usurpations and depredations. Until the 1949 Revolution the Catholic Church had been in the hands of the imperialists."

During my trip through China, I would occasionally hear of Christians, invariably older people, meeting privately to worship. Near Shenyang, formerly Mukden, in Manchuria, while I was visiting a vegetable commune, an official told of Catholics going into the city to worship, although from the outside the church itself seemed locked. What few churches were still open in China in 1966 were often defaced or burned by Red Guards. Despite the sizable foreign community in Peking, not a single Christian church was open to them. A mosque, attended mainly by members of the Pakistan Embassy and other Moslems of the diplomatic community, still functions. The Buddhist temples also have been barred. While in Hangchow, we visited the great Monastery of the Soul's Retreat, the Lingyin Sze, on the western side of the lake, which was first built in A.D. 326 and has been repeatedly destroyed and reconstructed since then. Audrey recalled that it was a working Buddhist shrine in 1966 when she visited it. "A monk in gray robes welcomed us into the temple and proudly showed us the newly gilded Buddhas and a beautiful giant Kwan-yin, the Goddess of Mercy," she said. "On the steps outside there was a young mother breast-feeding her baby son. His head was shaven except for a square topknot left there to fool the evil spirits into thinking the baby was only a girl and not worth bothering with."

But when we toured the temple, which in the big main hall has two magnificent nine-story stone stupas, sixty feet high, with finely carved panels of Buddhas and Bodhisattvas, there was no evidence that it was still a working shrine. There were no monks about, and a guide said the temple was "a historical relic preserved by the state." Damage to the statuary was done by a mob of Red Guards which descended on Hangchow in 1966. The mob was beaten off and the temple saved from complete destruction by a rural faction of local Red Guards. The state has since repaired the damage and the temple reopened to sightseers.

Under the state constitution there is freedom of religion in China. In practice, religion is frowned upon and attacked in Party propaganda and the schools. The Christian missionaries who once worked in China are linked with foreign colonialism. As we toured the Lingyin Sze, I asked Yu about the prevalence of Buddhism, once one of the great religions of China. "I have no knowledge of it," he replied.

Returning from Fancheng, the Ronning party spent three days in Nanking, the old Nationalist capital where I had met Audrey. She motored out to the Purple Mountain, east of the city, where I had asked her to marry me, and on the southern slope visited the Sun Yat-sen tomb. The blue-tile-roofed pavilion stands against the mountainside, and she climbed the three hundred-odd steps to the tomb, where a great white statue of the seated Father of the Revolution is seen as one enters. In a circular marble rotunda behind reposes the casket of Dr. Sun, brought there from Peking in 1929. Above the statue and the casket there had been mosaics of the white sun on blue flag of the Kuomintang Party, into which Dr. Sun had for a turbulent period brought the Communists. In June 1966, when she first returned to the tomb, Audrey had noticed that the mosaics of the Kuomintang flags were still there, but this time they were gone, leaving only the white ceiling. On the way back, they drove past the Ming Tombs and the amphitheater where in 1948 Audrey and her sister, Meme, had played in *A Midsummer Night's Dream* before the diplomatic community and their father, in a voice that rang out from the mountainside, sang "Jerusalem" at Easter sunrise service.

"Nanking is cleaned up," Audrey said. "The filth and the beggars are gone. I went up that street where I used to agonize so much over the cart horses which were always in such terrible condition. They aren't there any more.

"They showed us the new bridge over the Yangtze. It's a great achievement, most impressive—but we spent almost an entire day looking at it," she said, with a sigh. Construction on the new four-mile-long, two-level bridge spanning the broad Yangtze River was begun in 1960 and finished in 1968. The giant ferry that had carried Audrey's train across the Yangtze in 1966, and which I had used to travel to Pukow in 1949, was being used to haul freight. Trains, often two at a time, were traveling across the bridge together with a flow of cars, trucks, pedestrians and ox, donkey and horse carts. Along one side of the bridge were two giant Chinese characters reading "LONG LIVE OUR GREAT LEADER CHAIRMAN MAO TSE-TUNG." Each character was said to weigh five tons.

When we returned from the lake to the hotel, Ronning and Sylvia were there and I was enfolded and hugged by my father-in-law. He was in marvelous shape, his eyes agleam with enthusiasm at being back in China, and moving tirelessly, wearing out his considerable entourage. We broke open a bottle of Scotch, which I had brought from Hong Kong to celebrate Audrey's birthday, and, with the help of our Chinese friends, consumed it within the hour. By the time the Scotch had vanished amid an exchange of Chinese riddles and quips between Chester and his assorted Chinese hosts and escorts, we were ready for the banquet in a private dining room.

Ronning was being given the dinner by Ma Hsiang-kuang, a dignified man of military bearing dressed in a gray tunic who was the chairman of the Revolutionary Committee of Hangchow. Over a feast that featured Beggar's Chicken, baked in mud and so tender it parted at the wave of chopsticks, stuffed bean curd and special duck, Ma and Ronning exchanged innumerable ganbei (bottoms up) toasts in mout'ai, a powerful sorghum liquor. After half a dozen, Ma was declaring undying friendship between China and Canada "despite the rivers and mountains that separate us." None of the happy guests seemed to notice the slight to the Pacific Ocean. When I cautiously advanced a toast to Sino-American friendship, Ma looked at me somewhat pityingly and responded: "In spite of the aggressive actions of the American Government, the people of the United States and China will always be friends."

This was my first encounter with a chairman of one of Mao's key Revolutionary Committees, and I learned that, dinner chitchat aside, they were very serious, tough and powerful Party leaders.

By early 1967, utilizing the Red Guards and other revolutionary cadres, Mao had immobilized Party and government offices in the provinces and begun a gigantic purge of officials thought to be loyal personally to Liu Shao-ch'i or to his policies. To replace the Party apparatus and government administration while both were purged and reconstituted in keeping with his ideology, Mao called into being the Revolutionary Committees, organized in "three-in-one combination." The committees embraced representatives of the army, representatives of selected trusted cadres—meaning officials of the Party, government or technical managers—and delegates of the revolutionary masses, which usually meant militant Maoist workers or peasants. The chairman headed a guiding standing committee, which was always operational. The "three-in-one combination" ensured mutual surveillance, with each member empowered to report on the others or on the general performance of the committee as a whole to higher Maoist authority.

Between early 1967 and September 1968, with the extension of the Cultural Revolution to Tibet and Sinkiang in the far west, Revolutionary Committees were put in charge of each of the twenty-nine self-governing provinces, autonomous regions and municipalities on the mainland. As the political restructuring and screening of personnel went forward, these administrative units put Revolutionary Committees in charge of their subdivisions, that is, the hsiens or counties, cities and townships. Virtually every administrative unit in the country, including factories, farm communes with their subordinate brigades and production teams, schools, cultural groups and economic enterprises such as department stores, was also put under these new central committees.

In every Revolutionary Committee of any importance the army played a key role, actually leading the committee or acting as its ideological watchdog. Some two-thirds of the provincial Revolutionary Committees were headed by army men. Mao, confident then of the loyalty of the military under Defense Minister Lin Piao, his "closest comrade-in-arms," personally committed to the principle that the People's Liberation Army is "the main component of the state," thus placed his trust in the PLA, as he had done in every time of crisis or transition since Yenan days. This did not mean that China had passed into a period of military rule, as some foreign observers interpreted the movement of army men into key administrative posts normally held by civilians. In September 1971, when a military oligarchy challenged the Party leadership, Mao Tse-tung purged Lin Piao and other top military men, and shook up the military hierarchy in the provinces.

The PLA has always performed a twin mission, that of a revolutionary or political corps as well as that of a professional fighting force. In its revolutionary function, the army has been integrated with the Communist Party and acts as the chief conduit of the "mass line," propagating Maoist ideology through direct association and involvement with workers and peasants.

Tens of millions of people serve in China's militia, but the regular armed forces, totaling 2.8 million men and women, is not a large one for a country of 800 million people. In 1971 the United States, with a population of 208 million, maintained 2.7 million in its armed forces, while the Soviet Union, with a population of 245 million, deployed 3.3 million.

Wherever combat units are stationed in China, in addition to their military duties, they dispatch propaganda teams to carry out "Socialist education" among the local people. The soldiers also take part in factory and farm work, both as a political demonstration of their ideological integration with the people and as a spur to production. They raise much of their own food and make much of their equipment. Army men habitually move between regular military assignments and posts in the Party, government and economy. The role of the army has been entwined with that of the Communist Party since the thirties, when both Mao and Chou En-lai served as military strategists and political commissars in the Red Army at the onset of the revolutionary struggle.

We were up early the next morning despite a late night over a white porcelain jug of mou-t'ai purloined from the banquet table. There is an early-morning bustle and excitement in China which makes it hard to stay in bed beyond 6:30 or 7. By that time many of the Chinese have tumbled out, jogging about or doing mass calisthenics as the loudspeakers blare marching songs, others postured in the graceful traditional exercises of T'ai Chi-ch'uan. I saw more dawns in the interval of five weeks in China than in the preceding year in Scarsdale. Ronning was already bustling about as usual, getting his party, which struggled perpetually and hopelessly to keep up with him, to the breakfast table. He had once been a bronco buster in Alberta, and, as I hurried along, I thought that of all of his past occupations, sometime missionary, educator, air force officer, diplomat, he had probably been happiest running those horses across the plains. Some of the party breakfasted on a Chinese soup of noodles, greens, shrimp and chicken taken with steamed buns, while others had the foreign breakfast of scrambled eggs, ham and toast, and then we were in a convoy of cars heading for the hills to visit a tea commune.

The doors to our rooms at the hotel were left open, with clothes, cameras, jewelry and other belongings lying about. Theft is something foreigners do not worry about in China. Money, documents or other valuables can be left in an unlocked room or house or car on the streets, with the certainty that nothing will be stolen. A foreigner who loses a camera or handbag in a park can be quite sure that it will be turned in to the lost-and-found, then returned on inquiry. Once a taxi driver in Peking knocked on my hotel door and with apologies returned a banknote worth a few cents. He had not noticed it stuck to another bill when I paid a fare the previous day.

Traveling through China, one gets the impression of a society in which honesty is considered not a virtue but the norm of life. It is difficult to measure precisely the dimensions of the crime problem since no statistics are made available. But in factories and farms, managers look at you blankly when questioned about the prevalence of crime. Obviously, it is not a critical problem, although locks on some doors and bicycles suggest that thievery has not been eradicated. In every city visited by Audrey and me, we never saw the slightest evidence of anyone being afraid to walk at night in any neighborhood.

My request to visit a People's Court was never granted, but some information was available about the penal system. There are prisons where criminals are rehabilitated through ideological "re-education" and manual labor. Most of their cells have no locks. There is no escape in a regimented society in which all residence and travel must be registered. The same pervasive controls have been used to wipe out most crime, including drug traffic and addiction. For the most serious crimes, the convicted may be executed by shooting.

En route to the West Lake People's Commune, our cars followed a twisting road through the terraced hills to a pretty village which was the center of the Mai Chia Wu Tea Production Brigade. We walked across a stone bridge over a river flowing through a narrow gorge, where women were washing clothes on the rocks below, down a narrow street flanked by gray-tile-roofed cottages with walls made of lime, mud and brick, and into a larger house in a garden, where we were greeted by Ch'en Wu-yuan, a small sturdy woman, with short hair and white teeth and strong rough hands which showed work in the fields, who was the vice chairman of the Revolutionary Committee of the brigade. She wore a gray jacket over a blue-checked blouse and gray pants. She led us into a large elaborate sitting room with teak walls, furnished in the center with a classic rare old rosewood table, surrounded by chairs and rows of benches. "This was the house of the landlord and is now our meeting hall," Mrs. Ch'en said. And where was the landlord? "He works in the commune," Mrs. Ch'en replied. In other communes we also found that many landlords had survived and been absorbed into the communes, but they were marked ideologically and never fully trusted. On the wall was a portrait of Mao and below it a framed letter from Chou En-lai congratulating the brigade on its production achievements.

The brigade was a showplace for visitors. Audrey had visited it in

1966 and had been received in the same manner by Mrs. Ch'en, although the vice chairman, then called brigade commissar, did not recognize her. "The other thing that has changed," remarked Audrey, "is her Mao button. It has gone from the size of a dime to a silver dollar."

Mrs. Ch'en recited the history of the local people. "We were liberated on May 10, 1949, by the People's Liberation Army, and then Mao Tse-tung told us 'to stand up and become the masters of our own fate.' Then came the land reform and our people struck down the rich landlords and took the fields. In 1952 we started forming Agricultural Mutual Aid teams. In 1955 we formed Agricultural Producers Cooperatives, and in 1958 we set up the commune."

Mrs. Ch'en had slipped so easily over the frustration of the peasants and the turmoil which accompanied the transition from individual ownership of the land to collectivization. Through "Socialist education" the peasants were disabused of their hunger for individual ownership, a hunger that had once led many of them to rally to the Communist cause in response to the cry "Land to the tillers!" during the civil war. Mao once described his power to remold the peasants in these terms:

Apart from their other characteristics, the outstanding thing about China's 600 million people is that they are "poor and blank." This may seem a bad thing, but in reality it is a good thing. Poverty gives rise to the desire for change, the desire for action and the desire for revolution. On a blank sheet of paper free from any mark, the freshest and most beautiful characters can be written, the freshest and most beautiful pictures can be painted.

In June 1966, when Audrey toured the country, commune officials everywhere were reviewing their accomplishments by comparing current production with the period before "liberation," that is, pre-1949. Now they compared their production with pre-1949 and pre-1966—that is, prior to the Cultural Revolution, when they were often ruled by cadres loyal to Liu Shao-ch'i, the ousted Chief of State.

In June 1966 Mrs. Ch'en reported current production of 1,850 kilos (1 kilo = 2.2 pounds) of tea per hectare as compared to 45 kilos before "liberation." Now she provided three figures: 45 kilos pre-liberation, 1,650 in 1965, and 2,100 in 1970. The new propaganda emphasis was on showing a sharp upsurge between pre-Cultural Revolution and current production.

In June 1966 as the Cultural Revolution was getting under way, there were still portraits of Liu Shao-ch'i beside that of Mao in Hangchow as well as other cities of Southern and Central China. Now the portraits of Liu were gone, and down the village street on a board outside a nursery where rosy-cheeked tots of three and four sang songs in praise of Mao, there were wall posters denouncing "traitor Liu Shao-ch'i."

I saw only one anti-American poster in the village: an illustration on a wall, showing demonstrators holding placards reading in English "DOWN WITH NIXON" against a background of the crumbling New York skyline.

We strolled into the factory area at the edge of the village. On the terraced hillside, girls were plucking the green tea leaves from the plant rows baking in the brilliant sunshine. In the factory the grinders and other machinery processing the tea had been made in commune workships. The tea was Lung Ching, a select fragrant green tea of a flat leaf popular in the country and much in demand abroad. We sipped it from rice-China mugs with covers to retain the fragrance and the warmth and found the taste excellent.

We drove back to the hotel, stopping en route on the southern side of the lake to see the well-preserved, russet-colored Pagoda of Six Harmonies, built in 970 and towering nearly two hundred feet in thirteen tiers. We packed and in the evening took the train to Shanghai, riding in the comfortable upper coach of a double-decker passenger car.

CHAPTER 18

CHINA FIGHTS POLLUTION

As the train moved out of Hangchow northeast toward Shanghai, we could see the tall factory chimneys of Kungchenkiao, the northern industrial suburb of the city. Some belched black smoke, and I thought of the Hangchow municipal officials who told me of their efforts to spare the city from industrial contamination.

In Peking, three weeks earlier, Chou En-lai had spoken to Ronning of his concern about pollution. When Ronning had jokingly told the Premier that he personally would cook a Chinese meal for him if he came to Canada, Chou rejoined: "Do you still have fish to eat in your area or have they all died as a result of pollution?" More seriously Chou went on: "The greatest pollution has taken place in the most advanced industrial countries. Developing countries, like China, which are not as far advanced industrially, can benefit from the experiences of these countries and avoid similar problems."

In my tour of China, I found the people coping with the primary problems of the environment on the farms where more than four-fifths of the 800 million inhabitants of China live. The very shape of the landscape had been changed by giant water conservancy and land reclamation projects. The magnitude of the afforestation program was staggering. Tens of millions of trees have been planted. Saplings line the roads, are seen in every village and on mountainsides, and in the cities border the streets and stand in every garden and open lot. They beautify, contain the erosion of the earth and draw dust and fumes from the air.

The Hangchow region has been transformed into a major industrial complex since the Communist takeover without blighting the central garden city. As in other Chinese cities, planners have sought to restrict factories to the suburbs. Near Hangchow is the Tsien Tang Truck Plant, which assembles vehicles made from parts manufactured locally and shipped from elsewhere in the country. There are also iron and steel works and electronics, machine tool and chemical plants, as well as newly opened coal mines. The factories have been sited mainly in wooded suburbs, with surrounding vegetation intensively cultivated as screening and to absorb fumes.

Yang Shao-shen, a municipal official, talked to me about Hangchow's pollution problems as we sat in a pavilion of the Running Tiger Spring, where the people come to sip the fragrant local green tea made with the mineral water of the spa. "We are trying to deal with pollution before it becomes a serious problem. We are building special treatment facilities to convert waste water from factories into fertilizer for surrounding farms. One paper factory converted successfully after the peasants indignantly protested that fish were dying from waste discharged. Now the peasants get fertilizer and the fish are back." In other cities I also found factories attempting to convert end products into fertilizer. At the Peking Experimental Chemical Works, sulphuric acid fumes, once discharged into the air, are now being trapped and converted into fertilizer. However, on one farm commune officials said some chemical fertilizers had proven toxic to fish in the streams and irrigation canals, and their use had been discontinued.

In Peking and Shenyang, sewage, including human excrement, is treated and piped to communes in the surrounding countryside, where it is distributed as fertilizer through the irrigation ditches. Officials say the sewage makes excellent fertilizer and the farmers are pleased with the result. However, farther south in the Yangtze River valley, inadequately sterilized sewage of this kind has caused schistosomiasis, the dreaded snail fever, which has killed thousands of farmers. In schistosomiasis, snails are hosts for parasites bred in human excrement. Peasants working along the irrigation ditches and streams pick up the parasites, which attack the intestines through the skin. Chinese scientists, who have eradicated other diseases that have long plagued the peasants, believe that the disciplined population can be organized eventually to eradicate schistosomiasis and various skin diseases related to the use of sewage. Some progress has been made through spraying the irrigation ditches and streams, covering up the snails by throwing dirt over them, and more effective sterilization of the human excrement fertilizer, called "night soil" by the Chinese. Victims have been effectively treated by a traditional Chinese herb medicine, ground pumpkin seeds. In 1949, Chinese officials say, ten million peasants were suffering from schistosomiasis.

Millions of peasants and workers have been mobilized in the countryside and cities to dredge polluted waterways. In Shanghai, I looked incredulously at Soochow Creek. It runs beside the skyscraper Broadway Mansions, where I once lived briefly in the foreign correspondents' club that occupied the top three floors. The club has been converted into an excellent restaurant. In 1949, when I passed the foul Soochow Creek, crowded with sampans and filthy barges, walking across the bridge to the Bund, I habitually held my nose. The Communists have dredged the creek, making it respectably clean.

Some of the larger industrial cities, such as Shanghai, which has a serious smog problem, Peking, Wuhan and Shenyang, have moved polluting factories into special suburban districts. In Shenyang, where the Japanese built a forest of factory chimneys in the center of the city, many of them stand unused. Fei Li-jen, a member of the Revolutionary Committee in charge of city construction, told me that considerable industry had been diverted to the eastern district. The city is exposed frequently to winds from the southwest, and the relocation of industry to the eastern district has minimized the smog problem. Coal-burning furnaces are equipped to capture cinders from the smoke, which are used in the making of brick. Ashes are utilized in road-making and other construction. In factories all over China extensive use is made of end products usually discarded as waste in the United States. Bits of metal are collected and sawdust is pressed into firewood. In China, with its plenitude of manpower, these practices are economical, whereas labor costs in the United States make them impractical except as antipollution measures. This is also true of the widespread recycling of paper and other products, which is feasible in China but often prohibitively expensive in the West. There are workshops in China where expended electric light bulbs are salvaged by restoring the filament and vacuum-sealing the bulb once again.

I never saw in China a garbage can spilling over on a city street. Garbage and human excrement for fertilizer are picked up regularly by collectors, but the garbage is thin. The Chinese consume few containers, and what is obtained in the shops is usually used at home. There is little waste. The six-page newspapers, if purchased rather than read on a public billboard, are used as fuel or sometimes as insulating material.

Even in the industrial suburbs of the large cities of China, I never found air pollution as serious as in most towns in the United States. The difference was simply in the absence in China of any automobile traffic. This may be of significance to Americans, as they search for solutions to their environmental problems, although in general there are few parallels to be drawn between China and the United States. In Maoist society frugality is dictated by economic necessity and an ideology that discourages material incentives, unlike the United States, where affluence is feasible and an encouraged aspiration.

CHAPTER *19*

SHANGHAI

In Shanghai, we stayed at the old Cathay Hotel, renamed the Peace Hotel. A big square edifice with a tower surmounted by a pyramid, once the swankiest hotel in cosmopolitan Shanghai, the Cathay stands on the Bund, fronting the harbor on the corner of Nanking Road, then the most elegant shopping thoroughfare in the city. When we dined that night in the large restaurant on the top floor of the hotel, I recalled my last meal there. It was in early September 1949, when the Communists had been the master of this still untamed corrupt international city, the largest metropolis in China, for only four months and were having trouble digesting its individualistic population. Robert Guillain, a French correspondent of *Le Monde,* and I had strolled from Broadway Mansions to the Cathay for dinner. We had walked south across the bridge over the Soochow Creek, not far from where it empties into the Whangpoo River harbor, down the Bund past the tall buildings which had once housed the foreign banks, great trading companies and clubs. Many of the 100,000 foreign residents of the city had fled before the Communists, and many of the buildings were darkened and looking desolate. No drinks were being served at the Shanghai Club, which claimed the longest bar in the world. The foreign caretaker staffs left behind were wrestling with the Communists, who were gradually taking over the enterprises. The Communists were insisting that in the transition period the Chinese staffs be retained on full pay although business was at a standstill. When we entered the dining room of the Cathay, it was empty except for several score waiters, still attired in their immaculate white jackets. We dined alone in the great room, with

248

seemingly dozens of waiters hovering over us and colliding with each other. When I paid the bill and put the tip on the small silver tray, I glanced up to see scores of eyes riveted on the tray from all parts of the room. They had depended in great part for their livelihood on tips, but there had been no other guests that day. Unnerved, Guillain and I escaped into the night.

As the Peace Hotel, the Cathay had lost its glitter and bustle, and although efficiently managed, there was a feeling of camping in the worn, faded establishment, and the Chinese staff operated as if they were in an unaccustomed environment. The same could be said of the central part of the city, where the foreigners had worked and played. The foreign cars and taxis which once crowded the streets had been replaced by a few automobiles and trucks weaving through the cavalcade of bicycles and dodging around the motor and electric buses. The smartly dressed foreigners and Chinese, those slim beautifully coiffured Shanghai girls in their slit brocaded skirts, had been replaced by crowds in blue and gray tunics over baggy trousers. Because it was cooler in Shanghai than in Canton, they wore the tunics over their shirts and blouses, making the street scene duller than in the southern city.

The neon lights, advertisements over bars and cafés, had been taken down. The line of imposing, towering, foreign-constructed buildings along the curve of the river, which had included Jardine, Matheson & Company, the Hong Kong and Shanghai Bank, were now Communist offices. As in Canton, the face of Shanghai had lost its bright, affluent Western makeup and had become more of a Chinese city. There was the other aspect as well. If the affluent in expensive garb were absent, so were the beggars, the opium addicts and the other tattered, emaciated human debris that had littered the Nationalist-held cities. Shanghai streets were strangely quiet after 10 P.M., but beggar waifs no longer slept in the doorways and there was no need for the police trucks that had once toured the city each morning to pick up from the streets the bodies of those who had lost the struggle for life. The Maoist man looked healthy and vigorous, and he marched to command. The boisterous, unruly, individualistic people of Shanghai had been tamed. Of the 100,-000 former foreign residents, there were only a handful left, largely belonging to the Polish and North Vietnamese consulates and two, lonely, isolated British bank representatives. Ten million Chinese lived in the greater Shanghai area. The presence of foreigners had become unusual enough that hundreds of smiling, curious Chinese gathered in front of the Peace Hotel each day to glimpse the strangers in Western dress.

Audrey noticed changes since 1966. The Shanghai clock tower, which used to strike in the somber tones of London's Big Ben, now chimed on the half-hour with strains of the revolutionary song, "The East Is Red." The harbor, which had been semideserted for such a long time, was abustle with ships from Eastern and Western Europe, and the new merchant vessels being turned out in Chinese yards. In the harbor there were two of the six ten-thousand-ton merchantmen which the Chinese say they have built since 1966. "Before the Cultural Revolution," an official of the Shanghai Revolutionary Committee said in a briefing on the city, "we only repaired ships. Now we build them. We plan to build seven more this year and will soon build twenty- and thirty-thousand-ton ships. In the past all the naval vessels in the Whangpoo were foreign. Now we can build our own navy."

In the harbor there were naval vessels, some, apparently, ships seized from the Nationalists and others provided by the Soviet Union before 1960. There was also an active submarine base, which could be seen at a distance but could not be photographed.

The Revolutionary Committee spokesman said there had been a sharp increase in industrial production since 1966. "We make thirty-two-ton trucks here also," he reported, "in spite of the fact that the Soviet Union tried to impose an economic blockade on us." Shanghai as an industrial center obviously had grown. The fumes from the factory chimneys merged with the smoke from the vessels in the harbor in a smog that hung heaviest over the river.

We frequently saw overseas Chinese tourists, easily distinguishable by their more Western clothing, short skirts and narrow trousers and sports shirts worn by the men. Thousands of overseas Chinese are returning to their homeland to visit ancestral homes and relatives, and simply to view the new China. At Shum Chun and in Canton, I had seen lines of young men, some of them carrying Pan American and BOAC flight bags over their shoulders, coming into China, sent by their parents in Hong Kong, Singapore, the Philippines and other countries of Southeast Asia to become familiar with the mother country. They are treated as dual citizens in China and are given privileged treatment. In Canton, the capital of Kwangtung, which sent out more emigrants than any other province before 1949, there is a residential area set aside for overseas Chinese who have elected, as many do, to return to China at the end of their lives. In Canton, Shanghai, Peking and other cities, there are special overseas Chinese hotels, with travel and information centers to facilitate their journeys and to provide tickets for cultural events and entertainment.

Peking has treated the some fourteen million overseas Chinese of Southeast Asia gingerly since their host governments and peoples have viewed the energetic, shrewd Chinese immigrants suspiciously for political reasons and jealously because of their frequent business success. Overseas Chinese remittances to the homeland provide an important source of foreign exchange for Peking. The remittances, often forwarded through the Bank of China in Hong Kong, go to support relatives, sometimes wives of marriages contracted by parents while the bride and groom were only children. The biggest foreign group at each Canton Trade Fair invariably consists of overseas Chinese.

Although they may have ideological reservations, there is evident pride among overseas Chinese in the accomplishments of the People's Republic. Rich and foreign-educated Chinese will sometimes confide a longing to return home despite the loss of personal freedom and affluent living it would mean. In Changsha I spoke to a Chinese-Filipino businessman dressed in a white sports shirt, gray sports trousers and two-tone shoes, who had just been to Peking with his wife and two children. "I wanted to show the kids what their country is like," he said, in an American accent. "No rock music, but they were impressed."

Among the Chinese visiting the country from abroad are dozens of residents of the United States, including American citizens. They are generally given the same treatment as the others, although United States citizens are offered the choice of being classified as such or simply as overseas Chinese. On arrival, the overseas Chinese are issued passports, which serve as identity cards and are collected by Communist officials on departure. During my stay in China, the Nobel laureate in physics, Dr. C. N. Yang, of the State University of New York at Stony Brook, visited Shanghai to see his father, who was ill. Dr. Yang also saw his father-in-law, Tu Yü-ming, the former Nationalist General who was captured in January 1949 when the Communists overran his armies, the fleeing Hsuchow garrison. Dr. Yang reported that his father-in-law and other former Nationalist officers were living quite comfortably. He said that they drew salaries as members of the Chinese People's Political Consultative Conference, but that they were not doing "any job of any real significance" though they are "members in good standing in the community." Dr. Yang said that his impression was that Nationalist generals who surrendered were receiving better pay than those who were captured and much more than an average worker. Before he left China, Dr. Yang was received in Peking by Premier Chou En-lai.

Audrey was to remain in China to continue on to Peking with me, but Chester and Sylvia packed to leave the next morning for Canton. After arriving there they were to go to the Dao Chao People's Commune on the Pearl River Delta to observe the "harnessing of the tides." The commune had built 104 small power stations which take the ocean water brought in by the tides, dam it, and then release it to a lower level to turn turbines. In the morning when we gathered in the hotel lobby to go to the airport to say goodbye to Ronning and Sylvia (who would be going directly back to Canada from Canton), we were joined by two other Americans en route to Canton. They were Dr. Arthur W. Galston, professor of biology at Yale University, and Dr. Ethan Signer, an associate professor of biology at the Massachusetts Institute of Technology. Galston, a specialist in plant physiology, and Signer, in the genetics of bacterial viruses, had spent two weeks in China visiting the National Academy of Sciences in Peking, Peking University, Chung Shan University in Canton and Futan University in Shanghai. They had been given access to laboratories, libraries and conference rooms as well as to members of scientific staffs. Critics of the Vietnam war, they had spent seventeen days in Hanoi lecturing and giving seminars, and it was during this period that they successfully applied for admission to China. When they arrived in China, Dr. Galston was welcomed by Dr. Loo Shih-wei, who returned to the mainland in about 1947, after completing his doctorate at the California Institute of Technology in Pasadena. Galston had met Dr. Loo while he was a postdoctoral fellow at the Institute in 1943–44, and the two had exchanged letters and Christmas cards until the advent of the Cultural Revolution, when the Chinese broke off foreign contacts. Loo, whom Galston had given as a reference on his visa, was now at the Research Institute for Plant Physiology in Shanghai. He remained with the scientists during their entire tour.

I was delighted with my good fortune in encountering the scientists. As far as I knew they were the first American scientists to visit China in the last two decades and certainly the first to be allowed into Chinese research establishments. I interviewed them in their car as we drove out to the airport. Both men seemed a bit hesitant about speaking and somewhat edgy about how they might be received in the United States.

I assured them that the one-week tour of the American table tennis team had awakened a great desire among Americans for more contacts with and information about China, and that they would find little adverse political reaction. Signer, a dark young man with a thick mustache, seemed particularly tense, perhaps because his wife was momentarily expecting a baby and he was anxious about the journey home. However, during the lengthy ride to the airport they relaxed and discussed their interesting findings quite freely.

Galston said that Chinese scientists had developed "a lot of scientific information of which we are unaware." To give one example, he said, the Chinese had originated a method for mass-producing inexpensively hormone substances known as gibberellins, which when sprayed on plants significantly increase crop yields. The crystalline form used by American farmers is expensive and requires special technology to produce. The Chinese were making crude gibberellins on a large scale in farm communes, factories and at research institutes. In 1965 the Biochemical Institute of Shanghai had attracted world-wide attention by achieving the total synthesis of biologically active insulin.

Galston said they had become convinced that Western pharmacology had much to learn from traditional Chinese medicine. They also had observed in hospitals the successful use of acupuncture, another traditional technique of medical treatment, employing needles inserted at nerve points.

"We must also say," Signer interjected, "that Chinese scientists admire Americans as the world leaders in science, and they would be glad to accept advice and help if given in the right way. They would benefit from our technology tremendously."

The two scientists were able to provide firsthand confirmation that the National Academy of Sciences, known as Academia Sinica, and research institutes were operating again after the disruptions of the Cultural Revolution. But the publication of scientific journals had almost entirely stopped, and the trickle of information about Chinese science to the West had dried up. Since the Cultural Revolution the emphasis in Chinese research institutes had shifted to a very large extent away from pure research to applied science which would produce practical solutions for China's problems. Scientists are concentrating on developing techniques of spurring agricultural and industrial production.

Later I was to find that Chinese scientists also have felt the political impact of the Cultural Revolution. Together with other intellectuals who had been exposed to foreign thought and culture, they were harassed by the Red Guards and some research establishments were damaged. The "mass line" has also been applied to the scientific community, requiring association with and deference to ordinary workers and peasants, and the performance of some manual labor. Staffs have been screened for political reliability and some individuals sent to factories or communes to do manual labor while being ideologically re-educated. Often the chairman of the Revolutionary Committee heading a research institute would be a political cadre, while actual technical direction of the work would be in the hands of a vice chairman who was a scientist. The Party is seeking to break down the traditional social barriers between the technician and the ordinary Chinese, peasant and worker, so as to create fully integrated teams in production.

In the workshop of the Peking Heavy Electric Machinery Plant I encountered Hsu Tung-p'eng, a thirty-year-old scientist of the Peking Chemical Research Institute who had been in the factory for a year working on special problems. "I have been taking part in hard physical labor, but the workers often persuade me to do light jobs," Hsu said, peering at me through his black horn-rimmed glasses and glancing at the circle of factory officials about us. "They are re-educating me."

When we arrived at the gleaming new air terminal at Shanghai's Hungjao Airport, Dr. Loo Shih-wei, Galston's old colleague from Cal Tech, a gentle round-faced man in the usual worker's dress, was already waiting there with other scientists to say goodbye. The American scientists were ushered into a large private waiting room with Mao slogans emblazoned on the walls, while I joined the Ronning party in a similar reception room. There were not many people in the big terminal. Besides Pakistan's twice-weekly flights, only Air France of the other international airlines serves Shanghai. After an hour's wait, we were told that the flight was canceled because of bad weather in Canton. The plane had been waiting in bright sunshine on the tarmac in front of the terminal. Cancellations of this kind were a common occurrence. There is no elaborate radar guidance equipment at China's airports. China possesses some sophisticated electronic equipment, as evidenced by the launchings of an earth satellite and guided military missiles, as well as test explosions of hydrogen devices, but evidently not yet in sufficient quantity to install control instruments for flying in bad weather. Therefore when weather is dubious at either end, flights are simply postponed. The excellent safety record is some compensation for the frequent inconvenience. The scientists and the Ronning party piled into cars and returned to the hotel.

In the afternoon the Revolutionary Committee of the Shanghai No. 1 Department Store, the largest such shop in the country, agreed to receive us. Accompanied by Yu, my interpreter, we strolled up Nanking Road, looking in the windows of the smaller shops along the way. The foreign goods which once crammed these shops for the old elite had been replaced by simply made serviceable consumer items produced in China. Shanghai has more shops than any city in the country, but, apart from variety, the goods available can be found everywhere, as Audrey and I discovered in our travels. In small general stores in peasant villages, we would find the same inexpensive shoes, cotton and synthetic cloth, in the same colors and patterns, or other staple consumer items as in the Shanghai No. 1 Department Store, the Nanfang Department Store in Canton, the Peking Commodity Store or in shops in Hankow and Fancheng. Shopping in a number of cities is nevertheless worthwhile because of the wide variety of local handicrafts, such as the embroidery in Hangchow or the jade and ivory carvings in Peking. Prices are uniform throughout the country apart from small variations attributed to transportation costs.

The Shanghai No. 1 Department Store, known as Ta Hsing before 1949 when it was owned privately by the Sun Company, and the Peking Commodity Store are the finest in the country. Both stores, with their goods attractively displayed in showcases separated by wide aisles illuminated by fluorescent lighting, compare with some in the United States in appearance. The Canton store was dreary and poorly lighted in comparison

About 150,000 people each day throng through the five floors of the Shanghai store, looking at an array of goods of greater volume and variety than has been available since the Communist takeover. Significantly, colors are brighter and designs more varied than in 1967–69, the most austere years of the Cultural Revolution. There are transistor radios and small table television sets for sale, but almost all goods are basic, functional consumer items. There are virtually no goods that an American would classify as luxury items. All sales are for cash—no installment buying. Since there is no advertising in China, the salesclerks, mostly girls, are trained to help customers, particularly peasants from the countryside, find what they need. The store is open seven days a week, 8 A.M. to 9 P.M., and a special section is open from 6 P.M. to 8

A.M. to serve late-shift factory workers and peasants who bring their produce into the city in the early-morning hours.

We stopped at the stocking counter, where there were cotton and rayon socks of brighter color and design than the others on a display board under a sign reading "EXPERIMENTAL TYPES." I asked what it meant. A shy smiling salesgirl, who looked in her teens, explained that there had been complaints about the quality and style of socks, and the samples on display were the new line ordered from the factory.

Service in the store was excellent, and faster and more efficient than I remembered in GUM, the biggest department store in Moscow. The clerks still add up sums on the ancient abacus, clicking the beads in lightning fashion, but customers still got away more quickly than in GUM, where after waiting on line to buy, one had to wait on another long line to pay, then return to the line before the sales counter to pick up the purchase.

Sales were brisk, but certainly not pell-mell, largely because prices are deliberately pegged to depress demand for items other than necessities.

Only a few items are rationed, notably inexpensive cotton cloth at seven yards a person each year. But there is no rationing of more expensive wool, silk, rayon and synthetic cloth. In foods, grain and cooking oil are rationed, but most families seem to be able to get as much of these items as they require, and food generally is plentiful. The population looks well fed. Recent foreign observers traveling in the provinces of China open to inspection have not seen any evidence of hunger.

China remains far from being a free consumer society. In effect, the state exercises rationing through pricing, although the price structure has remained stable and there have been regular reductions in many categories of goods. The prices of drugs were slashed 50 percent in 1970, and plastic items, such as shoes and raincoats, went down 30 percent.

I picked out at random what I thought might be a typical customer for an interview to try to define average buying power. He was Chang Ming-yuen, a fifty-year-old worker behind the meat counter of the food shop adjacent to the department store. Calculated at the working exchange rate of 2.4 yuan to the U. S. dollar, the wages of urban workers in China range from $14.17 (34 yuan) to $45 (108 yuan) per month, with apprentices earning less. It turned out that Chang, a veteran worker who held the same job before the Communists took power, was better off than most. He and his wife have a joint income of 120 yuan, of which he earns 70 and his wife about 50 as a factory worker. In the department store itself, salaries for the employees varied from 40 to 90 yuan, with the average being 65.

Outlining the monthly budget for his family of six, Chang said they spent 60 yuan for food, while rent for their small three-room apartment was the average 3 yuan. Mr. Chang spends another 3 yuan on bus fare. He pays no income tax. Education and almost all of the family's medical costs are free, and entertainment is cheap, leaving the family with about 45 yuan a month for additional consumer items and to save, which Chang says he does.

When the Chang family goes to the Shanghai department store, they find that the cheapest shoes—those with canvas tops and rubber-composition soles worn by many Chinese—cost 3.70 yuan. If Chang wanted, however, to buy black leather dress shoes, the cost would be 17 yuan. An inexpensive blue cotton tunic, which many Chinese wear over a shirt, costs 7 yuan, with trousers priced at 6 yuan. A woman's sweater is 10 yuan. An alarm clock is priced at 15 yuan, and a wristwatch at 120 yuan. Transistor radios were cut 40 percent in price last year because the government wanted more people listening to its broadcasts. But the smallest, cheapest portable transistor, receiving only medium wave, was 31 yuan, while a better make with an additional short-wave band was 120 yuan. With prices at these levels, the Changs by Western standards lived in a sparsely furnished apartment.

Chu Sung-ling, a member of the Revolutionary Committee that runs the store, invited us into what looked like the board room of the management and seated us at a long narrow table laid out with tea and cigarettes. Like the rest of the store, the decor consisted largely of Mao slogans and portraits of the Chairman. There were thirty thousand different items on sale, and since the start of the Cultural Revolution there had been a 20 percent increase in the variety of goods, Chu informed us. Only a handful of items are foreign made. Survey teams and sales personnel in the shop are used to explore consumer attitudes and to advise on the projected volume of sales and the type of goods wanted.

The store is under the control of the municipal Department of Commerce, but operates with a great deal of autonomy. Twice a year the store draws up a buying plan in coordination with state commerce officials. Demand is estimated, but if there are goods left in stock, they can be returned to the central state distribution agency for shipment elsewhere. In addition to what is received from the central distribution center, the store may buy directly from factories and wholesale stores. It pays directly by check or cash, drawing for funds on its own bank deposits. The state expects each department store to make a 7 percent profit each year after all costs are accounted. Part of this profit is retained for a welfare fund for employees, but the bulk of it reverts to the state.

With our notebooks crammed with facts and figures about retailing in China, and wondering how the folks back at Gimbel's would feel about the whole thing, Audrey and I returned to the hotel to pack for our flight to Peking the next morning.

At dawn Canton was still being lashed by rainstorms and so, saying goodbye to Ronning and Sylvia and our scientist friends, commiserating with Signer, the increasingly tense expectant father, we went to the airport. Our Peking plane was also delayed, we found on arrival, but surprisingly the Canton plane was cleared to take off. Signer and Galston came puffing up, but Ronning was not to be seen. When we inquired if the Ronning party was also en route, Hung Jao, a Chinese official, calmly informed us that the Ambassador would be notified as soon as he had finished lunch. We were then summoned to the Peking-bound Ilyushin-18. The stewardess told the passengers where they were going in Chinese and English, warned them that in China taking photos from airliners is forbidden, and we were aloft. The landscape, gashed by great water conservancy canals and dams, seemed limitless. The fields, vivid green rice paddies in Central China, turned into varying hues of green, browns and grays as we came into the wheat and kaoliang country beyond the Yellow River. Then in brilliant sunshine, in the dry late spring air, we landed in the capital.

CHAPTER 20

PEKING

Peking, radiating out from T'ien-an-men, the Gate of Heavenly Peace, a city of seven million, lay shimmering in the hot May sun. The "yellow wind" had brought the dust, as it does each spring, from the Great North China Plain and diffused it in a fine haze that gave a mystic quality to the city of imperial palaces and temples ruled by the new Communist dynasty. The Gate of Heavenly Peace looked south on the great paved T'ien-an-men Square, where as many as one million people would gather on ceremonial occasions to hail Mao as he stood on the balcony of the vermilion gate with the Forbidden City behind him. On the west side of the square was the Great Hall of the People, a huge modern building that received a procession of visitors calling day and night on Chou En-lai. Far to the east, in the industrial suburb, plumes of smoke were visible from the smokestacks of the new factories, but there was no smog above the yellow-and-purple-tiled roofs of the Forbidden City or the purple-roofed magnificence of the Temple of Heaven to the south.

The city had grown in population but not lost its spaciousness, and at the center, where the old walled city once stood, these open vistas lent grace even to the ponderous Soviet-style architecture of the government buildings west of T'ien-an-men Square. On Changan Chieh, the Boulevard of Eternal Tranquillity, which is the broad east-west axis of the city and passes before the Gate of Heavenly Peace, a thin stream of cars, army trucks and buses ran down the center lane with battalions of bicycles moving on the outer flanks. At first glance, only the temples and the avalanche of life strewn with the pedicabs and carts drawn by horses and donkeys in the old narrow, native hutungs or alleyways seemed familiar to me. I had left a charming city with an imperial past in 1948, and returned to a metropolis which had the presence of a great world capital and a Communist future.

This was the most relaxed spring for Peking since 1966, when the city was first swept with the tumult of the Cultural Revolution. The capital was still bedecked with Maoist portraits, statues and slogans, but fewer than last year, and there were fewer paraders and loudspeakers shouting revolution at the citizenry. Mao himself had expressed weariness with the extravagances of the adulation cult. It had been a useful weapon for his followers to rouse the masses, especially the youth, in the most militant years of the Cultural Revolution. But worship of the cult did not always identify the faithful since even the opponents of the Maoists bowed before Mao's image and, as the Party leaders said, "waved the red flag to oppose the red flag."

The people of Peking were dressed in the ubiquitous proletarian blues and grays, but there was a flash of color now and then in a girl's blouse or skirt, and some of them wistfully undid their braids a bit so their dark locks would curl more softly. At home, some wore the brighter, prettier and better-quality clothes available in the shops. May Day had been a joyous spring festival day, and after the mass demonstration in the square before Mao, who appeared only briefly on the Gate of Heavenly Peace, there had been music and a sparkling galaxy of fireworks.

Foreign delegations, trade, political and diplomatic, were crowding the Peking Hotel, reserved for dignitaries, and the state guest houses, the theaters and official receptions, providing entertainment for the populace, who loved to gaze and chuckle at strange white, Asian and African faces peering out of the vintage sedans which went whipping by. For the foreigners, Chou En-lai seemed to preside over this spring thaw which had brought the American table tennis team to Peking in a subtly contrived political comedy, and which in turn was to lead President Nixon to arrange his visit to the Chinese capital. At diplomatic receptions, the Premier, dressed in a gray tunic, would walk with deliberate step along the lengthy receiving line bent in a square at one end of the great banquet hall, his intense brown eyes looking out from under heavy dark eyebrows directly at each guest as he firmly shook hands. To the outside world the visage of China was that of Chou En-lai, who managed the government on a day-to-day basis. The deposed Liu Shao-ch'i, who as Chief of State had been Premier Chou En-lai's immediate superior, was said to be vegetating on a commune, being "re-educated." The post of Chief of State was vacant.

Chou En-lai's most pressing problem was the reconstruction of the government, which had been shattered during the Cultural Revolution by the ideological purge and power struggle.

The government purge had been massive, but its extent could not be measured precisely. Government officials, apart from some in the Ministry of Foreign Affairs, and a few others, remained secluded. Diplomats were just beginning to have conversations of substance at the Foreign Ministry after a long interregnum of silence, but they had not been able to sort out the new administrative structure since no lists of officials with their titles had been published. As nearly as could be determined, in the State Council, the top government executive body, there were only two vice premiers actively working with Chou En-lai out of a total of fifteen listed before the Cultural Revolution. The others had been purged, suspended or assigned to other duties. About half of the 366 ministers and vice ministers had been denounced by one Maoist group or another and were no longer seen publicly. The 90 ministries or departments of the central government had been merged into 26, and the 60,000 administrative personnel whittled down to about 10,-000. Revolutionary Committees were in charge of each department. Part of the thinning out of government ranks was attributed to application of the Maoist principle of decentralization, in accordance with the Chairman's recent injunction to "simplify the administrative structure" of all state bodies.

The purge in the Communist Party had been even more extensive, extending to Teng Hsiao-p'ing, the General Secretary, who had controlled the Party machinery. When the Ninth Party Congress met in Peking in April 1969, only 52 of the 172 members and alternate members of the ruling Central Committee were re-elected. In the provinces more than 20 of the 28 top provincial leaders were purged, demoted or suspended as the Maoist Revolutionary Committees took over and screened the incumbent hierarchies. On each level of government and of the Party structure within the provinces, a comparable purge had taken place, affecting factories, communes, other economic enterprises, schools and cultural organizations.

In August 1966, meeting in plenary session to give its sanction to the

Cultural Revolution, the Party Central Committee had issued the call for a purge in these terms:

At present, our objective is to struggle against and overthrow those persons in positions of authority who take the capitalist road, to criticize and repudiate the reactionary bourgeois academic "authorities," and the ideology of the bourgeoisie and all other exploiting classes, and to transform education, literature and art, and all other parts of the superstructure not in correspondence with the Socialist economic base. . . .

In the economic administration, the purge struck the pragmatists who balked at putting into practice the Maoist rule, "Politics in command," and gave priority to production and technique over ideology. Officials and economic managers were struck down who "took the capitalist road" by relying on material incentives for workers and peasants rather than "Socialist education" to spur production. Intellectuals who emphasized the Chinese classics or were influenced by foreign ideas rather than Maoism, scientists who insisted on giving priority to theoretical over applied research, artists who did not devote their work entirely to furthering "Socialist education," all were hit by the purge. A general charge of being divorced from the masses in thought or attitude was used broadly to remove people from their jobs or demote them.

The purge went forward in two spheres. In one, Liu Shao-ch'i and his adherents were removed. Many of those linked to Liu in the provinces continued to fight for their jobs through the summer of 1968. Some, before being ousted, professed loyalty to Mao and joined in the general vituperative denunciation of their former patron. In the other sphere, there was a purge in the Maoist camp itself, as a savage internecine struggle developed over policy and power, with the line of the Cultural Revolution oscillating left and right as Mao pursued a zigzag course. It was these oscillations, sometimes manifested in armed struggle among rival coalitions of Red Guards and revolutionary workers and cadres, which projected such a turbulent picture of civil strife and anarchy to the outside world during the years 1966–68.

At the onset of the Cultural Revolution, Mao had leaned hard to the side of the leftists or radicals, whose most outspoken leader had been his wife, Chiang Ch'ing. He told the Red Guards, "It is right to rebel against reactionaries," and not to be afraid of disorder, encouraging them to seize and paralyze the work of the entrenched official bureaucracy. Mao also gave the instruction: "The People's Liberation Army should support the broad masses of the left," and obediently the military gave protection and logistic support to the Red Guards.

But there were those in the "Central Cultural Revolution Group," the committee set up by Mao to guide the Cultural Revolution, who were fearful of unleashing an uncontrollable revolutionary torrent that would wash away hard-earned economic gains and, instead of gradually purging and reforming the administration, throw it into chaos. Among these was T'ao Chu, for eight years the powerful Party leader of Kwangtung, who was called from Canton to Peking in 1966 to assume a major role in the leadership of the Cultural Revolution, ranking fourth behind Mao, Lin Piao and Chou En-lai. T'ao sent out Party work teams to propagate the Cultural Revolution while trying to put curbs on the rampaging Red Guards. In early 1967, T'ao, under attack by radical Red Guards, was purged and dismissed with seven others from the Central Cultural Revolution Group. T'ao was denounced as a rightist in essence and a counterrevolutionary. It was apparent that his conservative tactics had displeased Mao and his radical wife, Chiang Ch'ing.

The army, obeying Mao's injunction to support the left, had stood aside as radical Red Guards took over municipalities and made violent assaults on opposition groups. However, in early 1967 the army began to grow uneasy about the excesses of the radical Red Guards, which were paralyzing normal life in many areas of the country. When it moved in to protect vital installations and broke up some of the pitched battles among rival Red Guard and mass revolutionary groups of workers and cadres, organized in opposing coalitions of radicals and conservatives, Chiang Ch'ing intervened. In April she obtained a directive from Mao instructing the army to support the radical Red Guards and mass revolutionary organizations and to refrain from halting the factional battles.

In May, however, Mao and Chou En-lai saw a serious threat to their power developing on the left. Thousands of ultraleftist Red Guards stormed out of control through the streets of Peking. They attacked the Foreign Ministry, stripped its files and demanded that Ch'en Yi, the Foreign Minister, appear to answer their questions and confess. Placards began to appear denouncing Chou En-lai as a rightist. Only the intervention of a more moderate Red Guard faction prevented the destruction of the Foreign Ministry.

Courageously, Chou En-lai went to the Foreign Ministry to face the mob of ultraleftist Red Guards. He demanded the restoration of the files, refused the demands to produce Ch'en Yi and, pleading that he had not slept for twenty-four hours, declined to answer many of their questions. Chou succeeded in turning back this challenge, but, as Mao later professed, over the next months he and Chou En-lai evidently lost command of events in Peking to the ultraleftists. The army grew more restive in the interim.

In mid-July, Wang Li, an ultraleftist member of the Central Cultural Revolution Group, went to Wuhan, the Central China metropolis, to whip local army leaders into line. He and others with him were seized, with the approval of Ch'en Tsai-tao, commander of the Wuhan Military District, by a conservative mass organization, self-styled the One Million Heroes. Wang Li was released after the radicals in Peking brought pressure against the local commander. The incident was used to castigate Huang Yung-sheng, the powerful Canton military commander, and others for their opposition to the radicals. Under pressure from the leftists in Peking, the army relaxed its restraints for a few weeks and Red Guard disorders flared across the country. Intimidated army men allowed Red Guards to break into barracks and depots to seize guns and trucks for their factional war. In August hundreds of thousands of ultraleftist Red Guards again surged through Peking out of control. They burned down the office of the British Chargé d'Affaires, and attacked the Indonesian and Burmese embassies. Ch'en Yi was forced to go through repeated "self-examinations" and humiliated. An attempt was made to seize the files of the Central Committee. For two days Chou En-lai was isolated by mobs of Red Guards in the Great Hall of the People, standing off in discussions those who accused him of right-wing deviation.

Alarmed, Mao toured five provinces, viewing the disorder and seeking to quiet it. The Party Chairman and Chou En-lai then yielded to the army's appeals for the re-establishment of order. Lin Piao's troops moved into the capital to disarm and disperse the Red Guards. Severe fighting erupted, but the troops finally restored order. A purge began of radicals in the Central Cultural Revolution Group, on the charge that they and others were members of an ultraleftist "May 16" faction which had tried to seize power, leaving Mao only a figurehead. Wang Li was purged in August, and between September and February 1968 four other radical members of the Central Cultural Revolution Group were implicated in the "May 16" plot, which was said to have aimed at the ousting of Chou En-lai and the discrediting of the army leadership.

Among the ultraleftists who were purged and disappeared was Sydney Rittenberg, an American who was employed in the Party propaganda apparatus in Peking. Rittenberg organized the Red Guard Yenan Brigade, wore its arm band and took an ultraleftist line. He, among others, denounced the North Vietnamese for having expressed interest in peace negotiations with the United States.

The upheaval in Peking in the spring and summer of 1967 was so severe that Anna Louise Strong, the leftist American writer who worked for the Communists in Peking until her death in March 1970, observed to a friend: "Mao has let the genie out of the bottle. I don't know if he can get it back in." But Mao succeeded, ruthlessly purging close associates on the left whom he suspected of sympathy or complicity with the "May 16 group." When I arrived in Peking in May 1971, only four of the original eighteen members of the Central Cultural Revolution Group had not been either purged, transferred or had disappeared. Ch'en Po-ta, the director of the group, was last seen publicly in August 1970, and subtle allusions to him as "a big careerist" were being made in the press. Ch'en, a close aide to Mao, and editor of the chief ideological journal, *Red Flag*, had been No. 4 behind Mao, Lin Piao and Chou En-lai in the five-man standing committee of the Politburo, the top body of the Party. The surviving members of the Central Cultural Revolution Group were K'ang Sheng, the fifth member of the standing committee of the Politburo; Chiang Ch'ing, the wife of Mao; Chang Ch'un-ch'iao, the chairman of the Revolutionary Committee of Shanghai; and Yao Wen-yuan, the Shanghai editor who had written the first articles in 1966 denouncing Wu Han, which sounded the opening gun on behalf of Mao in the Cultural Revolution. At the Ninth Party Congress in April 1969, Chiang Ch'ing, and her two close Shanghai associates, Chang Ch'un-ch'iao and Yao Wen-yuan, were appointed to the Politburo and ranked ahead of the Chief of the General Staff, Huang Yung-sheng. Huang had been commander of the Canton Military District, when he was appointed Chief of the General Staff in March 1968. A protégé of Lin Piao, he received the post although he had been denounced by the radical Red Guards and had quarreled with Chiang Ch'ing. By early 1971, as military men assumed most of the key posts on the new Revolutionary Committees that were taking charge of the country's provincial administration, Huang moved ahead of Chiang Ch'ing in the hierarchy of the Politburo, ranking fourth behind Mao,

Lin Piao and Chou En-lai. Chiang Ch'ing and the leftists seemed in decline, but the struggle was not yet over.

In Peking, I was able to report a dramatic footnote to the affair of the ultraleftists. While dining at the United Arab Republic's Embassy one evening, I was told casually by an Asian diplomat of rumors of a mass trial at which a prominent Chinese diplomat had been sentenced to death. The facts, as I learned later that night after checking with a number of sources, were that Yao Teng-shan, a high-ranking diplomat who had been Chargé d'Affaires in Indonesia and involved there in the abortive leftist coup d'état in 1965, had been taken before a crowd of four thousand people in an indoor stadium in Peking, made to confess and denounced. Yao, an ultraleftist, had headed the revolutionary group which seized control of the Foreign Ministry for a time in the summer of 1967. He was accused of plotting to do personal injury to Chou En-lai and of holding Ch'en Yi, the Foreign Minister, as a prisoner. He was also charged with responsibility for the burning by radical Red Guards of the office of the British Chargé d'Affaires and the attacks on the Indonesian and Burmese embassies.

On March 2, just one hour before he was to leave Peking for London on leave, Chou En-lai called in John D. Denson, the British Chargé d'Affaires, apologized for the burning of the chancery and pledged that his government would pay the replacement costs. It appeared that Chou En-lai by humiliating Yao, who was subsequently imprisoned, was settling an old score and at the same time demonstrating that his government was a responsible one which did not approve of violence against foreign embassies. At the Yao mass meeting, attended by the staff of the Foreign Ministry and selected "foreign friends" who made sure that the word got out, there was one especially concerned spectator. He was Ch'en Yi, ill and still showing the physical ravages of his 1967 ordeal. Ch'en Yi had retained his title as Foreign Minister, but had remained inactive. When the old warrior who led the Third Field Army across the Yangtze to seize Nanking, died of stomach cancer on January 6, 1972, Chou En-lai delivered the funeral eulogy before an urn containing the ashes of the seventy-one-year-old revolutionary. At the Papaoshan Cemetery, Mao and the other top surviving leaders of the Revolution heard Chou En-lai praise the "staunch fighter for the Chinese people."

The human cost of the Cultural Revolution had been enormous. There had been hundreds of thousands of casualties in the factional battles among the Red Guards and other revolutionary groups. Other hundreds of thousands had been affected by the purges. The Maoists did not execute their opponents or put them in concentration camps. Deposed senior officials at worst remained under house detention. The lesser offenders were left in their jobs and "re-educated." Thousands were shipped into the countryside to do manual labor in the fields and undergo re-education and screening by the peasants and revolutionary cadres. Some would remain in the communes, and others would eventually go to new assignments in factories or to government and Party jobs. Other scores of thousands entered hundreds of May Seventh schools, where officials, managers of the economy and intellectuals do manual labor and are "re-educated by the poor and lower-middle peasants." The schools take their name from Mao's May 7, 1966, directive in which he said: "Going down to do manual labor gives vast numbers of cadres an excellent opportunity to study once again." A "student" entering one of the May Seventh schools, which are organized on a paramilitary basis, has no knowledge of how long he or she will remain or any assurance of a return to his previous occupation, although most return to their jobs. "Students" may remain from six months to several years. They are told that the most menial manual labor, such as hauling night soil, is not punishment for mistakes, a viewpoint attributed to Liu Shao-ch'i. "His aim was to turn cadres into intellectual aristocrats divorced from proletarian politics, from the workers and peasants and from production," the students are told. "Cadres so corrupted could serve his scheme of capitalist restoration for China." Mao holds that China will progress toward a classless society only if there is a continuing program of integration of intellectuals and cadres with the ordinary workers and peasants.

At the "Peking Eastern District Cadre School for Official Functionaries," 1,250 students, ages twenty-seven to fifty-seven, live in one-story dormitories, four to six to a room, men and women in separate dormitories. The students built the school themselves in November 1967 from bricks of the newly torn down Peking wall. They may keep in touch with their families by phone and visit home twice a month. Their former government department continues to pay their salaries while they undergo re-education, and their future is determined according to their "tempering" in the school.

Among the typical students at the school was Ming Kuai-san, thirty-eight, former deputy chief of the Education Division of the Cultural

Bureau in Peking. He works as a laborer in the rice paddies while undergoing reindoctrination. Mrs. Hsu Ying, twenty-six, a school-teacher, labors as a masonry worker. T'ien Chi-chen, former vice chairman of the now disbanded trade unions in Peking's eastern district, makes water pails in a school-run factory.

Millions of Red Guards, shock troops of the Cultural Revolution, did not come through the upheaval of 1966–68 unscathed. They were uprooted from their homes, lost their educational opportunities and had their career hopes blighted. Their tragedy exceeds most other human sacrifices of the Cultural Revolution. They became the debris of the Cultural Revolution, not because Mao willed it, but because the flood tide wrought changes in the society and suddenly they were bypassed. The "revolutionary successors," ranging in ages from twelve or thirteen to the early twenties, mostly middle-school and college students, but also young workers and soldiers, had responded to Mao's call and joined the Red Guards with a spirit blended of revolutionary dedication and romanticism, and personal adulation of the Great Leader. Millions of students abandoned their classrooms, and the schools closed. When the schools began to reopen in 1968, as the Cultural Revolution subsided and the militant mission of the Red Guards was ended, the "revolutionary successors" found themselves in a tragic dilemma. There were too few places in the schools for them. The middle-school curriculum consisted in 1966 of three years of junior and three years of senior studies. Now Mao, in his emphasis on practical as distinct from theoretical studies, shortened the course to five years. Going back to middle school was also made difficult for the Red Guards since the younger generation were clamoring for their places in the classrooms.

Many of the Red Guards had also lost their innocence and respect for authority. The college campuses had been their first target in sweeping away the old society, and they had paraded the faculty in dunce caps. In their factional struggles, many had developed a taste for power and status. Confronted by millions of idle youth, many of them rambunctious and demonstrating for jobs or return to school, the Revolutionary Committees began shipping hundreds of thousands of unhappy youths into the rural areas. Some were to come back to schools, factories and government jobs, but most were expected to integrate with the peasant masses in the communes. It was crude, but seemingly it was the

only way to absorb a "lost generation." The movement into the countryside also served the purpose of enriching the communes with new
talent and manpower. This would help progress toward attainment of
the Maoist dream of eliminating the differences between countryside
and urban areas, and promoting uniform economic development of the
entire country.

In Yenan, Audrey interviewed Miss Chou Yu-fung, an attractive
twenty-one-year-old student from Peking who has been working as a
peasant for the last two and a half years. Miss Chou and eleven other
members of her class of fifty-four high school students came to work in
the Willow Grove Brigade of the Liu Ling Commune near Yenan. They
lived in a cave dwelling, as Mao had once in the former Communist
capital, and worked with the peasants in the fields.

"It was difficult at first," Miss Chou told Audrey. "The living standards in Peking are higher and just climbing the mountains here took the
energy out of us. We couldn't tell a potato plant from a tomato plant."

Hsi Huai, vice chairman of the Yenan regional Revolutionary Committee, said that of the 24,000 students sent to the region, more than
a hundred have joined the Communist Party and about a thousand are
members of the Communist Youth League. He said that the young
intellectuals serve as well as learn from the peasants. Seven thousand
of them are working as scientists, and 1,200 are teachers or "barefoot
doctors"—those who are trained in first aid, sanitation and other basic
health subjects—300 have joined the army; 1,400 have been transferred
to industry, finance and trade, where they are workers or staff members; 2,400 have been assigned to supervise and work with 13,000 who
work as peasants in the fields or do other manual labor.

When Miss Chou was asked when she might go to the university, she
replied: "My main purpose here is to receive re-education. We came
determined to take roots and live here. If the country needs us elsewhere, we will roll up our beds and go."

Only one student of the group in the Willow Grove Brigade was
chosen to go back to the university this year. He was sent to Tsinghua
in Peking.

Following the turbulent phase of the Cultural Revolution many of
the colleges and universities were slow to reopen, and when they did,
their student bodies were sharply reduced in size. In the spring of 1971
the enrollment at Tsinghua University was 2,700, all freshmen, as com-

pared with a total of 12,000 in 1966. The enrollment at Peking University was also 2,700 as compared with 10,000 previously. Student enrollment will be increased gradually as the institutions of higher education respond to Mao's directive:

> It is still necessary to have universities; here I refer mainly to colleges of science and engineering. However, it is essential to shorten the length of schooling, revolutionize education, put proletarian politics in command and take the road of the Shanghai Machine Tools Plant in training technicians from among the workers. Students should be selected from among workers and peasants with practical experience, and they should return to production after a few years of study.

College entrance examinations have been abolished. Graduates of middle schools are accepted only after having completed at least three years of service in a factory, commune or the army. They are nominated for entrance by a committee at their production unit. The committees also propose workers and peasants who have excellent production records and potential, but whose middle-school education was as limited as two years. At Peking University about 10 percent of the student body is made up of these "veteran workers." All the entrants must be certified by their nominating committees as "ideologically advanced."

The emphasis in the curricula of the institutions of higher education is on practical studies that can be applied to production. Students combine studies with work in factories and farm communes. In Canton's Chung Shan University the biology department once specialized in zoology and botany. The substitute studies today are industrial biology, agricultural biology and Chinese medical herbs. Studies in the purely theoretical fields, the arts or classics have been either subordinated or eliminated. Writing and arts courses prepare students largely for roles in the propaganda apparatus.

Courses have been shortened from five or six years to two or three. At No. 3 Affiliated Hospital of Peking Medical College, the medical curriculum, which is at the university rather than the postgraduate level, has been shortened from six to three years. In general, the faculties of most colleges were still struggling in 1971 with the reorientation of their studies within the new Maoist ideological framework, and experiencing difficulty in adjusting to the changes and strictures.

Surprisingly, the Cultural Revolution had not severely damaged the economy, although there was a decline in industrial production in 1967–68. The Maoist tactic of employing the youth as revolutionary shock troops rather than summoning workers and peasants en masse had its practical value in that production was sustained apart from sporadic interruptions.

Industry and agriculture have resumed their steady growth. According to Japanese analysts, the modest Chinese industrial base grew at a good rate of about 10 percent in 1970 and 1971. Reporting 1971 as the successful first year of the Fourth Five-Year Plan, Peking said that there was a gain of 10 percent in the value of industrial and agricultural output. A record output of grain of 246 million metric tons, six million over that claimed in 1970, was reported. The abundance of food everywhere I went was an index of the success in agriculture.

In May 1971 there was a surface calm and sense of well-being in Peking that was somewhat deceptive. Concealed were the deep, jagged scars of the Cultural Revolution, which would take time to heal. The purge was not yet ended, and one could not be certain who would be toppled next before the power struggle was concluded. There were deep-seated resentments among those who had been displaced. Eventually it would become possible to weigh the human sacrifices of the Cultural Revolution against the gains of this historic revivalist movement. In the next weeks, I would be given opportunities to see the balance sheet more clearly.

CHAPTER 21

WALK IN PEKING

In Peking, we camped at the Hsin Ch'iao, an exceedingly plain but well-run hotel near the old foreign legation quarter southeast of T'ien-an-men. China Travel Service normally assigned foreign journalists and some diplomats, businessmen and tourists to the Hsin Ch'iao, while members of official delegations were put in the more spacious prewar Peking Hotel or one of the state guest houses. During the Nixon visit, the press corps was housed in the National Minorities Hotel, which tourists will be using more in the future. Built in the Soviet style, the six-story Hsin Ch'iao had a Western restaurant on the top floor where we breakfasted on pineapple chunks, scrambled eggs and strong coffee, and a Chinese restaurant on the lobby floor where we enjoyed our other meals. There was a massive blue sign at the entrance to the Chinese restaurant which, in the Chairman's words, said: "The east wind is prevailing over the west wind." This seemed a fair commentary on the food. In the lobby there was a large white plaster statue of Mao, which was removed in September as the Mao cult became more subdued. We had one of the regular rooms, just barely big enough for the twin beds, a desk, two easy chairs, a tiny closet and bath, but not big enough for Audrey's camera paraphernalia. There was no air conditioning, which we missed as the temperature flirted with ninety. A number of larger rooms and suites were occupied by Canadian and other diplomats waiting for completion of permanent quarters in the two big diplomatic compounds. On each floor there were service counters manned by willing guardians with impeccable manners, who would smile when you passed, get your laundry done nicely, clothes pressed on the spot (there was no dry cleaning available), bring tea, beer and telegrams at any hour, reserve restaurant tables and order dinner menus. Outside our door was a bookrack where we could pick up free of charge Mao's collected works, Volumes I to IV in several languages. All this cost us less than $30 a week, which made you feel that capitalist expense accounts and Socialist hotels were incompatible. In the lobby, journalists were blessed with an efficient cable suboffice. In the shop opposite, you could buy pears, Chinese-made shirts and lather shaving cream, among other necessities and souvenirs. A Mr. Chu, who spoke good English, presided over the China Travel Service desk in the lobby. Chu could produce with miraculous promptness tickets to anywhere and anyplace if those mysterious officials, presumably of the Ministry of Foreign Affairs, on the other end of his busy telephone approved.

Our room looked south, and we could see the sun glinting on the towers of the Temple of Heaven in the distance. Enormous heaps of old rocks, bricks and sand were piled on the other side of the street, down which we could see the children sliding in the daytime, while during the night—why night we didn't know—large steam shovels would noisily eat away at the mounds. They were the remains of the last section of the great south wall of the old Imperial City. It had been dismantled to make way for the new subway which ran to Chien-men, the South Gate, and beyond on its fourteen-mile circular route. Construction of the subway began in 1965, and it went into limited operation in October 1969, but only for some sixty thousand selected Chinese sightseers each day. For some reason, possibly because the subway, like the one in Moscow, serves also as an air-raid bunker, foreigners, except for members of official delegations, are barred from it. Ronning and Audrey went for a ride on one of the trains, which speed along at up to fifty miles an hour. Each of the sixteen elaborate stations is made of different-colored marble from Yunnan Province in the Southwest, and they vary in style of construction, color and lighting. "At first we had all the lights red, but we didn't realize that it would make it very dark so we changed to white lights," the subway commandant told Audrey. The young subway staff is still learning to operate the system, taped music and all. "They waved their little red books at us as our train went through the stations," Audrey said. "Each of the trains has six cars, and they are very proud of them. They tell you that the trains have been made in China, at a factory in Changchun up in the Northeast."

On our first day in Peking, we left the hotel, without disturbing Yu, who had flown up with us, and shared a room at the Hsin Ch'iao with China Travel colleagues, and walked north up Ch'ung-wen-men Boulevard, pausing at the little neighborhood park. At the southern end of the park was the cultural section, which meant army propaganda lecturers, occasional revolutionary song-and-dance ensembles and industrial exhibits. The rest of the green patch could have been an American park, with old men sitting on benches dozing in the sun or gossiping, grandmothers leading toddlers, and a group of chattering adolescent schoolgirls eating Popsicles bouncing along the stone walks. We crossed the Boulevard of Eternal Tranquillity, which is about three hundred feet in width, and strolled along some of the old hutungs that twisted among gray-walled compounds. Soon we came to a familiar group of gray-brick buildings with green-tiled roofs behind towering walls. I had known the compound as the Peking Union Medical College. The college had been established by the Rockefeller Foundation of New York in 1916 and, with the support of the foundation, became one of the most important institutions in the development of the Chinese medical profession. The Communists had dubbed it the Anti-Imperialist Hospital, in reaction to its American origins. Just before the Nixon visit to China in February 1972, when it was designated the hospital to treat members of the American delegation, the Chinese quietly and discreetly renamed it the Capital Hospital. Even-handed with their other ideological foes, the Russians, the Chinese also changed the name of the Anti-Revisionist Hospital, which cared for Soviet and East European diplomats, to the Friendship Hospital.

When I passed through the gates of the Peking Medical College for the first time in October 1946, some of the buildings had been given over to housing Executive Headquarters. This was the organization established by General George C. Marshall to bring about a cease-fire in the civil war. The American, Chinese Nationalist and Communist commissioners of the Headquarters sent out truce teams to investigate the frequent violations of the cease-fire agreement signed by the warring sides in January 1946. There were so many American officers on the scene that the Headquarters was called the "Temple of One Thousand Sleeping Colonels."

When I made my first call at Executive Headquarters as a part-time reporter for International News Service, I was still on terminal leave and wearing the uniform of an army infantry captain since there had

Students at a May Seventh school put on an ideological skit in praise of Mao Tse-tung.

All photographs in this section by Audrey Topping

Picking tea at a commune near Hangchow

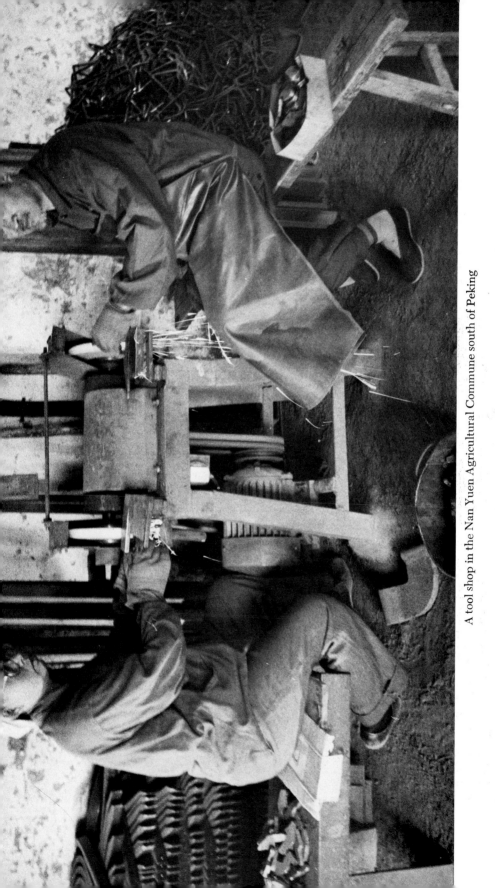

A tool shop in the Nan Yuen Agricultural Commune south of Peking

A family in their two-room house in the Nan Yuen Commune. She is a pediatrician and he works in the fields. *(Below:)* The bed at right is a typical kang, made of bricks with bedding on top. In the winter a fire is lit in the kang to warm the bed.

Officials of the May 3 Vegetable Commune south of Shenyang show produce.

Gathering rice seedlings for transplanting on the Nan Yuen Commune

A pupil at the Peking Deaf and Dumb School receiving acupuncture treatment
from an army specialist

Two students at the Deaf and Dumb School

Child and grandmother in their apartment of the housing for Cotton Mill No. 2 in Peking

Army men and other sightseers visiting the Great Wall on a Sunday

Tang Yu-hai, head of the newly opened iron ore mine near Anshan, the biggest steel center in the Northeast

The four-mile-long, two-level Yangtze River Bridge at Nanking, one of the great construction feats of the Communist state

Soldiers shopping for clothing in a Shanghai department store

Shop in a commune near Sian

Audrey Topping, the author's wife, with a family outside their cave dwelling in Yenan

Chester Ronning, Mrs. Topping's father, and Huang Hua, Peking's first permanent representative to the United Nations, lunching in a pavilion near the Summer Palace in Peking

The author tries out one of the 12-horsepower multi-use tractors at the Mini Tractor Factory in Shenyang

Red Flag Square in Shenyang

View of the Shanghai Bund

Youth Militia and young demonstrators line up along the road from the Peking airport to welcome Rumanian President Nicolae Ceausescu.

been no time to buy civilian clothes before my flight up from Manila. It was on this occasion that I met Huang Hua, the first in a series of encounters with him at critical junctures in his country's history. Huang Hua, lean and energetic, looking younger than his forty years, was head of the Communist press office and a personal aide to Yeh Chien-ying, the Communist commissioner. When I introduced myself as the new INS correspondent, who was also a language student, Huang Hua looked at me, then at my uniform, and then at me again with skepticism, but later he accepted me as bona fide and became friendly. Huang Hua enjoyed the company of American correspondents. Edgar Snow had once befriended him. In 1936 the American writer had given refuge in his Peking apartment to Huang Hua when as a militant leftist student he was in trouble with the Nationalist police. Later, Huang Hua served as Snow's interpreter in the Communist areas at the time Snow was collecting material for his book *Red Star Over China*, the first authoritative American work on the Chinese Communists. In February 1972, Huang Hua was in Africa attending a special session of the UN Security Council when he learned that Snow was near death in his home at Eysins, Switzerland, after a cancer operation. Mao Tse-tung had sent a team of Chinese doctors to care for the American writer. Huang Hua flew to Eysins for a final reunion with his old friend several days before Snow died.

Huang Hua spoke fairly good English, and at dinner in Peking's fabulous duck or Mongolian restaurants, over cups of hot hsiao hsin, yellow Chinese rice wine, he would fare well in the political repartee with Americans. As we became more friendly, he would visit me at my small, sparsely furnished room in one of the stone dormitories of the compound of the College of Chinese Studies, and we would talk about the future of his stricken country and about life in the United States. He was intensely curious about the United States, a harbinger of his future role as chief diplomatic expert and negotiator with Americans. Sometimes he would bring a book about America and ask my opinion of it. We debated the merits of the Soviet versus the American system. Huang Hua, already a hardened political revolutionary, was the first Communist with whom I engaged in close intellectual discussion. The most important thing he taught me was that my more or less typical Midwestern university education had not equipped me to cope with his Communist dialectics and that I had considerable important reading to do. Politically, the straightforward American officers at Executive

Headquarters were no more—probably less—prepared to deal with their Communist counterparts, or for that matter with the Nationalists. Both sides had learned in twenty years of bloody struggle that the civil war had to be fought through to the finish, and so they went through the ritual of talking cease-fire to please the Americans while they maneuvered for a kill. By January 1947 Executive Headquarters was closed and General Marshall had gone home, bitter about Communist hostility and muttering about Generalissimo Chiang Kai-shek, who said "hao hao"—"yes, yes"—to his suggestions and then went his contrary way.

While Executive Headquarters operated, I traveled on its truce planes to the battle areas free of charge, which was important. I had the title of INS Correspondent for North China and Manchuria, but was paid only $50 a month. Fortunately, I could draw on my army savings and life in Peking was cheap, especially with a room at the College of Chinese Studies. Dr. Henry Fenn, the director, a missionary educator, was very kind to me, although I was a strange bird among the missionary students and a few young business corporation types who made up the small student body. One of the best Chinese teachers was assigned to me for individual lessons, and I was free to flit off as my reporting duties required. The college was not fully recovered from the Japanese war and some rooms were rented out to nonstudents. My education broadened when an American ex-schoolteacher from the Midwest moved in down the hall in my dormitory. She was one of a number of American women, fascinated by China, who were drifting about the country from job to job. This one had been living with a Chinese general, and she told intriguing tales about warlords and high living that seemed to confirm everything Huang Hua was telling me about corrupt Nationalist generals. Later, when INS generously raised my monthly salary to $100, I moved out of the college and shared a Chinese house on Kwan Mao Hutung with Captain David Galula, a brilliant young French Assistant Military Attaché who was studying the language and enjoying the easy pleasures of Peking.

Sixteen years later, Galula, a colonel now married to Ruth Morgan, an American girl whom he had met in China, went to Harvard and completed his book, Counterinsurgency Warfare, before his death from cancer. I never collected from him a case of champagne, pledged in China to the first who would leave the estate of bachelorhood.

Within a week after my arrival in Peking, decked out in an ill-fitting pin-striped suit with massive shoulder pads made by a Chinese tailor on Morrison Street, I was expertly swapping stories with the other correspondents over luncheons at the elegant Peking Club. My principal agency competitors were John Roderick of the Associated Press, a bachelor epicure who insisted that the best life would allow a man to live six months of every year in Peking and the other half-dozen in Paris, and Reynolds Packard of the United Press, a fleshy, lusty man who felt he had to write to please the "Kansas City Milkman," the title of a book he later wrote exposing the foibles of his news agency.

I had my first run-in with Packard when I sprinted past him, abandoning dignity for ambition, to file a cable ahead of him on a big story. Pack took me to the club and, after three martinis, leaned across to me and said: "Kid, you're going to be a great newspaperman someday, but right now you are staining the tablecloth." After that, I behaved more decorously.

Pack and I were good friends when Walter Rundle, the UP Bureau Chief in Shanghai, came up to fire him. Packard, UP's chief correspondent in the Mediterranean during the war, was engaged in a running battle with his home office, and his salary was now more than it could afford. The moment of truth came for Pack after he filed a story picked up from the imaginative Chinese press. It was about a human-headed spider, and it caused a sensation around the world. Peebee, Pack's wife, also a newspaperwoman, had arrived in Peking by that time with her leg encased in a cast. Peebee, a gruff, solidly built woman, had been insulted in a New York bar by a man, kicked out in self-defense, aiming high, missed and broke her leg. When she and Pack were leaving, she cornered me on Legation Street and tried to persuade me to take an ugly, giant Chinese woman, known as the "Manchu Monster," who had been living in the Packard menage. I declined and didn't see the Packards again until many years later in Rome, where they were working for the New York *Daily News.* Pack had lost twenty or thirty pounds, grown a fierce long beard and had become an institution.

My first trip for INS into Manchuria was to Changchun, the old Japanese capital of the puppet state of Manchukuo. Shortly before Christmas 1946, accompanied by Jules Joelson, a serious pinched-faced correspondent of Agence France Presse, and Vladimir Drozdov, a pint-sized Russian correspondent who wore a big square fur hat with a red star on it, I took the train from Changchun south to Mukden. When the Communists blew up the tracks, our train ground to a halt and we sat in a crowded coach without heat or food for fourteen hours, exposed to the furious cold winds and snow of the Manchurian winter. Our Russian companion huddled closer to us as the Chinese, who hated the Russians after the looting of Manchuria in 1945, snarled, "Ta Pi Tze"—"big nose," at him. Drozdov, a great storyteller and tippler, worked for the *Russian Daily News*, which served the twenty thousand Russian émigrés living in Shanghai.

At breakfast time, my stomach was growling uncontrollably when I noticed that Joelson was holding a paper bag close beside him. He clutched it tighter when he saw me eying it. Jules had been to the far north of Manchuria, to Communist-held Harbin, and, on the strict instructions of his rather stern French wife, was returning to Peking with a kilo jar of the finest Russian caviar. Finally, yielding to my piteous whimpers for food, Joelson opened the jar and placed it between us. Joined by the eager famished Russian, we dipped into the caviar, eating it by the handful. I had no taste for caviar for years thereafter. When the Nationalists fixed the ripped tracks, we rolled on to Mukden, where I spent Christmas.

The dean of the correspondents was Walter Bosshard, of the *Neue Zürcher Zeitung*, the leading Swiss newspaper. A tall, dignified man with a shock of gray hair, he was a correspondent in the great tradition of adventurer and explorer, and lived of course in the best Peking style. He rented a house in Wang Fu Chien, one of sixteen owned by Prince Pu Lun, a cousin of Pu Yi, who later became the puppet Emperor of Manchukuo under the Japanese. I would sit beside his blazing fireplace in the main room of his Chinese house, polished wooden beams above us, and lovely scrolls and figurines all about, and listen to tales of mandarin statesmen, revolutionaries, warlords and famous concubines. At dinner there would be French wine and liqueurs made near Peking in a Catholic monastery, served by Bosshard's two long-gowned servants. Peking servants were the best in China, almost unreal as they moved wraithlike to anticipate your wish. Beyond the Peking red front door there was a courtyard with moon gates and flowers. When Bosshard retired, he lived in an Alpine chalet surrounded by his Chinese things. Some of his antiques he bought in Peking just down the road at the shop of Walter Plaut, a German who would sell his beloved wares only to customers he favored personally.

In his unhurried gracious way, Bosshard at times would scoop the rest of us. Once in 1947, all the correspondents flew to Changchun, which was encircled by the Communists, under fire and soon to fall. There, we visited the front and interviewed the Nationalist military commander. Communications were poor, and so we drew lots to determine the order in which our dispatches were to be sent by the cable office—all but Bosshard, who casually said his could go last. We slept that night on the floor of one of the row of pretentious white administration buildings of the former Manchukuo Government, which had been looted by Chinese mobs after the Japanese defeat. At daybreak, we trooped to the cable office to see if our dispatches had been radioed. Cunningly, hoping to get his dispatch out first, Roderick had marked it "urgent" without telling us, but to no avail. In Chinese fashion, the telegraph clerk had taken the last dispatch delivered, sitting on top of the pile, and Bosshard's cable had gone first. The Swiss fox had won again.

Much of Peking's social life whirled around Benjamin Welles, son of Sumner Welles, the Under Secretary of State, who was the *New York Times* correspondent, and his beautiful English wife, Cynthia. Among the gayest was an American Marine captain who was liaison for the Marine units in Tientsin and Tsingtao. A handsome man, he wore his uniform well and loved it, and adored the rare life in Peking. The captain saw the war through with courage, but he flinched when a routine order came to terminate his service as a reserve officer and go home, to his family. One morning the captain dressed immaculately in his uniform, put the barrel of his 45-caliber pistol in his mouth and pulled the trigger. There were many who found it unbearable to leave.

Audrey listened patiently to these twice-told tales as we walked back to the Boulevard of Eternal Tranquillity and west toward the Gate of Heavenly Peace, past the Peking Hotel.

Before the Communists came, there was a French Book Store in the Peking Hotel that had an international reputation for fine, rare Oriental books. It was run by a Frenchman, Henry Vetch, who had a theory that there was a relationship between spoken Chinese and the shape of the mouth and the written Chinese characters. He was a fine-featured man with intense eyes, whose life was Peking and scholarship. Vetch did not flee before the Communists, and after they came in, during the heated 1951 campaign against "counterrevolutionaries" Vetch was arrested with six other foreigners and accused of plotting to kill Mao and other Communist leaders by shelling the parade reviewing stand in Peking during the celebration of the October 1 National Day with a 60-mm mortar. Two of the foreigners, Antonio Riva, an Italian businessman, who was a former arms dealer and had specimens in his possession, and Ruichi Yakaguichi, a Japanese, were executed. The others were sentenced to prison, Vetch for ten years. I met him again after his release at a dinner party in Hong Kong on a veranda overlooking Repulse Bay. He was still enamored of the Celestial City.

Audrey and I reached the Gate of Heavenly Peace and looked south with awe at all ninety-eight acres of T'ien-an-men Square. The concrete expanse was marked with tiny squares with a number in each so that demonstrators could find their assigned places in the organized assemblies before the gate. During the early phase of the Cultural Revolution, as many as one million people, mostly youngsters, were summoned at times en masse into the square before Mao standing atop the vermilion gate. Mao's last appearance had been on May Day, but a disappointing one for many of the celebrants eager to see him. Appearing for the evening festivities accompanied by Lin Piao, and two nurses who have been seen with him often, Mao stood on the rostrum for only a few minutes. He sat at a table with Prince Norodom Sihanouk, the exiled Cambodian leader who resides in Peking, chatting for a few moments and glancing up at the firework displays, and then left. It was the first public appearance of the year for both Mao and the frail-looking Lin Piao, who had suffered in the past from tuberculosis and is said to have only one lung.

Continuing west past the gate on the Boulevard of Eternal Tranquillity, we came to the vermilion Hsinhua-men Gate and peeked past the two stone lions and two sentries into Nan Hai or South Lake Park, where, in the complete privacy of the walled compound amid the imperial cedars and pines, Mao, Chou En-lai and other top leaders live. They occupy residences and other pavilions of the Ming emperors, living amid imperial splendor in approved Socialist simplicity. No mention is ever made in the Chinese press of where the Party and government leaders reside, nor are photographs published illustrating their personal living styles. All the leaders dress plainly. Chiang Ch'ing, the wife of the Chairman, and Yeh Ch'ün, the wife of Lin Piao, who was also a member of the Politburo until she disappeared with her husband in September 1971, customarily wore an army uniform. The leaders were driven to their offices in limousines, usually of vintage Russian make, by chauffeurs in army uniform or dressed as ordinary workers. Nothing is published in China and very little is known of their family lives.

We walked back to the square and crossed to the south. On the west side was the Great Hall of the People, deliberately built some feet higher than the old Imperial Palace so the new governing dynasty could look down on the old. The emperors had forbidden commoners to erect any building taller than the spires of the sloping tiled roofs of their palaces. The imposing gray Great Hall was built in 1958, the year of the "Great Leap Forward," in the extraordinarily short time of ten months. All this from Audrey, who had already visited the Great Hall twice as the guest of Chou En-lai.

On the east side of the square were the large buildings housing the Historical Museum in the right wing and the Revolutionary Museum in the left wing. The museums were closed at the beginning of the Cultural Revolution, together with the Forbidden City and other historical repositories, to protect them from the unruly Red Guards, who had taken too literally the Lin Piao directive to eliminate the "Four Olds" — old things, old ideas, old customs, and old habits. In the closed museums and central public libraries in Peking, Yenan and other cities, the Maoists were also busy doing some rewriting and rearranging of historical perspectives to fit the new order. We walked past the 120-foot-high Monument to the People's Heroes, depicting episodes from the Revolution and texts in the calligraphy of Mao and Chou En-lai, which stands in the center of the square. Peasants, in from the countryside for a day of sightseeing, looked at us with more curiosity than the sophisticated Peking people. On holiday, most of them did not wear Mao buttons.

We turned east off the square, back toward the hotel, and walked along Legation Street, now dubbed Anti-Imperialism Street, where the old turreted diplomatic compounds of the American, French, British and other foreign embassies, and later consulates, had been located before the Communist victory. Only the Rumanian Embassy, opposite the former American compound, was still there. Prince Sihanouk was living amid the beautiful gardens of the old French Embassy, now a Foreign Ministry compound. The enclave, symbol of the old colonial foreign concessions, was otherwise completely under Chinese occupation. Most of the embassies are now in the new diplomatic quarter in the northeast district of the city, and most diplomats live comfortably, but not exquisitely as before, in modern apartment houses. St. Michael's Church, with its Gothic towers, was barred and desolate. The Wagon-lits Hotel, the famous hotel of old Peking, romanticized in novels and short stories, was shut. Charlotte Horstmann, who had an antique shop in the hotel, fled to Hong Kong, where she carries on. Fatigued, we entered the Hsin Ch'iao at the end of Legation Street, itself the site of the former German barracks, wondering what the Foreign Ministry planned for us the next day.

I had called at the Information Department of the Foreign Ministry earlier in the day and discussed my program. No assurance was ever given in advance that any of my requests would be granted, although my two principal requests eventually were met, that is, an appointment to talk to Chou En-lai and a visit to Manchuria, known now as the Northeast, which no Western correspondent had been allowed to do since the Cultural Revolution. The Information Department firmly controlled the activities of visiting journalists and those posted in Peking. There were many Communist correspondents, but only three Western reporters were permanently stationed in Peking, representing the Toronto *Globe and Mail*, Agence France Presse and DPA, the West German news agency. The Chinese permitted a woman journalist of Ansa, the Italian news agency, and one from Reuters, the British agency, to join them in the following months. Reuters had not been represented since Anthony Grey was seized by ultraleftist Red Guards on August 18, 1967, and kept in solitary confinement in a small room in his house for twenty-six months in retaliation for the arrests of Chinese by British authorities during rioting in Hong Kong.

Correspondents were able to move within Peking freely, but like other foreigners needed a special pass to go beyond the twenty-five-mile limit or into certain restricted areas. Permission was required from the Foreign Ministry and arrangements were made in advance to interview any official or make a professional visit to any state office, school, factory, firm or economic enterprise of consequence. The arrangements were not unlike those in Moscow, although Audrey found she was much freer to take photographs than in the Soviet Union.

The day-to-day arrangements were handled by Chi Ming-chung, of the Information Department, a fine-featured man who had served in London as a diplomat and spoke beautiful English with an Oxford accent. Chi had an unenviable job managing frustrated, impatient correspondents and at the same time making arrangements on their behalf with officials who viewed Western reporters uneasily.

Despite these pressures, which were at their height during the Grey case, when he endured notoriety abroad as the official who passed instructions to the incarcerated British reporter, Chi survived and seemed imperturbable.

I had one middle-of-the-night encounter with Chi, which was revealing of what he was like. Our phone rang at 3 o'clock one morning, and it was Chi politely asking if he could come to the hotel to see me. Speaking in his customary, cool, measured tone, he sounded as if he were suggesting afternoon tea. I waited for him at the hotel entrance, and soon the headlights of a black chauffeur-driven Mercedes were cutting through the darkness of the street and Chi emerged from the sedan smiling. With a graceful wave of his hand, he ushered me back into the hotel lobby to a divan in an alcove and ordered tea from an impassive attendant. Chi had doffed his buttoned-up tunic and was wearing a soft white sports shirt in deference to the heat, and there was only the barest trace of sleep in his eyes.

"Mr. Topping, just by chance," he began, "the clerk at the telegraph office who took your dispatch about Yao attended the meeting which you described. He noticed several errors—" Chi cleared his throat apologetically—"and he telephoned me." Chinese officials tell you there is no censorship in their country, although correspondents stationed in Peking sometimes file dispatches with inhibitions. Obviously, an official in the telegraph office reads outgoing press messages and the officials at the Information Department receive copies. Normally, dispatches are not held up, but if there is what is termed a factual error, an official may request that a correction be sent. In this instance, the clerk at the telegraph office, to spare me embarrassment, had held the dispatch, Chi informed me, smiling gently.

I had filed the dispatch, concerning Yao Teng-shan, the diplomat accused of responsibility for the burning of the British Office in 1967, about midnight after checking with several sources. There was no answer when I rang the Information Department. I had written that Yao reportedly had been sentenced to death, and this is what troubled the Chinese. There were one or two other errors cited. Chinese Communist officials may decline to provide information or give you incomplete facts which may distort your appreciation of a situation, but I never met an official who would tell me a bald untruth. I therefore accepted Chi at his word, and subsequently confirmed that he was accurate. I suggested that we go to the central telegraph office so that I could correct the dispatch. Chi welcomed this proposal as a fine idea, by his manner suggesting it had not occurred to him, and we proceeded to the telegraph office, where my telegram was altered to report imprisonment rather than death for Yao. Then back to the hotel, chatting about the weather, and with another graceful wave of his hand Mr. Chi was gone. We never discussed the incident again.

Each day's program was never given to me any further in advance than the previous day, and sometimes Chi would telephone as late as 11 P.M. to advise me of the schedule.

During our first days in Peking I visited a series of farm communes and factories. When I learned that the various central government ministries would not depart from their established custom and grant my requests for interviews, I realized how valuable these tours were. Each commune and factory was a world of its own, and specific questions about life in China were answered directly and frankly most of the time. There were differences among the communes and factories in terms of their development and prosperity, but work methods and organizational techniques were close to uniform throughout the country. "Know the anatomy of a single sparrow and you will know all sparrows," Yu told me, and he was right. Generally, I was taken to well-developed economic units, but they were not showplaces, nor did Chinese officials pretend they were typical. Constantly, I was told that China remained a backward country economically and that there was much work to be done to bring all communes and factories up to standard. Mao's injunction to develop one-third of a set of enterprises as models and then move onto another third for rapid development was commonly practiced. By correlating what I saw and the data gathered in various communes and factories, I began to piece together an appreciation of how the system worked. In China, where most doors in the capital remained closed to reporters, this was the only way to arrive at the composite that was reality.

The phone rang late that night. It was Chi. A farm commune awaited us in the morning.

CHAPTER 22

THE COMMUNES

In every school of the seventy thousand farm communes which encompass rural China and embrace about four-fifths of the nation's 800 million people, the children recite the tale of "The Foolish Old Man Who Removed the Mountains." It is a fable recounted by Mao in which the Foolish Old Man and his sons are ridiculed by another "wise" graybeard when they set out to dig away two mountain peaks which are obstructing the sun from the south. The Foolish Old Man persists, saying his descendants will carry on the digging for generations until the job is done. "God was moved by this," Mao wrote, "and he sent down two angels, who carried the mountains away on their backs." Mao went on to say that "our God is none other than the masses of the Chinese people," and if they work with the Communist Party, the two mountains of imperialism and feudalism can be cleared away. That was written in 1945, and today the peasants of China are told the story and asked to believe that if they persevere and work unceasingly, they can accomplish any task and overcome any obstacle. In a country still poor and backward, by the Communists' own definition, there had been many obstacles to the creation of a modern and prosperous agriculture. Over the centuries the land had become eroded, plagued by alternating flood and drought, and subdivided uneconomically by the peasant masses. There was not enough surplus produced on the land to finance the buying of the tractors and other machines needed to work the farms efficiently. When Mao ordered the organization of the communes in 1958, he turned to his designated God, the peasant masses, as the only

285

motive force open to him to finally lift Chinese agriculture from the encrustment of centuries of feudalism into the twentieth century. The communes he brought into being were structured so that the peasantry could be mobilized in tens of thousands to move mountains through sheer *people power.*

The communes or collectives now occupy 90 percent of the cultivated land, with the other 10 percent given over to state farms or wholly government-owned enterprises. Of varying size, the five communes I visited in Central, North and Northeast China ranged in membership from the approximately 10,000 people of the West Lake Tea Commune near Hangchow to the 38,770 people of the May 3 Vegetable Commune near Shenyang. Every commune controls a number of brigades or collectives, which are the basic accounting units, and these are further subdivided into production teams, which are the basic work units. Each production team is made up of the households of one or more villages.

The staggering changes in the shape and contours of the Chinese landscape are evidence of what *people power* generated by the communes can do. Thousands of peasants, without modern earth-moving equipment, mobilized by the communes, with primitive tools and bearing wicker baskets containing earth and stones on their heads, have built great dams and dikes and dug canals and thousands of miles of irrigation ditches. These form a network of water-conserving projects that protect the peasants from the age-old cycle of flood and drought.

Each commune that I visited had an achievement inspired by Maoist slogans to describe. At the August First Commune in the Northeast, the people show you a thirty-mile irrigation canal and tell you an incredible story of how fifty thousand peasants and soldiers dug it in eighteen days and nights. At the West Lake Tea Commune the peasants relate how in 1968 they struggled forty days and nights to fight back the waters of the Tsientang River, sometimes knocked over by the swift current as they stood in the water erecting dikes. Ten hectares of river bottom were reclaimed and converted into rice paddy fields in response to Mao's call for the communes to be self-sufficient in food.

The four-mile-long Yangtze River Bridge at Nanking, which some foreign experts doubted could ever be built, was completed in eight years by peasants, summoned from the communes, as many as fifty thousand of them laboring in a single day, moving earth by hand.

Much of the Maoist education of the peasant mass goes forward by emulation of successful models, and in every commune one hears Mao's instruction, "In agriculture, learn from Tachai." The extraordinary achievements of the three hundred people of a production brigade of the Tachai Commune at the foot of the Tiger-Head Hills in Shansi, in leveling, terracing and irrigating the starved, eroded land, are discussed in "Socialist education" meetings across all of China.

Apart from the personal power struggle, it was on the central question of the relationship of Socialist education and ideology to production that the great struggle between Mao and Liu Shao-ch'i turned, finally erupting in the Cultural Revolution.

The Cultural Revolution and the earlier Great Leap Forward were similar in that both were characterized by Mao's intuitive, romantic revolutionary style and his impatience with the practical day-to-day problems of administration. In 1958 when he ordered the headlong "Leap" into the organization of the farm communes, and in launching the revivalist Cultural Revolution in 1966, he felt the need for radical action if China was to be kept on the road to Communism as he envisioned it, a truly classless society: "From each according to his ability, to each according to his needs."

In both mass movements he unleashed a torrent of raw revolutionary energy that initially led to damaging excesses and loss of control over the society. When the communization of land was undertaken in 1958, a tide of revolutionary enthusiasm engendered by Mao obscured at first the serious errors that were committed. Having been brought relatively gently by stages to cooperative tilling of the land, the peasants were suddenly thrust into an accelerated program of collectivization that entailed the abolition of private property and the introduction of such innovations as common mess halls, which upset their traditional living style. An unrealistically intensive spurt in industrial development had also been ordered, and the peasants had been involved to such a degree that their energy was diverted from their primary agricultural tasks. By 1959, exhausted by extended working hours and resentful of forced communal living, the peasants began to balk.

The Maoist revolutionary zealots were compelled to yield to the pragmatists so that the damage could be repaired. Mao, in his own words, withdrew to the "second front," allowing Liu Shao-ch'i and Teng Hsiao-p'ing, General Secretary of the Party, to put the economy back in working order.

To get the peasantry back to work and restore output levels, certain private property rights were re-established. Peasants were allowed to own their own houses and personal possessions, including some farm tools, and most common mess halls were abolished. Private plots, where families had raised their own vegetables, were returned to the peasantry, and once more they were able to buy and sell things produced as a sideline, such as handicrafts, fruit, poultry and pork raised on the private plots. Some families began earning one-fifth or more of their income privately rather than through work in the collective. Some communes, deviating from the concept that the production team is the basic work unit, assigned output quotas to households and granted bonuses when they were exceeded. Subtle class distinctions began to re-emerge as some peasants grew richer.

The Maoists observed this retreat from Socialism with dismay. At the Tenth Plenum of the Central Committee in September 1962, Mao called for a revived battle against capitalism and rededication to the "class struggle." The army, which Lin Piao had just put through a "Socialist education" campaign, was in turn ordered into the countryside to reindoctrinate the peasantry. The cadres—party, government and commune managers—bowed to the Maoist directives, but most of them, preoccupied with production, made their obeisance rhetorically while declining in practice to return to the policies of 1958. Ideologically, the contest between the Maoists and the pragmatists boiled down to the question of which should take priority, production or Socialist endeavor looking forward to the creation of a classless society. The Maoists insisted that Socialist politics must remain in command and redness take precedence over expertness. Economically, the pragmatists wanted to rely on material incentives to spur production, while the Maoists asserted that the peasants could be inspired through "Socialist education" to lift up the economy. This ideological tug-of-war continued from 1962 until 1966, when Mao resolved the issue by touching off the Cultural Revolution.

It was not until I traveled in June to the Northeast, where the shock waves of the Cultural Revolution took effect later than in the regions to the south, that I could see clearly the abrasion of change in the countryside.

Audrey and I felt immediately the difference in atmosphere from that in other communes we had visited when we arrived at the August First Rice-Growing Commune north of Shenyang, accompanied by Robert Keatley of the *Wall Street Journal* and his wife. The commune apparently had not received any foreign visitors—certainly no Westerners—since the Cultural Revolution. We were greeted by San Kwang-ta, a tall, muscular, rather sullen-looking man, who was the chairman of the Revolutionary Committee, his deputy, Mrs. Tu Fu-ching, several other committee members, and Ch'en Wen-liang, a uniformed member of the PLA propaganda team assigned to the commune and the only one of the welcomers who could bring himself to smile. Army ranks were abolished in 1965 as an act of Socialist egalitarianism, and there is no insignia of rank on uniforms nor are army men introduced with titles. We were taken to a long room, in a one-story building, apparently used for conferences, decorated by a portrait of Mao and scrolls inscribed with four of his poems. A girl with braids poured hot water, rather than tea, evidently a sign of austerity, into our mugs on the white table, and when it cooled, dumped the tepid water on the earth-packed floor and gave us fresheners from her large thermos jug.

San began by formally welcoming us and then told us about the structure of the August First Commune. Like most communes it was a new, self-contained microcosm of rural China, with its own workshops, primary and middle schools, hospitals and shops. Its 19,000 people, of 4,000 households or families, lived on 8,000 acres of flat fertile land, mostly rice paddy fields, heavily traversed by irrigation ditches.

San told us the villages were organized into 73 production teams grouped into 15 brigades. The growing season was a short one in the rigorous northern climate, only 135 days, and the army, together with urban workers and students, was called in to help with the planting and the harvest. Off season, the commune peasants leveled the land, dug irrigation ditches and worked in the factories.

Suddenly the meeting room took on the atmosphere of a confessional as San, in a deliberate manner, began to intone the past ideological sins of the commune:

"Before the Cultural Revolution, the traitor scab Liu Shao-ch'i pursued a revisionist line, and some members of this commune began to revert to capitalism. They expanded their private plots endlessly, some to three times the original size. They took part in individual, not collective, cultivation and grain quotas were fixed for households. There were free markets. Some people who were running commune enterprises kept their profits, and there was speculation.

"But after the Cultural Revolution," San added grimly, "we smashed them. We carried out mass criticism and repudiation and greatly raised the consciousness of the people in the struggle between the revisionist line and the line of Chairman Mao. The people now cultivate for the Revolution."

San did not become more specific, but it was obvious that the peasantry had been reluctant to give up their private gains and that a hard struggle had taken place. The mood of well-being which we had seen in other communes was lacking here, although it was obviously an efficient work unit.

Although it was Sunday, normally the day of rest, most of the people, including children, appeared to be out working in the fields, and we saw only a few people in the tile-roofed houses made of bricks and mud. Presumably there were no days off during the short growing season.

San said a People's Liberation Army propaganda team of twenty members came to the commune in 1967 to carry out "struggle, criticism and transformation." San himself, who had worked in the Communist Party administration in Shenyang, and was obviously a troubleshooter, was sent to the commune in May 1970.

San said that the family private plots, each used mainly to raise vegetables, a few chickens and a pig, had been reduced to .016 of an acre per person. Private trade or free markets had been abolished. Handicrafts or food raised outside the collective must be bought or sold through a commune Supply and Marketing Cooperative. There is also a Loan and Credit Cooperative, where peasants may keep their savings at 4 percent interest or borrow at the same rate.

The PLA propaganda team has been cut down from twenty to twelve men, but its members still preside at "Socialist education" meetings to root out the old thinking.

San said the commune was steadily increasing its grain output and making progress toward the goal of self-sufficiency in vegetables and other food. In 1970 the commune turned over sixteen million tons of rice to the state. The state taxes each commune an average of about 6 percent of its income for use of the land. The commune is then paid in cash by the state for what output it turns over in excess of 6 percent. This money balance is distributed among the members of the commune in addition to their allotments of grain and other farm output after certain deductions are made. These deductions include the overhead expenses of the commune and funds for investment in equipment and other capital improvements at the commune, brigade and production team levels. There is also a welfare fund deduction of about 2 percent for care of the disabled, aged and others in need of aid. Each peasant is assured of the "five guarantees" of food, clothing, medicines, education and burial.

At death, the commune supplies a coffin and burial is in a crypt deep in the earth so there is no waste of the precious agricultural land. Once tradition required an above-ground shelter built of bricks and tile, or if the family was poor, of straw, preferably in a grove of mulberry trees. Now the communes have removed most of the ancestral grave mounds that once dotted the countryside. The elaborate ritual funeral with its procession, often with a Buddhist priest presiding, has also been eliminated. The ancestral shrines in the homes, containing the tablets of the dead, are no longer seen. What few remained appear to have been swept away by the Red Guards during their "Four Olds" campaign at the onset of the Cultural Revolution.

The ceremonies of the funeral and the wedding were once of great importance to the peasant, but a back-breaking expense. It is estimated that an average of one-seventh of the family budget went to finance these two ceremonies. Today, in place of the ritual funeral, the commune arranges a nonreligious memorial service for a deceased peasant at which his service to the state is extolled. To marry, a couple now just registers at a commune office. If the families desire it, a simple wedding party with toasts in the native wine and speeches by friends follows the registration.

The August First Commune was more mechanized than most, probably because of the short growing season and the relatively small indigenous work force for the land area. It had a central tractor station with fifteen machines, and there were another ten in the hands of the production teams. "If I had another twenty-five tractors, I could do without the bullocks, horses and donkeys," San said, referring to the animals the peasants now use in working their fields.

We strolled down a village street to the commune hospital, where we had an unexpected discussion about sex in China. It was a two-story building built around a courtyard, where patients seemed to be getting good basic medical attention, although without some of the comforts or frills of Western care. As we arrived, a sick man came to the hospital lying on a cart pulled by a bicycle. This seems to be the common way of bringing patients in. While in China, I never saw an ambulance charging down a street, or for that matter a speeding fire engine or police car with siren howling.

Walking through the corridors of the commune hospital with Yu, I saw a young woman in a white smock talking to a woman patient. At my suggestion, we entered what was obviously a dispensary, and I began to chat with the woman on duty, who was a nurse. We were soon joined by a doctor dressed in the ordinary tunic, baggy trousers and cap of a worker. I asked about the vigorously pressed birth control program in China.

The nurse said that the pill, a type developed in China that is taken twenty-one days in the month, was the most common method, overtaking the intrauterine devices which were still in wide use. All the birth control devices were distributed free by the hospital, in the dispensaries of the production teams. Abortions and male vasectomies were also provided without charge. Teams toured the countryside showing family planning films and handing out literature.

"We are also encouraging the boys and girls to marry late," the doctor added. "There is no fixed age, and postponing marriage is entirely voluntary. We suggest twenty-five for men and twenty-three for women in the countryside. We tell them late marriage is good for the country. It is better for their health, gives them more time to study and to make a bigger contribution to Socialist construction." In the urban areas even later marriage is urged, twenty-five or twenty-six for women and twenty-seven or twenty-eight for men. Under old Chinese customs it was common for families to arrange child marriages.

I then pulled a gaffe by asking if sexual relations outside marriage were common in view of the trend to late marriage. Yu, glancing about in embarrassment at the other Chinese who had crowded into the dispensary out of curiosity, lost his temper with me for the first and only time and snapped: "That's a silly question." But he put it to the doctor and nurse, who said that extramarital relations were rare.

The reaction to my question was revealing of the extent to which the Communist Party had engendered an attitude of puritanism toward sex and disapproved of promiscuity. In the revolutionary plays which dominate the Chinese stage and films, a romantic attachment is often implied but always thrust aside for the sake of duty to the Party, state and people. It was hard for me to believe that the Chinese, despite the new discipline, were not having considerable psychological problems in wrestling with the temptation to promiscuity. The Chinese are a highly sexed people, whose inclinations in the past were evidenced by large families and an accepted system of concubinage that is still practiced by some Chinese in the communities of Southeast Asia. With the lack of privacy in China today, the young people are not allowed many temptations. One sees them holding hands in the park or together on organized hikes into the countryside to help the peasants, taking part in mass sports or attending revolutionary theater performances. There was a period of looseness during the Cultural Revolution when as Red Guards boys and girls traveled and camped together and the birth rate went up. But discipline has been restored, and once again the marital bed, at least officially, exercises a monopoly on sex.

When we left the hospital, Yu was still in a bad temper. Getting back into a car to leave the commune, I remarked about how different moral attitudes were in the United States. He asked sarcastically: "You mean wife-swapping?"

When I spent a day in the Chinese-Vietnamese Friendship People's Commune, north of Peking, I had a better opportunity to get a close-up look at village life.

At the gate to the village compound of Shih Ke Chuang, peasants wearing Mao buttons came out with undisguised curiosity and broad smiles to welcome me, the first American they had seen in more than twenty years. The village, with 628 inhabitants, makes up one of the Chinese-Vietnamese Commune's 95 production teams.

Touring the commune, I saw fine red-brick buildings constructed to house the animal husbandry and central administration buildings. But the villages themselves had not been extensively rebuilt, although they were cleaner and more orderly than those I had seen before 1949.

In Shih Ke Chuang there are still old tile-roofed, small houses behind white walls made of lime-painted bricks and mud. The narrow streets are paved with stones, as are the small courtyards and floors of houses.

Mrs. Li Yang-shih, a fifty-four-year-old long-time inhabitant of Shih Ke Chuang, lives in a typical small two-room house, whose walls are decorated with the portrait of Mao and posters depicting scenes from revolutionary plays of the Peking Opera. She shares her house with three children. Her husband works in a carpet factory in Peking, and he bicycles home fourteen miles every Sunday rather than pay bus fare. The Li family sleeps on the traditional kang bed, which is made of brick with an oven for heating below. It is covered with straw mats and bedding. Water hauled from an outside well stands in a tall jar in a corner, and the main room is illuminated by a single electric bulb, which is the only utility Mrs. Li pays for. The house is owned by the family. In a tiny courtyard outside there are a few chickens and a black pig. The state supplies fodder on the condition that the pig be sold to the government slaughterhouse. The money is used to buy processed pork. Mrs. Li shops for cloth and other necessities in the village store, where prices are the same as those in Peking.

"I am happy now," she told me. "Before liberation I worked hard for a landlord."

For entertainment she likes to go to performances of an amateur troupe in the village and to see films shown by a touring projection unit. A loudspeaker in her house, which she can turn off, brings her wired music, mostly revolutionary songs, and political lectures.

Mr. Li earns 60 yuan a month, about $25 at the exchange rate of 2.4 yuan to the dollar, at his factory job. Mrs. Li from her job in a nursery and an unmarried daughter, who works in the fields, earn an additional 60 yuan—$25. On that income the family eats well, with dishes of rice, meat and vegetables. The two women are members of the commune.

The production team pays Mrs. Li's daughter in terms of work points. Generally each member of the team is classified in one of four grades, according to skills, physical ability and cultural and ideological development. Each grade, on a graduated basis, receives from seven to ten points for each day's labor. There are some nongrade peasants who receive less than seven points. The grade of each worker is decided by the work team after hearing the claim of the individual concerned. Many married women work on the teams, leaving their children in the commune's free nurseries or with grandparents, and thus increase the family income. According to the rules, pay for men and women is on a basis of equality, but in practice in some places some of the old discrimination persists, with women not being credited with work points according to the same criteria as men.

The commune or brigade can mobilize the production team for special jobs. In 1960 five thousand of the commune's total force of nineteen thousand workers labored for seven months to dam the Sha River to create a reservoir. Two hundred miles of irrigation ditches were later dug and pumping stations were built to give the region its first flood control system and continuing water supply in time of drought. Today the commune has rich, leveled farmland, with extensive fields of rice, wheat, soybeans, corn and orchards divided by tree-lined roads.

At the end of the year, each one of the brigades determines what share each of its production teams has earned from sales of output to the state. Then the production team redistributes earnings to its members proportionately according to the individual work points earned. Last year the Shih Ke Chuang team, which is one of the most productive in the commune, harvested 7.5 tons of rice and paid each worker an average of $0.62 (1.5 yuan) a day. This compared to the average rate of pay of $0.41 (one yuan) in other, less productive teams. Some 10,000 yuan ($4,166) were withheld by the production team for investment and used to purchase small tractors. During the year peasants draw advances in farm produce and money against their annual payment to meet daily living needs. If a family for some reason fails to earn enough to provide its necessities, an allotment is made from the welfare fund.

Each person in the commune is charged one yuan ($0.41) a year for medical care. This includes everything except the services of the commune dentist and the purchase of eyeglasses, which cost about $4.16 (10 yuan).

Medical treatment begins at the production team dispensary, two small rooms with white-lime walls and stone floor where Chinese herb medicine and Western medication are provided by Miss Lo Hui-ying, a pert twenty-four-year-old graduate of a six-month medical course. Miss Lo is one of 120 "barefoot doctors" in the commune, who work directly with peasants as part-time medical practitioners and also share in their labor. Her fellow "barefoot doctor" in the dispensary is on leave in Peking, where he is supplementing his two-and-a-half-year medical education. Miss Lo treats peasants mainly for minor ailments and finds them generally in good health. She gives them advice on sanitation and urges them to brush their teeth every morning, which they probably do judging by the white teeth one sees among the younger Chinese. When her patients have more serious ailments, they go to one of the commune's six medical centers served by fifty doctors. If a medical center sends a patient to a hospital in Peking for advanced treatment, the commune will pay the costs. But if the patient himself elects to go, he pays.

In Shih Ke Chuang adult education classes are held, and there is universal education available for children through the first three of the five years of middle or secondary school.

When I visited the Hei Lung Kuan secondary school, class was in session for four hundred students meeting in simple one-story buildings, with some forty students assigned to each classroom teacher. Hung

Yu-lo, a teacher and chairman of the Revolutionary Committee of the school, told me that it had been put under the supervision of a board of education made up of poor and lower-middle-income peasants since the Cultural Revolution. However, he said that examinations were still prepared by the teachers and given periodically during the two semesters of the year.

On the wall of Hung's office was posted the class schedule for that day for the second-year students. It called for seven forty-five minute periods. The initial period was given over to study of Mao's works. This was followed by Chinese language and literature, mathematics, agricultural biology, musical instruments and singing revolutionary Peking Opera, politics and ideology, and, finally, a marching and sports period on the red-clay outdoor fields where there are a basketball court and gymnastic parallel bars.

When the students leave school, they must put in three years of manual labor. Then they can compete for entrance into a college, for which they must be nominated by a committee that includes peasants of their village. "Academic grades are not the only criteria," Hung told me as we walked between the classroom buildings emblazoned with Maoist slogans. "They are judged in an all-around way, taking into account their political and cultural development."

Miss Sun Fu-chi, a thirty-year-old graduate of the Peking Teachers Training University, who was wearing braids and a gray tunic over a white blouse, was teaching agricultural biology to her second-year class. The ages of her forty-seven students varied because the school had been closed during 1966–68 when the Cultural Revolution was in its tumultuous stage and some of the Red Guard boys and girls were trying to make up the lost years. The students sat two-by-two at wooden desks writing with fountain pens in copybooks. They had just studied some plants under microscopes. On a wall, a slogan in large characters declared: "HEIGHTEN OUR VIGILANCE AND DEFEND OUR MOTHERLAND."

Miss Sun used a paperback textbook that has been revised since the Cultural Revolution to include more practical applications. It was marked "provisional and experimental."

The secondary schools, like the universities which have been reopened, are still suffering from a lack of precise directives as to how to revise their curricula. They have only rather vague guidelines, drawn on the basis of Mao's generalities about the need to emphasize practical studies and the ideological struggle.

In another classroom, politics was being taught. The teacher, Miss Han Lu-chu, had written on the blackboard a denunciation of "revisionist traitor Liu Shao-ch'i."

As we left the school, Ma Ching-chang, the vice chairman of the commune's Revolutionary Committee, confessed that he, too, had for a time been led astray ideologically by the ideas of Liu Shao-ch'i and P'eng Chen, the purged Mayor of Peking. Ma said he had been "unable to distinguish between the proper road to Socialism and capitalism" and had been removed from his post as vice director of the commune, and subjected to mass criticism by the people. Later, after studying Mao's work, Ma said, he had become ideologically rehabilitated. When the Revolutionary Committee of the commune was formed in March 1968, Ma, an impressive-looking, obviously intelligent man of forty-five, had been elected vice chairman. Driving out of the commune, I waved goodbye to Ma, and the vice chairman waved his red book of Mao quotations in reply.

My tour of various communes and what data I had gathered on nationwide agricultural performance left me with the impression that China was close to a solution of its central economic problem: the creation of an annual farm surplus. Such a surplus is vital to finance internal development and pay for the imports of raw materials and machines required for industrialization. In 1960 the Party Central Committee adopted the guideline: "Agriculture is the foundation and industry is the leading factor," thus accepting, as it does currently, that the wherewithal to transform China into a modern industrial state must come in the first instance from the land. Until China's infant industry can grow large enough to compete strongly on world markets, about three-fourths of her exports must continue to be raw and processed agricultural products.

When I left China in 1949, I reported that it was unlikely that the Communists would be able to rescue the country from its economic bog. The problem then essentially was that the fast-expanding population was consuming everything produced by primitive Chinese agriculture, and, in fact, grain was being imported to make up a deficit. I added one qualification to this gloomy prognosis: If the Communists could sustain the momentum of their Revolution and fundamentally transform Chinese society, then the gap between production and consumption might be closed and a surplus to fund industrialization created.

Mao has done just that, I believe, on the basis of my glimpse of the new China. In the commune system Mao found the means of mobilizing the peasant masses to move the mountains he spoke of in his adaptation of the fable of the Foolish Old Man. The peasant masses, roused out of the torpor of feudalism and inspired to adopt a new frontier spirit, have reshaped the land with their water conservancy projects and broken the cycle of drought and flood.

Although agricultural development varies from area to area, most communes report a doubling or even quadrupling of production since 1958, when the communes were founded. Allowing for local ideological refurbishing of statistics, every reliable indicator—official reports of record harvests, the abundance seen in local markets, and the reduction in wheat imports—points to a great upsurge in farm output. The Chinese say their steady increase in grain production has been achieved without reliance on the new miracle high-yield grain strains developed in the Rockefeller-funded International Rice Research Institute in the Philippines and elsewhere. The strains have resulted in a "green revolution" in India and other countries. Chinese farm officials speak of their own improved seed varieties and also attribute high yields to irrigation, greater use of chemical fertilizer and multiple cropping. Nevertheless, the Chinese say much work remains to be done before a significantly larger portion of the land can be diverted to exportable cash crops, such as nuts, cotton, tobacco, rice, vegetable oil, fruits and other produce for canning, and animal products.

The present modest farm surplus can be attributed not only to success in production but also to the birth control program. Farm output is rising proportionate to population. The peasants have become more amenable to birth control because they no longer must depend on having sons who will till their land and care for them in old age. The commune welfare fund affords old-age insurance where needed.

Chou En-lai warned us, however, at dinner one evening, that "old customs take lots of hard effort to overcome." He quoted Mao as saying that one must not believe everything that is said in the countryside about birth control and the equality of women. "In some places it is still like the old days. First there is a girl born, then a second, third, fourth and fifth, until there are nine girls. By then the wife is forty-five, and only then can she stop trying for a son. Is this equality?"

Jokingly, I told Chou En-lai that as the father of five daughters I could see the problem. "No sons?" asked Chou, raising his thick black eyebrows. "Topping is tired," someone said. "No," rejoined Chou quickly. "Mrs. Topping is tired. I'm talking on behalf of women."

Notwithstanding Mao's reservation, and the absence of reliable detailed birth statistics, there does seem to be a decline in the birth rate, varying from area to area, but apparently averaging below 2 percent. In the communes the younger couples, either because of late marriage or contraception, seem to be raising more families of only one, two or three children. In the villages opposition is voiced, particularly by women, to the old-style large families. Nevertheless, even if this trend continues, there will be more than a billion Chinese by the end of the century.

Ideologically, the communes seem stable enough so that there is not constant interruption, as before, in the rhythm of production. The ideological pendulum, which swung between the Maoist rigidity of 1958, when the communes were first organized, to the emphasis on material incentive during the ascendancy of Liu Shao-ch'i, has come to rest at a center position of relative moderation. But the PLA propaganda teams are still active in the communes, and there are PLA or militiamen on every commune Revolutionary Committee, reflecting the Maoist conviction that the fight against incipient capitalism must go on endlessly. The Chinese peasant by nature is an industrious, acquisitive being with a taste for good living. His frugality is not an end in itself, but an expression of savings in the aspiration toward relative affluence. Mao's Socialist education aims at replacing this materialism with a commitment to the Communist goal of "From each according to his ability, to each according to his needs," and dedication to the support of world revolution. But it seems doubtful that the peasant, conditioned by millenniums of lonely struggle for self-betterment, can be purged of his yen for profit unless Maoist ideological strictures are applied rigorously for generations. Recognition of this reality is implied in the compromises that Mao has made. Today, between 4 and 7 percent of the cultivated land is given over to private plots, although in 1958 he sought to abolish them. The peasant is paid according to his work and size of harvest, not his need. The peasant remains owner of his house and personal possessions and tools, rights he lost temporarily in 1958. In the village of Shih Ke Chuang officials laughed and dismissed as "foreign inventions" reports of communal mess halls and dormitories, choosing to forget that a move was made in that direction during the "Leap." Mao or his successors may decide once again to force the pace of collectivization. In 1971, however, although the slogan in every commune was "Politics in command," I discerned more of a preoccupation with the priorities of production than the cadres cared to state.

Although the peasant is regimented as a laborer, he is not a robot, nor does he live in an anthill, as is sometimes pictured abroad. In the village, the individual household continues to be the basic social unit and family attachments and affections remain strong. In the early years of the Communist campaign against the habits and thinking of the old society, ideological barriers were erected between children and their parents. There were tensions, and children reported to Party commissars on the ideological sins of their elders. Through common indoctrination over the years, this ideological generation gap has been closed. Ancestor shrines in the homes have been replaced by portraits of Mao or photos of the revolutionary operas, but children are openly devoted to their parents. Grandparents share households and customarily take care of small children. Most elderly people live with their children, although there are "respect-for-the-aged" homes in the communes.

On my return to China in 1971, I found the peasant typically to be the same intelligent, good-humored person I knew in 1949. In manners, he displayed the same gentle civility and earthy sophistication that are his natural cultural heritage. There was something else as well, a new pride and confidence in himself and his country. He tells you that China has shaken off the feudal past, become self-reliant and taken its rightful place in the world. He has obeyed Mao's injunction to stand up and walk with dignity.

The peasant lives in a monolithic state. He has never known parliamentary democracy, or freedom in the Western sense, and he does not know it now. Yet he has more of a voice in the management of his village affairs than ever before. He is freed from the bullying landlord, the usurer, the corrupt official. The woman has won freedom from child marriage, concubinage and slavery, enjoys equality before the law and in the economy, the right of divorce and abortion. Illiteracy has been reduced, according to official statements, to about 10 to 15 percent of the population, mostly the aged or infirm, giving the peasant a new social mobility. When the Communist state was founded in 1949, about 80 percent of the population was illiterate.

These are the gains, together with greater material well-being on the average, which the peasant weighs against the loss of some of his former individualism. (Yes, there are too many ideological meetings and lectures, everybody agrees.) Someday the peasant may yearn for other freedoms. Someday he may want television sets and refrigerators in addition to bicycles and sewing machines. Just now, he is obviously content with the balance sheet of past and present.

CHAPTER 23

REMEMBER THE BITTER PAST

One sparkling clear morning in Peking, Audrey and I, accompanied by Yu, drove to the Forbidden City and after showing our pass to a sentry entered through the Flowery Gate at the southeastern corner of the compound. The fabulous Imperial Palace, rebuilt in the fifteenth century by the Ming emperors, stands close to the center of the Imperial City. To the south of the palace stands the Gate of Heavenly Peace, and between this gate and the palace are lovely public gardens, the Sun Yat-sen Park on the west side of the Altar of Earths and Harvests, and on the east, the People's Cultural Park. In the eastern garden, where once emperors went to worship at the Temple of the Imperial Ancestors, the peasant and worker subjects of the new dynasty now stroll among the cypress and willow trees or pause to play chess or table tennis as overhead loudspeakers blare revolutionary songs and Communist political lectures.

Within the vermilion walls of the Forbidden City, the emperors of the Ming Dynasty and later the Ch'ing or Manchu Dynasty had their personal apartments. During the Cultural Revolution many of the palace's priceless art treasures were taken to secret storehouses to protect them from the Red Guards as the campaign against the "Four Olds" raged. Despite the ideological incantations sounded during the Cultural Revolution against all vestiges of the old society, we did see in China ample evidence of the regime's long-term concern with the preservation of historic buildings and the classic art treasures. The palace grounds within the Forbidden City were closed to the public during our stay in Peking, as they had been except on rare occasions since the Cultural Revolution, but they have since been opened and new exhibitions of antiquities are on view at the Palace Museum.

When we toured the palace grounds on a previous occasion, the Foreign Ministry had arranged for us to visit the closed apartments and temples in the Forbidden City. The magnificent rectangular 250-acre grounds are secluded by 35-foot-high vermilion walls and a 150-foot-wide water-filled moat. At each corner of the Forbidden City there is a tower surmounted by pavilions with yellow-tiled roofs. Inside the walls, the visitor passes through a succession of golden- and purple-tile-roofed palaces and temples, bearing such names as the Palace of Heavenly Purity and the Hall of Perfect Harmony, guarded by stone and bronze phoenixes, dragons and animal figures, and separated by great cobbled courtyards. In the Imperial Garden, we saw workmen restoring the red-pillared pavilions, standing amid the royal white peonies and cypress, and joined by carved stone arched bridges. Some of the marvelously fashioned vases, furniture and draperies have been returned to the emperors' personal apartments, and they can be seen through large windows. Here and there on the walls one could detect the smear of a Maoist slogan painted by the Red Guards, but most of the defacing marks have been removed. In one courtyard workmen were putting up a large standing plaster sign inscribed with Maoist slogans, but it was being constructed so as to stand apart from the ancient wall. The work being done suggested that the palace would be reopened soon.

When we traveled to the Northeast, we also saw restoration work being done on the Eastern and Northern Ch'ing Tombs near Shenyang. The Eastern tombs had been neglected and weeds had begun to grow through some of the pagoda roofs.

On this particular morning, we were visiting the only section of the Forbidden City which was open to organized visits by the Chinese public. We had been invited to see an exhibition housed in the Hall of the Worship of the Ancestors in the northeast section of the Forbidden City. It was an exhibition, contrasting strangely with its surroundings, that was revealing of the means used by the Communists to secure and hold the loyalty of the Chinese masses. Long lines of people, mostly schoolchildren, under the supervision of their teachers, and young soldiers, were waiting to enter the cobbled courtyard that leads to the temple. Across the portico of the Hall of the Worship of the Ancestors, in white characters on red banners, was inscribed: "LONG LIVE THE INVINCIBLE MAO TSE-TUNG THOUGHT, LONG LIVE THE COMMUNIST PARTY, LONG LIVE THE GREAT LEADER CHAIRMAN MAO." In the high-ceilinged temple, arranged in a sequence of tableaux were life-sized sculpted brown-clay figures depicting the sufferings of peasants under the landlords and Nationalist officials in pre-Communist China. Groups of schoolchildren were being taken from tableau to tableau and at each station given a lecture by an exhibition guide which concluded with the cry uttered with clenched fist: "We will never forget the bitter past."

The realistic clay figures had been brought from the province of Szechwan and were said to record the exploitation of peasants there by the landlord, Liu Wen-chai, who was also described as a "Kuomintang warlord." In 1948, we were told, he controlled more than thirty thousand acres of land scattered over more than forty counties, and had built twenty-eight palaces on his properties. A young woman guide showed us around the exhibition, reciting the shocking misdoings of the landlord with crisp efficiency. We were shown first some of the torture instruments said to have been used on unruly peasants, including a boxlike affair in which a manacled prisoner was held as drops of water fell on his head. We were informed that the only known survivor of this torture was a woman who is now vice chairman of the Tang We People's Commune in Szechwan. There were tableaux showing the tattered peasants being compelled to pay extortionate rents. Others showed them being beaten, their daughters being dragged off to serve the pleasure of the landlord, and peasants imprisoned in cages. The final scene showed triumphant peasants and Communist soldiers joining together to slaughter their oppressors, the landlord and his henchmen. At this final tableau each group of children shouted in unison: "Long Live Chairman Mao!"

Hundreds of thousands of Chinese, the guide said, had seen this "class education exhibition organized so that the young will know what it was like in the Kuomintang times and the older generation will never forget." The exhibition was opened at the beginning of the Cultural Revolution. It replaced a display of tomb figurines of the period fifth century B.C. to ninth century A.D. and clay figures of the Chou Dynasty. The guide told us: "This exhibition follows Chairman Mao's teachings that art and literature should serve the broad masses." We saw a miniature replica of the Szechwan exhibit in the Museum of the Ming Tombs north of Peking. Many other miniatures are displayed throughout the country.

The Szechwan exhibition is one of the many means used by the Communists to inculcate a sense of gratitude in the Chinese for their present-day living conditions. In schools, factories and communes there are frequent discussion meetings, usually given some such name as "Remember Bitterness and Think of Sweetness," at which members of the older generation tell vivid stories of starvation and maltreatment by landlords and Nationalist officials before the establishment of the Communist government. Most of the new revolutionary stage productions, including five operas, two ballets and three pure musical numbers, produced under the leadership of Chiang Ch'ing to replace the stylized traditional Peking Opera, deal with the theme of the sufferings of the people under the landlords and Nationalist officials, who are also accused of working with the Japanese invaders. These productions not only dominate the stage but also are seen constantly on television, in skits put on in schools, factories and communes, and are heard on the radio or over public loudspeakers, and their tunes sung as popular songs.

In this unending "Socialist education" campaign, the Communist Party is mainly concerned with making the young aware of and grateful for the improvement in living conditions. Before the Cultural Revolution there were signs of restiveness among the youth, who were beginning to yearn for the more worldly pleasures, such as more style in dress and better consumer goods. Most of the older people need no convincing about the disabilities of life under the Chiang Kai-shek Government. In their minds, they tend to lump together, not only the inequities of the old land tenancy system, the inefficiency and corruption of many Nationalist officials, but also the deprivations suffered as a consequence of some thirteen years of Japanese invasion and civil war into a blanket, sometimes oversimplified indictment of the past regime. During my tour of China, ordinary people consistently expressed to me support of the Communist Government, not in a romantic revolutionary or ideological context, but simply in terms of better present-day living conditions, security and revulsion from their pre-1949 experiences.

Once walking through a village of the Nan Yuen Commune south of Peking, I noticed a grizzled old peasant grinding grain in a shed. He was Chao Yu-ching, a sixty-seven-year-old miller, and I asked him what he thought was Mao's greatest accomplishment. "Since the liberation,

Mao has brought us a lot of happiness," Chao replied without hesitation. "I am no longer worried about my food and clothing. Before I worked as a hired laborer and earned twenty yuan [$8.33] a year. Now I earn five hundred yuan [$208.33] a year. Before liberation, I had to work very hard. I had to get up when the stars were still shining in the sky and I went home when it was dark. The food was bad and I ate husks and chaff. We would get better food such as steamed buns only at the autumn or New Year festival."

In the Peking No. 3 Cotton Textile Factory, Audrey and I selected at random a thirty-one-year-old woman, Ma Shu-ching, who was working at a table correcting faults in cotton cloth. Seventy percent of the six thousand workers in the factory are women. Mrs. Ma said she came from a poor peasant family. "My father was killed by our landlord," Mrs. Ma said. "The landlord wanted to take my older sister, and my father tried to stop him. My sister ran away to some relatives. When the landlord came and asked my father where my sister was hiding, he would not tell him. So they killed him. When we found his body, he had one leg cut off." A small shy woman, wearing a white smock and hair covering, Mrs. Ma's eyes became moist as she told her story. Mrs. Ma now earns 58 yuan ($24.16) a month at her forty-eight-hour-a-week job. Her husband, who is employed in the telegraph office, earns 70 yuan ($29.16). They have three children, two in elementary school and another in a nursery. Mrs. Ma's mother lives with them, and she looks after the children.

Driving back to Peking from the Ming Tombs in the Western Hills, I saw an old man in the fields driving two donkeys along. He was wearing a large straw peasant's hat and a bleached jacket and pants. I stopped the car, went into the field and asked him to compare his old life with his present way of living. The herdsman, who is seventy and lives with his son in the Ming Tomb Commune, looked at me quizzically through wise eyes and said deliberately: "Things are better now. I understand the meaning of life now because I am happy."

In a large workshop of the Peking Heavy Electric Machinery Plant, I stopped at the bench of a young apprentice, Chu Ya-cheng, an eighteen-year-old graduate of three years of secondary school who had been working for one year in the heavy-electric-motor shop, and asked him what he thought was the single most important thing that Mao had done for him. "For someone like me, who comes from a poor family," Chu replied after thinking for a few moments, "before the liberation

I could never have afforded to go to school. Now, thanks to the Party and Chairman Mao, I have received an education and a chance to work in this modern factory."

The official history of every commune, which is taught to the children and is told to visitors, always has a before-and-after section. At the May 3 Vegetable Commune, south of Shenyang, Yang Shih-shung, a member of the Revolutionary Committee, told us: "About 80 percent of the land in this area was owned by landlords and rich peasants. Under the evil rule of the old society, my entire family was wiped out except for myself. My father, a laborer hired by the landlord, was beaten to death. My mother went to beg for a living and died of starvation. My younger sister was sold as a slave, and my younger brother died of the winter cold."

Some of these stories may have been embellished over the years with retelling, but they are obviously generally accepted by the young. There is no one around in mainland China to demur. Many thousands of the accused landlords were executed after mass trials in the purges that followed the establishment of Communist rule. The surviving landlords and rich peasants, and sometimes their descendants as well, are marked as being of questionable class origin and they lead circumspect lives.

Going to the ballet is the brightest and liveliest way of taking in a tale about the bad old days. One night, we attended a gala performance of the *Red Detachment of Women*, in which the evil old landlord is pursued and demolished by a bevy of beautiful ballerinas, dressed in what would be described in New York as "hot pants." The production is one of the most popular of the revolutionary Peking operas put on the stage by Chiang Ch'ing, and it is a potpourri of modern music with vivid romantic themes, Soviet-style ballet, and melodramatic gestures reminiscent of the purged Peking Opera, which featured the stylistic posturings of emperors, concubines, mandarins and generals. During his visit to Peking, President Nixon would see a performance of the *Red Detachment of Women* in the Great Hall of the People.

The theater is an occasion in Peking, as it is in New York, and before the curtain we dined at the Big Duck Restaurant near the Drum Tower. The meal, eight sumptuous courses, was ordered two hours in advance at 4 yuan ($1.67) per person. This time, however, when the brown crisp basted duck ready to be sliced was brought out in traditional fashion at the end of a long skewer for the inspection of the guests, I felt sorrow for the duck. I had been out to the Chinese-Vietnamese Commune, which supplies ducks to the restaurants of Peking and observed the forced feeding of the fowl. The famous ducks of Peking are white, yellow-billed birds which are fed a soupy mixture of flour, kaoliang, maize and soybean cakes. Each duck is taken to what looks like a small farm water pump with a pipe attached. The pipe is inserted in the bill and the mixture is pumped into the duck. When the duck is approaching maturity and slaughter, this is done once every six hours. "They like it," the feeder of the ducks assured me with a grin. But it took a full week before I was eating duck again with my former relish.

The ballet was at the T'ien Chiao or Heavenly Bridge Theatre near the Temple of Heaven in the southern district of Peking. It was a small, plain-looking theater with a double-tiered balcony, and illuminated signs flanking the stage flashed rows of Chinese characters to keep the audience posted on what was going on. The orchestra was roped off and presently television klieg lights were switched on and in walked General Javier Tantalean Vanini, the Peruvian Minister of Fisheries, in a bemedaled uniform, and Mirko Tepavac, the Yugoslav Foreign Minister, in a sports shirt. Most of the tickets had been distributed through official organizations. PLA men were sitting in blocks of seats, and in the balcony there were many overseas Chinese, conspicuous by their narrow trousers and short skirts, and foreigners.

The curtain rose. Opening scene according to the program: "Wu Ching-hua, daughter of a poor peasant, is chained to a post in the crude dungeon of tyrannical landlord Nan Pa-tien on the island of Hainan. Her eyes burn with hatred. If only she could smash the tiger's lair to smithereens."

The slave girl is played by the prima ballerina, Hsueh Chin-hua, a beautiful lithe girl in her twenties. Her name is not mentioned on the program because the Chinese prefer to give prominence to an artistic group rather than an individual star, nor is information provided on her ballet training. Up until 1959, Soviet teachers were working with the Peking Ballet Company. Its repertory included *Giselle* and *Swan Lake* as late as 1964, when Chiang Ch'ing launched her revolutionary productions. Miss Hsueh's style shows the Soviet influence as well as the special acrobatic skills of the Chinese dancers.

As the slave girl, Miss Hsueh is costumed in a red pants suit with golden ballet slippers, and she wears her hair in a single long heavy braid.

The slave girl escapes the dungeon with the landlord in pursuit. She is captured, beaten into unconsciousness and left for dead. A Red Army cadre and his messenger Pang enter in disguise. After hearing her story, "with profound proletarian class feelings," they tell her where to seek the Red Army. At the revolutionary base the slave girl finds the people celebrating the formation of the Red Detachment of Women, all dressed in blue-gray short pants uniforms and shouldering rifles. The slave girl joins, and the Red Army cadre uses her story to educate the people: Only by taking up guns and following Chairman Mao and the Communist Party to wage revolution can the oppressed people achieve emancipation. A raid is carried out on the landlord's citadel, but he escapes when the slave girl in her hatred fires on him, prematurely giving the signal for the main attack. Disgraced, the slave girl takes further political indoctrination and is awarded another chance to carry the gun and chase the enemy. She also learns from the Red Army cadre: Only by emancipating all mankind can the proletariat achieve its own final emancipation. The enemy attacks, and in a heroic defense of a mountain pass the Red Army cadre sacrifices himself. Then the Red Army counterattacks and captures the lair of the landlord, who is shot. The slave girl takes the place of the martyred Red Army cadre. Revolutionary masses flock to join the Red Army. Battle songs resound to the heavens: Forward, forward under the banner of Mao Tse-tung, forward to victory!

As a curtain falls, upon it appear the smiling features of Chairman Mao at the center of a sun radiating rays of light. The audience has been enthusiastic, hissing the landlord and applauding his death. The cast comes forward triumphantly, waving their little red books, and the audience joins in singing "Sailing the Seas Depends on the Helmsman." A typical night at the revolutionary Chinese theater is ended.

Westerners might very well leave the theater repelled by the obvious propaganda content of the production, but this is not the reaction of the Chinese audiences. The revolutionary productions are conceived as popular morality plays for the consumption of the unsophisticated Chinese masses. In this context, they are effective theater. The audiences stream out of the theaters humming the catchy tunes and subtly bent to the Maoist view of life—"Remember bitterness and think of sweetness!"

CHAPTER 24

THE NORTHEAST

Like a serpent, the Great Wall undulated over the hills below us as our Ilyushin-14 sped north from Peking to Shenyang, the city once called Mukden by the Manchus. Our plane was a twenty-four-seat Soviet-made turboprop with blue fuselage walls, blue, newly washed, cotton-covered seats, and a smiling stewardess who served jasmine tea and dried fruits to the passengers. Robert Keatley, the Washington correspondent of the *Wall Street Journal*, a bespectacled young man who looks like a State Department protocol officer, but has a puckish sense of humor that would get him quickly fired from any such job, and his wife, Ann, a pert girl who met Bob and learned Chinese while a student in Hong Kong, were traveling with us. Why the Chinese had decided to give a visa to the *Wall Street Journal* while ignoring such newspapers as the Washington *Post* and the Los Angeles *Times* was a subject of much discussion among us. I theorized that the Chinese were demonstrating their openness by admitting the correspondent of a newspaper whose name indicated that it was the organ of those archvillains in Peking's ideological constellation: the evil capitalist barons who were bossing the United States.

Yu, who was traveling with us, was quite excited since he had lived in Shenyang as a boy for six years while attending secondary school. "In 1954 my parents and teachers warned me not to eat anything without cleaning it because the Americans had dropped germs," Yu recalled. "We killed flies and mosquitoes and other germ carriers." When I told Yu I didn't believe the stories of the Korean War about American germ

310

warfare, he became quite indignant and said that an investigation team had confirmed the facts. This exchange was one of many reminders that, despite Ping-Pong cordiality, there existed a reservoir of bitterness among the Chinese. Young people, such as Yu, had been educated to blame the United States for helping Chiang Kai-shek in the civil war, the Korean War, defense of the Nationalist Government on Taiwan, the Vietnam war, and it would not be easy to offset these sentiments so that uninhibited relationships could develop between Chinese and Americans.

We flew over the Liao River, leaving behind red-clay valleys and jagged mountains, and ventured on to the greener lands of the south Manchurian Plain. The cultivated fields were larger, more tractors were at work furrowing the land than in North China. Surprisingly, there were extensive rice fields in addition to the kaoliang, wheat and soybean I remembered. In keeping with Mao's policy of decentralization and local self-sufficiency, rice has been cultivated despite the short 135-day growing season and the harsher northern climate. We were told that the greater Shenyang area, once a major grain importer, had become virtually self-sufficient.

At the cavernous, once again nearly empty Shenyang air terminal we were met by five Chinese, who introduced themselves as representatives of China Travel Service and our hosts for the five-day stay in the Northeast. Somehow our hosts communicated a sense of being more important officials than functionaries of China Travel Service. Only a very few foreigners had been permitted to visit the Northeast since the Cultural Revolution. Our hosts hovered over us rather nervously, and we had the feeling that our visit was an anxious innovation for them. Shenyang, the fifth largest city of China after Shanghai, Peking, Tientsin and Canton, was the capital of Liaoning Province. The Liaoning Revolutionary Committee had not been formed until May 10, 1968, later than most other provincial committees, indicating that political and ideological difficulties had persisted.

We drove from the airport in four cream-colored Russian Volga sedans through old mud-walled villages on the outskirts of the city, and then past blocks of gray-brick buildings to our hotel on the main square of the largely Japanese-built western district of the city. The hotel, largest in the city, was the Liaoning, and the name of the open circular plaza was the Red Flag Square. When I visited the city during the civil war in 1946–49, the hotel built by the Japanese was known as the

Shenyang Railway Hotel and the plaza as the Sun Yat-sen Square, a name evidently discarded during the Cultural Revolution. The scene was very different from the one I had left in 1948, when Mukden was a battered, starving city besieged by the Chinese Communists.

In January 1948, Lin Piao's Red Army columns had succeeded in isolating the Mukden garrison of 200,000 Nationalist troops. Disregarding urgent American military advice to break out of the encirclement and link up with Nationalist forces to the southwest at Chinchow, the well-armed Nationalists in their yellow padded uniforms had sat too long behind static defenses, allowing Lin Piao to draw a fatal noose tight about a perimeter some sixty miles in diameter. There were four million people in the perimeter's rural area, but their farm output could not feed the 1.2 million in Shenyang, its population swollen by refugees.

When I flew into Mukden for the last time in the late summer, it was a tortured city. Pillboxes dominated the empty streets lined with boarded-up shops. The big red-brick factories stood gaunt and silent, bombed by American planes during the war, looted by withdrawing Russian troops in 1946, and now abandoned. Three China-based commercial airlines, including Major General Claire L. Chennault's Civil Air Transport, were bringing supplies for the garrison and some of the civilians. About 300,000 people were subsisting on bark and leaves, and pressed soybean cakes, ordinarily used as fertilizer or fodder. Thousands were going blind because of vitamin deficiencies, and other thousands, many of them children, were being wasted by noma, pellagra, scurvy and other diseases of malnutrition. I walked down the desolate streets past the emaciated bodies of dead in the gutters, pursued by unbearably pitiful child beggars and women crying out for help. People were offering bribes or fighting at the airfields for places aboard planes, which brought in supplies and took about fifteen hundred people out each day. At the airfields, I saw American-supplied Chinese Nationalist planes, P-51 Mustang fighters and two-engined transports, taking off loaded with personal possessions of Nationalist officers or other valuables purchased in the dying city for virtually nothing.

Mukden fell on November 1, 1948, after its garrison commander, General Chou Fu-sheng, defected, and the bulk of the defending force had been wiped out in a belated break-out sortie.

As Audrey and I entered the old Shenyang Hotel, the city seemed strangely quiet to me. I still recalled vividly the drone of the airlift planes overhead and the crack and boom of artillery in the distance.

Now the skies were clear. On the broad thoroughfares there were more trucks and cars than I had seen in Shanghai or Canton, but here again there were the endless muffled processions of bicycles making up the bulk of the traffic. I found the quietude weird. The large high-ceilinged marble lobby of the hotel and its broad corridors were empty except for the staff, who looked at us with curiosity. It seemed that the Keatleys, Audrey and I, and our interpreters were the only guests in the hotel, which could accommodate many hundreds. One morning I did glimpse in a reception room a group receiving an ideological lecture, which might have been a tour party, but otherwise the corridors, large dining rooms and lobbies were clear of other guests. When we took meals in the hotel, the Keatleys and ourselves dined alone at a round table in the corner of a deserted dining room, ordering from a delicious à la carte Chinese menu and washing down numerous courses with mou-t'ai and excellent beer.

One evening, the Keatleys, Audrey and I, carrying a jug of mou-t'ai from the dinner table, went into the hotel bar. It had changed. In 1948 there had stood at the long hardwood bar in the darkened lounge clusters of American civilian pilots who were flying the airlift planes, Chinese Nationalist officials and officers, Russians of the joint Soviet-Chinese administration of the Chinese Changchun Railway, American consular and economic aid officials, and army officers of the Joint United States Military Assistance Advisory Group. They were paying for their Scotch, gin and vodka in American dollars. Prices in Mukden had soared to one million times the prewar index, and a stack of the local Manchurian dollars were needed to pay for a drink.

Although one-fourth of the Mukden population was starving, you could buy any kind of food or drink if you had money. The beggars crowded outside the restaurants in the city, holding out their hands to rich well-fed Chinese officials who emerged laughing and belching after their elaborate dinners.

In the bar, the American pilots debated how long they should remain in China flying support for the Nationalists, for which they were being paid thousands of dollars each month. The Russians grumbled about having nothing to do because both Manchurian railways were cut, the one leading north to Communist-held Harbin and the Siberian border, and the line that ran southeast to Soviet-occupied Port Arthur and Dairen. The American advisers joked cynically and despairingly about corrupt, cowardly Nationalist generals who would not take their advice. The aid officials spoke bitterly about the hopelessness of trying to feed the starving population and accused the Communists of driving refugees into the Mukden perimeter to aggravate the famine. The talk and the drinking would go on into the morning hours, almost desperately, as if each man feared going out into the city to confront its realities.

Now the long bar was closed and looked seedy under naked light bulbs. In the bar lounge, a pretty Chinese girl who worked in the hotel played Ping-Pong with an army man, both enjoying the game hugely. There were also pool and billiard tables, but no players. The only other people were two young men in a corner playing cards. We asked for a light from one, and when we began to play pool, they laughed and joined us. I asked them in Chinese if they were from Shenyang. They laughed again and said, no, no, they had been in Shenyang for months but were from Hanoi. Our new-found North Vietnamese acquaintances looked us over with interest when I told them we were Americans, but they kept playing pool with us, exchanging jokes with each other in Vietnamese. They were small men, dressed in Western-style open-necked shirts and trousers, and probably were being trained at one of the Shenyang industrial establishments. Soon, they bid us good night in Chinese and departed with smiles. When we left, the old man was clearing the abandoned bar and the lounge was deserted.

On the afternoon of our day of arrival, the Keatleys and ourselves were invited to separate briefings. The Chinese had arranged that we would spend some time apart visiting different places, a tacit concession to the competitive attitudes of capitalist journalists. In a large reception hall, with five sofas, and ten chairs lined against three walls, we sat at one end of the large rectangular room facing the curtained doorway. There was a fine tea table before us on the beige, flowered carpet. On the sofa beside me sat Wang Yu-chuen, a round-faced man in army uniform who identified himself as a member of the Foreign Affairs Section of the Revolutionary Committee. Wang, quite obviously a political officer, spoke in Chinese with a half-smile on his face, his heavy-lidded eyes never leaving mine. Wang's two companions sat silently.

Wang outlined a program of visits to factories and farms in Shenyang and a tour of Anshan, the coal and steel center. He then remarked that the program had been prepared in a rather subjective manner. I replied that we did want to look at things from the Chinese viewpoint, and in any case, I added jokingly, according to Maoist-Leninist thought, what was termed objective was only the intellectual superstructure of class interest.

"I don't agree," Wang retorted. "We understand that a Western journalist, although he comes from a different background, can write fair reports. There are some journalists, who are in the pockets of capitalists, who have written that in our country two men must share a pair of trousers and that we kill our elder generations. Journalists who come here and see our society can expose the nature of these rumors by reporting the facts."

I asked Wang if in addition to the prepared program we could visit the Shenyang Academy of Fine Arts or the Conservatory of Music. In Peking, I had requested a visit to the Academy of Art, and an interview with one of its members, Yan Di, the painter. The Foreign Ministry had not answered the request.

Wang replied that after the Cultural Revolution, the academy, the conservatory and the College of Agriculture had been moved out of Shenyang into the Liaosi agricultural region west of the city. He said that it had made no sense to have an agricultural college situated in a city. "As for the art and music students, they have been sent out to become integrated with the peasantry," Wang said. "They had become divorced from the masses."

In the countryside, the students and faculty of the Shenyang Conservatory of Music were learning to serve the new musical world born of the Cultural Revolution. Previously, music conservatories had not shied away from foreign music and had developed instrumentalists good enough to perform on concert stages in Moscow and other cities abroad. But now, the Cultural Revolution had rejected Western and Russian music. Tchaikovsky, among other foreign composers, was denounced as a "bourgeois idealist," although the frequently played "Yellow River Concerto," composed by a contemporary Chinese group, had romantic passages reminiscent of Tchaikovsky and Rachmaninoff.

The walls of the theaters were inscribed with a quotation from Mao's talks at the Yenan Forum on Literature and Art in May 1942: "All our literature and art are for the masses of the people, and in the first place for the workers, peasants and soldiers; they are created for the workers, peasants and soldiers and are for their use." Chiang Ch'ing had for years attempted, in the face of opposition from moderates in the Party, to reorient the performing arts totally to Maoist themes of class struggle. When the Cultural Revolution began, and Mao returned in triumph to

Peking, his wife became the patron of the new revolutionary Peking Opera and ballets. Their plots and music were the epitome of art as propaganda. The classics were converted into easily understood morality tales in which the heroic Communists in alliance with the peasants always triumph over wicked landlords in cahoots with Kuomintang villains and Japanese imperialists. "Make the past serve the present and foreign things serve China" was another Maoist injunction to the performing arts. Chiang Ch'ing introduced the piano as an accompanying instrument in the new Peking Opera so that harmony could be enlisted in the communication of revolutionary truths to the masses. When the faculty and students of the Shenyang Conservatory returned from the countryside where they were being "integrated with the masses," they would be ready to play for the new conductor.

At the Nan Yuen Agricultural Commune, south of Peking, I once encountered some of the intellectuals among the many thousands of students, teachers, artists and technicians who have been sent to the countryside for re-education. Wang Wen-lung, vice chairman of the Revolutionary Committee, told me that there were about 150 intellectuals, students and former officials doing manual labor in the rice paddies of his commune. They included some who came originally from the area and others whom the peasants call "outsiders." "It is difficult for them at first, and it takes about half a year for them to become skilled in the fields," Wang said. "Some will settle down here with their families, others will go back to the cities and factories, and some will be recommended to universities."

Some of the students have found life in the villages unbearable. In Hong Kong, British officials told me, among the more than one thousand refugees who escape to Hong Kong each month, many are young people fleeing from assignments to the villages.

Before we left Shenyang, Wang arranged a discussion of the status of the Academy of Art with Pao Kuan-li, the member of the Revolutionary Committee in charge of education. Several other members of the committee were present in the meeting in the hotel, speaking on other subjects, but only Wang, aroused by my interest in the academy, interposed his remarks as Pao spoke.

Pao was a gaunt-looking man, wearing the usual tunic and black horn-rimmed glasses. He was obviously of academic background, and by his demeanor I hazarded that he had recently been through trying times. Pao told us that the Academy of Art and other colleges had been sent to the countryside to undergo "a period of struggle, criticism and transformation" and were learning from the experience of Tsinghua University in Peking. "Classes are being held on a smaller scale. We have recruited some students from among the workers, peasants and soldiers. Education is being combined with practical work."

What Pao was saying indicated to me that the colleges of the Northeast were in the same state of flux and transition as at Tsinghua. Peking had given them a broad ideological line to pursue, but not detailed instructions as to how it was to be implemented. The administrators were still trying to work out an educational plan, including new curricula and systems of instruction. They were also "re-educating" faculties and searching for new students of approved proletarian and peasant background.

Pao said that before the Cultural Revolution there had been faculties in the Academy of Art for oil painting, Chinese painting, sculpture, design and printing. "The students and teachers have now gone down to the masses, who are "re-educating them. They are creating new works, closer to the masses, about the life of the soldiers and peasants," Pao said. Wang interjected: "We are preparing large exhibitions of art done by workers, peasants and soldiers in cooperation with the art teachers and students. Among them is one popular work entitled 'Never Stop Struggling as Long as You Are Alive.' It is a painting depicting the story of our heroic soldiers fighting the Soviet revisionist troops when they invaded Chen Pao Island on our frontier. Yes," Wang said enthusiastically, "a new upsurge in art is taking form."

"In fine arts education," Pao chimed in, "we have broken away from the old methods. In the countryside, the students take part in manual labor and train workers, peasants and soldiers. Art must serve proletarian politics. The old art served a minority, not the broad masses. We hold that art serves the masses by following the Mao Tse-tung line. The academy is trying to overcome its shortcomings through struggle, criticism and transformation." When I asked about the preferences of the students, Wang replied: "Before the Cultural Revolution, enrollment in the academy varied from one faculty to another. The largest was in oil painting, about thirty to fifty students. The academy was not well run. It was criticized a great deal, especially by workers and peasants. In the work at the academy, the figures of workers did not resemble actual workers, and also the peasants did not look real. The academy closed the door on the workers and peasants in keeping with Liu Shao-ch'i's revisionist line. For example, in cooperation with workers, soldiers and peasants, the sculpture faculty devoted itself to making the huge sculpture in the circle."

Outside, in the center of Red Flag Circle, there towered a thirty-foot statue of Mao, erected on a base more than twenty feet high with sculptures on the sides depicting Communist revolutionary struggles. It had been put up on October 1, 1970, the twenty-first anniversary of the founding of the People's Republic.

Wang said it had taken the students two years to complete the Mao statue. "More than one hundred models were made, small and large," he said. "Then to improve the work, criticisms of the masses were invited. Finally, the masses granted approval."

It was difficult for me to accept these words of an army political commissar as the definitive edict on the evolution of art in Maoist China or to regard the giant statue in the Red Flag Circle as representative of its ultimate expression. What Wang had told me, I had heard elsewhere on my trip and read in the tracts of the Cultural Revolution. The radicals had applied vigorously Mao's injunction in his introductory address to the Yenan Forum on Literature and Art: ". . . to ensure that literature and art fit well into the whole revolutionary machine as a component part, that they operate as powerful weapons for uniting and educating the people and for attacking and destroying the enemy, and that they help the people fight the enemy with one heart and one mind." When Mao delivered this instruction in 1942, the Communists were embattled against the Japanese and in quasi-civil war against the Nationalists. In 1966, when Mao unleashed the Cultural Revolution, and the tenets of the Yenan Forum were reaffirmed, he was engaged in a mortal struggle within the Party, and it had been precisely the literary medium that had been employed by Wu Han and other enemies for personal and ideological attacks on him.

But in 1971, as the violence of the ideological conflict subsided, there were a few hints of an evolution toward greater tolerance, at least as regards the classics, both in the fine arts and literature. When I left Peking for Shenyang, there had reappeared in the shops the essays on the classics, *Research on Ancient Chinese Society,* written by Kuo Mo-jo, president of the Academy of Sciences. In 1966, when the Cultural Revolution purge began, Kuo had declared that his book of essays should be burned. The classic *Book of History* was also in the bookshops amid the long rows of technical manuals. In the fall, a larger number of classics, including novels, would be sanctioned for sale. Given the Chinese taste and enormous talent for the arts, expressed even in Mao's own poetry and calligraphy, I thought it unlikely that the society could long accept viewing the arts solely as the claw of man, the political animal.

When we left the hotel in the morning, there was Mao, in army greatcoat, his right arm upraised, confronting us. Hundreds of sight-seers were milling about the base of the statue. The people, although about 90 percent are Han, emigrated from North China, showed traces of the facial characteristics of the Manchus, the indigenous tribes of the Northeast. Features were bolder. The faces were open, frank; eyes were more slanted, and cheekbones higher and wider. The girls had round faces and rosy complexions, seemingly all wearing their hair in thick braids. The adults were dressed like the people of North China, in blue and gray tunics and baggy trousers, but small children were garbed in brightly colored jackets and some wore white hats.

Hundreds of people were crowded around the foot of the stone steps leading to the hotel, hoping for a glimpse of a foreigner. Once Shenyang, the largest metropolis of the Northeast, was an international city, but now foreigners were rare birds indeed. The large Japanese community had been repatriated after World War II. The White Russians, whose restaurants once lent a cosmopolitan touch to Shenyang, had emigrated to the Soviet Union, Australia, Canada and other countries.

When the Sino-Soviet ideological split burst into the open in 1960, Moscow abruptly withdrew 1,400 of its technicians who had been working on 250 aid projects in the Northeast. The Soviet engineers took with them the blueprints for the projects which Moscow had contracted to complete. I found the Chinese still bitterly complaining about the "tearing up of the contracts." Strangely, I thought, I heard no recriminations about Soviet dismantling of the Japanese-built factories in the Northeast as "war booty," when their troops withdrew in 1946. According to the Pauley Mission Report, the Russians stripped Manchuria of nearly $900 million in industrial equipment.

When we visited the Shenyang No. 1 Machine Tool Plant, one of the largest in the country, employing six thousand workers, we were told of the condition in which the factory was found when the Communists seized it in 1948.

"We took over a ruined building," said Wang Min, chairman of the

Revolutionary Committee. "Horse shit and broken glass. That is all we got!" Wang said the Chinese Nationalists, after they took over the factory, which was making armored cars, from the Japanese, sold the equipment and turned the workshops into stables.

I asked Wang if the factory had been looted by the Russians. The question obviously disconcerted Wang, and he glanced at his colleagues who were also sitting about the table in the factory reception room. "The Russians came, but the equipment had already been sold by the Kuomintang." He hesitated, and then added: "Of course, they took some. But then we liberated Shenyang, and the Russians, who were then under Stalin, helped."

After discussing the Communist strategy in the civil war, Wang returned to the subject, seemingly worried that he had not provided a convincing explanation. "Now, Stalin came for the purpose of helping us, not to loot. Only the imperialists and the Kuomintang looted and humiliated us. We will never forget Stalin and we will never forgive Khrushchev for tearing up the contracts."

Wang had run into a contradiction between Maoist ideology and recorded history. Stalin's portrait is displayed in China with those of other Socialist heroes, Marx, Engels and Lenin, since Mao's relations with Stalin were excellent during the Korean War and up to the Soviet leader's death in 1953. The Russians officially did not become villains until Peking's relations with Moscow began to deteriorate seriously after the Soviet Communist Party's Twentieth Congress in 1956, at which Nikita Khrushchev made his secret speech denouncing Stalin.

As we toured Shenyang, I could see that the Communists had made impressive progress, not only in restoring Shenyang's devastated factories, but also in rapid expansion of the industrial base. Chu Wei-jen, the member of the Revolutionary Committee in charge of industry, told us that production was 33 times what it was in 1949 and 53 percent greater than in 1966, the first year of the Cultural Revolution. The population of the city had nearly doubled since the war, to 2,000,000, with a worker force of 600,000. In the larger plants, machine tools, heavy machinery, chemical, metallurgical, textiles and others, about 30 percent of the workers were women. In the city's myriad small neighborhood factories, more than half were women.

The winters are harsh and long in the Northeast. The winds sweep across the Manchurian Plain, pick up eddies of dust curling among the mud-walled villages on the outskirts of the city, and send them whipping down Shenyang's streets. History has left Shenyang architecturally a hybrid city. The old Manchu town lies in the eastern district, its earth wall leveled by the Communists. In the west is the new city founded by the Japanese, with open plazas, broad thoroughfares, large public buildings with elaborate porticoes, and gray-brick office buildings and apartment houses. There are long rows of villas with gardens behind gray walls where Japanese officials and army officers lived. The Chinese have added red-brick apartment houses, some of their façades painted in brave blues and greens which challenge the brooding light.

The chimneys of the factories begin their westward march in the center of the new city and become lost in a forest of smoking stacks in the Tiehsi heavy-industry district. Shenyang is virtually one giant workshop, and for its workers there is not much in the way of public diversion from the monotony of the factory shifts. There are cultural parks and dozens of small cinemas, but in these, as in the factory auditoriums, the amusement fare is heavily ideological.

On Sunday afternoon, we went to the park of the Northern Imperial Tombs. We joined the cheerful sightseers, drank soda pop and went boating on the lake. We walked through an archway, past twelve statues of imperial beasts, through the Dragon Gate and into the walled compound of the tombs. Near the tombs there were no portraits of Mao. At sunset, in the rich golden light, the Manchu temples and the tile-roofed pavilions seemed to come alive again, assigning the smokestacks of Shenyang to another world.

CHAPTER 25

INDUSTRY

We drove quickly through the dun-colored villages encircled by fences of reeds and bamboo on the outskirts of Shenyang, past the maize and cabbage patches rimmed with reed fences to catch the wind-blown dust and winter snowdrifts, and then rode south on the two-lane blacktop road dodging past horse carts and occasional tractors. The road to Anshan, the great iron and steel city, sliced straight across the broad fields, the rice paddies checkered among stands of soybean and maize planted in alternate rows for the greatest yields. The vivid green landscape was generous in its scope, but every bit of land had been cherished and planted, nothing wasted. The bright morning sun glinted on the waters in the irrigation ditches and shone on pools where peasants cast their fishnets and white, yellow-billed ducks paddled, circling in panic when our cars roared by. The peasants, working together in teams, standing in the water among the rice sprouts, watched us pass. Some of the production teams had planted red banners in their fields, and two or three times we saw peasants clustered on a bank listening to lectures by army propaganda teams.

Suddenly, Anshan loomed on the landscape, shrouded in haze spewed by the smoke curling from the chimneys of the blast furnaces and steel mills. This was the pride of China's embryo heavy industry. With the factories of Shenyang and the coal mines of Fushun, the Anshan mills made up the most important industrial complex in a land still straining to master modern technology. About 150,000 men and women labored in the iron and steel industry out of Anshan's total

322

population of one million. Ten blast furnaces jutted upward in the center of the city, with the mills all about them.

The smoke haze drifted over the residential areas, broad thoroughfares with trees and flower beds defying the smog. The gray-brick Japanese-built dwellings are interspersed with the new brick apartment houses extending out to the suburbs, where the claws of the excavation shovels had ripped off the tops of the mountains for iron ore to feed the furnaces.

Anshan is proof to the Chinese of their entry into the industrial age, and when we visited the No. 9 Blast Furnace, built by the Japanese, Soong Ming-chou of the Revolutionary Committee told us, "When the Japanese left, they told us: 'You can't run it. It will become a kaoliang field.' The Japanese were wrong." At a rolling mill, built by the Russians in 1956, we watched huge red-hot sheets rolled expertly by remote control in a mile-long shed, and a foreman told us: "After 1960 the Russians would not give us spare parts, so we made our own."

However brave the Chinese effort, as we walked through the iron and steel plants, we could see the equipment was aged, that productivity lagged behind the more automated works of the United States, Western Europe and Japan. The Chinese were trying to close the gap through makeshift innovations, work discipline, ideological dedication and frugality. The tin-helmeted workers, laboring in the intense heat amid the cascading sparks of the furnaces, often lacking safety devices standard in the West, received no bonus pay other than an extra payment of 35 Chinese cents a day (15 U.S. cents) for food.

From the foreign-made steel plants, we were taken to a new Chinese-built enterprise, the Chi Ta Shan iron ore mine on the outskirts of Anshan. The mine, in construction and operation, illustrated the principles that Peking was relying on to expand industrial production despite shortages of capital and modern technology.

The Chi Ta Shan mine complex was wrapped around two mountains imbedded with iron ore. We drove up a dirt road that curled around one of the peaks to a midway station, where we were greeted by the chairman of the Revolutionary Committee, T'ang Yu-hai, and taken into a shack. At a table covered with a white cloth, we were briefed on the mine.

The chairman was a sturdy, confident, forty-year-old engineer, a graduate of Shenyang Northeast Technological Institute. Married, with two children, he lived in an apartment in Anshan. In many large industrial enterprises, such as the Shenyang No. 1 Machine Tool Plant, the chairman of the Revolutionary Committee is a political cadre who depends upon a vice chairman to run the technical operation. However, T'ang actually bossed the production operation, and served also as the vice secretary of the Party committee of the mine. Of the twenty-five-man Revolutionary Committee, twelve members were political and managerial cadres, seven were from the army including leaders of the propaganda teams, and six were worker representatives. Like all administrators in Chinese industrial establishments and in farm communes, T'ang and his fellow cadres on the committee were required "to integrate with the masses" by taking part in manual labor. T'ang said that he and his staff put in their time on Saturdays or by taking out one or two months each year for their manual labor. T'ang told us that construction of the mine had begun in January 1969 and one year later it was producing processed ore for the Anshan blast furnaces. He reeled off construction statistics of the first year: 21,000 square meters of surface building, 30 kilometers of railroad, 22 of high-voltage transmission lines, 14 of piping and 12 of roads. "Once," T'ang said, "it would have taken us four to five years to do all of this. But after the Cultural Revolution we were able to do it in one year thanks to the teachings of Chairman Mao Tse-tung." I did not doubt the achievement claimed by T'ang. It had been accomplished by throwing in vast numbers of workers.

We drove up to the leveled mountaintop, where the ore was being scooped up by huge excavation shovels and put into twelve-ton dump trucks. When I noted that the trucks were French, Yu quickly remarked: "We are now producing thirty-two-ton trucks in Shanghai." T'ang proudly showed us an innovation that had made it unnecessary to transport the ore off the mountaintop. The trucks carried the ore to the edge of the mountain, turned around and backed up, then dumped their load down a natural slide which had been hacked out of the mountainside. The ore tumbled into the valley, where it was picked up again and put into the cars of an electric railway that carried it to the mine's processing plants. The mine, which employed 2,500 workers, was producing three million tons of processed ore and hoped to double that output.

The most revealing thing about the mine, as it related to the Chinese economy as a whole, was the fact that the iron ore being mined was of a 30 to 31 percent content, which is low. A Western company probably would find such a mine uneconomic to work, requiring at least a 50 percent grade of ore to make the enterprise profitable. The Japanese had hauled high-grade ore from as far as Hainan Island in the South China Sea to feed Anshan. However, the Chinese were mining the low-grade ore in the Anshan region, not only because of availability of plenty of cheap labor which made the production economic, but also in keeping with the Maoist principle of local self-sufficiency.

Unlike the Soviet Union and other East European Communist states, Mao has opted for decentralization and local "all-around development." Each hsien or county had been given the target of becoming self-sufficient in light-industry products and food. "See the country as a chessboard," each square self-sufficient but related, Mao told his people. The principle extended even to a city such as Shenyang, which traditionally has had a high degree of specialization in heavy industry, and met much of its other needs from sources elsewhere in the country. Despite the short northern growing season, the Shenyang region is now virtually self-sufficient in food. Light-industry plants and scores of small neighborhood workshops have been established to supply the needs of the workers in heavy industry. Within each factory and farm commune, managers try to develop "all-around" self-sufficiency so as to reduce to a minimum what must be asked from the state. In China's labor-intensive production system, this pattern is economic, while it would be wasteful in the more advanced, specialized industrial countries. For China, it also has other advantages. It reduces pressure on the country's inadequate transportation system. Industrial development is carried forward more evenly throughout the country. Thus, in the interior, near Fancheng, Audrey found a cotton textile mill more modern than the No. 3 Plant which we were invited to visit in Peking. Before World War II, industry was concentrated largely in the eastern coastal region and the Yangtze River valley. Mao is determined to industrialize the country as a whole, reducing the differences in living standards among the regions and between the urban and rural areas. The policy of decentralization has also given China the capacity to absorb a nuclear blow or invasion and to carry on in the unaffected part of the country without crippling dislocation of the economy.

The Keatleys and ourselves stayed in Anshan at a large, newly renovated guest house. Audrey and I had a freshly painted bedroom, with brightly colored comforters on the twin beds, a tiny sitting room with lounge furniture, and a narrow bathroom whose balky plumbing revealed the advanced age of the building. We took our Chinese meals, a marvelous array of dishes of Northeast and North China, alone with the Keatleys at a large round table in a private dining room. On impulse, after one exquisite meal, we walked into the kitchen to congratulate the cook, a rotund, bald Chinese in a clean white apron. The kitchen was immaculate, which I found extraordinary. The restaurant kitchens of the old China, while just as accomplished in their culinary magic, were notorious for their lack of sanitation. One learned to accept monster cockroaches underfoot and rats cavorting on the rafters over the restaurant tables. Foreigners who were wise in the ways of the country survived by eating only hot foods, shunning salads and taking only hot drinks, unless the liquid was bottled or one was certain it had been boiled. On my return, noting the cleanliness, I cautiously began to eat cold dishes and did not suffer the old stomach tribulations. In the villages, I was told by the "barefoot doctors" that there was much less dysentery, which once was endemic with many Chinese.

Our evening in Anshan, spent in a lounge of the guest house, was a political one, and rather heated at that. A discussion had been arranged for us with T'ien Chih-chang, the member of the Anshan Revolutionary Committee responsible for production. A tough doctrinaire Party man, T'ien was obviously more concerned with the politics of Anshan than its production. "There is no such thing as production without political significance," he told us as we sat with a group of Chinese officials on sofas arranged in a square in the center of the sparsely furnished lounge. T'ien, whose manner I found smug, was the only official in China who provoked me into an angry exchange. The Chinese Communists are hypersensitive to any kind of bullying by foreigners, and losing one's temper is almost always counterproductive. I knew this, but I found T'ien particularly provocative.

T'ien began by inviting questions, and I asked him for the figures on Anshan's steel output. The Chinese make only a few hard economic statistics public, and have been particularly secretive for some reason about revealing their steel production. However, Premier Chou En-lai recently had told Edgar Snow that the country's average production during the past five years had been between 10 and 18 million metric tons, a very modest figure when compared to Japan's 1971 production of 88.6 million tons. (Peking later reported a 1971 production figure of 21 million tons, an increase of 18 percent over the previous year.) In view of Chou's frankness, a departure from the secrecy of the past decade, I thought T'ien might be more forthcoming. However, apart from claiming steady increases in production since the onset of the Cultural Revolution, he declined to give figures. Unlike other Chinese officials we had met, he was also evasive in answering all specific questions, put by Keatley or myself, about over-all production operations in his area. T'ien then launched into a lengthy ideological lecture rich with overly familiar Mao quotations, which even left some of his Chinese colleagues dozing, until I stopped him with a request that he be more specific. He snapped back sharply, "You interrupted me," and then began to talk in more concrete terms.

T'ien's overly cautious manner and his emphasis on the political suggested that Anshan had experienced serious difficulties during the Cultural Revolution. Chou En-lai remarked to Snow that steel output had been adversely affected by revolutionary struggles in 1967 and 1968. The Anshan workers have always been regarded by Peking as an elite force, but one can imagine their attitudes when their bonuses, extra pay for overtime and other material incentives were eliminated during the Cultural Revolution as a revisionist return to the "capitalist road."

"Material incentives corrode man's soul and create a hotbed of individualism," T'ien told us. He said that Mao had ratified a constitution for the Anshan iron and steel complex that was intended to "smash the revisionist line for the restoration of capitalism." The constitution called for "keeping politics firmly in command," meaning that ideological considerations would be paramount. Party leadership would be strengthened. A vigorous mass movement to rouse the workers would be undertaken. A system would be instituted whereby cadres took part in manual labor and workers in management. A struggle would take place against the "revisionist line" which put production and material incentives ahead of political considerations and allowed the directors of industrial enterprises to exercise full control in defiance of Party leadership.

Without specifying what had happened in Anshan during the Cultural Revolution, the stated aims of the constitution reflected clearly the nature of the shakeup which had taken place. In Anshan and in the factories of Shenyang, Peking and other cities I visited, posters were displayed everywhere denouncing "the revisionist line of the traitor Liu Shao-ch'i who had taken the capitalist road," and encouraged material incentives. The intensity of the propaganda campaign indicated that Maoists felt that many workers still had to be indoctrinated to accept the fixed wage scale and forgo their former extra income derived from incentive bonuses, payments for piecework and overtime.

There is a uniform graduated scale of wages for urban workers throughout China, with revolutionary criteria for determining how a worker should be classified. In general, factory workers are graded in eight pay categories, ranging from 34 yuan ($14.17) to 108 yuan ($45.00) monthly. "We determine the category of a worker by his total contribution to the country, including length of service and development of skills," Ch'en Chang-yi, a member of the Revolutionary Committee that runs the Peking Experimental Chemical Works, explained. He said that ideological involvement and reliability are also taken into account. A worker can move up in grade, but he is not demoted. Skill tests for promotion are given each year by committees of workers. An apprentice can graduate to Grade 1 at 34 yuan ($14.17) after two to three years.

Under the codes, men and women receive equal pay. I found, however, a few instances of discrimination, especially where women were working on a part-time basis. Managers of Socialist enterprises are not very different from their capitalist counterparts in using what means are available to hold down costs. In China, a manager of a factory is judged in good part by the profits he turns over to the state, in much the same way that a Western factory manager is rated by his board of directors according to how much money he makes for the stockholders.

Since the Cultural Revolution, salaries paid to senior Party and government officials, enterprise managers and specialists have been held down as part of the drive against material incentives. At the Shenyang No. 1 Machine Tool Plant, which employs 6,000 workers, the chairman of the Revolutionary Committee, a senior Party man, was earning 140 yuan ($58.33) monthly as compared with the top worker scale of 108 ($45). The chairman of the Chi Ta Shan mine was earning 108 ($45). In Peking, a master ivory carver who had worked at his bench for thirty years was earning 100 ($41.66), while a doctor in a hospital was receiving 145 ($60.41). In a Chengchow textile plant, the chief engineer is paid 188 ($78.33), while the head of the plant gets 166 ($69.16). The system allows a skilled factory worker with long experience to earn more than his department head. The same worker, if his wife also has a job, may have a family income that exceeds that of the head of the factory.

This graduated wage scale is in itself a tacit acceptance of a material incentive system and a compromise with the Communist principle: "From each according to his ability, to each according to his needs."

While differences in income are being narrowed, a spread of about ten to one persists. Some university professors, for example, earn as much as 350 yuan, more than ten times the wages of the factory worker paid minimum scale. The Maoists deplore this broad disparity, although it is much less than in the more highly structured, technically advanced Socialist societies of the Soviet Bloc. The Maoists attribute the wide differentiation in income in China to the "revisionist influence" of Liu Shao-ch'i in the past, and say they are struggling against it. And in agriculture as well, where there is a graduated compensation system and toleration of private plots, Mao has sanctioned some compromises to meet the practical needs of the society in its present stage of development.

The ceilings that have been imposed on salaries, intended to inhibit the rise of a privileged bureaucracy which Mao believes would impede evolution to Communism, exemplify only one of the curbs imposed during the Cultural Revolution on the status of managers of the industrial economy.

When visiting factories, it is difficult to get managers to state their rank and responsibilities. Responding to Mao's dictum that the cadres and intellectuals must integrate with the masses, senior administrators usually describe themselves as "ordinary workers," and dress as such.

In Anshan, we visited an alarm clock factory where an incident took place that demonstrated how many managers had been humbled during the Cultural Revolution. At the factory, whose workers assemble nearly a half-million clocks annually for domestic sale and export, we were received by Chang Yu-ming, a thin, finely featured Chinese with graying hair, who was the chairman of the Revolutionary Committee. Chang, a technical rather than political cadre, who had built up the factory, briefed us on his enterprise, and we toured the shops where the workers, mostly women, dressed in white smocks, were assembling the clocks.

Replying to questions, Chang told us, in a rather nervous manner, that before the Cultural Revolution there had been a material incentive policy in the factory, but it had now been abandoned. One of our escort officials, obviously a political officer, whom we called "Smiley" because he always seemed to wear a half-smile, interrupted the chairman.

"Chairman Chang used to be the director of this factory, but at that time he did not study the works of Chairman Mao," Smiley said. "He invented all kinds of material incentives to raise production, including rewards for overfilling quotas and piecework. The workers were opposed to this. 'Where are you leading us,' they asked, 'to Socialism or capitalism?' The director replied, 'I am director. I have final say.' He would not listen." Chairman Chang nodded. Embarrassed and flushed, he looked at his deputies sitting about the table.

"During the Cultural Revolution," Smiley continued, "I came to this factory and found the workers severely criticizing the director until he said, 'Now I understand better what mistakes I have made.' The workers took the director to an exhibition showing the old life and told him, 'You wanted to lead us back to the old society by following the material incentives policy.' After this experience and being re-educated by the workers, the director decided to study the works of Chairman Mao and he was elected to the post of chairman of the Revolutionary Committee. Now the workers work for the country, not for money."

Smiley glanced at the chairman, laughed and said, "The chairman did not mention that experience. Maybe he did not want to lose face. So I am doing it for him." The chairman now was pale and his hands trembled.

Smiley said, "There is a changed relationship between the chairman and the workers. He does not have the final say. He is a technician and he and the workers learn from each other."

Looking at the chairman, who was wearing a brown tunic and dark trousers of slightly better texture than his workers, Smiley said, "The chairman put on his fine clothes because of your visit. As soon as you leave, he will put on his working clothes." The chairman nodded.

I interrupted Smiley to ask the chairman how he handled overtime problems. "You know," the chairman replied eagerly, "they work overtime voluntarily to make innovations that will improve production. There is no regular paid overtime. Sometimes we have to persuade the workers who stay to go home for health reasons."

As the discussion ended, I thanked our hosts for their frankness. Smiley, a gentle-looking man whose eyes crinkled pleasantly, giggled.

During the Cultural Revolution, a massive purge was carried out of industrial managers who were loyal to the Liu Shao-ch'i apparatus and others who simply gave priority to boosting production rather than to ideological considerations. Thousands were sent to May Seventh schools or to the countryside for re-education and eventual reassignment if they were deemed reformed. Others were demoted or transferred, such as in the Peking Experimental Chemical Works, where an army representative became chairman of the Revolutionary Committee and the former plant director was relegated to a more junior post. Many first-class managers who had been denounced but were too difficult to replace remained in their jobs but were "re-educated" and locked into a Revolutionary Committee system of administration that ensured they would be kept under surveillance by reliable Maoists and subject to their veto.

I encountered a management situation of that kind when I visited the Peking Heavy Electric Machinery Plant. Wei Ching-shen, the head of the plant, which employs 5,300 workers, welcomed us in a reception room that was the functional equivalent of the board room in an executive suite of an American corporation. The only furniture was plain wooden chairs drawn up to a long narrow table on which jasmine tea and cigarettes had been placed. The walls were of unfinished white plaster but, like the stone floor, were scrubbed clean.

Wei, a small, mild-looking man of fifty years, wearing a plain gray cap and tunic, was flanked during the interview by Ma Kuei-tang, head of the sixteen-man army propaganda team, and Miss Yeh Yu-hua, a thirty-three-year-old design worker. The triumvirate, all members of the Revolutionary Committee, was typical of the "three-in-one combination," including managers, army representatives and worker delegates, which we found in virtually all the major plants we visited.

When I asked Wei if he had been the director of the plant before the establishment of the Revolutionary Committee on February 14, 1968, Miss Yeh interrupted by saying, "Yes, he was formerly General Secretary of the Communist Party of the plant. He is now the same man physically, but he has greatly changed since the Cultural Revolution." Miss Yeh, a handsome, confident woman wearing braids, and a worn olive-drab jacket over a gray blouse, glanced at Wei. As an aide took notes, the committee chairman confessed that before the Cultural Revolution his staff had been "divorced from production and the masses. We did not take part in manual labor and we had bureaucratic airs." Wei said, "The pernicious revisionist influence of Liu Shao-ch'i" had influenced the management of the factory. Material incentives and rewards had been put in command, and the development of technology and expansion of production had been given priority over politics. But now, Wei said, with the help of the workers and the army propaganda team, the factory had passed through a period of struggle, criticism and transformation and was being run completely according to Maoist doctrine.

Since the Cultural Revolution, Wei said, in keeping with the Maoist precept, "Better troops and simpler administration," the factory's administrative staff had been reduced from five hundred to about two hundred. Similar reductions in administrative staff had been reported to us in virtually every farm and industrial unit we had visited.

Ma, the uniformed head of the factory's army propaganda team, said his men had been there since June 1967 "to safeguard and defend our red political power and to consolidate the dictatorship of the proletariat." After factory sessions, he said, members of the team go to the apartments of the workers, who live in the housing complex nearby, for further discussion with the families. Every employee of the factory was expected to spend about one hour a day studying Mao's writings. The fact that four years after they were first sent into the factories the army propaganda teams must still carry on their work was a good indication to me that ideology was still not yet the master of materialism among the workers to the extent that Mao would like.

Ma told me that his men spent one-third of their time in productive manual labor in the factory. An infantry officer, Ma wore no identification of unit or rank on his olive-drab uniform with red collar epaulets. When I asked Ma if he and his men were able to maintain their military skills despite their political assignment, he said they were ready to go to the front if "imperialists or revisionists impose aggression on our country." By "imperialists" he meant the United States, and by "revisionists" the Soviet Union.

In touring the Heavy Electric Machinery Plant, I was surprised to see the workshops decorated with placards and pink streamers welcoming me. "We warmly welcome our American friend," one streamer said. It was the most effusive reception that I had received in visiting more than a score of factories and communes. In each I had been received with courtesy, but with varying degrees of friendliness and enthusiasm. When I toured the Shenyang No. 1 Machine Tool Plant, an elderly worker began to applaud as he saw the party approach, the expected reaction when an official delegation pays a visit, but one of the officials escorting me silenced him with a curt aside. At most factories and communes, officials would make some remark about friendship between the peoples of the United States and China. With the advent of

Ping-Pong diplomacy, many Americans attached too wide significance to this sort of remark. They saw it as evidence of a thaw in relations between the United States and China. In fact, references to friendship between the Chinese and American people, despite differences between the two governments, were being made by Mao as early as 1945, and the Chinese Communist attitude has never changed in principle since then. Speaking before the Seventh National Congress of the Chinese Communist Party on June 11, 1945, Mao said: "We oppose the U.S. Government's policy of supporting Chiang Kai-shek against the Communists. But we must draw a distinction, first, between the people of the United States and their government and, second, within the U.S. Government between the policy-makers and their subordinates." The Chinese position has tactical, ideological and historical roots. Tactically, it is an attempt to separate Americans from support of U.S. Government policies which the Chinese Communists regard as antagonistic. Ideologically, no Communist accepts that a non-Socialist government is freely and fully supported by the people of that country. Historically, many Chinese still remember the humanitarian work done by American individuals, missionaries and others, and the United States opposition to colonialism in China, although by demanding most-favored-nation rights we shared at times in the exploitation of the country by Britain and the other European powers.

Leaving the Heavy Electric Machinery Plant, I felt a sense of pity for Wei, as I did later in Anshan for the chairman of the alarm clock factory. It seemed to me that they and many of the other purged or "re-educated" cadres had been trapped either in the power struggle between Mao and Liu Shao-ch'i or in the swing of the ideological pendulum. Going back to 1958–59, the period of the Great Leap Forward, one found cadres denounced first for failure to press forward more boldly with Mao's policy of radical collectivization, then criticized for being overzealous. Even now, in the aftermath of the Cultural Revolution, many of the overly radical cadres who were once in the forefront of change-making are being purged or spanked while the formerly criticized moderate or conservative officials are gaining power again. I had the impression in meeting scores of cadres in factories and on farms that, after being badly buffeted by the ideological and political fluctuations of the last decade, many were more interested simply in staying out of trouble than anything else. The Cultural Revolution had denied them some of the customary material rewards accorded the bureaucracy and stripped them of the trappings of special status. In place of these incentives, ideological pressures and the implied threat of being sent to the countryside or a May Seventh school had been substituted. Mao had succeeded in inhibiting the growth of a Soviet-style bureaucracy, highly structured and enjoying class privileges. But it is yet to be demonstrated whether ideological incentives are enough to keep the Chinese bureaucracy functioning loyally and efficiently. To some degree it is now safer and more rewarding in China to be a skilled worker rather than a manager or cadre.

Walking through the shops of the Peking Experimental Chemical Works, a plant employing 2,300 persons, situated in the southeastern suburb of the capital, I selected at random a worker to interview. He turned out to be Chou Chieh-hua, a muscular five-foot eight-inch pleasant-looking man dressed in a blue cap, tunic and trousers. He is the foreman of a crew of ten who install new machines and repair others. Chou has been with the plant since it was built in 1959. Construction began in 1958, in the year of the Great Leap Forward, and was completed a year and a half later. By going to night school, Chou completed six years of secondary school, which helped him qualify for his job.

Chou works the standard six-day, forty-eight-hour week. This does not include the half to one hour spent each day studying the works of Mao under the guidance of the army propaganda team. He is off on Sunday. Chou earns 71 yuan ($29.58) a month, and his family is comparatively very well off and is able to save money because three others also work. With two of his four children holding jobs and two in school, his wife recently became an apprentice in the factory at 18 yuan ($7.50) a month. A nineteen-year-old son operates a lathe at an apprentice scale of 21 yuan ($8.75). Another seventeen-year-old son is earning 17 yuan ($7.08) as an apprentice in a food-processing plant.

If his wife has another child, she will be able to keep her job at the factory. Women workers, who make up one-third of the employees, are entitled to fifty-six to seventy-two days of paid maternity leave and special rest periods for the first seven months after returning to their job. There is a free day-care nursery in the factory.

The family lives a half-mile from the factory in a sparsely furnished apartment of two small bedrooms with tiny outside balconies, a kitchen and lavatory. It is a factory-owned apartment house and they pay 7 yuan ($2.92) a month rent, which is higher than the average. Electricity for illumination and gas for the cooking stove, central heating and water costs another yuan ($0.41) per month.

With food costing about 10 yuan ($4.16) per person, the family is left at the end of the month with 59 yuan ($24.61) to buy consumer goods or save in the People's Bank at 4 percent interest. Prices are high for everything except basic staples, so they do not buy much. Chou thinks they eat well with pork or beef or fish at least once a day. One good meal is eaten in the clean, well-tended canteen. Chou has ulcers and is able to get the eggs-and-milk diet prescribed for him.

The Chou family has never had to draw welfare payments. In each region of the country, a minimum per capita income has been fixed for urban workers. Around Peking the cost-of-living scale is pegged at 12 or 14 yuan ($5.00 to $5.83) a person per month. When family income is below the per capita minimum, the factory is required to pay a subsidy that brings it up close to the general standard.

The state has established uniform social benefits for factory workers. Each worker is guaranteed free medical care, but members of his family who do not work in the factory are entitled only to payment by the factory of 50 percent of their medical costs. In some factories, such as the one that Chou works in, the workers have founded cooperatives to pay the additional 50 percent of the medical costs of family dependents. Each family gets complete coverage by contributing less than one yuan ($0.41) a month. When a worker suffers an occupational accident or illness, the factory pays all medical costs and his full salary. For other extended illnesses, workers get 60 percent to full payment of their salary, according to length of service, during the first six months of the illness and thereafter 60 percent. Welfare payments are available to ease family hardships. Education is free.

When Chou got married, the factory gave him the required three-day holiday. Now he gets seven days a year vacation, divided among the main festival holiday periods. The factory provides much of the Chou family's entertainment. In the factory auditorium they attend films, mostly propaganda shows comparing the "bad old days" under Chiang Kai-shek and the landlords with their present life. An amateur troupe puts on similar stage shows mostly drawn from the revolutionary Peking Opera.

Periodically, Chou is caught up in some special production drive. When the Peking Machine Tool Plant produced its first 2,500-kilowatt compressor, Chou tells you proudly that his crew worked twenty-four days and nights to install it in their factory. Since the Cultural Revolution, he has been hearing about the nefarious deeds of "the traitor scab Liu Shao-ch'i" and his revisionist line which kept production low. Chiang Chung-ying, an army man, has become chairman of the Revolutionary Committee and has replaced Tsang Hua-ping as head of the factory. The administrative staff has been reduced from 14 sections to 3, and 200 of the 360 personnel sent to work in the shops. Chou learns from the wall posters that the output of synthetic ammonia, used for fertilizer, has been raised after a big production drive from 27,000 tons a year in 1966 to 43,000 in 1969.

In 1968 there was great excitement in the plant when it was announced that Japan, under United States pressure, had refused to land a cargo of methyl alcohol which had been contracted for and shipped. Chou and his fellow workers were told that "to break the strangling economic embargo imposed by imperialism and revisionism," the Revolutionary Committee had decided to set up its own methyl alcohol workshop. The efforts and experiments involved in bringing into being the workshop dominated the wall posters for some time, until finally methyl alcohol, a chemical needed in the national defense plants, was being produced regularly.

Chou finds life in the factory pretty exciting. He remembers the "bad old days" and feels he is well off now. More than anything else, he says, he is grateful to Mao for the opportunity to become a skilled worker. Chou expects to work in the factory until he is sixty, when he will be entitled to retire at 70 percent of regular salary. Mrs. Chou can retire at fifty, also at 70 percent of salary. The normal retirement age for women is fifty-five, but in the chemical plants and other factories such as cotton textiles, where the work is hard, the age is fifty. If they retire at the usual age, the Chous may move in with one of their married children, as many grandparents do, and care for their grandchildren while the parents go to work. For families who make this arrangement, the state tries to make available a larger apartment. But under the rules the Chous may elect to continue to live in the factory apartment house after retirement. When Chou dies, the factory will arrange a nonreligious memorial service in the auditorium at which fellow workers will describe his achievements. Cremation will also be arranged by the factory.

We returned to Shenyang from Anshan and before leaving that city visited the Mini Tractor Factory, where, to Audrey's amusement, I tootled around the grounds in a 12-horsepower tractor built to pull a plow or a cart. The factory is producing about 450 of these a month as part of a drive to modernize Chinese agriculture.

In the factory, all the machines are painted either green or gray, revealing one unique Maoist approach to industrialization. Green designates a piece of equipment which has been manufactured in the plant itself, while gray means it has been supplied by the state. Many, if not most, of the smaller machines are painted green. Like every factory, the tractor plant must keep an official count of the number of minor and major innovations instituted by workers. Mao seems to have boundless faith that through ideological indoctrination the ordinary worker can be roused to increase production and through homemade innovation renew much of the antiquated character of Chinese industrial plant. In our tour of the Northeast industrial heartland, the central themes had been innovation, self-reliance and self-sufficiency. Short of the foreign exchange needed for large-scale imports of machinery and technology, determined never again to be dependent on foreign aid, Mao was summoning his industrial workers, in much the same way as he had roused the country's farmers, to leap forward through *people power.* What I had seen in the Northeast convinced me that in his approach to industrialization Mao was more than a romantic revolutionary. He had obtained a release of creative energy among the industrial workers that had boosted production without the massive investment of capital that might have been required in other countries. But China was still only barely over the threshold of the industrial age, while her competitors, Japan, the Soviet Union, the United States and Western Europe, were making great strides into the postindustrial electronic era. In the Northeast I had only seen one computer, a primitive experimental model, although I had been told there is a model in serial production for the operation of lathes. Presumably at China's nuclear and missile installations and in some research institutes there are advanced computers in use. But in industry China is still utilizing in its most advanced plants many adaptable techniques and equipment that have become obsolescent in Japan and the West. Unless there is a major intake of machinery and technology from the more sophisticated industrial countries, China is more likely to fall further behind than gain, despite the people power mobilized by Mao.

Certainly, in the next years, China will steadily increase its imports of modern technology and equipment, but the country will also continue to employ its labor-intensive production methods taking advantage of its large reserves of manpower. These methods, as well as the adaptable and easily manufactured machines that have been developed in China, are suitable for application to the other less-developed economies of Asia, Africa and Latin America. For these countries, China will exert an attraction as a society similar to their own, which by its own ingenuity and labor has lifted itself out of poverty, disorder and dependence.

In Shenyang, with the weather bad in Peking, we were put aboard an excellent railway sleeper for the overnight journey back to the capital. As the train clattered south, I lay awake in the darkness in my bunk and thought of the last time I had left Mukden for Peking, flying out of the besieged city overcome with horror of the suffering and corruption I had witnessed. Whatever else the people of Shenyang may lack today, they now have dignity, security and hope. Against the perspective of Mukden 1948, they had made progress indeed.

CHAPTER 26

CHINESE NEEDLING

Upon our return to Peking, Audrey and I were invited to visit the Peking No. 3 Deaf and Dumb School, where acupuncture was being used in a new revolutionary treatment of deafness in children. It was a time in the capital when acupuncture, an art of healing employing needles that had been practiced in China for thousands of years, suddenly had become the central topic of conversation, and indeed of impassioned debate at virtually every diplomatic party.

For the first time since the onset of the Cultural Revolution in 1966, a large group of the foreign diplomatic corps in Peking had been taken on a tour of Chinese cities. In a hospital in Wuhan, the Central China metropolis on the Yangtze River, they had been permitted to observe major surgical operations, in which acupuncture was used as the sole anesthetic while the patient remained conscious throughout, speaking at times to the operating team, sipping juice and eating orange slices.

Since the Cultural Revolution, the Maoists had encouraged the practice of acupuncture and the use of traditional Chinese herb medicine in conjunction with Western medical techniques. Institutes were established to determine the scientific basis for the effectiveness of acupuncture in certain cures and to develop it further. The Chinese press reported that acupuncture was being used to treat illness ranging from forms of paralysis and arthritis, and other ailments where there was no advanced atrophy, to such simple disorders as stomach-aches and headaches. A hospital in Hunan reported some success in utilizing acupunc-

339

ture as a therapy in treating mental illness, and elsewhere experiments were being conducted in the alleviation of blindness.

The foreign diplomatic community in Peking, which included a number of doctors, had not taken the new emphasis on acupuncture seriously, mainly because in the past Western doctors had dismissed the art as quackery. They were dubious also because there was a strong ideological character to the claims, with Mao being credited with inspiring astonishing cures. However, after some of the diplomats witnessed the apparent startling innovative use of acupuncture in anesthesia, a debate raged between those who believed the Chinese had made an important medical breakthrough and others who claimed that what was being practiced was hypnosis or the placebo effect, in which a patient is made to respond through autosuggestion.

When I met Audrey in Hangchow, she, her sister and father had only several days earlier been to Wuhan, where they had seen the use of acupuncture anesthesia in major surgery. After testing the technique in thousands of operations, Chinese doctors were now exposing it to examination by foreigners. Like the diplomats, Audrey, the first Western journalist to witness acupuncture anesthesia, had been impressed.

Through an observation dome in the Wuhan hospital, with Professor Chu Fa-tzu, head of the surgical department, explaining the procedures, she had watched a surgeon spend twelve minutes removing a tumor from the throat of a fully conscious fifty-four-year-old woman. Twenty minutes before the surgery began, an acupuncturist had inserted two very fine, flexible needles about two centimeters into each wrist. An acupuncturist at each wrist whirled the needles between thumb and two fingers until the patient reported a numbness in the throat.

"When the incision was made," Audrey said, "the woman didn't twitch, but I did."

Seconds after the last suture was tied, the patient sat up, ate some orange slices, put on her robe, thanked the operating team and walked out. On the way, she stopped to wave her little red book of Mao's quotations at Audrey and the other amazed Canadian observers.

Dr. Chu said that the needles had been inserted into nerve centers controlling the afflicted area of the body. "It is very difficult to explain exactly what happens," he said. "There are about five hundred nerve points in the body that we know we can use. We know the results we will get, but we cannot explain exactly why we get them."

The Canadian party also witnessed open-heart surgery on a thirty-three-year-old woman, who, in addition to the needles in the wrists, had an additional needle in each forearm. The purpose of the operation was to enlarge the valve between the left auricle and the left ventricle of the heart. After the chest incision and the removal of a rib and some tissue, the heart was exposed. Gauze dipped in a Chinese herbal medicine was used to prevent excessive bleeding. The surgeon picked up the patient's heart and held it in his hand. An attendant walked into the room with orange sections in a glass bowl and offered them to the patient. She smiled and refused, but sipped juice through a straw as the surgery was carried out, and she was wheeled off smiling.

Although Audrey was impressed by what she had seen, she was hesitant as a layman to report medical observations to the *Times* until we reached Shanghai and spoke to Dr. Galston, the Yale biologist, and his colleague from M.I.T., Dr. Signer. They had witnessed and been permitted to photograph major surgery employing acupuncture anesthesia at Peking Hospital No. 3. In one operation, Dr. Galston told me, they had watched an ovarian cyst "as large as a baseball" removed from a fully conscious woman and then shown to her, at her request, on a tray, immediately after the operation. In the operations observed by Galston and Signer, the needles were kept vibrating electrically to sustain the anesthetic effect.

The surgery utilizing acupuncture anesthesia is conducted in operating rooms with aseptic procedures and equipment comparable to that in the West. An anesthesiologist is present, in addition to the acupuncturist, prepared to administer conventional anesthetics, which remain in use in China. As in the United States, patients receive fifty milligrams of meperidine, a sedative, before surgery.

During our stay in China, we learned that acupuncture anesthesia was being used commonly in a growing number of cities in a variety of operations, including gastrectomies, thyroid adenomas, tonsillectomies, laryngectomies and in dental surgery. At the Hun Shan Hospital in Shanghai, the technique was being employed in brain surgery. Patients remained conscious and conversed with members of the operating teams while brain tumors were being removed.

Chinese doctors said that acupuncture anesthesia was preferable to anesthetics in the cases of patients who suffer from poor functioning of the liver, kidneys or lungs, high blood pressure, debility from serious disease or shock or oversensitivity to anesthetics. With the patient conscious, the doctor has the advantage of being able to communicate with him during an operation. They also say that it is especially suitable for use in China's vast countryside and mountain areas, since acupuncture anesthesia does not require complex apparatus and costs practically nothing to administer.

Apart from whatever may be the medical value of acupuncture anesthesia, it was also true that patients in China are readied for surgery through ideological indoctrination. If one was to judge by the enthusiasm demonstrated by patients in waving their little red books before and after operations, ideological conviction was an important mental conditioning factor in helping them to sustain surgery. At the Peking No. 3 Deaf and Dumb School, we saw another example of how the Maoists apply ideology in medical treatment.

The school, one of four in Peking, was located in a walled compound with a cobbled courtyard and a cluster of red-brick one-story buildings constructed in 1958 when the school was founded. Some of the 128 boys and 111 girls, ages eight to twenty-two, who make up the student body live at home, but others from counties surrounding Peking live in dormitories. They have a teaching staff of twenty-six. We were told that there are similar schools in every province of China, many of them located in the larger cities.

We were welcomed by the Revolutionary Committee and members of the army propaganda team, who escorted us into a long narrow conference room where we were seated at a table covered with a blue cloth. On the walls were portraits of Mao, placards bearing quotations from his works and photographs of distinguished persons who had visited the school, among them Prince Norodom Sihanouk.

Audrey, Yu and I sat opposite Wang Chen-ying, the uniformed leader of the army propaganda team assigned to the school. He was flanked by Yeh Hu-hsu, a sixteen-year-old girl in braids who wore a Red Guard arm band, and Fang Shou-suan, a doctor of the army medical team that was treating the deaf students with acupuncture.

Wang told us that the use of acupuncture in the treatment of deafness was discovered by an army medical team working in a deaf and dumb school in the Northeast. When the team experienced some success, other army teams were sent all over China to set up new schools and to introduce the new methods into existing schools. An army medical team of two doctors and an attendant joined the Peking No. 3 School in November 1968.

"We began to work in December, but none of us knew how to treat the deaf and the dumb," Wang said. "Hospital doctors were refusing to treat them, saying the illness was incurable. But the army medical team took the view that nothing is incurable. Mao teaches us that if we undertook struggle only under favorable conditions, then the shaping of history would be too easy. If we understand our problems, we can master them. So we studied Mao's writings on contradictions. He says that in studying any process, if it is complicated and composed of more than two contradictions, first find the main one and concentrate on settling it.

"What was the main contradiction here?" Wang asked. "From case histories, we learned that most deafness was caused in one- to three-year-olds as a consequence of a high fever, brain inflammation or other diseases. Then the vocal organs, although they were actually in good condition, would degenerate from lack of use into a diseased state. Dumbness was often caused by deafness, so this was the first contradiction. To solve this we must first cure the deafness.

"Then we studied Chairman Mao's teachings on practice. He says, 'If you want to know the taste of a pear, you must eat it.' We tried the needles on our own bodies to find the proper acupuncture points rather than experimenting on the deaf and dumb. One team member drove a needle into a certain point and felt as if he had been electrified. Another drove a needle into a point in the ear and felt as if he had been struck by a thunderbolt. We were all healthy men and sometimes feared that we would injure ourselves, but with Mao's thought, 'Everything for the people,' in mind we continued the experiments. After repeated trials we discovered the acupuncture points that cured deafness. Now after a year's treatment 90 percent of the students have a certain capacity for hearing.

"The next contradiction," Wang continued, "is dumbness. After the students' hearing is recovered we teach them how to speak. In little more than a year, of 238 students, eleven have been completely cured and have gone into regular schools. Some of our remaining students can shout 'Long Live Mao Tse-tung' and sing 'The East Is Red.' We can thank Chairman Mao's teachings for this."

Miss Yeh, the teen-age Red Guard student, spoke to us in a slightly thick voice, her phrases rather stilted, but clearly intelligible. "Today we welcome you," she said, looking at us shyly. "When I was two years old, I became ill and as a result became deaf and dumb. My younger sister was the same. We didn't get treatment until we came to the school when I was fourteen. Chairman Mao sent the PLA team here, and we regard them as our most beloved people. Up until one and a half years ago, I was still deaf and mute. Now I can talk, and shout and even sing: 'It is Chairman Mao who has given me the power to speak. I will follow him to make revolution all my life.' "

Miss Yeh may have been coached to make her statement, but her whole demeanor also conveyed sincere conviction and pride in being able to speak. The prize student was a nineteen-year-old who they said had recovered his ability to hear and speak after one year of treatment and had now been accepted in the army. "He can even speak on the telephone," one teacher said.

Dr. Fang, one of the army doctors, took us through the classrooms, where the students sat behind ordinary desks while the teacher stood before a blackboard. The walls were hung with language charts, pictures of Mao and his slogans.

The curriculum was in four parts.

In the first classroom the children were taught the finger language from charts and by mimicking the teacher. Then the treatment course was explained to them.

In the second classroom acupuncture treatment was begun to restore hearing. We watched as an army medical attendant inserted the needles in the arms and in the region of the ears. I stood over a boy and then a girl, both ten or eleven years of age, as they underwent acupuncture. The child would rest one side of the head on the desk. The needle would be inserted near the exposed ear and spun. When the child uttered a cry, presumably as the nerve was stimulated, the needle would be quickly removed. None of the children hesitated in accepting treatment as the acupuncturist made his rounds.

The students initially are subjected to a ten-day course of treatment and then rest for seven days before acupuncture is resumed. "For the first course," Dr. Fang said, "we have a special set of points. Then we check the progress report, and, depending on the results, another set is plotted for the second course." The doctor said that the "acupuncture spurs the nerve system and adjusts the hearing nerve. We use several points. The acupuncture points near the ears have quick but temporary effects, while the points farther away, as in the arms and hands, have a slower but permanent effect. On some students, the effect is quick, and we get good results in six months. Most cases take about a year, and in some cases, where the deafness was caused by brain injury or inflammation, it is very difficult.

"If we can get the child to hear from a distance of three meters, we know it will be all right. We then carry on until the hearing reaches twenty meters. Then we stop acupuncture and concentrate on teaching him to speak."

In the third class basic sounds are taught to the students, and in the fourth they are instructed in how to speak without reliance on the finger language. It is difficult, Dr. Fang said, to persuade the students that they must not revert to gestures regardless of how difficult it is to use the vocal chords. In the third and fourth classes, where science, history and mathematics are taught, the students are required to answer questions orally. Dr. Fang said that younger students responded better to the treatment.

Before we left the school, a dozen boys and girls of the student body who had partially recovered their ability to hear and speak enacted a revolutionary skit for us, dancing and singing "The East Is Red" in brave but uncertain voices. It ended with the performers shouting, "Long Live Chairman Mao!"

We drove out of the school compound deeply stirred, but uncertain as to whether we had witnessed evidence of a significant advance in the treatment of the deaf and dumb unmatched in the West or primarily an exercise in ideological fervor. My sensing was that we had seen a process involving both factors and that they were related.

Western doctors, such as Dr. Samuel Rosen, professor of otology at the Mount Sinai School of Medicine, have begun to visit the deaf and dumb school to observe the acupuncture and other Chinese techniques. He believes it will take time, perhaps years, before these studies permit conclusive judgments. Western doctors have seen audiograms indicating improvement in hearing ability, but present research data are inadequate and three or four years of testing will be required before sufficient medical evidence can be accumulated. The Chinese themselves are proceeding pragmatically, without any pretentions that they can yet define the scientific basis for the results they have achieved. They consider the acupuncture treatment to be still experimental, and so far applicable only in cases where deafness is attributable to certain diseases of early childhood. Meanwhile, overseas Chinese in Hong Kong and Macao have begun to send their children afflicted by deafness to the schools in mainland China.

Certainly, in China ideology is an important positive aid in therapy. It recalls the faith healing of the early Christian Church, and what is practiced today at Lourdes in France. There is a similarity in that believing on the part of the patient is a significant factor in spurring recovery. At the Peking No. 3 Deaf and Dumb School, the manifest conviction of the students that adherence to Maoist teachings could solve their problems had the quality of religious fervor, and strengthened their will to engage fully in the difficult course of hearing and language therapy.

Earlier, in a visit to the Mineral Spray Sanitarium near Anshan in the Northeast, we saw how Chinese doctors use a mix of ideology, traditional Chinese medicine, including acupuncture, and modern Western medical techniques in the treatment of patients suffering from arthritis and other chronic diseases mainly of the joints.

The buildings of the sanitarium were scattered over a lovely wooded estate traversed by the mineral water streams which fed thirteen hundred baths. Chang Yu-chen, the head of the sanitarium, told us that some of the older buildings had been constructed by the Japanese and the estate used by officers for boisterous drinking parties. At one time, Emperor Pu Yi of Manchukuo had used the estate, and one could imagine him and his retainers taking their tea in the old traditional pavilions among the pines.

The sanitarium, staffed by 60 doctors and 110 nurses, received patients, mostly ordinary workers, from all over the country. Treatment and transportation were paid for by the state. The patients, who continue to receive their wages while at the sanitarium, pay half of their 20-yuan-a-month food bill while their factory or other enterprise foots the balance.

We toured the therapy rooms, inspected modern equipment for radiation, heat and electrical treatments. There were facilities for massage, mineral baths, application of local clay heated to 140 degrees Fahrenheit and acupuncture. Western and Chinese herbal medicines were dispensed.

I strolled through one of the buildings where patients are housed, two to a room, and selected a room at random to visit. It was a small room, with unpainted but well-scrubbed walls, large enough to accommodate its two hospital beds but not much other furniture. The two women patients assigned to it and another patient visiting from a nearby room were chatting as I entered. On a small desk there was a straw-covered tea thermos. Towels hung on a string against the wall. There were two chairs in the room, a coatrack in the corner but no clothes bureau, and the occupants' personal possessions apparently were in chests at the foot of the beds. Although crowded, the room was immaculate.

I spoke first to the oldest woman, Mrs. Wang Yen-chu, forty-three, the mother of three children, who was employed in Anshan as a suit-maker. She was a slight woman, who wore her hair cut short, and was dressed in a gray-blue tunic worn over a spotted white blouse. Mrs. Wang, who had been in the sanitarium for six months for paralysis of the legs, described her treatment.

"First, I had to liberate my mind so I could look down on my illness and have the ideological power to defeat it," Mrs. Wang said. "I was also given mineral baths, hot clay, electrical treatments and acupuncture. Later, when my mind was set free, I came to realize that I cannot remain in bed and that I must do physical training and work. Now I have begun to walk." Mrs. Wang, who had been sitting on her made-up bed, got to her feet to demonstrate her restored agility.

Miss Hu Chieh, a rheumatism patient, was a short, broad-faced, smiling girl of twenty-four, unmarried, who drove a bulldozer for a factory in the Northeast province of Heilungkiang. She had first gone to her factory hospital for treatment, and had been reassigned to the sanitarium, where she had been given mineral baths, hot clay applications and Chinese herbs but no acupuncture. "I am feeling much better," she said. "The treatment has been quite effective." The fingers of her left hand were still stiff, and as therapy she was knitting a blue sweater.

The third woman was Chiang Li-jung, a young electrical worker from the Chi Ta Shan iron mine in Anshan. Three months earlier she had arrived in the sanitarium on a stretcher suffering from stiffness in the joints, but was now walking.

Miss Hu, at my request, outlined their daily schedule: "We wake up at 5:30 A.M., brush our teeth, wash and do physical training. At 6:30 we listen to a news program, then we walk and chat, and prepare for treatment—that is, the struggle against our illness. At 11:30 we have lunch. We have fish or meat at every meal. Then we walk again, and at 12:30 we have a nap before our second treatment of the day. At 4 o'clock we have a study period to arm our minds to fight our illness. At 8:30 we listen to the radio, and at 9 we go to sleep."

By what she said and by her demeanor, Miss Hu conveyed the whole sense of the organization, motivation and mood of the sanitarium. It was one of a highly disciplined, ideological attack on illness, making maximum use of the limited material resources available to the medical staff and the patients.

Since the Cultural Revolution Chinese doctors have been prodded and urged to make greater use of ideological suggestion in medical treatment. The Maoists have also encouraged the new emphasis on traditional Chinese medicine, including acupuncture. This has not been a xenophobic movement away from Western medicine. On the contrary, such Western doctors as Dr. Rosen and the noted cardiologists, Drs. Paul Dudley White of Boston and E. Grey Dimond of the University of Missouri–Kansas City School of Medicine, report that the Chinese are making use of the latest Western techniques. The total Chinese medical effort is one of marrying the traditional with the new, in keeping with the Maoist dictum: "Make the past serve the present and foreign things serve China."

While Drs. Rosen, White and Dimond, who visited China in 1971 and observed operations employing acupuncture anesthesia, were sufficiently impressed by the results obtained by the Chinese use of acupuncture to urge serious American research into the techniques, other medical authorities in the United States have abruptly dismissed the whole concept. Some of the skepticism stems from experience with quacks who have claimed to practice acupuncture and the exotic theories concocted in the past to explain how it is supposed to work.

According to one legend, acupuncture was developed 3,600 years ago by Emperor Huang Ti after he found that those wounded in battle by arrows were sometimes relieved of ailments in other parts of the body. More sophisticated theories and a philosophy of acupuncture were developed later and recorded around 1000 B.C. in the most ancient of Chinese medical books, *The Yellow Emperors' Classic of Internal Medicine.*

Acupuncture, in traditional Chinese medicine, is a treatment designed to keep the Tch'i, or what is sometimes referred to as the "vital energy force," flowing through the body unimpeded. This force is said to be controlled by the interplay of two forms of energy, the Yang, which is positive and masculine, and the Yin, which is negative and female. The life force flows from organ to organ along an invisible network of channels, the main ones being known as meridians, six of

Yang and six of Yin. If the flow is blocked, illness results. The acupuncturist seeks to eliminate the illness by stimulating the meridians at one or more of 365 nerve points so that the life energy force will resume unimpeded circulation. In traditional medicine, the acupuncturist makes a diagnosis of the illness by reading palpitations of the pulse.

The modern Chinese acupuncturist does not base his work on these traditional concepts, although he believes his predecessors stumbled on a medical art that produced results. He frankly concedes that his approach is empirical, that the scientific basis has not yet been established, and he welcomes Western research toward that end. He has refined his techniques to a point where he claims that there is as much relationship between him and some of the acupuncture quacks which have disillusioned Western doctors in the past as there is between the ancient alchemists and modern chemists. One of his refinements has been acupuncture anesthesia. To his many distinguished medical detractors in the West who insist that acupuncture has been combined with ideology to induce hypnotism or a placebo effect, Chinese doctors have an answer. They point to acupuncture treatment of animals which has produced effects similar to those with humans. "The rabbit and the cat, as far as we know, have not been influenced by the thoughts of Chairman Mao," a Chinese surgeon told Dr. Rosen.

The Chinese are a practical people. It is dubious that, at a time when they are shedding old customs and superstitions, they would foster the practice of acupuncture by the "barefoot doctors" in scores of thousands of village clinics, as well as central hospitals and research institutes, for reasons ulterior to what they believe is sound medical practice. Typically, foreigners were not invited to observe the modern acupuncture techniques until the Communist Party was convinced that the practice could bear critical scrutiny.

To me the mystery of acupuncture poses the same challenge that all China offers Westerners. It is something to be explored without preconceptions.

CHAPTER 27

PREPARE AGAINST WAR

Wandering along the boulevards of Peking and down the narrow congested hutungs, we often had to step around piles of gray bricks heaped before doorways leading into compounds that enclosed public buildings, shops and homes. Inside the compounds, excavations were in progress and dust rose into the humid June air. Bunkers were being built and tunnels dug, a network that was equipped with electric lighting, telephones, ventilators and dining halls. All this was part of China's massive air-raid shelter construction project.

Thus the Peking subway was built to serve a dual function as a sophisticated shelter for government offices equipped with the required communications gear. In Shenyang we watched children gleefully slide down the curved cement backs of street entrances to shelters. In a giant machine tool plant, we came upon a party of workmen building an underground workshop. In the center of an Anshan factory compound, a large shelter for the workers loomed. According to Chou En-lai, there are networks of tunnels under the great majority of China's large and medium-sized cities. But I also saw in the villages the protrusions of underground bunkers.

When asked about the shelters, Chinese officials would make cryptic replies, usually saying only that they were for defense. But Chou En-lai was more explicit one evening in May 1971 at a private dinner for Chester Ronning in Peking. In 1969, Chou said, during the clashes between Chinese and Soviet troops over border differences on Chen Pao Island in the Ussuri River, the Soviet Union prepared for an offensive war against China. "More than a million Soviet troops were stationed along our borders," he said, "from Siberia to Kazakhstan, and mobilized in the Mongolian People's Republic. Faced with this situation, China was compelled to make preparations for war. We began to dig air shelters everywhere. It cannot be said," Chou continued, "that China intends to invade the Soviet Union because air-raid shelters are being dug throughout our country. It is very clear that our actions are solely defensive."

Secret Sino-Soviet talks on the border dispute, begun in October 1969, were still in progress while I was in Peking. In the talks, I learned, the Chinese indicated their readiness to define the boundary along the present line of control with some minor rectifications. They insisted, however, that the Russians concede formally that the present frontier was imposed by Czarist Russia on China by means of "unequal treaties." The Russians steadfastly have rejected the offer, obviously fearing that such an admission would be used later by the Chinese to demand major territorial readjustments. There may be cause for Soviet apprehension if one examines Chinese attitudes today and the Czarist bequest to the Soviets.

For centuries, the Russians stubbornly pushed eastward into Asia. Under the Soviet Government, the territorial penetration persisted until the 1940s. Moscow's greatest gains, however, were made in the nineteenth century, when the Czars pressed against the crumbling Manchu Empire. The Ch'ing emperors were compelled to enter into a series of agreements ceding vast territories. These included stretches in the Far East, north of the Amur River, extending to Kamchatka and east of the Ussuri to the sea, embracing the sites of such major modern cities as Khabarovsk and Vladivostok. In Central Asia, the penetration was into Turkestan, where the Soviets eventually established the republics of Kazakh, Turkmenia, Kirghiz, Tadzhik and Uzbek. The indigenous inhabitants of these Soviet republics are largely of Turkic stock, like the peoples who live on the other side of the border in Sinkiang, that part of Turkestan still under Peking's suzerainty. The Russians drew their line of conquest without respect of the ethnic and natural entities. Independence movements which flared up periodically in Turkestan were crushed by Moscow, or, if they erupted in the Chinese-controlled areas, either by local warlords or by forces dispatched by Peking. On the Soviet side of the border, Russian settlers were sent in to secure the region, while Peking populated Sinkiang with Chinese of

Han extraction. Nevertheless, the ethnic and other problems persist on both sides of the border, contributing to the instability of this extensive section of the Sino-Soviet frontier.

Farther east, after the turn of the century, the Chinese were confronted with uprisings in Mongolia, encouraged by the Russians, and in Tannu-Tuva, which was an integral part of Outer Mongolia. In 1915 the Chinese Republic bowed to the pressure and entered into an agreement with the Mongols and Russians for an autonomous Outer Mongolia under Peking's suzerainty. After the 1917 Bolshevik Revolution the province became an independent People's Republic and is now closely linked to Moscow and garrisoned by Soviet troops. The Russians annexed Tannu-Tuva in 1944 as an autonomous republic.

With the defeat of Japan, Moscow resumed its eastward march, prodding Nationalist China into yielding treaty rights in the Manchurian ports of Dairen and Port Arthur. These ports were restored to Peking after the Chinese Communists took power, but the Russians also made it plain that no further major border adjustments were to be expected.

China, with less than half the land area of the Soviet Union but more than three times its population, looked into the undersettled expanses of Siberia and Soviet Central Asia, and pondered the past. Through the 1950s the Chinese suppressed their resentments and irredentist sentiments for the sake of ideological solidarity and because they were urgently seeking Soviet economic, technical and military aid, especially in the development of nuclear weapons. Then each of these inducements to remain compliant disappeared.

Chinese ideological ties to Moscow became frayed after the Twentieth Soviet Party Congress in 1956 when Nikita Khrushchev denounced Stalin, who had died three years earlier, as a paranoid tyrant. Mao had no great reason to grieve for Stalin. The Chinese Communists had been bullied by Stalin, and from 1927 on his advice had led them into costly reverses at the hands of Chiang Kai-shek. Speaking to the Eighth Central Committee on September 24, 1962, Mao confided that Stalin never trusted the Chinese Communists, believing them independent-minded Titoists except for the three-year period from the time of Peking's intervention in the Korean War in 1950 until his death in 1953.

Nevertheless, Mao was annoyed with the denunciation of Stalin, one of the heroic figures of the Communist world, by the upstart Khrushchev. The castigation of the Stalin cult of personality was by inference a criticism of the adulation of Mao in China. With the passing of Stalin, symbol of Soviet infallibility, the Chinese Communists began, at the 1957 World Conference of Communist Parties in Moscow, to challenge Soviet leadership of the international Communist movement.

"At the Conference I tried fruitlessly to persuade the Soviet Union from going too far along the revisionist path," Chou En-lai recalled in his reconstruction at the Ronning dinner of the events leading up to the Sino-Soviet split. "Then in June 1959 Khrushchev broke the Sino-Soviet Agreement on Nuclear Cooperation. In September, Khrushchev went to meet with President Eisenhower to begin his exercise in flirtation with the United States," Chou said.

Khrushchev entered into the nuclear assistance agreement with the Chinese Communists in 1957, hoping that they would then become more amenable to his leadership. Peking did not prove docile. Then, evidently apprehensive about the possibility of being drawn by Peking into a thermonuclear war with the United States over Taiwan or the offshore islands of Quemoy and Matsu, Khrushchev abruptly terminated his nuclear assistance pact with the Chinese Communists.

In 1958 Chinese Communist and United States military forces had come perilously close to a clash over Quemoy. The Chinese Communists had bombarded Quemoy and threatened to invade the island, which together with Matsu had been used by the Nationalists for harassment raids against the mainland. United States naval and air units were deployed to shield the island. The crisis faded when the Nationalists, under United States pressure, tacitly agreed to stop using the offshore islands as bases for commando raids on the mainland.

In 1960, Chou En-lai recalled, "The Soviet Union broke the agreement with China to promote industry and construction. All the Soviet experts and technicians were withdrawn from China. But China still had patience and did not pay too much attention to the breaking of contracts which were important to China."

In June 1960, during this phase of the rapidly developing Sino-Soviet dispute, I flew to Moscow for a three-year tour. On June 12, a few days after my arrival, the first hint in the Soviet press of public polemics in the dispute between Peking and Moscow appeared in a *Pravda* article which denounced unidentified "leftists." Soviet censorship would not pass any dispatch which speculated that *Pravda* was, in fact, referring to the Chinese. But Soviet reticence and patience rapidly eroded thereafter. At the end of the year, when the last full World Conference of Communist Parties took place in Moscow, I obtained details of the bitter Sino-Soviet quarrel that was taking place at the closed meetings. Without much hope of getting the news out, I filed a dispatch. I was astounded when Soviet censors allowed it to pass. My dispatch, the lead story that day in the *Times,* detailed the nature and seriousness of the rift. The Russians had decided to let their ideological contest with the Chinese come more into the open.

Despite this progressive deterioration of relations, Chou En-lai evidently still hoped for some kind of rapprochement when he attended the Twenty-second Soviet Party Congress in Moscow in October 1961, but he was quickly rebuffed. If the Chinese, who were suffering at home from bad harvests and the economic dislocation of the "Great Leap Forward," still were looking for large-scale Russian aid, they were now completely disabused. In Khrushchev's statement of his Party's twenty-year economic program, the emphasis was heavily on development of the national economy and raising the living standards of the Soviet people, leaving the other Communist states largely on their own.

I watched Chou En-lai sit unsmiling among the other foreign Communist leaders on the stage of the auditorium of the new Hall of the Congresses in the Kremlin as one Russian leader after another denounced the Albanians, the close ideological allies of the Chinese. It was, in fact, as the Congress delegates knew, an attack on Peking. Khrushchev accused the Albanian leadership of practicing the methods of the Stalinist cult of personality. When Chou's appeal for a halt to public attacks on "fraternal" Socialist states went unheeded, the Chinese Premier left Moscow while the Congress was still in session. After Chou's exit from Moscow, the polemics between Peking and Moscow escalated rapidly, fragmenting the international Communist movement.

Between June 1959 and October 1961, the Chinese-Soviet alliance in effect dissolved, and with it vanished the ideological restraints which had inhibited the re-emergence of the historic national antagonisms between the neighboring giants. During the intense debate on such broad ideological questions as the inevitability of war with the United States, the concept of peaceful coexistence with non-Socialist states, the kind of support to be given to national liberation movements, there have been so many shifts in the positions of both the Chinese and the Russians as to render meaningless the bulk of the polemics except in the historical context. One is left with the summary impression that the ideological debate has been, in the main, a façade for the conflict of national interests and the competition for leadership of the Communist world and the developing nations of Asia, Africa and Latin America.

To the dismay of the Russians, beginning in 1960, with the visit to Moscow of Liu Shao-ch'i, then Chief of State, the Chinese began to insist on the need for a readjustment of the 4,500-mile border, the longest frontier between any two nations. In February 1964, on the proposal of a worried Khrushchev, a Chinese-Soviet boundary commission met in Peking, but the talks were suspended when the Chinese insisted on Soviet acknowledgment that the border had been imposed by the Czars through "unequal treaties."

Soon afterward, Mao suggested that Turkestan and the Amur region ceded by the Manchus might one day be reclaimed peacefully from the Soviet Union. On July 10 he told a group of Japanese visitors: "About one hundred years ago, the region to the east of Lake Baikal became Russian territory, and since then also Vladivostok, Khabarovsk and Kamchatka. We have not yet asked the Soviet Union for an accounting." Mao's remarks told the Russians publicly what they had already learned in private exchanges: the territorial question was now an open issue between the two countries.

After the ouster of Khrushchev in October 1964 the Chinese made another probe to determine if a rapprochement was possible with Leonid I. Brezhnev, the new Soviet Party leader. At the Ronning dinner, Chou En-lai recalled that China, hoping for a change in policy, sent a delegation to Moscow in 1964 to celebrate the anniversary of the October Revolution. "We discovered that the change in leadership was not a result of a change in Party policy," Chou said, "but was motivated by a struggle for power in the leadership, which was very disappointing to the Chinese." The following February, Chou related, Mao met the new Soviet Premier, Aleksei N. Kosygin, in Peking. Mao told him that because China and the Soviet Union had differences in principle, the polemics would go on for ten thousand years. Kosygin commented that that would be too long, Chou said, and Mao replied that since the Soviet leader had said so, a thousand years were deducted, which would still leave nine thousand years for polemics.

Chou also told of the conference he had had with Kosygin in 1969 when the Soviet leader was on his way home from the funeral of President Ho Chi Minh of North Vietnam. Kosygin had requested a meeting at the Peking Airport, and Chou talked with him for three hours. Chou said that he and Kosygin were in agreement that in order to improve relations the two countries should open boundary negotiations. Their understanding on the basis of the talks provided: First, the dispute on principle should not hamper the normalization of state relations. Second, the two countries should meet in Peking at the vice-minister level on the questions of disputed boundaries in the Ussuri-Amur region. Third, the negotiations should be free of any threat. To this end, before the negotiations on the boundary alignment, the two sides should reach agreement on provisional measures to maintain the status quo and halt armed conflict.

The negotiations continued during our visit, but so far as could be discerned without any real hope of agreement among Chinese officials or Russian diplomats.

The immediate territorial question is minor and relates largely to whether the border should run down the center of the Ussuri River bed, as the Chinese contend, or on the Chinese bank, as the Russians insist. It is the long-term implications which deter the Russians from signing a provisional agreement fixing the *de facto* frontier. For Moscow to acknowledge that the Czarist treaties were "unequal" would leave the larger territorial questions unsettled, and this possibility alarms the Russians, who stir uneasily before the weight of the Chinese masses on their borders.

Although the Sino-Soviet border was quiet in 1971, the Chinese dug their air-raid shelters with undiminished energy. A senior British diplomat told me he thought the shelter program was being pressed perhaps more for psychological reasons than for protection against Soviet attack. It was true that the program had the effect of making the Chinese people more amenable to the disciplines imposed by the regime. I thought, however, that the energy and resources being put into the shelter program, and other defense measures, suggested serious Chinese concern about the possibility of another confrontation with the Soviet Union.

In 1972 the Chinese were still reacting to the shock of the 1969 border crisis when various Communist parties hinted to them that the Russians were considering a nuclear strike if Peking kept its troops pressing against the frontier. The Chinese had accepted Kosygin's offer to resume boundary talks in sharp awareness of the degree to which China was exposed to nuclear strikes by Soviet bombers or the missile launchers emplaced along the border. The Russians might have been bluffing when they spread rumors of a possible nuclear strike, but the Chinese were not that sure. A year earlier they had watched anxiously the Soviet invasion of Czechoslovakia and the subsequent proclamation of the Brezhnev Doctrine, asserting the Soviet right to intervene in another Socialist state if the interests of the Socialist camp were threatened by those deemed enemies by Moscow. A pre-emptive nuclear strike at Chinese nuclear and missile development centers would have been presented to the world by Moscow as a move to shield it from the danger of a Chinese-inspired thermonuclear war. The superbly equipped Soviet conventional forces on the Chinese frontier were powerful enough to break through the Chinese divisions which Peking had massed there. For the Russians, there would be, of course, the serious risk that once they moved into China, their forces would become mired in interminable guerrilla warfare, leaving them in a vaster bog than the Americans had stumbled into in Vietnam. Weighing all the factors, the Chinese agreed to the border talks, calculating that it would give them more time to prepare their defenses. The Chinese were concerned not only with their ability to stand up to the Russians over the territorial issue. Looking ahead, they were also intent on strengthening their position in the sharpening contest for power and influence in Asia and in the world arena generally.

Apart from speeding up the shelter program, other measures have been taken to give the country the capability of absorbing a nuclear blow and still keep fighting. Industry has been decentralized. In rural communities, under the Maoist slogan "Prepare against war and natural calamities," large reserves of grain are being stored. At the Nan Yuen People's Commune south of Peking, I was shown the reserves of the Huai Fang Agricultural Brigade. Officials said there were more than 300,000 pounds of rice for the 3,680 people of the brigade, with a further reserve of 700,000 pounds held in state bins nearby. "These reserves are for use in case of drought, other calamities or war," a Communist Party official told me. "We have air-raid shelters in the village in case aggression is imposed on us." At the end of 1970, according to Chou En-lai, China as a whole had a grain reserve of forty million metric tons, which is a sixth of the record bumper crop harvested that year.

In the two years following the opening of the Peking border talks, China made good progress in the development of its embryo nuclear-weapons arsenal. The International Institute for Strategic Studies, in its annual report published on September 3, 1971, said that China has succeeded in producing a medium-range missile. Peking apparently deployed about twenty of them, mainly in northwestern and northeastern areas flanking the Soviet border. United States experts believe the Chinese will have eighty to one hundred such missiles operational by the middle or late 1970s. These have a range of 600 to 1,000 miles. In February 1972 Pentagon officials reported that the Chinese had deployed new missiles with a range estimated at 1,500 to 2,000 miles. The new missiles, which can be stored underground in hardened silos because of their liquid propellant, presumably have brought Moscow within range. China has also increased its nuclear air strike capability, according to the Institute, by producing at least thirty TU-16 medium bombers, a Soviet type with an operational range of 1,500 miles. At least one nuclear submarine is under construction. The Chinese were believed in 1972 to have a stockpile of less than two hundred nuclear weapons.

China has developed the capability, probably in 1970, of test-firing an intercontinental ballistic missile. Some Pentagon experts believe the Chinese late in 1970 fired a three-stage missile from a new launch site in northeast Manchuria into western Sinkiang Province, over a 2,200-mile course. A ballistic missile which can travel over 3,000 miles is classified as an ICBM, and it is calculated that the Chinese missile could have been fired at least 3,500 miles. In 1970 and again in 1971, the Chinese orbited earth satellites, demonstrating their progress in rocketry. Test-firings of ICBMs into the Indian Ocean were evidently planned. By the middle or late 1970s China was expected to have a force of ten to twenty-five ICBMs equipped with thermonuclear warheads and with a range of 6,000 miles. The Chinese would then have the capability of striking cities in European Russia and the United States.

The Chinese have developed their nuclear program on a base of technology and equipment supplied between 1957 and 1959 by the Russians. Since then they have relied on their own limited resources and a cadre of Chinese scientists and technicians trained in Soviet and earlier in American universities and laboratories. They exploded their first nuclear device in October 1964, paradoxically—and coincidentally, Chou En-lai assured us—one day after the ouster of Nikita Khrushchev from the Soviet leadership. Since then a series of explosions have been detonated at the Lop Nor testing area in Sinkiang Province, including that of a three-megaton thermonuclear device, equivalent in strength to the force of three million tons of TNT, which presumably is intended as an ICBM warhead.

While developing their nuclear weapons, the Chinese, like the French, have evidenced no interest in the various proposals that they join in nuclear arms limitation or in a ban on testing. When I met with Chou En-lai at the conclusion of my stay in Peking, he discussed China's determination to continue with its testing program.

"We do it precisely for the purpose of breaking down the nuclear monopoly and blackmail and to bring about a complete solution to this problem," Chou said.

"First of all, we are not a big power, although the extent of our territory is vast and we have a vast population. From the point of view of power, we are rather weak and backward. Second, we are in an experimental stage in our testing of nuclear weapons. We cannot call ourselves a big nuclear power. Third, every time we conduct a nuclear test which is necessary in a limited way, we issue a statement as follows: 'We will not at any time and under any circumstances be the first to use nuclear weapons.' Never! We advocate that all countries of the world regardless of their size should sit down together and agree on complete prohibition and complete destruction of nuclear weapons."

The Chinese nuclear arsenal is minuscule compared with those of the United States and the Soviet Union, and doubtlessly Peking would be delighted if the great powers would agree to destroy all nuclear weapons. In the category of land-based ICBMs alone, the United States stockpile in 1971 was put at 1,054 and that of the Soviet Union at 1,510, compared with the 25 which the Chinese are likely to have late in this decade. It is most unlikely that China will achieve anything approaching nuclear parity with the United States and the Soviet Union in this century or that the Chinese will strive to do so. Their current modest program probably is already consuming more of China's limited resources than it can afford.

What Peking seems to be striving for is an adequate nuclear deterrent to enable China to deal politically on terms of equality with the Soviet Union, and the United States and Japan, if it becomes a nuclear power. For a credible deterrent, the Chinese must have a second-strike capability, that is, the capacity to absorb a nuclear blow and still be able to inflict on any would-be attacker an unacceptable level of casualties and damage in return. The massive air-raid shelter program and the policy of decentralizing industry are part of Peking's effort to build a deterrent to nuclear attack. In the years before China attains a minimal nuclear striking force, the Chinese count on its infantry being able to go underground in the event of war and to emerge in great enough numbers to envelop any invading force. Later, this capability would become part of the second-strike defensive strategy.

Once Peking has developed what it feels is an adequate deterrent, the Chinese may become more interested in joining arms control negotiations. Given the overwhelming superiority of Soviet and American nuclear forces, it is unlikely that Peking would hazard a first strike with its limited nuclear arsenal. Apart from the suicidal character of such a move, Chinese military policy has been essentially cautious. Despite their ideological trumpeting of the virtues of armed revolutionary struggle, the Chinese have shown no inclination to become involved in foreign military adventures. While the Chinese are ready to support national liberation movements politically and with advice and weapons, the Maoist doctrine of revolutionary war holds that every insurgency must win its own armed struggle. In relations with other major powers, the Chinese habitually have avoided risking armed conflict except when they have felt their frontiers threatened, as in the Korean War after United States forces crossed the 38th parellel and in the border clashes, with India in 1962 and with the Soviet Union in 1969.

Since the opening of the border talks in Peking, the Soviet Union has continued its military build-up along the frontier with China and in the Mongolian Republic. The Soviet forces, which, according to Western estimates, number about three-quarters of a million men, have an enormous advantage over the Chinese divisions in terms of modern aircraft, tanks, guns, communications and back-up industries. The Russians have the capability of devastating China if they elected to strike with their full nuclear and conventional weaponry.

Mongolia, heavily dependent on Moscow's economic and technical aid, has become a giant military base area for Soviet tank divisions, air forces and rocket installations. A senior Western diplomat who had been posted in Mongolia told me he had observed the Russians improving airfields and building permanent barracks for troops rushed there during the 1969 crisis. The Russians make no effort to conceal their activities from passengers traveling on the railroad between Ulan Bator and Peking. The open build-up serves as a constant warning to the

Chinese. The Soviet forces in Mongolia constitute essentially a strike rather than a defense force. The Chinese, faced with the prospect of a lasting confrontation with Soviet military forces superior in strength to their own, were compelled to look for new political and diplomatic arrangements in the world to bolster their position vis-à-vis Moscow. The task was given to Chou En-lai, and he responded with a search for new allies and Ping-Pong diplomacy.

CHAPTER *28*

THE UNITED FRONT

In the spring of 1971, Chou En-lai was performing on the world stage as a master juggler of ideology and diplomacy. His sleight-of-hand was effective, and his policies appeared contradictory only to those not privy to the tactics and strategy of the Chinese Communist leadership. As the ostensible No. 3 man, behind Mao Tse-tung and Lin Piao in the Politburo of the Communist Party, Chou continued to espouse support of "national liberation movements" and world revolution. As Premier and architect of Peking's foreign policy, he busied himself welding together a coalition of "small and medium-sized nations" to stand against his chief antagonists in the world arena, those he dubbed the "superpowers," the Soviet Union and the United States. Chou sought adherents in a broad spectrum of ideologies, ranging from the independent Communist leaders of Rumania and Yugoslavia to the military dictatorships of Pakistan and Peru. It seemed that every nation that had a grievance or clash of interests with the United States or the Soviet Union could get a sympathetic hearing from Chou En-lai in the ornate colonnaded reception rooms of the Great Hall of the People or from other officials in the plush-carpeted conference rooms of the ministries of Foreign Affairs or Trade.

When the seventy-six-member Italian Government economic delegation trooped through Peking, they were told that China favors expansion of the Common Market and other nations so that the European Continent would be shored up against United States influence.

General Javier Tantalean Vanini, the bemedaled Minister of Fisheries in the ruling Peruvian military junta, was slightly flabbergasted but pleased when he was assured that China stands beside South American nations in insisting on the extension of the limit of territorial waters to two hundred miles.

Two sisters of the Shah of Iran were charmed when they were congratulated on their brother's successful fight to get American and British oil companies to pay higher oil royalties to his government.

When Peking is sparring with a government, such as that of Japan or Australia, which is unfriendly or wedded to the Chiang Kai-shek regime on Taiwan, Chou En-lai has invited leaders of the opposition parties to his capital. At the next general elections, the opposition Australian Labor Party intended to win votes by attacking government policies which in 1971 led Peking to withhold the usual contracts for the import of millions of tons of surplus Australian wheat.

During my stay in Peking, Chou En-lai's most important guest was President Nicolae Ceausescu of Rumania, who is also the General Secretary of his country's ruling Communist Party. An extravaganza welcome, which staggered me by its size, was arranged for this prime candidate for Chou En-lai's "united front" against the superpowers, and particularly the Soviet Union. It was an expression of Peking's gratitude for the independent neutral stand which Rumania had taken, unlike the balance of the Warsaw Pact Bloc, in the ideological and border dispute between China and the Soviet Union. Ceausescu had resisted strong demands from Leonid Brezhnev, the Soviet Party chief, that he join in a general condemnation of China. When the Rumanians suffered their disastrous floods in 1970, the Chinese sent substantial economic aid.

At Peking Airport, when the Rumanian President's Ilyushin-18 jet rolled to a halt, Chou En-lai, attired in a gray tunic, was waiting in a giant square of thousands of Chinese servicemen, students, delegations of national minorities in their native dress, and citizen delegations from Peking. The Rumanian President, hatless and dressed in a dark suit and a red tie, and Madame Ceausescu, in a white dress, entered a black limousine after the airport welcoming ceremonies, and our car joined the motorcade which raced toward the capital. Over an eight-mile section of the route from the airport into Peking, through T'ien-an-men Square to a state guest house, the Chinese had assembled nearly a half-million people in organized cheering squads to welcome the Rumanian guests. In rows usually three or four deep, the people cheered incessantly, waving their red books of Mao quotations, while overhead loudspeakers blared revolutionary songs. Most of the crowd seemed to be middle-school students, the girls having shed their usual blue tunics and pants for gaily colored skirts worn well below the knee. The schoolchildren waved brightly colored paper flowers and streamers, many of them tirelessly jumping up and down as they shouted in unison "Welcome!" There were thousands of young militia men and women wearing bandoleers and carrying bayoneted rifles. Soldiers hammered enormous kettle drums and clanged cymbals.

At first, I found the spectacle great fun. But as we went mile after mile, staring into the faces of the demonstrators, all behaving alike and shouting alike and on command, I suddenly felt apprehensive. A Frenchman who had lived in Peking for some time glanced at me, smiled and said, "A little frightening, isn't it?" I agreed. There was something frightening about the power of the Peking regime to summon within a few hours in any major city a half-million people, with red banners flying and drums beating, to shout tirelessly in unison any given slogan, welcome any friend or denounce any designated enemy. The studied indifference of the citizens of Peking to the arrival of President Nixon on February 21, 1972, in contrast to the welcome accorded Ceausescu, was another expression of disciplined response to the orders of the Party that are conveyed through committees in neighborhoods, factories, enterprises and schools.

In the evening, I attended a banquet for Ceausescu in the Great Hall of the People, at which Chou En-lai hailed Rumania for defying "brute force," an allusion to the Soviet Union, in safeguarding its independence. The next day, the Rumanian party left for a week's tour of the country. When the delegation returned, I was invited to attend the customary farewell "Friendship Meeting" for a visiting fraternal delegation. But it turned out to be not so customary a meeting.

When I entered the Great Hall of the People in the late afternoon of June 8, thousands of Chinese officials, phalanxes of uniformed army men and citizen delegations were already dutifully gathering in the "Hall of Ten Thousand People," a three-balcony auditorium that seats 10,300 and is used for Party Congresses and mass rallies. Brown leather seats faced a stage draped with red curtains framing a large portrait of Mao Tse-tung. At all seats there were simultaneous-translation facilities to accommodate twelve languages. There was a loudspeaker at every second seat and a microphone at every fourth seat. Over the balconies and on the walls, made of sound-absorbing plastic, were draped banners hailing Chinese-Rumanian friendship. The high ceiling was studded with lights, with a huge red star glowing in the center that symbolized the leadership of the Chinese Communist Party. The star was encircled by leaves representing rank-and-file members of the Party, while three additional concentric circles of lights, according to the official explanation, "symbolized the workers, the soldiers and the peasants who are following the Party from victory to victory."

At the appointed hour every seat was filled, the diplomatic corps in the section before the stage, with the foreign press just behind them. I fiddled with the translation equipment and found five language channels in use in an order revealing of Chinese preferences: Chinese, Rumanian, English, French, Russian. Once Russian had been the principal language taught in the schools; now it was English.

Ordinarily, the "Friendship Meetings" opened smack on time, with Chou En-lai and the chief guest filing onto the stage followed by members of their delegations who had been involved in the official talks and the negotiations on the wording of a final communiqué. A buzz arose from the diplomats and newsmen as the opening of the meeting was delayed without explanation. Chou En-lai and Ceausescu were still locked in their final negotiating session, and a hitch had developed. For more than an hour, the audience sat waiting in their seats before the diplomats and newsmen were ushered into an adjoining reception room and served orange squash while they clustered about speculating. Two and a half hours after the scheduled time, the klieg lights for the television cameras were switched on, and the delegations, looking strained, took their places at a table which extended the length of the stage. No explanation or apology for the delay was offered, and texts of the speeches were not distributed to the newsmen present as was the normal practice.

When the speeches began, the points of difference between China and Ceausescu emerged. When the Rumanian President spoke, Chou toyed unsmiling with a white embossed teacup and flipped impatiently through a manuscript which might have been a translation of Ceausescu's remarks. The Rumanian took a stand, by implication, with the Chinese leadership against Soviet meddling in the affairs of other Communist parties. He said that "each Party must formulate independently its line and strategy" and that relations among parties must be on a basis of equality and noninterference. But Ceausescu did not mention Moscow directly, nor would he make a pointed attack on the Soviet Union.

The Rumanian's speech had obviously been patched together after much wrangling. The simultaneous-translation facilities went out of whack as the interpreters struggled without texts to keep pace. Two Chinese interpreters were recruited to stand behind the rostrum at the left side of the stage, to read the amended text.

Then Chou spoke. After assuring his audience that China had no intention of assuming the role of a superpower "neither now nor ever in the future," the Premier called on small and medium-sized nations to unite and resist bullying by the superpowers. "We will always stand together with oppressed countries in firmly opposing power politics of the superpowers."

Later, I was told that the final negotiating session and the issuance of a joint communiqué had been delayed when Ceausescu balked at subscribing to the branding of the Soviets as "social imperialists," a term coined by the Chinese.

The contretemps continued at the banquet, to which we went directly, since there was no time to dress after the delay at the "Friendship Meeting." It was held in the gold-and-white colonnaded banquet room of the Great Hall of the People, which can accommodate five thousand guests. The dais table was just below a stage, which Chou and Ceausescu ascended to make their speeches as klieg lights mounted in the walls of the hall revolved and illuminated the scene for the television cameras and photographers.

Chiang Ch'ing, the bespectacled wife of Mao Tse-tung, made a surprise appearance, discarding her usual army uniform for a severe gray suit and a white handbag. She chatted with Prince Sihanouk, while the military orchestra played the Cambodian leader's romantic composition, "Nostalgia for China." Yeh Ch'ün, Lin Piao's wife, was there wearing her usual army uniform, as were many of the Chinese guests seated at round tables of ten with Rumanians and members of the diplomatic corps. The foreign press was sequestered at special tables in the rear of the hall, watched over by members of the Foreign Ministry Press Department. The farewell banquet was being tendered by the Rumanian Embassy, and we dined on a mixture of Rumanian and Chinese food, prepared by the expert chefs of the banquet hall, that puzzled the palate and sometimes defied the use of chopsticks.

The Soviet Ambassador, Vasily S. Tolstikov, a squarely built veteran Party man, grimly speared a Rumanian delicacy as he listened to Chou resume his attack on Soviet policies in East Europe. "Certain people vilify what they call 'nationalism,' " Chou said in his speech, "but as a matter of fact they are using this as camouflage in a wild attempt to carry out interference, control, exploitation and plunder against other countries." Ordinarily, the Soviet Ambassador would be expected to walk out. Tolstikov was pinned to his seat by a rhetorical device used by Chou. While denouncing the "superpowers," as bullying imperialists, Chou never mentioned the Russians by name. If the Soviet Ambassador had walked out, he would have tacitly conceded that the Russians had been scored as imperialists, an epithet which the Communists, until the Chinese innovation, had reserved for non-Socialist states, especially the United States.

All this was highly amusing for the Yugoslav diplomats attending the banquet. For a decade, in this same hall, the Yugoslav Chargé d'Affaires had regularly walked out of official banquets before the dessert was served as his Chinese hosts made their long-standing denunciation of "Tito revisionism." Then, in 1969, tensions began to ease between Peking and Belgrade, and the Yugoslav envoy began to get his share of the litchi nuts which topped off banquet menus.

The Rumanians were hardly out of China, heading for North Korea, North Vietnam and Mongolia, when Mirko Tepavac, the Yugoslav Foreign Minister, showed up to put the seal on his country's rapprochement with China. The diplomatic corps, obedient as always, and a trifle weary as always of banquet speeches, paraded back to the Great Hall of the People. In accordance with Chinese protocol, the number of guests had been cut from the usual 750 for a chief of state to 250 for a foreign minister, and there were fewer dishes. Instead of Chou En-lai, the second man in the government, Li Hsien-nien, a Vice Premier, did the honors. But the rhetoric aimed at the Russians by the Chinese was no less barbed. Like Ceausescu, however, the Yugoslav Foreign Minister was not prepared to take as hard a line as the Chinese. A dark, attractive, amicable man, Tepavac gently told the Chinese: "We are not a priori against the great powers; we are against the policy: from a position of strength, and the right of the stronger."

The Rumanian and Yugoslav visits were benchmark events in Chinese foreign policy and of crucial importance to their "united front" strategy. After the Soviet invasion of Czechoslovakia in August 1968, and the subsequent enunciation of the Brezhnev Doctrine of the right to intervene in a Communist state if the orthodox system was threatened, the Chinese reacted in alarm together with other independent-minded Communist states. The others included their close ideological allies: the Albanians, Yugoslavia, which started taking its own path to Communism as early as 1948, and Rumania, which had developed an independent foreign policy despite its nominal inclusion in the Warsaw Pact Bloc under Soviet leadership. The Chinese also saw an opportunity to expand their influence within the international Communist movement by standing up to the Brezhnev Doctrine.

As illustrated during the Rumanian and Yugoslav visits, the Chinese effort to weld an entente in Eastern Europe was only partially successful. Living in the shadow of Soviet power, Rumania and Yugoslavia, while valuing Chinese psychological support, could not afford to take a strong anti-Soviet stand. The Chinese were capable of extending limited economic aid despite their limited resources, as they did for Rumanian flood relief. In 1970 the Chinese made new aid commitments totaling $709 million, mainly to Pakistan, Peking's strategic counterpoise to India, Tanzania, where a showpiece railroad is being constructed to broaden influence in Africa, and Zambia. This was in addition to the ongoing military and economic programs for North Vietnam and Albania. But Rumania and Yugoslavia know, as do other countries which are being urged by Peking to take a more militant attitude toward the Soviet Union or the United States, that China does not have the military strength or material resources to render decisive support in any kind of a showdown with one or the other of the superpowers. Nevertheless, for the Rumanians and Yugoslavs, their visits to Peking did have the desired psychological effect on the Soviet Union. Worried about Chinese Communist influence in East Europe, in September Brezhnev visited Belgrade and signed a new declaration reaffirming Yugoslavia's political independence and her right to develop Communism in her own way. At the same time, Soviet pressure on Rumania eased as the Russians, concerned about the Chinese diplomatic offensive and the forthcoming visit by President Nixon to Peking, moved to consolidate their East European flank. If the Chinese approach to Rumania and Yugoslavia did not realize all of Peking's objectives, the Soviet reaction at least showed that China could successfully apply political leverage against the superpowers through "united front" tactics to achieve limited results.

For the sake of bringing about the broadest possible "united front," China revised the tactics it had employed up until 1965, a year of intense militant international activity.

Lin Piao's primer for world revolution, "Long Live the Victory of People's War," was published on September 3, 1965. Its doctrine of revolutionary struggle based on Maoism implied that Peking rather than Moscow was to be the center of the projected world Communist movement. Discarding the Soviet concept that revolution should be based on the urban workers, Lin propounded the Maoist theory, drawn from Chinese experience, that the countryside alone can provide the bases from which revolutionaries can go forward to victory. Then extrapolating a world outlook, Lin said:

> Taking the entire globe, if North America and Western Europe can be called "the cities of the world," then Asia, Africa and Latin America constitute "the rural areas of the world." Since World War II, the proletarian revolutionary movement has for various reasons been temporarily held back in the North American and West European capitalist countries, while the people's revolutionary movement in Asia, Africa and Latin America has been growing vigorously. In a sense, the contemporary world revolution also presents a picture of the encirclement of cities by the rural areas. In the final analysis, the whole cause of world revolution hinges on the revolutionary struggles of the Asian, African and Latin American peoples who make up the overwhelming majority of the world's population.

The article stated that Socialist countries should regard it as their duty to support these revolutionary struggles. But it also emphasized self-reliance and the principle that each people must make their own revolution, accepting foreign aid only as a supplementary support and never depending on it. Vietnam was held up as a classic example of how through "people's war" the most powerful adversary, in this instance the United States, could be defeated.

Within this context the Chinese saw themselves obliged to aid revolutionary or "national liberation movements" with weapons, economic aid, advice, political and propaganda encouragement, but not with troops. The doctrine also did not allow for the total "export of revolution." A revolutionary movement had to have tenable native roots in a country before it would attract Chinese support.

Lin's article was published just as Peking was suffering a series of stunning and unexpected foreign policy reverses.

In 1964—by the Chinese calendar, the Year of the Dragon—China emerged from the economic difficulties caused by the distortions of the 1958–59 "Great Leap Forward" and a series of bad harvests. The De Gaulle Government recognized Peking, and it seemed that China was breaking out of the diplomatic quarantine imposed by the United States, and would soon enter the United Nations. Peking detonated its first nuclear device, Nikita S. Khrushchev, the ideological archfoe of Mao Tse-tung, was toppled by his Kremlin rivals, and Chinese prestige within the international Communist movement soared. Confident and elated, Chou En-lai embarked on a series of tours of Africa and Asia to rally "the broadest united front" against the United States and to wean the Afro-Asian movement from Soviet influence. A spate of aid missions and cultural delegations debouched from Peking into the Afro-Asian world, and militant support was extended to "national liberation movements." The "encirclement of the cities of the world" seemed to be beginning.

"The world revolutionary situation is excellent," exulted Chou En-lai; then, one year later, the Premier conceded that the situation had turned temporarily "unfavorable," and he looked upon a policy in ruins.

Chou En-lai had been instrumental in arranging for the convening of a second conference of Asian and African leaders, a follow-up to the successful 1955 Bandung meeting. The Chinese had planned to use the conference to assert its leadership of the Afro-Asian world. Then a shocked Chou En-lai learned that China would not be able to muster the necessary majority either to bar the Soviet Union from the conference as a solely European nation or to subscribe to a denunciation of United States policy in Vietnam. Asian and African leaders, preoccupied with their pressing practical problems of nation-building, were unwilling to antagonize the United States and the Soviet Union or sacrifice what the Chinese Foreign Minister, Ch'en Yi, contemptuously described as bread from the two leading industrial powers. A bitter quarrel ensued between the Chinese and some of their erstwhile friends among the Afro-Asians, and the conference foundered. Other strains developed, particularly in Black Africa, when governments found the Chinese too assertive in their ideology and meddling in their internal affairs.

In Vietnam, Peking suffered the humiliation of its warnings being ignored by the United States, which extended its bombing close to the Chinese border. Hanoi swung from a pro-Chinese position in the Sino-Soviet ideological dispute to a neutral stance, inviting greater Soviet aid.

Chinese leadership of the Asian Communist parties splintered when Peking declined to enter into a joint aid program for North Vietnam with Moscow. Another crushing blow to Chinese aspirations in Asia came in October when the Indonesian Communist Party was massacred after an abortive leftist coup against the rightist army generals.

These disappointments engendered a sense of isolation and encirclement in Peking. As antiaircraft batteries were set up around Chinese cities and the training of militia accelerated, Foreign Minister Ch'en Yi cried out: "If the U.S. imperialists are determined to launch a war of aggression against us, they are welcome to come sooner, to come as early as tomorrow. Let the Indian reactionaries, the British imperialists and the Japanese militarists come along with them. Let the [Soviet] modern revisionists act in coordination with them from the north! We will win in the end."

The preoccupation with foreign affairs receded as the internal tremors of the Cultural Revolution were felt in late 1965. Peking, responding in the traditional manner to internal turmoil, turned its back on the world. Most of Peking's doors were closed to foreign visitors. Most of its diplomats were summoned home.

It was not until 1969, when the Chinese leadership was confident that the upheaval of the Cultural Revolution had been contained, that China began to actively re-engage with the world. In April of that year, the Ninth National Congress of the Communist Party was summoned to legitimatize the results of the Cultural Revolution and to lay down the line and define foreign policy.

The new Party constitution, adopted at the Congress, declared Maoism to be the theoretical basis and the guiding doctrine for Communist world revolution. The constitution stated:

Mao Tse-tung thought is Marxism-Leninism of the era in which imperialism is heading for total collapse and socialism is advancing to a world-wide victory. . . .

Comrade Mao Tse-tung has integrated the universal truth of Marxism-Leninism with the concrete practice of revolution, inherited, defended and developed Marxism-Leninism and has brought it to a higher and completely new stage. . . .

The Communist Party of China upholds proletarian internationalism; it firmly unites with the genuine Marxist-Leninist parties and groups the world over, unites with the proletariat, the oppressed people and nations of the whole world and fights together with them to overthrow imperialism headed by the United States, modern revisionism with the Soviet revisionist renegade clique as its center and the reactionaries of all countries, and to abolish the system of exploitation of man by man over the globe, so that all mankind will be emancipated.

By implication, the constitution again designated Peking as the ideological center of world revolution. Mao had taken on the mantle of Lenin, and the current tenants of the Kremlin had been denounced as renegades of the world Communist movement.

However, the principal report to the Congress, delivered by Lin Piao as Vice Chairman of the Party, indicated clearly that there had been a tactical shift from the militant foreign policy line pursued in 1964–65. The primary emphasis was now on national interests, mainly the confrontation with the Soviet Union and problems of defense, rather than ideological encouragement of national liberation movements. In fact, Lin made no direct mention of his theory of "people's war" and the encirclement of the cities of the world. He did pledge support of revolutionary struggle throughout the world, but in a broad, vague frame of reference that encompassed youth and blacks in the United States and "the laboring people of the Soviet Union in their just struggle to overthrow the Soviet revisionist renegade clique." At the same time, Lin stated explicitly: "We have always held that the internal affairs of each country should be settled by its own people."

In theoretical terms, Peking remained dedicated to world revolution. But this ideological goal was no longer a matter of first priority. The overriding concern had become national security. The confrontation with the Soviet Union had sharpened the feeling in Peking of precarious isolation and encirclement which had been expressed in Ch'en Yi's outburst in 1965. Now, not only had the Soviet military presence on her borders increased enormously, but China saw a new specter on her other flank in the shape of the growing economic and potential military might of Japan.

In October 1971, speaking to a group of Americans in Peking about the need to be prepared against attack, Chou En-lai said: "Suppose the Soviet Army goes straight to the northern bank of the Yellow River, the Americans go to the southern banks of the Yangtze River, and Japan invades and occupies Tsingtao in Shanghai and India joins in and invades Tibet?" To an American, this kind of speculation appears fantastic. To a Chinese Communist, in the light of his country's history, such a concerted attack is not impossible and therefore there is contingency planning in Peking for just such an eventuality.

To break out diplomatically and politically from its isolation, Peking could not go back to the narrow, militant revolutionary foreign policy of 1964–65. In any case, it had failed, and the leadership had become disillusioned with many of the Afro-Asian nations that had been assiduously courted in these years.

Instead, the concept of the "united front" was broadened, and Chou En-lai appealed for a coalition of small and medium-sized nations that would stand against the superpowers. The theoretical basis for the "united front" was contained in Lin Piao's report to the Ninth Party Congress. After noting that Peking was ready for peaceful coexistence with states of different social systems, Lin declared: "All countries and people subjected to aggression, control, intervention or bullying by U.S. imperialism and Soviet revisionism, unite and form the broadest possible united front and overthrow our common enemies."

To facilitate the search for new allies and international influence, Peking decided to actively seek entry into the United Nations. Quietly, Peking dropped two preconditions for accepting a seat in the world body that had effectively ruled out any prospect of membership earlier. These were demands for basic organizational changes and revisions of the UN Charter, and withdrawal of the 1950 resolution condemning China as an aggressor after Chinese "volunteers" entered the Korean War.

In October 1971, when Peking was admitted to the United Nations and the Chiang Kai-shek Government on Taiwan expelled, the call for a "united front" of the small and medium-sized powers was sounded in the General Assembly and Security Council by Chiao Kuan-hua, the head of the Communist delegation, and Huang Hua, the permanent representative. The United Nations became the new forum for furthering the "united front" strategy pressed by Chou En-lai in his meetings with diplomats in the Great Hall of the People. China intends to draw into a loose entente as many nations as possible which have a stake in limiting or inhibiting the influence of the superpowers. If this tactic is successful, as the central power of such an entente, China will acquire diplomatic leverage to contend with the Soviet Union and the United States in the pursuit of its national interests.

CHAPTER 29

THE WAITING GAME

When we returned from the Northeast to Peking on June 8, I was troubled by my lack of contact with Chinese officials who could speak with authority about the evolution of relations with the United States. My conversations with lower-echelon officials at diplomatic receptions elicited only perfunctory remarks. Yet I knew that we were on the threshold of a new era in relations between Peking and Washington. Only three officials in the guarded atmosphere of the Chinese capital were in a position to give me the information I sought. These were Chou En-lai and his two closest advisers on American affairs, Ch'iao Kuan-hua, whom I had last seen in 1961 at the dinner party given by Ch'en Yi in his Geneva villa during the Conference on Laos, and Huang Hua, who was now packing for his ambassadorial post in Ottawa.

I had requested an interview with Chou En-lai when I visited the embassy in Ottawa to pick up my visa, and then again when I called at the Information Department of the Foreign Ministry upon my arrival in Peking. On May 21 I renewed my request in a letter to the Premier, stating: "I have asked for an interview with you because I feel it is essential at this time for the American people to have a statement of position of your government in clear terms, and if possible, in your own words so there can be no mistake." Since the founding of the People's Republic on October 1, 1949, no American newspaperman had been permitted to interview Chou En-lai and publish the text of his replies.

When we returned to Peking, there was a puzzling evasiveness on the part of Chinese officials as I tried to get some statement of their

374

government's attitude toward the United States. I was told that my request to see Chou En-lai was still pending. There was reason enough why I could not see Ch'iao Kuan-hua, since I knew he was hospitalized with a recurring lung ailment. But I could not understand why I had not been received by Huang Hua. He had entertained and gone sightseeing in Peking with the Ronning party and had told Audrey that he was looking forward to seeing me. At the government reception for Nicolae Ceausescu, the Rumanian President, Ch'en Ch'u, the director of the Information Department, had made a point of telling me that Huang Hua was indisposed with a stomach ailment, but that he would see me before I left China. When Huang Hua postponed his departure for Ottawa for a month and failed to show up in accordance with the usual protocol for the receptions welcoming the first Canadian Ambassador, Ralph E. Collins, the embassy was also told that Huang Hua was ill.

Huang Hua might well have been troubled at this time by an old ulcer complaint simply because he was working under intense pressure. I did not know then that he was involved in the highly secret negotiations preparatory to Nixon's visit to Peking. When Henry A. Kissinger, the chief White House adviser on national security, arrived secretly in Peking on July 9 for a forty-nine-hour visit to discuss arrangements for the presidential visit, the top Foreign Ministry official who greeted him at the airport was Huang Hua. In September, when I dined with Huang Hua in Ottawa at his embassy, with a trace of a smile, he expressed regret that he had not been able to see me in Peking. The Chinese guard their secrets well.

In early June I waited impatiently in Peking for a reply from Chou En-lai, unaware that the exchanges between Peking and Washington on a Nixon visit had reached a decisive stage. For me, time was getting short. My three-week visa had expired on June 10. This was not in itself a problem since the Chinese seemed amenable to my staying on. In fact, a ten-day trip to Yenan and Sian had been proposed. Earlier, I had asked permission to return to Yenan, where I had seen the Chinese Communist leaders in November 1946. But now I was more concerned by what might be happening to the *Times* project for publication of the Pentagon Papers.

I had received no message from Rosenthal except one, as Audrey's dispatches and my own began appearing in the *Times* together, which said: "AUDREY ON FRIDAY AND SEYMOUR ON SATURDAY BUT WHATS

HOLDING UP COPY FROM JOANNA." Joanna was our four-year-old daughter. In our message traffic with Jim Greenfield, the Foreign Editor, his middle name, Lloyd, the code word which Rosenthal and I had agreed upon for the Pentagon Papers, had not been mentioned. June 14, the tentative date for publication of the first set of articles and texts, was only four days hence. I began to fear that the project had been somehow stymied. I decided to return to New York immediately.

On June 11 I took Audrey up to the roof of our Peking hotel, where we could not be overheard, and, as we sat in the hot sun leaning against the far revetment wall, I told her for the first time about the Pentagon Papers.

Early in March 1971, Neil Sheehan, an investigative reporter of the *Times* Washington Bureau, through hard digging and ingenuity obtained forty-five of a forty-seven-volume history of the United States role in Indochina, covering the period of involvement from World War II to May 1968, when peace negotiations opened in Paris and President Johnson announced his intention to retire. The lengthy, documented history had been commissioned by Robert S. McNamara in mid-1967 when he was Secretary of Defense. When Sheehan became privy to the history, of which only fifteen copies had been made, it was still classified "top-secret." Although the Papers' contents were historical in character, they were also politically explosive. The documents revealed not only the origins of the United States entrapment in the Vietnam bog, but also details of the covert sabotage operations against North Vietnam by the Kennedy and Johnson Administrations as well as the deception practiced in the distortion or withholding of critical information about United States activities in Indochina from the Congress and the public.

Soon after Sheehan became aware of the existence of the Papers, he approached James Reston in Washington to inquire whether the *Times* would be prepared to publish the highly sensitive material. Within a week, Sheehan had an affirmative answer, subject to the usual reservations that the editors would scrutinize the material before making a final judgment. Max Frankel, the Washington Bureau Chief, returned from a trip and joined Sheehan in delving into the three thousand pages of narrative and more than four thousand pages of appended documents. Frankel flew to New York to brief Rosenthal, myself, James L. Greenfield, the Foreign Editor, Gene Roberts, the National Editor, and several others who had to be brought initially into the highly secretive news operation. Greenfield, a former Assistant Secretary of State for

Public Affairs under Dean Rusk, with experience in handling and analyzing government documents, was put in charge of the team preparing the papers for publication. Additional writers to work with Sheehan, editors, researchers and clerks were added to the team as needed under conditions of utmost security. Our first task was to establish the authenticity of the documents, although we all had the fullest confidence in Sheehan's reliability and skill as an investigative reporter. I knew Sheehan well personally, and his wife, Susan, a talented writer for *The New Yorker* magazine, first having met him in Saigon in January 1963 when he was working for the United Press. Born in Holyoke, Massachusetts, the son of a dairy farmer, a graduate cum laude from Harvard, he was then twenty-seven years old, a tireless and dedicated reporter. In 1964 he joined the *New York Times*, serving in Indonesia and Vietnam, while I was based at Hong Kong as Chief Correspondent Southeast Asia.

Greenfield soon told Rosenthal and myself that further checking and a study of the documents had convinced him of their authenticity. The operation then went into high gear, competitively spurred by information that some of the material had been seen by others, specifically a group which intended to publish some of the material in book form in the summer.

It was apparent that many weeks would be required to correlate and select information in the documents before it could be prepared coherently for publication, and this process went forward initially in Washington with Gerald Gold, a gifted editor who was an assistant to Greenfield, working closely with Sheehan. On April 22 the operation was expanded with additional staffers and moved into a suite in the New York Hilton behind locked doors.

On April 29, Rosenthal, Greenfield and myself were called by Harding F. Bancroft, a lawyer who was an executive vice president of the paper, to a meeting in the board room of the *Times* on the fourteenth floor, where the Publisher, Punch Sulzberger, had his offices together with other of the corporate executives. Reston came up from Washington for the meeting. The subject was the Pentagon Papers. When Rosenthal and I entered the board room, we were vaguely troubled by the number of people present, apprehensive that the more people aware of our possession of the Pentagon Papers, the greater the chance of a leak. If the government was informed of our project, it would probably move to seize the Papers or halt publication through a court injunction.

We were surprised to see Louis M. Loeb, a partner of Lord, Day & Lord, corporate counsel to the *Times* for twenty-three years, and two of his legal associates. Others present included the Publisher; Bancroft; Ivan Veit, another executive vice president, who supervised the *Times* publishing enterprise which planned to put the Pentagon Papers in book form; James C. Goodale, the general counsel of the paper; and Sydney Gruson, then Assistant to the Publisher.

As the News Department did on all stories which might bring legal repercussions, Rosenthal had informed Goodale about our plans to publish the Pentagon Papers. Goodale, as was the normal practice in cases requiring extensive research or possible court litigation, had consulted with Lord, Day & Lord. Goodale, who had become familiar with the philosophy of the News Department in his years at the paper, was to remain sympathetic and helpful to Rosenthal and the other editors throughout the complicated Pentagon Papers affair.

It was the obligation of Loeb and his associates to point out possible legal pitfalls, and they did so scrupulously and emphatically. But, it seemed to the editors present, they did so without sensitivity to the broader questions of the public interest and the journalistic responsibility of the *Times*. They read from the federal secrecy codes extracts pertinent to the dissemination of classified information which stipulated penalties for violations of up to imprisonment for ten years. Whereupon Reston wryly remarked that he would be delighted to go to jail on this one, and if the *Times* did not publish, he would be glad to do so in his own weekly, the Martha's Vineyard *Gazette*. All the editors present contended that the codes were not applicable since the documents were historical in nature, did not affect national defense, and the press had repeatedly published, without penalty, classified material of similar nature in the public interest.

I also advanced my conviction that publication of the Papers was vital to the national debate that was in progress on an issue that transcended the Vietnam war. What was revealed in the Papers would help the Congress and the public determine if new safeguards were needed against secret arbitrary action by the Executive Branch. The meeting ended with the Publisher ruling that we would go forward with the preparation of the Papers for publication, but he withheld his final decision as to whether to publish pending an exhaustive review of all considerations. It was evident that the problem was weighing heavily on the forty-five-year-old Publisher. In the tradition of his family and of the paper, he had always stood by the editors, regardless of risk or cost. I believed, as did Rosenthal, that he would do so again. But Punch had to decide himself what was the true national interest, evaluate the warning of his legal consultants on possible government prosecution of the *Times*, and estimate how the reputation of the paper might be affected. The project also would cost, at a time of economic recession, hundreds of thousands of dollars in staff commitments, additional columns of space in the paper, and anticipated legal fees when the issue inevitably would go into the courts.

For these reasons, Rosenthal and I were concerned as we left the board room and walked down the corridor to the elevators. I remarked to him: "Our jobs also may be on the line here." He looked at me, his brow creased, and he nodded. We both knew if the *Times* did not publish the Papers, our position at the *Times* might become untenable. Apart from our personal conviction that we had an obligation to our readers, it was dubious that we would be able to retain the loyalty and respect of the staff if we failed to print the Papers.

I told Audrey, as we sat on the roof of the Hsin Ch'iao, that it was hard for me to conceive that the Publisher would balk at publication of the Pentagon Papers, but the pressures on him to desist were enormous and probably had increased during my absence. I told her that I intended to return to New York immediately. If I found on arrival that a decision had been taken not to print the Pentagon Papers, I might feel compelled to resign. Audrey approved of my plans. She decided to go on to Sian and Yenan for news and photo coverage, and we would meet in New York. The next morning, Audrey flew to Sian with a party of resident foreign correspondents, and I made ready to return home.

Early on the morning of June 13 I was awakened by a Chinese porter who brought a telegram from Rosenthal. We had gone to press with the Pentagon Papers and the first installment would be published that morning. I sat for a long time on the edge of the bed, my face in my hands, silently thankful.

Punch had decided to publish despite the risks. Rosenthal, backed by Reston and others, had stood like a rock throughout, insisting not only on printing the stories by the *Times* reporting team but also the pertinent texts, although publication of the classified documents themselves might make the *Times* more vulnerable to government prosecution.

In the evening, Audrey telephoned from Sian and I told her the news. "Great!" she shouted over the bad telephone line. It was Sunday and I told her that I would be leaving for New York on Wednesday. On Tuesday morning I called at the Information Department of the Foreign Ministry to say goodbye. Chi and his superior, Ma Yu-chen, an urbane but tough diplomat who was responsible for supervising the activities of foreign correspondents, received me pleasantly. We sat on sofas in the beautifully carpeted reception room, sipped tea, and they listened sympathetically as I explained that my presence was required in New York because of the repercussions stemming from publication of the Pentagon Papers. Although Chinese media had not, and would not, make mention of the Papers, senior Chinese officials were aware of the published material from *Reference News,* a compendium of monitored foreign news agency reports distributed daily to specified offices on a need-to-know basis. They were keenly interested in the Papers.

Then Chi casually expressed surprise that I would not be going to Nanking. This was the first time I had been told that I would be allowed to go to Nanking, and I said so. Chi's eyebrows arched. Earlier I had repeatedly requested permission to revisit Nanking, but had finally given up hope. Now it was obvious that the Foreign Ministry did not want me to leave the country immediately and the Nanking trip had been offered as an inducement to delay my departure. Eager to see the city where I had lived for two years and met Audrey, my hopes of seeing Chou En-lai once more aroused, I agreed to delay my departure for several days, meanwhile making a side trip to Nanking.

When I returned to the Hsin Ch'iao Hotel, there was a cable from Rosenthal:

TOPPING WOULD APPRECIATE SOONEST DETAILED ITINERARY YOUR HOMEWARD JOURNEY STOP REASON IS THAT RESTON MIGHT POSSIBLY MEET YOU IN HONG KONG OR ENROUTE IF FEASIBLE STOP ALSO PLEASE KEEP IN MIND EYE WOULD LIKE YOU TO RETURN AS SOON AS FEASIBLE STOP EVERYTHING WELL UNDER CONTROL STOP ENORMOUS REACTION TO SHEEHAN PROJECT BUT OUR FAN IS IN GOOD WORKING ORDER REGARDS.

I knew it was as close to a summons home as Rosenthal would send me. Tied up with the Pentagon Papers, Rosenthal would need me to run the news operation. I ran out of my hotel, jumped into a taxi and returned to the Foreign Ministry, catching Chi and Ma just before they left for lunch. I assumed that the Foreign Ministry saw all cable traffic between foreign correspondents and their home offices, and that Ma might have anticipated my return. I told him developments in the

United States necessitated that I leave the next day as scheduled. That night, in a private dining room of the Peking Hotel, the Information Department gave a farewell dinner for me, at which I completed negotiations for the future entry of *Times* correspondents into China. I cabled Rosenthal to "continue keep fan running," and the next morning at 6:30 A.M. I left the Hsin Ch'iao for the airport.

I boarded the Chinese jet airliner, an IL-18, which made the daily nonstop flight to Canton. I would have to stay overnight in Canton because the plane arrived too late to make the train to Hong Kong. My traveling companions included Roland Carter, the British Ambassador to Mongolia, who was returning to London for reassignment, his wife, a British diplomatic courier and two Canadian bankers. The flight was a smooth one in brilliant sunshine, but suddenly we banked and the stewardess told us we had been diverted to Changsha because an engine had begun to fail. We landed easily at the Changsha Airfield, an important Chinese Air Force base in the South Central province of Hunan and rolled past long lines of MIG-17 and MIG-19 fighter planes. Our plane was parked in a line of civilian aircraft, and we walked about 150 yards under the boiling sun to a small passenger terminal.

We had landed in the midst of a Chinese Air Force training exercise, and one MIG-19 after another swooped down onto the field, their parachute brakes billowing out behind them. While work progressed on an engine of our aircraft, we were taken to a small dining room in a building at the rear of the terminal where we lunched on excellent local Chinese dishes and beer. When we returned to the terminal, I saw that the fighter planes as they landed were being towed by trucks past the terminal and several had been parked just to the left front of the building, where they were being serviced by mechanics. I thought it peculiar since there were obviously servicing facilities, including sheds, elsewhere on the airfield, which was lined with dozens of military aircraft, almost all MIG-17 and -19 fighters. It was almost as if the planes were being shown off to us. I walked onto the tarmac and stood a short distance from the fighters being serviced. The air force personnel, dressed in work fatigues, ignored me.

The silver fighters, glistening in the sun, seemed fairly new. They were modified versions of the Soviet-type MIG-19 and apparently built in a plant reported to be situated near Shenyang.

In the early 1960s, when the Russians cut off military aid to Peking, the Chinese Air Force was crippled. Not only was its source of aircraft eliminated, but also spare parts and jet fuel. The Chinese began to develop their own military aircraft industry. At the Shenyang plant, the MIG-19 was copied and then improved in a series of modified models. The latest modification, designated the F-9 by American experts, was said to be considerably advanced and different in important respects from the Soviet aircraft. It is a twin-jet fighter said to fly at more than twice the speed of sound—roughly 1,400 miles an hour—with a combat radius of 300 to 500 miles. In 1971 the Chinese were believed to be producing about ten of these a month. The Chinese have supplied some of their models of the MIG-19 to Pakistan and North Vietnam.

The MIG-19 was already being phased out by the Russians in the early 1960s and being replaced by the MIG-21, a delta-winged fighter radically different from the 19. The Chinese managed to obtain a few of these in the 1960s, either from the Russians before aid was suspended or through third countries, such as Indonesia, which had received them from Moscow. The Chinese may have been unable to copy the MIG-21 en masse, although some have recently been spotted in China by foreign military attachés. Some features presumably were adapted to the Chinese models of the MIG-19. The Chinese MIG-19 is described by foreign experts as a highly serviceable fighter, although it is outclassed by the Soviet MIG-21, the newer 23, and United States F-4 Phantom fighters. The Chinese had also begun recently to produce the Soviet-type TU-16 medium bomber, some of which had been obtained from the Russians in the early 1960s.

Altogether, the Chinese are estimated by the Institute for Strategic Studies to have about 2,800 combat aircraft, including a fleet of about 150 obsolete IL-28 light bombers which were also supplied by the Russians in the 1960s before the aid cutoff.

The Chinese are producing their own jet fuel, and judging by the brisk air force activity I saw at several airfields, there is no longer any shortage.

After several hours of waiting, we were told that we would continue our journey to Canton in another plane. We carried our hold luggage from the IL-18 airliner to a smaller plane. The British diplomatic courier had been wearily toting his sealed bags of official mail around the airfield all afternoon, not able to leave them out of his sight. Gratefully, he accepted the help of Roland Carter and myself in hauling the bags to our new aircraft.

We landed at Canton at 4:15 P.M., some ten hours after I had left the

Hsin Ch'iao Hotel for the Peking Airport. I felt fatigued as we debarked and trudged in the sultry heat toward the terminal. I was met by a representative of China Travel Service, and to my surprise, he separated me from the other passengers and led me into a small side waiting room. Within a few minutes, as I sat sipping tea, a tall Chinese came into the room and was introduced as Mr. Yang, the responsible member of the Foreign Affairs Section of the Revolutionary Committee of Canton. "Mr. Topping," he said in Chinese, "Premier Chou En-lai would like to see you. Will you return to Peking?" I looked at him, slightly dazed, nodded my head and asked: "When?"

"The plane leaves at 5 o'clock," Mr. Yang said. It was then 4:25 P.M. "I must telephone my office in Hong Kong," I replied. "They are expecting me tomorrow."

"You will be driven to a hotel to make your call," Mr. Yang said. "The plane will be held." He rose, smiled, shook hands and left.

The China Travel Service man led me to a car and at high speed we drove to the Tung Fang Hotel, where I had stayed on arrival in China. Chinese characteristically attach great importance to old personal ties, even if the past contacts were casual, and so I was welcomed back by the desk clerks at the Tung Fang with more warmth and broader smiles than on my first visit. The China Travel man spoke to them in an urgent whisper, and my call to the *New York Times* office in Hong Kong was put through in less than five minutes. Ian Stewart listened in more amusement than I could muster to the word that I was flying back to Peking that night. We arranged that he would relay my message by telephone to Rosenthal. The Chinese had no objection to my reporting that I had been summoned by Chou En-lai on condition that the information not be published in advance of the meeting. The Chinese also had agreed to inform my traveling companions from Peking so they would not think that I had strayed or been kidnaped à la Fu Manchu.

We sped back to the airport. Bureaucracy could not be surmounted despite the fact that the airliner with its passengers was waiting for me on the tarmac. With an apologetic smile, the China Travel man led me to a counter, where I bought a ticket back to Peking. I grumbled only when asked to pay the excess baggage charge once again. When at 5:15 P.M. I boarded the same aircraft that had brought me to Canton an hour earlier, the same stewardess, a large, broad-faced girl, greeted me without a twitch of astonishment. I sank in my seat opposite a Mr. Urbanski, the Polish Consul in Shanghai, who looked at me with more than ordinary curiosity, and then we were airborne, en route, I thought, to Peking.

We had been in the air for some two hours when it was announced that the weather was bad in Peking and we would spend the night in Chengchow, the capital of Honan Province in North Central China. We were taken by bus from the airfield to the Chengchow Guest House, a large hotel evidently built with Russian help in the fifties. Done in the ornate Stalin style of Soviet architecture, with cavernous lobbies and dining halls but small guest rooms, the building could have easily housed several hundred guests, but it seemed virtually empty. It evidently was kept open to accommodate visiting delegations. A Foreign Ministry tour for the Peking diplomatic community had just passed through. The rooms were clean and fairly comfortable, but the fixtures were cracking and the plumbing was rusting. When normal tourism, which had been discontinued during the Cultural Revolution, was resumed, the Chengchow Guest House would be put to good use.

We breakfasted the next morning on eggs, toast, Chinese preserves and strong coffee. Urbanski and I shared a table, the only foreigners among the passengers apart from some overseas Chinese. Our only common language was a few words of English that Urbanski knew. We communicated mostly with the exchange of sighs and glances of impatience as we waited for our journey to Peking to be resumed. In mid-morning we were bused back to the airfield, where we waited two hours for clearance from Peking. Before our plane took off, Urbanski collected a fistful of anti-Soviet propaganda pamphlets in a half-dozen languages which were lying on tables in the waiting room for the education of travelers.

As our plane neared Peking, my excitement rose. I speculated on the circumstances under which I would see the Premier and what he might say. In any case, journalistically, it would be a coup. No American newsman had been granted an exclusive interview with Chou En-lai in two decades. I clambered impatiently off the plane at Peking Airport and found Mr. Chi of the Foreign Ministry Information Department waiting for me. This in itself was unusual. When I had arrived in Peking the first time, I had half-expected that an official might meet me, the first American newspaper editor to be admitted to the People's Republic. That vision vanished on the deserted tarmac, especially as I carried my own bags to the taxi. Now my sense of expectation rose still further as the graceful Mr. Chi greeted me. "I am sorry we did not get word before you took off for Canton," Mr. Chi said. As we waited in the terminal for my passport and internal travel documents to be passed by the Foreign Affairs Section, we talked about the weather. Then Chi said: "And what would you like to do over the next several days?" I looked at him in stunned disbelief. In my Walter Mitty reveries aboard the plane, I had seen myself whisked from the airfield and ushered into the presence of the Premier to hear some great headline-making announcement. Reality intruded. I had been summoned back to await the pleasure of Chou En-lai.

This manipulation of an American innocent was to have its parallel during the visit of James Reston less than four weeks later. Scotty and his wife Sally arrived in Canton on July 8, and were told that plans for their flight to Peking had been changed. They were to remain in the Canton area for two days and then proceed by rail to Peking. When they demurred and asked to fly to Peking at once, they were told it was out of the question. After their arrival in Peking on July 12, over lunch with Foreign Ministry officials, Reston was given "a little news item." Henry A. Kissinger had been in Peking from July 9 to 11.

Mr. Chi delivered me back to the Hsin Ch'iao Hotel, where further blows awaited me. I encountered William Attwood, the publisher of *Newsday*, the Long Island newspaper. Bill and his wife, Sim, had been in Peking for two weeks as the guests of Prince Sihanouk and had also asked to see Chou En-lai. Bill and I took the measure of each other and decided that candor would be the best strategy. I told my story, and he informed me that he had been told by Ma Yu-chen of the Information Department that if he delayed his departure, a certain responsible official might see him the following week.

Meanwhile, unaware of the blows dealt the hopes of Attwood and Topping for exclusive interviews, Bob Keatley of the *Wall Street Journal*, who had been rummaging amid the museums of Yenan, was in a high state of excitement. He, too, had been told without explanation to rush back to Peking with his wife, Ann, and this he did with visions of an exclusive interview with Chou En-lai dancing in his head. Audrey was also having her share of fun and games. Yu, our interpreter, who had accompanied Audrey to Yenan, told her coyly: "Why don't you telephone Top in Peking?" Audrey protested that I was gone. When Yu insisted, Audrey said, "Well, I will call Peking just to show you." Another piece was added to the Chinese puzzle when I answered the telephone at the Hsin Ch'iao. Soon, the Keatleys and Audrey were on a special plane heading back to Peking for our rendezvous with Chou En-lai. The Keatleys, Attwoods and Toppings were reunited in the Hsin Ch'iao. Their common dream of exclusivity had been foiled, but nevertheless a unique and fascinating evening with Chou En-lai, his first dinner with American newsmen in twenty-five years, lay ahead.

Over the weekend, we were asked by the Information Department to stand by in the Hsin Ch'iao for a summons from Chou En-lai. There was no telling when the call might come or at what hour Chou would see us. He often worked through the night until 5 A.M. Every few hours Ma or Chi would telephone to make sure that we were still in the hotel and to urge us not to stray. We waited for three days.

Rosenthal kept me informed as the Pentagon Papers controversy dominated attention in the United States. Aware of my chagrin at having been away from New York at this challenging moment, he cabled me on June 18:

WE ALL MISSED YOU BUT KNOW WAS FOR WONDERFUL PURPOSE. REACTION AROUND WORLD CONTINUES ENORMOUSLY STRONG BEHIND THE PAPER AND THE SERIES AND COURT CASE NOW UNIVERSALLY RECOGNIZED AS LANDMARK IN JOURNALISM AND LAW FONDLY.

Three installments of the Pentagon Papers had been published—on June 13, 14 and 15—before United States District Judge Murray I. Gurfein issued a temporary restraining order on June 15. On the evening of June 14, John Mitchell, the Attorney General, had wired the Publisher asking the *Times* to refrain from further publication of the Papers and to return the documents to the Department of Defense. Punch had flown to Europe that morning, but by telephone authorized Rosenthal to proceed with our publication schedule. The Publisher returned to New York forty-eight hours later to announce his determination to fight the case through. In his absence, Harding Bancroft telephoned Robert C. Maridan, the Assistant Attorney General in charge of the Internal Security Division. "We refuse to halt publication voluntarily," Bancroft told him.

Lord, Day & Lord, whose lawyers had argued so strongly against publication, were not disposed to fight the case in court. The excuse was a conflict of interest. When Herbert Brownell, senior partner at Lord, Day & Lord, had been Attorney General during the Eisenhower Administration, he had drafted the Executive Order establishing the categories of classified government information.

Overnight, Bancroft and Jim Goodale, chief counsel for the *Times,* found Professor Alexander M. Bickel of Yale Law School and got him to agree to represent the *Times* in court the next morning.

On June 21, Rosenthal messaged me:

FEDERAL JUDGE GURFEIN RULED RESOUNDINGLY SATURDAY IN FAVOR OF TIMES ON FREEDOM OF PRESS AND NATIONAL SECURITY ISSUES AND REFUSED TO GRANT INJUNCTION. HOWEVER BAN ON PUBLICATION IS CONTINUED THROUGH TUESDAY PENDING GOVERNMENT APPEAL BEFORE FULL COURT OF APPEALS. LIKELIHOOD IS CASE WILL GO SWIFTLY TO UNITED STATES SUPREME COURT. TIMES IS COVER STORY ON TIME AND NEWSWEEK AND REACTION AROUND COUNTRY CONTINUES HEAVILY FAVORABLE REGARDS.

While these events were transpiring, I paced my room and the corridors of the Hsin Ch'iao agonizing over my absence from New York and wondering when the call would come from Chou En-lai. In fact, the culmination of the Pentagon Papers court fight did not come until I was back in New York on June 30, when the Supreme Court ruled against the government and allowed the *Times* to resume publishing the Papers. In May 1972, publication of the Papers would bring the *Times* a pulitzer prize for public service.

Later in the afternoon of Monday, June 21, Mr. Chi telephoned to say that we were to dine with Chou En-lai at 6:15 in the Great Hall of the People.

CHAPTER 30

AN EVENING
WITH CHOU EN-LAI

Shortly before 6 P.M., the Attwoods, Keatleys, Audrey and I left the Hsin Ch'iao Hotel and climbed into three cars dispatched by the Foreign Ministry. The motorcade moved swiftly up Legation Street, turned west on the Boulevard of Eternal Tranquillity and sped toward the Great Hall of the People on T'ien-an-men Square. I looked out at the broad thoroughfare, virtually empty except for processions of bicyclists returning home from work, and thought of the events preceding this dinner at which Chou En-lai would be host to American correspondents. Three months ago there had been no apparent breach in the wall of hostility which had separated the United States and China for two decades.

Yet, in hindsight, one could see how the evolution of the world situation and the initiatives undertaken by Chou En-lai and Richard Nixon over a four-year period had led to a reopening of communications between China and the United States. If not for the Indochina War, Ping-Pong diplomacy or some similar ploy might have been put into play by Peking in 1970 to restore communication between China and the United States.

As long ago as November 26, 1968, Peking had, in fact, proposed a meeting in Warsaw with delegates of the incoming Nixon Administration. The forum was to be the private ambassadorial talks which began in 1955 and continued for 134 fruitless meetings, first in Geneva and then in Warsaw. The talks had been in a state of suspension since January 1968 because of Chinese unwillingness to reconvene.

The diplomatic gambit in November 1968 toward the Nixon Administration was undertaken for a complex of reasons.

The turbulent phase of the Cultural Revolution had ended and Chou En-lai could safely turn his attention to foreign affairs. Peking was eager to extricate itself from the isolation into which it had blundered as a consequence of the ideologically militant foreign policies of 1964–65. Relations with the Soviet Union were deteriorating, and there was a sense of insecurity in Peking in the wake of the Moscow-led Warsaw Pact invasion of Czechoslovakia. The Chinese had also been intrigued by an article written by Nixon thirteen months before his election to the presidency. In the October 1967 issue of the quarterly *Foreign Affairs*, in an article titled "Asia After Vietnam," Nixon wrote that "any American policy toward Asia must come urgently to grips with the reality of China." He said that "taking the long view, we simply cannot afford to leave China forever outside of the family of nations, there to nurture its fantasies, cherish its hates and threaten its neighbors." It was not a conciliatory article, but it left an opening for an exercise of diplomacy. "Within two weeks of my inauguration I ordered that efforts be undertaken to communicate our new attitude through private channels, and to seek contact with the People's Republic of China," President Nixon recalled in his State of the World Message to Congress in February 1972.

The Chinese probe of the Nixon Administration's intentions foundered forty-eight hours before it was to begin on February 20, 1969. Complaining about the defection on January 24 of Liao Ho-shu, a Chinese diplomat in the Netherlands who was subsequently granted asylum in the United States on February 4, Peking canceled the scheduled February 20 meeting. Peking's charge that Liao had been incited to defect by the Central Intelligence Agency seemed to be a cover for other considerations which had arisen in Peking to require that the Warsaw meeting be postponed. The Chinese may have decided to delay the discussions until after the Ninth Party Congress, which was summoned into session on April 1, 1969, to legitimize the shifts in power and policies stemming from the Cultural Revolution.

Disappointed, President Nixon worked to revive the Warsaw talks. On July 21 it was announced that American citizens traveling abroad would be permitted to bring home $100 worth of goods produced in China and that United States scholars, students, scientists, physicians and newsmen would henceforth be permitted to travel freely to the mainland. In August 1969, William P. Rogers, the Secretary of State, urged Peking several times during an Asian tour to resume the Warsaw talks.

On January 8, 1970, Lei Yang, the Chinese Chargé d'Affaires in Warsaw, and Walter J. Stoessel, Jr., the United States Ambassador to Poland, meeting in an unusually cordial atmosphere, decided to resume the formal ambassadorial meetings on January 20. In the year which had elapsed, Chinese interest in exchanges with the United States had heightened. The military confrontation with the Soviet Union had sharpened in 1969 following border clashes in Central Asia and the Northeast. Peking, at a disadvantage in terms of military strength vis-à-vis the Soviet Union, saw an opportunity to influence the power equation by flirting with the United States. Similarly, Nixon and Kissinger hoped to inject a Chinese factor into the United States–Soviet equation that would tend to make Moscow more accommodating to American policies. The bitter Soviet reaction to the announcement of the forthcoming Sino-American talks was revealing of Moscow's fears that the balance of forces in the world might be tipped to its disadvantage.

Ambassador Stoessel and Lei Yang, the Chinese Chargé d'Affaires, met on January 20 and again on February 20 amid cautious optimism that progress was being made toward easing antagonisms. At the February 20 meeting, Stoessel conveyed an offer from President Nixon that a senior American official travel to Peking to discuss means of bettering relations between the two countries. Then on May 19, twenty-four hours before the envoys were to meet again in Warsaw, Peking canceled the session "in view of the increasingly grave situation created by the United States Government, which has brazenly sent troops to invade Cambodia and expanded the war in Indochina." The disruption of the talks was part of the price paid by the Nixon Administration for mounting the strike by American and South Vietnamese troops against North Vietnamese and Vietcong sanctuaries in Cambodia. However, in a few weeks' time, while lending support to the ousted Cambodian regime of Prince Norodom Sihanouk, the Chinese let it be known that they would resume the contacts at a suitable time.

In the next months, President Nixon sent a series of secret messages to Peking in which he persuaded the Chinese that it was his intention ultimately to withdraw from Indochina and that he was committed to normalizing relations with Peking. During his European tour in 1969, the President had confided to President Charles de Gaulle and

Rumanian President Nicolae Ceausescu, both in touch with Peking, that he was determined to arrive at an accommodation with China. Other channels, as well, were utilized to draw Peking into talks.

In December, Mao told Edgar Snow in a private conversation that he would be happy to talk to Nixon, either as a tourist or as a President, and that the Foreign Ministry was studying the matter of allowing Americans to visit China.

Soon afterward, the exchange of signals between Peking and Washington intensified. On March 15, 1971, the State Department removed the ban on travel to China by Americans in general. The first public Chinese response came on April 7 when the United States table tennis team, participating in a tournament in Japan, was invited to play in China. According to Chou En-lai, it was Mao who decided to invite the team while the Foreign Ministry was still hesitant. On April 16, in a speech to the American Society of Newspaper Editors in Washington, President Nixon expressed the hope that he could visit China, but said he was far from certain that it could happen while he was in office. By April exchanges were in progress between Peking and Washington on the possibility of a presidential visit to the Chinese capital. The Chinese were also trying to take the measure of the men they were to meet. In early April, Ronning was closely questioned by Chou En-lai about Nixon. In the days immediately preceding our June 21 dinner with Chou, Chinese officials casually questioned Audrey and me about Kissinger, asking about his background, his personality and influence. We had become so inured to Chinese curiosity about American leaders and the United States in general that it did not occur to us that the visit of a presidential envoy was imminent. Certainly, there had been no slackening in the press in Chinese attacks on the United States, especially on the central issue of Taiwan, which for twenty years had impeded any substantial improvement in relations between Peking and Washington.

In the Warsaw talks, the Chinese had consistently stood by two conditions for any basic change in relations with the United States. As arrangements were made for President Nixon to fly to Peking, Chou En-lai was insistent that there would be no change in these conditions, which were:

First, the U.S. Government undertakes to immediately withdraw all its armed forces from China's Taiwan Province and the Taiwan Strait and dismantle all its military installations in Taiwan Province.

Second, the U.S. Government agrees that China and the United States conclude an agreement on the five principles of peaceful coexistence.

The five principles, endorsed in 1955 at the Bandung Conference of African and Asian States, are: mutual respect for each other's territorial integrity and sovereignty, mutual nonaggression, mutual noninterference in internal affairs, equality and mutual benefit, and peaceful coexistence.

Since the United States is bound by its 1954 Mutual Defense Treaty with the Chinese Nationalist Government to defend Taiwan and the adjacent Pescadores, the first of these conditions had been unacceptable. To Peking respect for territorial integrity meant United States recognition that Taiwan was part of the People's Republic of China.

While there was no resolution of the deadlock, Chou En-lai was, nevertheless, disposed to talk to President Nixon because the Chinese had detected a new flexibility in the American position. In the context of internal American politics, the Chinese estimated correctly that President Nixon, a Republican and a conservative, could muster more support and would have broader scope to bring about a change in the Taiwan policy. Chou En-lai was also keenly aware that the American people, disillusioned by the experience of the Vietnam war, were wavering in their attitudes toward Asia. He believed that American public opinion was now more susceptible to persuasion and could be a potent ally in bringing about changes in United States policy. This was part of the Chinese motivation for Ping-Pong diplomacy, and our own dinner with the Premier. He would tell us frankly that American visitors could help to mobilize their fellow countrymen to bring about the withdrawal of American forces from Taiwan and Indochina.

Our motorcade halted in T'ien-an-men Square, and we walked up the stone steps to a side entrance to the Great Hall of the People, guarded by a single army sentry.

We entered at the center of a long carpeted hallway and on our left saw Chou En-lai walking slowly toward us with six other Chinese officials clustered about him. He wore a well-tailored gray tunic, with a Mao emblem inscribed "Serve the People" above the left breast pocket, with matching trousers and brown sandals over black socks. His right arm, slightly stiff from an old injury, was held bent at his side. He was grayer than when I had met him last, but the bushy eyebrows were still bold and black and he remained extraordinarily handsome, almost theatrically so.

As we went forward to meet him, I could see that at seventy-three he was thinner and had become somewhat frail, although his fine bone structure, erect carriage and incandescent personality veiled the changes of age. I had last seen him in July 1954 at the conclusion of the Geneva Conference when he went to the airport to say goodbye to Soviet Foreign Minister Molotov. His usually mobile features were impassive as he shook hands with the burly Stalinist and watched him board the two-motored camouflaged plane that was to take him back to Moscow. For the onlookers at the Conference Chou En-lai had been the most dramatic figure, striding about Geneva in the cooler weather in a long, narrow black coat and a tall, broad-brimmed, black hat. Once John Foster Dulles, the American Secretary of State, entered a conference room and found Chou En-lai the only other negotiator there. The Chinese Premier extended his hand in greeting. Dulles, muttering "I cannot," turned on his heel and walked out of the room, his hands locked behind his back. The 1954 sojourn in Geneva was the last occasion on which Chou En-lai, the principal architect of Chinese foreign policy, the most worldly and widely traveled of the top Peking leadership, visited a Western country. His subsequent travels were confined to Eastern Europe, Africa and Asia.

"Welcome," said Chou En-lai, shaking hands with each of us and leading the group into an adjoining room to a two-step platform. "We shall have our photos taken here. Stand wherever you like." Our photos with the Premier, which are usually taken as a souvenir for every banquet guest or for publication, were delivered to our hotel room at 5 A.M. to be sure that we would have them before our departure from Peking. The news that we had a "friendly conversation" with the Premier was to be published in a six-line item at the bottom of the *Jen Min Jih Pao*, the official Party newspaper, in the same format and space assigned to the initial visit of Kissinger to Peking.

As we walked into the Fukien Room, where we were to dine, Chou said to Audrey: "The last time you were here we had dinner with your father, Chester Ronning." Turning to me, smiling, he added: "At that time she made use of the opportunity to note some words of opinion and wrote a story about it. It goes to show the prowess of a correspondent's wife."

The Fukien Room was furnished in brown and cream. At one end there was a semicircle of conference chairs. The spacious room was dominated by a huge painting of a group with red banners fluttering standing atop a Kansu mountain peak high above a cloud-shrouded valley.

The Chinese officials in the party included Chang Wen-chin, Chief of the West European, American and Oceanic Affairs of the Foreign Ministry; P'eng Hua, a director of the Information Department; Ma Yu-chen, who looked after foreign correspondents; and two interpreters, Chi Ch'ao-chu, a former Harvard student, and T'ang Wen-sheng, known to her American friends as Nancy. Miss T'ang is the American-born daughter of T'ang Ming-chao, who until 1949 was the editor of the *Overseas Chinese Daily* in New York City and was then an official in Peking dealing with cultural relations with foreign countries.

Before the dinner Ma told me privately that at the end of the evening I would be handed the Premier's answers to a list of sixteen questions I had submitted three weeks earlier appended to my request for an interview. I was surprised and delighted, but was also presented with a journalistic dilemma. Ma told me the replies would be given to me exclusively, and now I was in a quandary as to how many of these questions I should pose verbally at the dinner and thus share the replies with Attwood, whose reports were being widely syndicated by the Los Angeles *Times*, and Keatley.

The Premier guided us past an exquisite lacquer screen to a round table set with blue and white porcelain, silver knives and forks, ivory chopsticks, glasses for Chinese wine, beer and mou-t'ai, and place cards.

"According to the Chinese custom," Chou said, "the guests should sit opposite the hosts at the head of the table." Audrey and I were seated in the places of honor opposite Chou En-lai, with the Chinese menu, embossed with the national red and gold seal, between us. The Attwoods were on our right and the Keatleys on our left. We had been joined by Kao Chun-chung, the director of protocol, and a woman secretary who recorded the conversation in a Chinese shorthand.

Small dishes of cold chicken and paprika, stuffed crab meat, spiced pork, bean curd and string beans, ham, mushrooms and cucumber were set near each plate.

Chou En-lai apologized for recalling me from Canton, noting that I was hurrying home because of the Pentagon Papers. The Premier compared the publication of the Pentagon Papers by the *Times* with the release by the State Department in 1949 of the China White Paper backgrounding the United States involvement in the Chinese civil war in the period 1944–49. "They published the China White Paper to defend themselves, but it was a great shock to the world," Chou said. When I stated that the *Times* had printed the Pentagon Papers, despite the opposition of the government, because we felt it was in the interest of the United States, Chou remarked: "Not only in the interests of the United States, but of the whole world. It would be a glorious thing if the United States withdrew from Vietnam. The United States would win the acclaim of the peoples. The *New York Times* is to be highly commended."

Our small brandy glasses were filled with mou-t'ai, a clear 120-proof liquor. We had been drinking it at banquet tables the length of China, finding it a powerful but pleasant liquor that slid down far more easily than vodka.

Chou raised his glass in a toast to the withdrawal of American troops from Indochina, and asked: "Can you all drink mou-t'ai?" "Oh, yes," I replied. "We believe that when trade develops this will be one of your most successful commodities."

"Well, we probably won't be able to supply so much mou-t'ai," Chou said laughing, "because it is produced only in a certain locality." He recalled that it was the Chinese Red Army on the Long March which had found the Mou T'ai River in Kweichow Province and discovered that its waters were ideal for making the sorghum liquor. "This liquor won't go to your head," Chou assured us, "although you can light it with a match."

The history of the epic six-thousand-mile Long March records that the Red Army halted for a time at Tsun-yi in Kweichow in January 1935 for a crucial political conference at which Mao consolidated his leadership of the Party. Chou, then a lean, bearded and resourceful soldier, the Red Army's Chief Political Officer, apparently lost out to Mao at that conference in terms of political power, although they have worked closely together thereafter.

The remarkable political durability of Chou En-lai in the recurring power struggles within the Party may be explained in part by the manner in which he has repeatedly and gracefully yielded top positions to such leaders as Mao, and then in turn to Liu Shao-ch'i and Lin Piao, both purged in turn, and others when he sensed that political circumstances required his acceptance of a lesser role.

The Long March began in the Southeastern province of Kiangsi in October 1934, as the Red Army sought to flee the onslaughts of the Chiang Kai-shek troops, and ended in the refuge of the Northwestern province of Shensi in October 1935. Chou ended the march on a stretcher, having become seriously ill during the latter part of the journey.

"Actually," said Chou En-lai, raising his glass pensively, "after drinking for thirty years, I am giving it up." The Premier explained: "In spirit I am always young, but my material base is getting older and older." Despite this allusion to his health and the protests of his young interpreter, Nancy T'ang, Chou continued to knock back mou-t'ai toasts throughout the dinner, declaring: "I will not pretend to drink, let me have real liquor."

Agaric consommé, a cloudy broth with a jelly-like mushroom floating in it, was put before us. It was soon followed by sea cucumbers, abalone sea slugs, which the Chinese assured us were good for inhibiting hardening of the arteries.

Chou reminisced about how he had entertained many Americans between 1938 and 1946 in Yenan, Chungking and Nanking. He had not had a dinner meeting with American newspapermen since 1946, when he left Nanking after the breakdown of his peace talks with the Chiang Kai-shek Government.

"I still like to recall those seven or eight years," Chou said. "Now, as Premier, I am not so free. For instance, I say just one word and you note it down."

The Premier had watched with amusement as we scribbled under the table, pausing intermittently to stab frantically with our chopsticks as the superbly prepared gourmet dishes passed before us. Now there were chicken slices, shrimp and peas, steamed and delicately flavored with green peppers and ginger.

"Well," I said rather lamely, "this just illustrates the importance of China in the world."

"We can only say that China is comparatively important, not so very important," Chou replied. "China will never become a superpower. It is not easy to be a superpower. You must have control over the atom bomb, look into everything all over the globe, strive for hegemony and compete with other superpowers. All this results only in bringing about the opposition of peoples. Why suffer all that? We have benefited from the experience of the other superpowers [the Soviet Union and the United States] and decided we shall not attempt it."

As for space shots, Chou commented: "It's a heavy burden on the American taxpayers. We have so many things to solve on earth—why go to the moon? It is a waste—a great waste, and the people must pay for it."

While commiserating with the American people over their economic problems—"The profits of monopoly capitalists are increasing steadily"—Chou did not see disaster ahead for the United States. "The American people will be able to solve their problems," he said. He also had a word of sympathy for any man who becomes President. "Being President of the United States is a terrible job. No matter what you do you are criticized. The President cannot do anything right."

As the shad, served with sweet and sour sauce and sprinkled with crushed almonds, arrived on huge platters, Attwood purred in pleasure: "Chinese food is so much better in China." Miss T'ang reported that shad came from the confluence of a fresh-water river and the sea.

The Premier, who had been speaking strongly in support of the liberation of women, whom he said had been "suffering for thousands of years," quipped, "I suggest we men also liberate ourselves and take off our coats." He doffed his tunic, draped it over the back of the chair, and returned to the table in a soft white short-sleeved shirt with open neck.

During the dinner conversation, Chou En-lai revealed an understanding of English by reacting to our remarks before they were translated, and in several instances he corrected his interpreters in Chinese. On occasion, Chou will utter a sentence or two in English, but at our dinner he confined himself to Chinese. The Premier learned to speak French and some English during the years 1920–24, when, already a revolutionary, he was a student in Paris and made side trips to Britain, Germany and Belgium. It was in Paris, in 1922, that he joined the Chinese Communist Party and shortly thereafter met Ho Chi Minh, whom he described in later years as "my big brother." Presumably the Premier continues to read in French, but his spoken French has fallen into disuse.

Attwood asked Chou En-lai about the outlook for Taiwan over the next six months.

"It is difficult to answer when one puts a time limit on it," the Premier said.

"In the first place, Taiwan is Chinese. Historically, it has been a province of China for a long time. Because of the Sino-Japanese War of 1894, Taiwan was occupied by Japan following the Treaty of 1895. But in 1945, at the conclusion of the Second World War, in accordance with the Potsdam and Cairo declarations Taiwan was returned to the embrace of its motherland and once again became a province of China.

"Topping and Ronning were in Nanking for our entry. They saw the new replace the old in April 1949.

"In January 1950, President Truman acknowledged these facts in a statement. Truman recalled that Taiwan had already been returned to China, was a matter of internal Chinese affairs, and that the United States had no territorial ambitions in regard to Taiwan. Truman said further that the question between the mainland and Taiwan could be solved by the Chinese people themselves. Thus we can say that the position of the American Government toward the new China was defined before the whole world," Chou continued.

"Then suddenly, in June 1950, the position was changed, and the American Seventh Fleet was dispatched to the Taiwan Strait."

The Premier was referring to the statement made by President Truman on June 27, two days after the North Korean attack on South Korea. Altering the United States position, which previously had been unequivocally that Taiwan belonged to China, the President stated: "The determination of the future status of Formosa [Taiwan] must await the restoration of security in the Pacific, a peace settlement with Japan, or consideration by the United Nations."

The Seventh Fleet arrived in the Taiwan Strait as the Chinese Communists were preparing for an assault on the island.

Chou, his demeanor now cold and deliberate, said: "At that time, China had nothing to do with the Korean War. It was an interference in China's internal affairs.

"Now we demand that all American forces be withdrawn from Taiwan and the Taiwan Strait, that the United States respect the sovereign independence and territorial integrity of the People's Republic of China and that there be no interference in our internal affairs. On our part, we respect the independence and territorial integrity of the United States, and we will not interfere in your internal affairs. Once this problem is resolved, then all other problems can be solved and China will be able to establish diplomatic relations with the United States. This has been our consistent position for the past fifteen years since the opening of the Sino-American talks in 1955. We have no other demands," Chou said emphatically.

The Premier was asked how he thought Taiwan would be united with the mainland, by negotiation or by force, and what would happen to the two million refugee mainlanders on the island, as well as the twelve million Taiwanese.

"First," Chou replied, "the Taiwanese are Chinese. Not only those mainlanders brought over by Chiang Kai-shek, but also the overwhelming majority of the people who live on Taiwan are Han. They speak the same dialect as the people of Fukien. There are minority nationalities on Taiwan, but there are also a lot of national minorities throughout China. Our policy is one of equality.

"As to how Taiwan will be returned to China, and how it will be liberated, that is our internal affair. Mr. Topping knows that when I was about to leave Nanking [in 1946], they asked if I would come back. I said I surely would. Since then we have returned to Nanking. We will also return to Taiwan. It will not be all that difficult.

"There is a simple fact involved here that is worth the attention of our American friends. Even Chiang Kai-shek is opposed to the so-called two Chinas, and he is also opposed to the one China and an independent entity of Taiwan. So, although in the past we have been both allied with Chiang Kai-shek and hostile to him, on this question we share a common point of view. There can be only one China. That is a fact, and a way can be found."

Noting that Taiwan has a living standard second only to Japan in Asia, Chou was asked what would happen to the living conditions of the people. Chinese leaders, insisting that the administration of Taiwan is an internal matter, have, as a matter of policy, declined to answer questions of this kind. However, at the farewell dinner given to me by the Information Department before my departure for Canton, I had argued that the American people would never be persuaded to favor Peking's takeover of the island until they knew what the fate of the Taiwanese would be. There had been talk in the United States of a bloodbath if the Communists occupied the island. Now Chou En-lai undertook to partially answer this question, in a statement which other Chinese officials at the dinner later described as being of great importance.

"It is impossible that we would lower the living standards on Taiwan," Chou said. "On the contrary, when Taiwan is returned to China, the living standards will be improved.

"First, taxation would be decreased, as it has been here. Second, there would no longer be debts, because the motherland would help construction. China has no internal or external debts, which must be considered a small achievement on our part. Third, there would be no income tax. So the Taiwanese would receive the same income and salaries, which are low, but without income tax. Fourth, if there are unemployed people among those who went to Taiwan from the mainland, they may return to their homes and we will not discriminate against them.

"If Taiwan returns to the motherland, the people will be making a contribution, so the motherland, far from exacting revenge on them, should reward them, and we shall reward them."

In an obvious gesture to officials of the Chiang Kai-shek Government, Chou said:

"You may know that we gave the last emperor of China, Pu Yi, his liberty in Peking as a free citizen. Unfortunately, he died three years ago, but his wife and younger brother, who is married to a Japanese, are still here in Peking. Then there are the high-ranking officers of Chiang Kai-shek's army who were captured during the war. They are now in Peking and looked after well. So we can say, in returning to the motherland Taiwan will receive benefits and not be harmed and relations between the United States and China will be bettered. If all American forces were withdrawn from Taiwan and the Taiwan Strait, it would be glorious. This action would be acclaimed and friendship would result. Under these circumstances, the world would change."

From behind a screen, our waiters, young men and women, wearing white tunics, Mao buttons and beige pants, emerged again to fill our glasses and bearing new dishes. A bean puree was served, cold, thick and sweet. With it came pastries made of sweet ground soybean dipped in sesame seeds and sandwiched in almond paste.

Attwood, unaware as the rest of us that arrangements were well advanced for the Kissinger visit and that he would arrive eighteen days hence, asked if the Premier was prepared to receive the President or his emissary.

"That is such a big question," Chou replied with a smile. "Nixon himself has said that he would like to visit China. Since he has said that, he will know himself under what circumstances he will want to come to China." Chou's cryptic reply did not reveal to us anything he preferred not to reveal, but characteristically, neither did he deceive or mislead us simply to guard an important secret.

Would Chou En-lai visit the United States so that we could reciprocate his hospitality?

"I am certain that day will surely come. Whether it comes slowly or quickly depends on the efforts of both sides. It depends on you, in the first instance, to help mobilize public opinion. We have already opened up contacts between the peoples of the United States and China using the Ping-Pong ball."

When I noted that the Chinese were better at Ping-Pong than the Americans, Chou replied: "But we do not play basketball quite as well as you."

Chou said that contacts between China and the United States for scientists, writers and others "will gradually increase."

"We will also go to the United States. We must do some preparatory work. Our people did not realize that contacts would develop so quickly. Our table tennis team, already invited, is preparing and will be the first to go. People of other circles have also been invited, but some preparation must be undertaken."

Watermelon and bananas were served as the dinner drew to a close. As we rose, Chou En-lai spoke again of Taiwan, the problem central to the future evolution of United States–China relations. He gave us a hint of how he hopes the United States will resolve its dilemma of adhering to its treaty obligations in defense of Taiwan while seeking better relations with Peking:

"If the United States Government withdrew all its armed forces from Taiwan and the Taiwan Strait and no longer regarded Chiang Kai-shek as the representative of China, then the logical result would be that Chiang Kai-shek and Taiwan would be matters of Chinese internal affairs. This would constitute recognition of the People's Republic of China as the only lawful government representing China. There cannot possibly be two Chinas, or one China and one Taiwan. Therefore the treaty concluded with Chiang Kai-shek, signed in 1954 and ratified in 1955, known as the United States–China Mutual Defense Treaty, would become null and void."

It seemed to me that Chou was implying that Peking would not require a formal renunciation of the treaty by the United States. Taken together with his remarks earlier in the evening, what Chou seemed to be saying was that the problems of Taiwan and the establishing of diplomatic relations could be solved if the United States simply left the island, allowing Peking to work out a deal directly with its inhabitants.

The Premier walked with us to the side door by which we had entered the Great Hall of the People, and warmly bade us good night.

As we waited on the steps of the building for our cars, I asked Ma if I might now have the Premier's written replies to my questionnaire. Ma said he would contact me later in the night, and we drove back to the Hsin Ch'iao Hotel.

The telephone rang near midnight as I was writing my dispatch. It was Ma. "The Premier in his replies at dinner went much further than expected, and we see no point in giving you the written answers to your questions," Ma said. Disappointed, I pressed Ma to allow me to see the written answers in any case. There had been questions, such as the prospects for the release of a few Americans held prisoner in China, which had not been touched on at dinner. Ma rang back shortly and said definitively that I would not be given the written replies.

Another surprise awaited me. We had agreed before the dinner to allow Ma to check direct quotes in our dispatches against the Chinese transcript prepared by the secretary at the table. About 1 A.M. I went to the Foreign Ministry with my dispatch, only to be told by Ma that the copy would not be cleared until the next afternoon. Presumably, Chou wished to see the quotes himself. All the dispatches were cleared the next day without any corrections required by the Chinese.

The night before we left Peking, Audrey and I dined with Yu, our interpreter, in splendor alone in a large room of the Little Duck Restaurant on Anti-Imperialist Street. We had come to regard Hsiao Yu, as we called him, with respect and affection. A dedicated Communist, he had performed as his government expected him to, with dignity, great efficiency and detachment, and yet he had proved a warm, personable companion who satisfied our professional needs honestly. Americans will find that there are many Chinese Communists like him, and that it is possible, despite ideological differences, to communicate directly and openly with them.

The next morning, with the Attwoods, we boarded a plane for Canton, and on the following day at the border we walked across the railway bridge at Lo Wu.

THE LEADERSHIP

As we flew back to New York from Hong Kong, going the short way, via Bangkok, Tashkent and Copenhagen, the face of Chou En-lai kept flashing through my mind. His features, since the advent of Ping-Pong diplomacy, had become the visage of China to much of the world. Yet Chou did not wield ultimate power, nor did he pretend to. Up until 1965 he walked behind Liu Shao-ch'i, the heir apparent to Mao Tse-tung. When Liu was toppled, although Chou had been in the forefront of the Cultural Revolution, he bowed to Mao's designation of Lin Piao as his "closest comrade-in-arms and successor," and stood by dutifully as this commitment was written into the new Party constitution at the Ninth Congress in April 1969. Thereafter, on ceremonial occasions, Chou En-lai walked two or three steps behind Lin Piao, who followed Mao.

Lin Piao preferred seclusion, like Mao, emerging with him only on important public occasions. Foreigners had seen him last in June when Mao received Rumania's President Ceausescu. Lin was a thin, frail-looking man, sixty-four years old, largely bald, which is unusual for a Chinese, with heavy black eyebrows and dark beard showing through pale skin. Habitually, he wore a baggy army uniform. Mao and Lin, closely associated since the Long March in the thirties, were alike in many ways. They blended peasant earthiness with the mystic qualities of the guerrilla leader, the ascetic revolutionary and the ideologue with a world outlook, although they spoke no foreign language and had not traveled abroad except to the Soviet Union. Lin went to the Soviet

Union in late 1938 or early 1939, remaining for three years for treatment of a battle wound and chronic tuberculosis. Given his age, only fourteen years junior to Mao, who was seventy-seven, and his poor health, some in Peking doubted the wisdom of relying on Lin Piao for the succession.

Although Lin was dubbed Mao's "closest comrade-in-arms," the Party Chairman entrusted daily management of the country to Chou En-lai. Mao, the visionary, the ideologue and the strategist, worked effectively and comfortably with Chou, the pragmatist, the administrator, the tactician. Peking waited to see if Lin Piao, and his military supporters, would continue to tolerate a leadership constellation in which, although anointed successor, he did not head Party or government. An event was impending that would bring ambitions to the fore and put old loyalties to the test. On New Year's Day the Peking press had proclaimed 1971 as the important year in which "we are going to greet the fourth National People's Congress" (NPC), and it was awaited in the fall.

Technically, the NPC is the highest organ of state authority, its members elected every four years by provincial congresses. In fact, it is a rubber-stamp parliament controlled by its standing committee, which in turn is directed by the Party. The importance of the forthcoming NPC, the first since the Cultural Revolution, was that it would provide the public platform for the proclamation of crucial decisions taken secretly by the Party's Central Committee. A new state constitution was to be approved to replace the 1954 constitution, denounced as a "bourgeois document" during the Cultural Revolution. A draft circulating privately named Lin Piao as Mao's successor. The NPC would also elect a new Chief of State to replace Liu Shao-ch'i, and it was on this question that conflict within the ruling hierarchy might erupt.

As the replacement of Liu Shao-ch'i, Lin Piao might reasonably expect to inherit, not only the post of Party Vice Chairman, but also that of Chief of State, making him head of government and the superior of Chou En-lai. This would not only subordinate Chou, but it would also put Lin Piao in charge of two of the three pillars of power in China, the government and the army, which he controlled as Defense Minister. Once before, Mao had in effect yielded two pillars of power—control over the apparatus of both the Party and the government—to a potential rival leader, Liu Shao-ch'i. It was uncertain that he was willing to take the risk again.

In June, one couldn't say whether Lin Piao would be so impatient for power that he would lean against Chou En-lai and incur the displeasure of Mao. But there was one ominous sign. Systematically, the army had been expanding its hold on the administrative structure in the provinces. Military men held a preponderance of the senior posts in the Revolutionary Committees. It had been assumed that the army would begin gradually to withdraw from its dominating role in local government once the apparatus of the Party had been repaired.

Mao reasserted his authority over the central organs of the Party at the 1969 Congress, but the rebuilding of the provincial committees, shattered by the Cultural Revolution, had been complicated by ideological strife and political rivalry. The process took three years and was not completed until August 1971. The results were disconcerting for those who had been apprehensive about the pre-eminence of the military. In the new committees, of 158 leaders, 59.5 percent were military men, 34.8 percent were civilian cadres and 5.7 percent were delegates of mass organizations. Twenty committee first secretaries were military men, eleven of them were commanders of military forces in one or more provinces, and nine were professional soldiers acting as political commissars. Of the nine other first secretaries, all but one were civilians who had held positions as commissars of military commands. The military were thus effectively in control of the new provincial Party apparatus which exercised supreme power on the local level.

In Peking, at the center of power, the military were also strongly entrenched. Huang Yung-sheng, the Chief of the General Staff, ranked fourth after Mao, Lin Piao and Chou En-lai, in the Party Politburo. He had edged past Chiang Ch'ing, Mao's wife, with whom he had quarreled during the Cultural Revolution when she had stood up for the radical Red Guards. The composition of the new provincial committees showed that the local officials who had sided in the Cultural Revolution with the policies of Chiang Ch'ing and other radicals in Peking had lost out to more conservative soldiers and civilians. It was Lin Piao who had appointed Huang, his long-standing protégé, as Chief of the General Staff. The lines seemed drawn for a showdown between the Maoists and the military on the eve of the convening of the NPC, and back in New York at the end of August, I waited for the drama to unfold.

On September 21 dispatches from Peking reported the unexpected cancellation of the October 1 National Day parade, which had been held every year since the founding of the People's Republic. Chinese officials said that the celebration would be conducted "in another form," but it was obvious that a political crisis had erupted within China. From September 13 to 15 all civil and military flights had been suspended. This had been the practice in the past when the leadership was confronted with a challenge to its authority. Cancellation of the parade meant that the Politburo would not appear, as was the custom, on the reviewing stand of the Gate of Heavenly Peace. If there had been a purge or reshuffle of the hierarchy, the line-up on the gate would have revealed the new order. Speculation all over the world centered on Mao, spurred by a French radio report that he was ill or dead.

On that first day, September 21, one hour before the *New York Times* was to go to press with a front-page story reporting the speculation about Mao, I got through by telephone to the Information Department of the Foreign Ministry in Peking. Chi, who answered, was startled out of his customary imperturbability when I identified myself. There were no regular New York–Peking connections then. When I asked Chi to confirm or deny the reports about Mao, he replied that the line was bad and he had to check the switchboard. There was a long silence before Ma Yu-chen, his superior, came on the line, and said: "We usually do not answer questions on the telephone, but this is an exceptional case. The pernicious rumors about Chairman Mao Tse-tung are untrue. He is in very good health." The *Times* carried Ma's statement in the first edition, but we still did not know the nature of the crisis in China, and speculation during the next days turned to the health and status of Lin Piao.

On September 25 I flew to Ottawa for a meeting with Huang Hua, who had presented his credentials as Ambassador to Canada. The timing of my trip was coincidental with the events in China. Huang Hua had invited me to visit him weeks earlier. The furnishing of the Chinese Embassy offices had been tastefully completed in Western decor interspersed with a few Chinese paintings and other art objects. There was a packet of Chinese cigarettes on the rosewood side table beside my easy chair in the private reception room where I waited for the Ambassador.

Huang Hua, now sixty-one, graying, slightly heavier than when I had known him but still trim in well-cut Western clothes, greeted me warmly. "It has been a long time," he said, as he seated himself on the divan and offered me a cigarette. Our last meeting had been a chance encounter at Moscow's Sheremetyevo Airport in 1961. Audrey and I were flying from our post in Moscow to London for a short holiday, while Huang Hua and his talented, attractive wife, Ho Li-liang, were en route from Peking back to his ambassadorial post at Accra, Ghana. Assigned to Accra a year earlier, he had built his embassy into a center of Chinese influence in West Africa. We boarded the same British airliner, and after a time Huang Hua, who was attired in British tweeds, brought me from our economy section to his first-class compartment for a talk. As we flew over the Soviet Union, he told me of growing Chinese disillusionment with the Russians. In 1966 Huang Hua took over the Cairo Embassy, the key Chinese post in the Middle East. He was the only ambassador who was not summoned home in the first years of the Cultural Revolution. When he returned in late 1970, he and his wife asked to attend a May Seventh re-education school, where he worked in a machine shop. He talks proudly of that experience of "reintegrating with the masses," completed not long before he met Henry Kissinger in Peking.

In his Ottawa office, Huang Hua was receiving a parade of American politicians, scholars, writers and businessmen soliciting his views and eager to obtain visas for China. They left charmed by his affable and hospitable manner, notwithstanding that he had remained the same tough-minded dedicated Communist revolutionary I had known in China.

As Huang Hua sat near me on the divan, smiling and asking about Audrey, I could detect that he was harried. His embassy was deluged with inquiries. "You will hear many more rumors," Huang Hua said, when I noted tentatively that reports of all kinds about Mao and Lin Piao were flying about. Seeing he was disturbed, I dropped the subject.

Huang Hua asked me to stay for a "very informal dinner." A small table was brought in and quickly laden with superbly prepared Chinese dishes, among them my favorite northern delicacy, chiao tze, a highly spiced ground meat wrapped in fine dough. We reminisced about early days in China, and I asked him whether, if Leighton Stuart had been permitted to go to Peking in 1949, it would have been possible to establish diplomatic relations. Shaking his head, Huang Hua replied: "The United States was pursuing an aggressive policy." There is a deep bitterness in Huang Hua, common to the whole Yenan generation of Chinese leaders, that is bared when they speak of the past. This is a reality that will brood for a long time over the negotiating tables.

Over jasmine tea and small Chinese cigars, we discussed the debate in the United Nations on Chinese representation. Huang Hua was incensed over the American attitude. Reversing a twenty-year policy, the United States had declared its readiness to accept the seating of the People's Republic, but on condition that the Chiang Kai-shek Government on Taiwan retained a seat. For two decades, Peking steadfastly had rejected this "two-China" solution. Huang Hua was quite sure that his government would not be admitted that year to the United Nations. When Peking was voted in by the General Assembly on October 26 and the Nationalists expelled, Peking was surprised and not fully prepared to take part in the business of the world body.

Although Huang Hua was hopeful that some good would result from the Nixon visit to Peking, he expressed lingering Chinese suspicions. He said Peking might yet have to contend with a plot to encircle and divide China. He spoke earnestly of the possibility that the Americans might attack from Southeast Asia, Japan in the Northeast, and the Soviet Union and India from the West. Once again, these fears which I had heard expressed so often since the mid-sixties. Huang Hua and I talked for almost three hours before we said goodbye and I flew back to New York. We would meet again in November when he would become Peking's permanent delegate to the United Nations.

The Peking mystery became more intriguing on September 30 when Tass, the Soviet press agency, announced that a Chinese Communist jet had violated the air space of Mongolia on the night of September 12 and crashed. Nine badly burned bodies, bits of documents and firearms were found aboard the plane. A senior Russian diplomat told me that the bodies were so badly charred that identification was impossible beyond the fact that one of the dead was a woman. The jet had been bound for the Soviet Union. Before it took off, there had been a meeting of the Peking leadership. Afterward, Huang Yung-sheng, the Chief of the General Staff, and other top military figures disappeared. The others, also members of the Politburo, included Wu Fa-hsien, the air force commander; Li Tso-p'eng, the navy political commissar; and Ch'iu Hui-tso, chief of logistics for the armed forces. There was speculation that some of the top military leaders had attempted to flee to the Soviet Union in the jet after a losing showdown with Mao and Chou En-lai.

Then, abruptly after October 8, the Chinese press and radio omitted all mention of the name of Lin Piao, and portraits of him were removed from public places. The little red book, *Quotations from Chairman Mao Tse-tung*, whose foreword had been written by Lin Piao, of which more than 700 million copies had been printed, vanished from Peking book-shops. (In February 1972 a new edition was to appear with the Lin preface deleted.)

What appeared to be allusions to Lin Piao, denunciatory and vitu-perative, sprouted in the Chinese press. In *Red Flag*, the theoretical journal of the Party, there was criticism of the "bourgeois ambitionist" who had promoted the cult of Mao to further his own interests. Here was an echo of Mao's impatience with the extravagance of the cult when he talked to Edgar Snow in December 1970. There had been a need for a personality cult to stimulate the masses, Mao had said, but it had been overdone. Was this remark an expression of irritation with Lin Piao, foremost propagator of the cult?

In November 1971 the press emphasized that the armed forces were now under "the direct leadership and command of Chairman Mao." Previously, the missing Lin Piao had been cited as exercising "direct command." Once again, the slogan was revived: "The Party commands the gun and the gun must never be allowed to command the Party." Mao was reasserting his authority over the army at the center and in the provinces, and the slogan evoked memories of the 1959 purge of P'eng Te-huai, Lin's predecessor as Defense Minister, who had wanted a professional army subject to less political interference. The parallel with P'eng Te-huai seemed even more valid on December 1 when a joint editorial in the Peking press declared: "In our Party's history those bourgeois careerists, conspirators and persons having illicit relations with foreign countries, who clung to opportunist lines and engaged in conspiracies, could not but bring ruin, disgrace and destruction upon themselves in the end." P'eng also had been accused of illicit contacts in Moscow. He had favored better relations with Nikita Khrushchev so that modern arms could be obtained from the Soviet Union.

It seemed likely that foreign policy had been the central issue in a power struggle between the Lin Piao faction and the Maoists just before the convening of the NPC. Mao's continued jousting with Moscow had brought China close to war with the Soviet Union in 1969, a war that could not be won given Moscow's overwhelming preponderance in modern weaponry. Uneasily, the Chinese military leaders had observed the rearming of Japan while India was being supplied with the latest jets and other modern equipment by Moscow. The Chinese were producing good small arms and making progress in nuclear missilry, but only the Russians could supply the additional sophisticated equipment needed to transform China quickly into a first-class military power. Now, Chou En-lai was about to enter into a negotiation with the American President that would widen the gap between Peking and Moscow.

Less than six weeks before the arrival of Henry Kissinger in Peking for his second visit preparatory to the Chou-Nixon talks, the Lin Piao faction confronted Mao, then the military leaders disappeared, and the Chinese jet crashed in Mongolia en route to the Soviet Union. In January, Wu Fan-wu, of the Foreign Ministry, told a visiting French delegation that Lin Piao was alive but had been "politically eliminated."

Mao, employing his enormous personal prestige, as in 1959 and in 1966 when he unleashed the Cultural Revolution, had won again. As the Party Chairman and head of the Military Affairs Commission, he had not been opposed by the army as a whole but rather by the power clique which had exercised direct command over the armed forces. Among those who rallied to the side of "the Great Leader" was Yeh Chien-ying, the vice chairman of the Military Affairs Commission and a former marshal of the army. Mao now turned over Lin Piao's military functions to the old stalwart.

But the victory was a hollow one. The succession of purges since 1966 had exacted a terrible toll, sending many of the most talented and experienced leaders into limbo. Once Liu Shao-ch'i and his allies had been disposed of, pursuing his "zigzag line," Mao had struck to the right within his own Cultural Revolution Group, eliminating T'ao Chu because he had not been radical enough. In 1968, when the ultraleftists crowded him, he swung the purge ax to the left. Ch'en Po-ta, the head of the group and Mao's personal confidant, was among those who disappeared. The only members of the group who survived politically were the Shanghai radicals: Chiang Ch'ing, Chang Ch'un-ch'iao, and Yao Wen-yuan. In the latest purge, hitting out to the right again, Mao had purged the military men he used in 1967 to subdue the ultraleftist Red Guards. Of the twenty-one members of the Politburo elected at the 1969 Congress, only ten were still active, the rest having been purged or were incapacitated for other reasons. The Revolution was devouring its children.

Mao and Chou En-lai reigned in 1972, but the Peking hierarchy was aged and more fragile than the façade in the capital indicated. When the Nixon party was in China, Chou remarked about the comparative youth of members of the delegation, wistfully noting that after the long Revolution in China there had been too little time for those who had fought to govern.

Mao, at seventy-eight, and Chou, at seventy-three, were in indifferent health. Ranking third after them in the Politburo was Chiang Ch'ing.

Mao took Chiang Ch'ing, a Shanghai actress, as his fourth wife shortly after she went to Yenan in 1939 as a political student. They have two daughters. Before the Cultural Revolution she had not occupied a significant role in public life. After becoming prominent in 1966, the press recounted how Chiang Ch'ing had gone to Shanghai in the early 1960s to carry on her revolutionary cultural work because she had not been allowed to operate freely in Peking. Liu Shao-ch'i and P'eng Chen, the purged Mayor of Peking, were accused of relegating her to obscurity. In Shanghai, Chiang Ch'ing was befriended by the Mayor, K'o Ch'ing-shih, and she collaborated closely with two of his aides, Chang Ch'un-ch'iao and Yao Wen-yuan. Yao, who was writing criticism of the theater, films and art, was particularly useful to Chiang Ch'ing since he actively shared her Maoist concept of literature as a propaganda weapon of class struggle. When Mao arrived in Shanghai in late 1965 to mount his counterattack against Liu Shao-ch'i, Chiang Ch'ing was waiting for him with her two close friends, and the Chairman never forgot the help they gave him.

In April 1972 Chang Ch'un-ch'iao and Yao Wen-yuan ranked fifth and sixth in the Politburo after Yeh Chien-ying, the seventy-two-year-old military leader. After them came Li Hsien-nien, the sixty-five-year-old Deputy Premier to Chou En-lai, an economic specialist who was a possible successor to Chou in the government, and Tung Pi-wu, eighty-five years old, who acted as the ceremonial Chief of State.

The Shanghai radicals were the only fairly young leaders among the influential in the Politburo. Chiang Ch'ing was in her mid-fifties. Chang Ch'un-ch'iao, who had become chairman of the Shanghai Revolutionary Committee and was to be host to President Nixon during his visit to that city, was sixty. Yao Wen-yuan, vice chairman of the Shanghai Committee, was in his forties. Little was known abroad about the background of Chang and Yao, who had been relatively obscure municipal officials before 1965.

At the end of February, I called on Huang Hua on the fourteenth floor of the Roosevelt Hotel, where he lived with his UN delegation until March, when the Chinese purchased the Lincoln Square Motor Inn on West Sixty-sixth Street and turned it into a mission headquarters and residence. During our conversation, I asked him about the problem of the aged Peking leadership.

"There are good young people in the Central Committee and in the Revolutionary Committees such as the committee in Shanghai," Huang Hua replied. "But the important thing is the collective wisdom of the masses. After the Cultural Revolution it was the masses which gave us confidence in the future."

I left the Roosevelt Hotel less confident than Huang Hua about the prospects of the ruling hierarchy and stability in China. Since 1966 the purges had shaken and stripped the Central Committee and, below it, the Youth League. There was no solid evidence that the Chinese Communist Party had solved the ultimate problem of arranging an orderly succession at the summit, any more than the Soviet Party, which had been racked with power struggles, had succeeded in finding such a political mechanism. I was sure that there were good young people waiting in the middle echelons of the Party, but like Chang and Yao of the Shanghai group, they lacked broad experience. China would need strong, skilled inspirational leadership if the country was to remain unified, disciplined and on the Maoist path. In the provinces, the conservatives were still powerful. There was a heavy residue of bitterness after the widespread purges of the past six years which might spawn new dissidence.

Yet there was more than ideological rhetoric in Huang Hua's observation about the "collective wisdom of the masses." Mao had carried through a broad-based popular revolution, and in the matrix of Chinese society he had furrowed a deep, well-defined line of development that would not be diverted easily. When Mao died, his successors would enshrine the "Great Helmsman" and his ideology to endure as Lenin lives in the Soviet pantheon. Mao's writings already were scripture to the masses. In the unpredictable future, the invocation of Mao's authority would help to ensure continuity of domestic and foreign policy.

EPILOGUE:
NIXON IN CHINA

After a quarter of a century of hostility and recrimination, the television images of President Nixon in China had a dreamlike quality. The Republican leader who had been in the forefront of the anti-Communist crusade in the 1950s being received by Mao Tse-tung in the Chairman's secluded study where so many ideological polemics against the United States had been composed. Mao, smiling and speaking animatedly to Nixon, shaking hands and then holding the President's hand cupped between his own. In the state guest house, the President helping Chou En-lai into his overcoat. At the banquet in Shanghai, seat of power of the radicals, the Premier standing to attention as a People's Liberation Band played "The Star-Spangled Banner." And after the images of those other ritual pleasantries flickered out—the Nixons and Secretary of State William Rogers at the Great Wall, Mrs. Nixon shopping and inspecting a commune school, Chou En-lai and the President strolling beside Hangchow's West Lake—there was the reality of the eighteen-hundred-word communiqué.

The reservoir of Chinese bitterness and suspicion had not been drained during "the week that changed the world," as Nixon described his visit in a farewell banquet toast. The communiqué did not provide for normal diplomatic relations, although the President in the private talks had suggested an exchange of permanent delegations. Nor did it pretend that the two governments ideologically were no longer in adversary postures. Much of the document was couched in separate statements of divergent political positions. Nonetheless, immensely sig-

413

nificant steps had been taken toward closing the gap between the two countries, and arrangements were made for diplomatic contacts and people-to-people exchanges to narrow it further.

The Peking leadership had been impelled by paramount considerations of national security to enter into negotiations with the United States. Mao's crucial stake in the success of the negotiations was clearly indicated when the Chairman received the President immediately after his arrival on February 21, 1972. Ordinarily, Mao did not confer with a visiting chief of state before Chou En-lai had probed his attitudes. By seeing Nixon in advance, Mao committed his personal prestige to the success of the visit. His meeting with the President was the signal that spurred the Chinese media to extraordinarily lavish coverage of the American delegation.

Like Nixon, who had a personal political investment in a presidential election year in making his visit appear successful, Mao was motivated in part by pressures of internal politics. After the struggle with Lin Piao and his military adherents, there was a need to demonstrate the correctness of "Chairman Mao Tse-tung's Revolutionary Diplomatic Line." The overriding concerns, however, of Mao and and Chou En-lai related to foreign policy and national security.

Since the mid-sixties the Chinese Communists had been plagued by a nightmare of encirclement by the Soviet Union, India, Japan and the United States. In the months before the Nixon visit, the anxieties in Peking sharpened, and there was more preoccupation with the dangers, real or imagined, of the encirclement and dismemberment of China than with the quarrel over Taiwan.

In August 1971 Peking saw the Soviet Union and India conclude a twenty-year treaty of "peace, friendship and cooperation," which the Chinese interpreted as a military alliance aimed at China. The division of Pakistan after the Indian invasion of the East in November 1971 in support of the Bangladesh movement reduced to impotence the state which Peking had counted upon as a counterpoise to India on the subcontinent. Ignoring the revolutionary aspirations of the Bangladesh forces and the mass killings perpetrated in the East by the Pakistan Army, which might have been expected to throw the ideological support of the Chinese Communists to Bangladesh, Peking backed Pakistan without qualification in the United Nations debate. Emphasis was put solely on the need "to oppose aggression and interference, be concerned for the security of nations and safeguard the independence,

sovereignty and territorial integrity of the countries of the world."
Chinese diplomats told me that the dismemberment of Pakistan had set
a dangerous precedent. It was obvious that Peking was worried about
its own outlying provinces. What, for example, if the Tibetans should
declare their independence with Indian and Soviet support, or the
native Taiwanese theirs with American and Japanese encouragement?

In a government statement on December 16, after the collapse of
the Pakistan Army in the East, Peking said: "The present sudden invasion of Pakistan by India with the support of the Soviet Union is precisely a repetition on the South Asian subcontinent of the 1968 Soviet
invasion and occupation of Czechoslovakia." Here again was the persis-
tent echo of the fear expressed in Peking after the border clashes with
the Soviet Union in 1969 when Moscow massed an overwhelming preponderance of military force on the Chinese frontier. Mao and Chou
En-lai had never doubted that Moscow would intervene militarily in
China if it became feasible, as in Czechoslovakia, to install a more pliant
regime in Peking.

To the northeast of China, Peking looked upon Japan as a growing
menace in a ring of hostile powers. Japan had become capable of
quickly producing a nuclear arsenal with highly effective delivery systems. China could not hope to match Japan's industrial capacity or
technical sophistication in this century. The Chinese blamed the United
States for the rapid economic and accelerating conventional military
build-up of Japan. In August 1971, Chou En-lai told James Reston:
"Economic expansionism is bound to bring about military expansionism. And this cannot be restrained by the [U.S.-Japanese Mutual
Security] Treaty." When Reston noted that the Premier seemed really
worried about Japan, Chou En-lai replied: "Because you know we suffered a long time, for fifty years. Such calamities can be prevented by
opposition from us and from the Japanese people together."

The assurances of peaceful intent proffered by Premier Eisaku Sato
and his Liberal-Democratic Party did not disabuse Peking of its conviction that the Japanese Government was bent on military, political and
economic policies counter to Chinese interests in Asia. Tokyo maintained diplomatic ties with the Chiang Kai-shek Government, and Japan had become the largest foreign investor in Taiwan. The visit of
Andrei A. Gromyko, the Soviet Foreign Minister, to Tokyo in January
1972 and the continuing discussions of possible Soviet-Japanese development of Siberia deepened Chinese suspicions.

The United States, with its bases extending from Japan to Taiwan to Southeast Asia, backed by the Seventh Fleet and Polaris submarine patrols, was regarded in Peking as the southern link in the encirclement of China.

The Chinese encirclement thesis could be challenged on many grounds. It ignored the pacifist sentiment in Japan and the extreme vulnerability of that country to nuclear attack. With its tight concentrations of population and industry, Japan would be compelled to proceed with caution in any future confrontation with a nuclear China. India, beset with internal problems, showed no disposition to provoke China, even though its military forces had been strengthened by Soviet arms. Nevertheless, the threat of encirclement had become so firmly rooted in Maoist thinking, particularly as it related to distrust of the Soviet Union, that breaking the ring had become Peking's prime foreign policy concern.

Surveying the powers occupying positions on the periphery of China, it was logical that Peking should seek an opening to the United States. There was no compelling reason for national antagonisms to persist indefinitely between the two countries. The conflict in Korea, and the confrontations in the Taiwan Strait and Southeast Asia, had stemmed from the Cold War, in which China and the Soviet Union had been allied against the United States. Now China and the United States had a common interest in containing Soviet expansionism in Asia. By 1971 the Chinese had been persuaded that the Nixon Administration intended to disengage militarily from Southeast Asia. American public opinion had become more amenable to a solution of the Taiwan problem. Peking estimated that a relationship could be developed with the United States that could be exploited as a counterweight against Japan as well as the Soviet Union.

It had become imperative for Peking to enter into liaison with the United States, but the way was blocked by the Taiwan issue. The Chinese were too deeply committed to "liberation" of the island to allow major concessions. When President Nixon and Chou En-lai met in Peking, however, they were able to agree on a formulation which cleared the way for broader negotiations. It was stated in the communiqué in these terms:

The Chinese side reaffirmed its position: The Taiwan question is the crucial question obstructing the normalization of relations between China and the

United States; the Government of the People's Republic of China is the sole legal government of China; Taiwan is a province of China which has long been returned to the motherland; the liberation of Taiwan is China's internal affair in which no other country has the right to interfere; and all U.S. forces and military installations must be withdrawn from Taiwan. The Chinese Government firmly opposes any activities which aim at the creation of "one China, one Taiwan," "one China, two governments," "two Chinas," and "independent Taiwan" or advocate that "the status of Taiwan remains to be determined."

The U.S. side declared: The United States acknowledges that all Chinese on either side of the Taiwan Strait maintain there is but one China and that Taiwan is a part of China. The United States Government does not challenge that position. It reaffirms its interest in a peaceful settlement of the Taiwan question by the Chinese themselves. With this prospect in mind, it affirms the ultimate objective of the withdrawal of all U.S. forces and military installations from Taiwan. In the meantime, it will progressively reduce its forces and military installations on Taiwan as the tension in the area diminishes.

By accepting that "there is but one China and that Taiwan is a part of China," Nixon relieved the apprehension in Peking that the United States or Japan might support the independence movement among the native Taiwanese or grant them self-determination by sponsoring an internationally supervised plebiscite. The underground independence movement on the island had been ruthlessly repressed by the Nationalist Government, but it had been kept alive abroad by Taiwanese émigré organizations in the United States and Japan. The Chou-Nixon communiqué severely crippled the movement.

No timetable was set for the withdrawal of American forces from Taiwan, but their presence in any case was largely a token one. Before the Nixon visit, all regular patrolling of the strait by the Seventh Fleet had been halted, together with the CIA-supported U-2 flights over the mainland. Of the 8,200 American servicemen on the island, some 6,000 were manning two airfields for transports and other installations in support of operations in Vietnam. They were progressively withdrawn as the American presence in Indochina was cut back. The other military on Taiwan were involved in the defense of the island as advisers to the Chiang Kai-shek Government or were service troops manning electronic intelligence equipment for the monitoring of mainland transmissions.

The island was shielded from Communist attack by the United States commitment under the 1954 Mutual Defense Treaty and the well-armed but untested 540,000-man Nationalist Army. More than 80 percent of the men in the army were native Taiwanese draftees of uncertain loyalties. They were officered largely by aging mainlanders. Under the treaty, which is of indefinite duration but may be terminated by either party on one year's notice, the United States was not obligated to maintain its own forces on Taiwan. It pledged only to join in resisting "armed attack and communist subversive activities directed from without" against Taiwan and the adjacent Pescadores.

While insisting that the treaty was illegal, Chou En-lai in his talks with Nixon tacitly accepted that it was not expedient for the United States to renounce it immediately. After Nixon's departure, the defense commitment was reaffirmed in Taipei by Marshall Green, the Assistant Secretary of State for East Asian and Pacific Affairs, who went from China to eleven friendly nations in the region to reassure them that Washington would continue to fulfill its obligations. In deference to Chinese Communist sensitivities, the treaty commitment to the Nationalists was not mentioned in the Chou-Nixon communiqué.

The Taiwan formulation was, in fact, consonant with Chou En-lai's practical approach to the eventual assertion of Peking's authority over Taiwan. The Premier was confident that a deal could be worked out with the mainlanders and the native Taiwanese after the United States withdrew all its forces from the area. A measure of his confidence was the informal assurance he gave Nixon, not stated in the communiqué, that China would refrain from the use of force in the Taiwan Strait, a concession that Peking had been unwilling to make in the past.

Without the physical presence of the American military, the Chinese Communists believed that resistance to union with the mainland would begin to erode on Taiwan, and at an accelerated rate after the death of the eighty-four-year-old Generalissimo Chiang Kai-shek. Insecure and nostalgic for their native provinces, some of the mainlanders might respond to the overtures from Peking. Under the Chiang Kai-shek Government, the native Taiwanese had prospered economically, but they had been repressed politically, not given anything approaching a fair share of power or positions in the Administration. Eventually, a Taiwanese faction might be persuaded to seek an accommodation with the mainland in exchange for some degree of autonomy.

There were autonomous regions in China in which Peking allowed considerable local government and tolerated preservation of native minority cultures. The Communist Party, however, insisted that all regions abide by Maoist ideology. For many native Taiwanese, accustomed to individual land ownership or running their own business, adjustment to a Maoist-type collective society would be difficult even if Peking was amenable to a period of transition. It would be another in the series of disruptive shocks dealt the Taiwanese people since World War II. In 1945, after fifty years of Japanese colonialism, the United States allowed the Chinese Nationalists to take over the island without ensuring them against the mass killing and looting which followed the occupation. In June 1950, when Ch'en Yi's Third Field Army was preparing to embark for Taiwan and so end the civil war, the United States halted the process by interposing the Seventh Fleet in the Taiwan Strait. During the next two decades, United States aid was pumped into Taiwan, encouraging the development of an economic and social system completely different from that on the mainland. With the publication of the Chou-Nixon communiqué, the native Taiwanese braced themselves for still another adjustment. Inevitably, they would have to make the choice between reuniting with the mainland or further conflict.

I felt that the native Taiwanese might in the long term profit by opting for stability by returning to the sway of Peking rather than to continue being objects of tension and pummeling among the great powers. The United States has a moral obligation to do what it can to ease the hardships of the native Taiwanese in any transition that may be ahead of them. This should not be done by intervention, but by negotiation with Peking. In the Chou-Nixon communiqué, the United States not only recognized Taiwan as part of China, but it also subscribed to the Bandung principles, which Washington had declined to do during the Warsaw talks because of the implications for Taiwan. The communiqué stipulated that the two countries "should conduct their relations on the principles of respect for the sovereignty and territorial integrity of all states, nonaggression against other states, noninterference in the internal affairs of other states, equality and mutual benefit, and peaceful coexistence."

The communiqué did not explictly extend to China any promise of American help if it should become the victim of Soviet or Japanese aggrandizement. Just as Chou would not collude with Nixon in an Indochina settlement that his North Vietnamese allies might find prejudicial, the President guarded the interests of Japan, the principal American ally in Asia. The communiqué stated: "The United States places the highest value on its friendly relations with Japan; it will continue to develop the existing close bonds." On the Chinese side it was stated: "[China] firmly opposes the revival and outward expansion of Japanese militarism and firmly supports the Japanese people's desire to build an independent, democratic, peaceful and neutral Japan." The President failed to convince Chou that the Mutual Security Treaty would provide an adequate brake on Japanese rearmament or that the orientation of the Sato Government was in the direction of peace and equitable arrangements in Asia.

The communiqué did not mention the Soviet Union, although relations with Moscow were discussed. Chou and Nixon were cautious in discussing third-party governments since a record of the conversations was kept, giving both sides protection against a contrived leak to gain political advantage. The President exercised care to avoid any risk to his forthcoming negotiations with the Soviet leadership on such issues of paramount importance to the United States as arms control in the SALT negotiations, the Middle East and European security.

Nevertheless, the Chinese succeeded in enhancing their security arrangements. The communiqué contained what President Nixon referred to upon his arrival back in Washington as "some rules of international conduct which will reduce the risk of confrontation and war in Asia and the Pacific." The communiqué stated:

Progress toward the normalization of relations between China and the United States is in the interests of all countries.

Both wish to reduce the danger of international military conflict.

Neither should seek hegemony in the Asia-Pacific region and each is opposed to the efforts by any other country or group of countries to establish such hegemony; and

Neither is prepared to negotiate on behalf of any third party or to enter into agreements or understandings with the other directed at other states.

Both sides are of the view that it would be against the interests of the peoples of the world for any major country to collude with another against other countries, or for major countries to divide up the world into spheres of interest.

Within this framework, the Chinese felt they could negotiate for more specific security safeguards, and they agreed to open a direct channel of communication between the two countries. The communiqué stipulated:

The two sides agree that they will stay in contact through various channels, including the sending of a senior U.S. representative to Peking from time to time for concrete consultations to further normalization of relations between the two countries and continue to exchange views on issues of common interest.

The Chinese declined to send a representative to Washington as long as a Nationalist Embassy was situated there. On March 7 it was agreed that the two countries would maintain a channel of communication in Paris through their embassies there. The first meetings took place between Ambassador Huang Chen, a sixty-four-year-old member of the Central Committee, and Arthur K. Watson, the fifty-two-year-old United States Ambassador, the former chairman of the board of International Business Machines' World Trade Corporation, who was appointed to the Paris post in 1970 by President Nixon.

The Chou-Nixon agreement on the "rules of international conduct" was a limited one, but it achieved a subtle shift in the world balance of forces. Peking was no longer in hostile confrontation with both of the two nations which possessed a first-strike nuclear capability, the power to devastate China to the extent that it could not retaliate effectively. The Soviet Union had been nudged into a triangular relationship with China and the United States in which it would have to weigh new risk factors before making an overt move against either of the two other powers. This inhibition represented a gain for the United States as well as China. The President could not state it publicly, but he had sought and obtained in Peking a new and important lever in bargaining with the Soviet Union on the range of issues between the two countries. The prospect of an accommodation with the Soviet Union had thus been enhanced.

The Chou-Nixon communiqué also signified that security arrangements in the Asia-Pacific region would be discussed by the United States on a triangular basis with Japan and China. Peking remained convinced that its long-term interests lay in encouraging the Japanese people to install a leftist government committed to disarmament and neutrality. Openly, the Chinese were seeking to woo Japanese voters through contacts with Japanese opposition political parties and businessmen. But while a conservative government was in power in Tokyo, the United States channel provided the Chinese with an opening to influence military policy in Japan, which was determined within the framework of the Mutual Security Treaty. Japan in turn could use the American channel to seek better relations with China.

The results of the Nixon visit were hailed throughout China as a triumph for "Mao Tse-tung's Revolutionary Diplomatic Line." When Chou En-lai returned to Peking on February 29 from Shanghai, where he said goodbye to President Nixon, he was given an exuberant welcome by five thousand people, with drums beating and cymbals clanging, exceeding any ovation rendered the Premier in recent years.

President Nixon encountered a generally favorable response in the United States. There was some criticism that he had made substantial concessions to the Chinese, particularly on Taiwan, without obtaining anything concrete in return. The criticism was shortsighted, in my view, and did not take into account the enormous benefits to be derived from resuming communication with nearly one-fourth of the human race. The United States was given a means of influencing and moderating Chinese foreign policy. During the talks with Chou En-lai, the President made a start that was not recorded in the communiqué. In addition to the informal assurance that Peking would refrain from the use of force in the Taiwan Strait, Chou accepted the fact that the United States could not tolerate any Chinese threat to its ally Thailand after the withdrawal of U.S. forces from Indochina.

The communiqué also had to be scrutinized in a historical perspective. What concessions were made by the United States represented rectifications of the mistakes of the containment policy. This was implied by the President when he said on return to Washington: "The primary goal of this trip was to re-establish communication with the People's Republic of China after a generation of hostility." It was attained twenty-two years after Truman told Leighton Stuart he could not go to Peking to talk with Mao and Chou En-lai.

The two governments also undertook to foster people-to-people contacts and exchanges in such areas as trade, science, technology, culture, sports and journalism. The Chinese proceeded in developing these contacts in a deliberate and measured manner so that the United States would continue to feel pressure for full normalization of relations with Peking through severance of diplomatic ties with the Nationalist Government. For this reason, and others, China did not let its doors swing open quickly and fully for Americans.

China is not an open society in the Western sense, and there were many sections of it, as well as geographical areas, that would remain closed to most foreigners for some time. Much of the fabric of the society had been unraveled by the Cultural Revolution, and more time was needed for the reweaving. As the Chinese frankly told visitors, some areas of the country remained backward, and there was no desire to expose them to foreign inspection. Other areas were closed for reasons of military security. Facilities for receiving visitors were limited.

The United States and China have much to gain in mutual enrichment through people-to-people contacts. It would be well, however, for Americans who go to China to be aware that judgments on the achievements of the last two decades are more valid in the frame of reference of the improvements in the life of the people rather than in comparisons between the Chinese and American societies. The stages of development, internal problems and characteristics of the United States and China are so diverse that ideological, social and cultural transplants between the two will not be easily made. The Chinese, disillusioned by their experience with the Russians, sensitive to foreign encroachment and proud of their own achievements, looked forward to exchanges on a basis of mutual benefit, but they did not intend to borrow funds, goods, techniques or technology to the extent that they would become dependent on the United States.

It had been a long journey between the two Chinas. In a way, Audrey and I celebrated its completion on December 27, 1971, the seventy-seventh birthday of Chester Ronning. Chester flew in from his home in Alberta, and, together with other friends, four members of the Chinese delegation to the United Nations General Assembly came to our home in Scarsdale for a luncheon birthday party. Ch'iao Kuan-hua, the Vice Minister of Foreign Affairs, who was to be Chou En-lai's chief adviser during the Nixon talks and Kissinger's partner in the hard negotiation of the communiqué, delayed his departure for Peking so he could attend. Huang Hua could not come because of a Security Council meeting, but his wife, Li-liang, a counselor of the permanent delegation, Fu Hao, another delegate, and Nancy T'ang, who was to be one of the chief interpreters during the Nixon visit, joined us.

It was the first time that members of the Chinese delegation had been in a private American home, and the party was a joyful one, full of laughter. Before the arrival of the guests, the Scarsdale police, the New York police and agents of the Federal Bureau of Investigation came in turn to the door, incredulously asking the same question: "The Chinese are coming?" They gazed in disbelief as Audrey showed them in turn the festive table and hooted: "It's only a birthday party!" Then they withdrew to the garden behind hedges and trees to furnish security as the Chinese arrived in two rented vintage Cadillacs.

We gathered around the fireplace in the lounge of the old house, and we talked about old friends and recalled common experiences. It was a time of reunion, and there was warmth and ease in the companionship that had once been so typical of Americans and Chinese when they mingled. Could it not be so again? At the table we drank mou-t'ai brought by the Chinese and ate American turkey served by our children. Ch'iao Ku'an-hua and Chester traded toasts, jokes and riddles in Chinese.

When it was time to go, Ch'iao Kuan-hua invited me to ride back to New York with him, and with Nancy T'ang perched between us we were soon driving south on the Bronx River Parkway in the long green chauffeured Cadillac.

Ch'iao, dressed in a black tunic and black overcoat, stretched out his long legs and peered out at the fine houses near the Parkway. "It must be expensive to live in such houses," he remarked. We looked at the gray and black Canadian geese strutting on the river bank, stretching their wings and pointing their beaks into the pale winter sun. We talked about his country and mine, about the past and the future.

"The Vietnam war has caused so much suffering, but the United States may be coming out of it a better and more moral nation," I said. "I have traveled about the country and spoken to young people on many campuses. If I were a foreigner, after talking to the youth I would feel more confident about the future role of the United States in the world."

"We rely on the youth," said Ch'iao Kuan-hua.

"In Vietnam, in our relations with China and other countries, we thought we could make changes to fit the American image," I said. "Leighton Stuart, the missionary, Kennedy and the others, each thinking that he was doing the moral thing, tried it. If we have learned anything in these last two decades, I hope it is the realization that one people cannot impose change upon another. If there is to be lasting change, it can only come from within a society."

"That is the most important thing to understand," said Ch'iao Kuan-hua.

We drove on, each in his own world, but not apart.

APPENDICES

I. The Mutual Defense Treaty between the United States and Nationalist China, signed on December 2, 1954

The Parties of this Treaty, Reaffirming their faith in the purposes and principles of the Charter of the United Nations and their desire to live in peace with all peoples and all Governments, and desiring to strengthen the fabric of peace in the West Pacific Area,

Recalling with mutual pride the relationship which brought their two peoples together in a common bond of sympathy and mutual ideals to fight side by side against imperialist aggression during the last war,

Desiring to declare publicly and formally their sense of unity and their common determination to defend themselves against external armed attack, so that no potential aggressor could be under the illusion that either of them stands alone in the West Pacific Area, and

Desiring further to strengthen their present efforts for collective defense for the preservation of peace and security pending the development of a more comprehensive system of regional security in the West Pacific Area,

Have agreed as follows:

ARTICLE I

The Parties undertake as set forth in the Charter of the United Nations, to settle any international dispute in which they may be involved by peaceful means in such a manner that international peace, security and justice are not endangered and to refrain in their international relations from the threat or use of force in any manner inconsistent with the purposes of the United Nations.

425

ARTICLE II

In order more effectively to achieve the objective of this Treaty, the Parties separately and jointly by self-help and mutual aid will maintain and develop their individual and collective capacity to resist armed attack and communist subversive activities directed from without against their territorial integrity and political stability.

ARTICLE III

The Parties undertake to strengthen their free institutions and to cooperate with each other in the development of economic progress and social well-being and to further their individual and collective efforts toward these ends.

ARTICLE IV

The Parties, through their Foreign Ministers or their deputies, will consult together from time to time regarding the implementation of this Treaty.

ARTICLE V

Each Party recognizes that an armed attack in the West Pacific Area directed against the territories of either of the Parties would be dangerous to its own peace and safety and declares that it would act to meet the common danger in accordance with its constitutional processes.

Any such armed attack and all measures taken as a result thereof shall be immediately reported to the Security Council of the United Nations. Such measures shall be terminated when the Security Council has taken the measures necessary to restore and maintain international peace and security.

ARTICLE VI

For the purposes of Articles II and V, the terms "territorial" and "territories" shall mean in respect of the Republic of China, Taiwan and the Pescadores; and in respect of the United States of America, the island territories in the West Pacific under its jurisdiction. The provisions of Articles II and V will be applicable to such other territories as may be determined by mutual agreement.

ARTICLE VII

The Government of the Republic of China grants, and the Government of the United States of America accepts, the right to dispose such United States land, air and sea forces in and about Taiwan and the Pescadores as may be required for their defense, as determined by mutual agreement.

ARTICLE VIII

This Treaty does not affect and shall not be interpreted as affecting in any way the rights and obligations of the Parties under the Charter of the United Nations or the responsibility of the United Nations for the maintenance of international peace and security.

ARTICLE IX

This Treaty shall be ratified by the United States of America and the Republic of China in accordance with their respective constitutional processes and will come into force when instruments of ratification thereof have been exchanged by them at Taipei.

ARTICLE X

This Treaty shall remain in force indefinitely. Either Party may terminate it one year after notice has been given to the other Party.

IN WITNESS WHEREOF the undersigned Plenipotentiaries have signed this Treaty.

DONE in duplicate, in the English and Chinese languages, at Washington on this second day of December of the Year One Thousand Nine Hundred and Fifty-four, corresponding to the second day of the twelfth month of the Forty-third year of the Republic of China.

For the United States of America:
JOHN FOSTER DULLES
For the Republic of China:
GEORGE K. C. YEH

II. The Joint Communiqué of the People's Republic of China and the United States of America, issued in Shanghai on February 28, 1972

President Richard Nixon of the United States of America visited the People's Republic of China at the invitation of Premier Chou En-lai of the People's Republic of China from February 21 to February 28, 1972. Accompanying the President were Mrs. Nixon, U.S. Secretary of State William Rogers, Assistant to the President Dr. Henry Kissinger, and other American officials.

President Nixon met with Chairman Mao Tse-tung of the Communist Party of China on February 21. The two leaders had a serious and frank exchange of views on Sino-U.S. relations and world affairs.

During the visit, extensive, earnest and frank discussions were held between President Nixon and Premier Chou En-lai on the normalization of relations between the United States of America and the People's Republic of China, as well as on other matters of interest to both sides. In addition, Secretary of State William Rogers and Foreign Minister Chi Peng-fei held talks in the same spirit.

President Nixon and his party visited Peking and viewed cultural, industrial and agricultural sites, and they also toured Hangchow and Shanghai where, continuing discussions with Chinese leaders, they viewed similar places of interest.

The leaders of the People's Republic of China and the United States of America found it beneficial to have this opportunity, after so many years without contact, to present candidly to one another their views on a variety of issues. They reviewed the international situation in which important changes and great upheavals are taking place and expounded their respective positions and attitudes.

The U.S. side stated: Peace in Asia and peace in the world require efforts both to reduce immediate tensions and to eliminate the basic causes of conflict. The United States will work for a just and secure peace: just, because it fulfills the aspirations of peoples and nations for freedom and progress; secure, because it removes the danger of foreign aggression. The United States supports individual freedom and social progress for all the peoples of the world, free of outside pressure or intervention. The United States believes that the effort to reduce tensions is served by improving communication between countries that have different ideologies so as to lessen the risks of confrontation through accident, miscalculation or misunderstanding. Countries should treat each other with mutual respect and be willing to compete peacefully, letting performance be the ultimate judge. No country should claim infallibility and each country should be prepared to reexamine its own attitudes for the common good. The United States stressed that the peoples of Indochina should be allowed to determine their destiny without outside intervention; its constant primary objective has been a negotiated solution; the eight-point proposal put forward by the Republic of Vietnam and the United States on January 27, 1972, represents a basis for the attainment of that objective; in the absence of a negotiated settlement, the United States envisages the ultimate withdrawal of all U.S. forces from the region consistent with the aim of self-determination for each country of Indochina. The United States will maintain its close ties with and support for the Republic of Korea; the United States will support efforts of the Republic of Korea to seek a relaxation of tension and increased communication in the Korean peninsula. The United States places the highest value on its friendly relations with Japan; it will continue to develop the existing close bonds. Consistent with the United Nations Security Council resolution of December 21, 1971, the United States favors the continuation of the cease-fire between India and Pakistan and the withdrawal of all military forces to within their own territories and to their own sides of the cease-fire line in Jammu and Kashmir; the United States supports the right of the peoples of South Asia to shape their own future in peace, free of military threat, and without having the area become the subject of great power rivalry.

The Chinese side stated: Wherever there is oppression, there is resistance.

Countries want independence, nations want liberation and the people want revolution—this has become the irresistible trend of history. All nations, big or small, should be equal; big nations should not bully the small and strong nations should not bully the weak. China will never be a superpower and it opposes hegemony and power politics of any kind. The Chinese side stated that it firmly supports the struggles of all the oppressed people and nations for freedom and liberation and that the people of all countries have the right to choose their social systems according to their own wishes and the right to safeguard the independence, sovereignty and territorial integrity of their own countries and oppose foreign aggression, interference, control and subversion. All foreign troops should be withdrawn to their own countries.

The Chinese side expressed its firm support to the peoples of Vietnam, Laos, and Cambodia in their efforts for the attainment of their goal and its firm support to the seven-point proposal of the Provisional Revolutionary Government of the Republic of South Vietnam and the elaboration of February this year on the two key problems in the proposal, and to the Joint Declaration of the Summit Conference of the Indochinese Peoples. It firmly supports the eight-point program for the peaceful unification of Korea put forward by the Government of the Democratic People's Republic of Korea on April 12, 1971, and the stand for the abolition of the "U.N. Commission for the Unification and Rehabilitation of Korea." It firmly opposes the revival and outward expansion of Japanese militarism and firmly supports the Japanese people's desire to build an independent, democratic, peaceful and neutral Japan. It firmly maintains that India and Pakistan should, in accordance with the United Nations resolutions on the India-Pakistan question, immediately withdraw all their forces to their respective territories and to their own sides of the cease-fire line in Jammu and Kashmir, and firmly supports the Pakistan Government and people in their struggle to preserve their independence and sovereignty and the people of Jammu and Kashmir in their struggle for the right of self-determination.

There are essential differences between China and the United States in their social systems and foreign policies. However, the two sides agreed that countries, regardless of their social systems, should conduct their relations on the principles of respect for the sovereignty and territorial integrity of all states, nonaggression against other states, noninterference in the internal affairs of other states, equality and mutual benefit, and peaceful coexistence. International disputes should be settled on this basis, without resorting to the use or threat of force. The United States and the People's Republic of China are prepared to apply these principles to their mutual relations.

With these principles of international relations in mind the two sides stated that:

- Progress toward the normalization of relations between China and the United States is in the interests of all countries,
- Both wish to reduce the danger of international military conflict,
- Neither should seek hegemony in the Asia-Pacific region and each is

opposed to efforts by any other country or group of countries to establish such hegemony; and

- Neither is prepared to negotiate on behalf of any third party or to enter into agreements or understandings with the other directed at other states.

Both sides are of the view that it would be against the interests of the peoples of the world for any major country to collude with another against other countries, or for major countries to divide up the world into spheres of interest.

The two sides reviewed the long-standing serious disputes between China and the United States. The Chinese side reaffirmed its position: The Taiwan question is the crucial question obstructing the normalization of relations between China and the United States; the Government of the People's Republic of China is the sole legal government of China; Taiwan is a province of China which has long been returned to the motherland; the liberation of Taiwan is China's internal affair in which no other country has the right to interfere; and all U.S. forces and military installations must be withdrawn from Taiwan. The Chinese Government firmly opposes any activities which aim at the creation of "one China, one Taiwan," "one China, two governments," "two Chinas," and "independent Taiwan" or advocate that "the status of Taiwan remains to be determined."

The U.S. side declared: The United States acknowledges that all Chinese on either side of the Taiwan Strait maintain there is but one China and that Taiwan is a part of China. The United States Government does not challenge that position. It reaffirms its interest in a peaceful settlement of the Taiwan question by the Chinese themselves. With this prospect in mind, it affirms the ultimate objective of the withdrawal of all U.S. forces and military installations from Taiwan. In the meantime, it will progressively reduce its forces and military installations on Taiwan as the tension in the area diminishes.

The two sides agreed that it is desirable to broaden the understanding between the two peoples. To this end, they discussed specific areas in such fields as science, technology, culture, sports and journalism, in which people-to-people contacts and exchanges would be mutually beneficial. Each side undertakes to facilitate the further development of such contacts and exchanges.

Both sides view bilateral trade as another area from which mutual benefit can be derived, and agreed that economic relations based on equality and mutual benefit are in the interest of the peoples of the two countries. They agree to facilitate the progressive development of trade between their two countries.

The two sides agreed that they will stay in contact through various channels, including the sending of a senior U.S. representative to Peking from time to time for concrete consultations to further the normalization of relations between the two countries and continue to exchange views on issues of common interest.

The two sides expressed the hope that the gains achieved during this visit would open up new prospects for the relations between the two countries. They believe that the normalization of relations between the two countries is not only in the interest of the Chinese and American peoples but also contributes to the relaxation of tension in Asia and the world.

President Nixon, Mrs. Nixon and the American party expressed their appreciation for the gracious hospitality shown them by the Government and people of the People's Republic of China.

INDEX

INDEX

UNION   OF   S

TANNU-T

Urumchi ⊙

S I N K I A N G

Lop Nor

K

T S I N G

AKSAI
CHIN

Islamabad ★

Indus R.

LADAKH

PAKISTAN

40°N

30°N

50°N

70°E

80°E

90°E

New Delhi ★

I N D I A

N E P A L

Katmandu ★

T I B E T

Chame

⊙ Lhasa

BHUTAN

BANGLADESH

Dacca ★

20°N

BURM

CHINA

⊛ Capital of China
⊙ Chinese provincial capitals
★ Other capitals
•••••••••••••• Disputed international borders
——— ——→ Topping's route, May 20 to June 24, 1971

0   100   200   300   400   500

MILES

90°E